EMMA WASSERMAN is an associate professor of religion at Rutgers University and the author of *Death of the Soul in Romans 7*. She specializes in early Christian history and maintains a particular focus on the letters of Paul and on ancient ethics and cosmology.

Apocalypse as Holy War

THE ANCHOR YALE BIBLE REFERENCE LIBRARY is a project of international and interfaith scope in which Protestant, Catholic, and Jewish scholars from many countries contribute individual volumes. The project is not sponsored by any ecclesiastical organization and is not intended to reflect any particular theological doctrine.

The series is committed to producing volumes in the tradition established half a century ago by the founders of the Anchor Bible, William Foxwell Albright and David Noel Freedman. It aims to present the best contemporary scholarship in a way that is accessible not only to scholars but also to the educated nonspecialist. It is committed to work of sound philological and historical scholarship, supplemented by insight from modern methods, such as sociological and literary criticism.

John J. Collins
General Editor

THE ANCHOR YALE BIBLE REFERENCE LIBRARY

Apocalypse as Holy War

Divine Politics and Polemics in the Letters of Paul

EMMA WASSERMAN

Yale
UNIVERSITY
PRESS

NEW HAVEN
AND
LONDON

"Anchor Yale Bible" and the Anchor Yale logo are registered trademarks of
Yale University.

Copyright © 2018 by Yale University. All rights reserved. This book may not
be reproduced, in whole or in part, including illustrations, in any form (beyond
that copying permitted by Sections 107 and 108 of the U.S. Copyright Law and
except by reviewers for the public press), without written permission from the
publishers.

Quotations from the Bible are from New Revised Standard Version Bible,
copyright © 1989 National Council of the Churches of Christ in the United
States of America. Used by permission. All rights reserved.

Yale University Press books may be purchased in quantity for educational,
business, or promotional use. For information, please e-mail sales.press@yale
.edu (U.S. office) or sales@yaleup.co.uk (U.K. office).

Set in Adobe Caslon type by Newgen North America, Austin, Texas.
Printed in the United States of America.

Library of Congress Control Number: 2017959971

ISBN 978-0-300-20402-5 (hardcover : alk. paper)

A catalogue record for this book is available from the British Library.

This paper meets the requirements of ANSI/NISO Z39.48-1992 (Permanence
of Paper).

10 9 8 7 6 5 4 3 2 1

JKM Library
1100 East 55th Street
Chicago, IL 60615

For Helen, Caitlyn, and Rose, with love

Contents

Acknowledgments

I have accrued many debts to colleagues and friends during the course of writing this book, and it is a great pleasure to acknowledge them here. Stanley Stowers read the manuscript at various stages, and our ongoing conversations helped to sustain me during the long period of writing and revising. I am grateful to Stan and also to Larry Wills and Bernadette Brooten, who generously listened to me air my frustrations and aspirations with warmth and good humor. I am especially indebted to Adela Collins, who read the introduction and book proposal in its early and its more developed forms. Her early criticisms of the project were crucial in helping me to shape the book that it has become. Saul Olyan also supplied judicious commentary on chapter 1, Jim Johnson worked on the introduction, and discussions with John Collins helped me to sharpen and refine my arguments in important ways.

This book was written during two years of leave from Rutgers University, and I thank my colleagues and Dean Jimmy Swenson for supporting me in these ventures. Since I arrived at Rutgers almost ten years ago, my colleagues in the department of religion have provided me with a wonderfully supportive and collegial home for my teaching and research. Jim Jones and Tia Kolbaba happily read anything I sent them and offered innumerable words of encouragement and sage advice. I owe a special debt to Jim Johnson, who in the years leading up to his retirement in 2015 worked tirelessly to shape his more juvenile charges into something that plausibly resembled well-adjusted, politically savvy academic adults. It is a great honor to work in the department he built and to count him still as a mentor and friend. My fellow juvenile, Tao Jiang, has been a wonderful friend and co-conspirator. Our regular meetings to discuss "how the writing is going" helped to ward off bouts of sabbatical loneliness and self-doubt.

It was an honor to spend a year at the Radcliffe Institute for Advanced Study, where I served as a fellow in 2011–2012. I made many new friends at Radcliffe and thank Deans Judith Vishniac and Elizabeth Cohen for making our time together so relentlessly interesting and memorable. I am particularly grateful to David Stern and Jesse Rainbow, who patiently listened and encouraged me as I worked half-formed ideas into the arguments that became the basis for this book. I learned a great deal also from several colloquia and seminars where I presented parts of this work. I especially thank the members of the Boston Patristics Group, the Columbia New Testament Seminar, and graduate students at the Harvard Divinity School, where Karen King and Laura Nasrallah graciously invited me to present my work. I express my appreciation to the Schoff Fund at the University Seminars at Columbia University for their help in publication.

My editor at the Anchor Yale Bible series, Bert Harrill, championed the project in its early forms and supplied helpful comments and criticisms as it neared its end. I am grateful to him, to the editorial board of the Anchor Yale Bible series, and to the two anonymous peer reviewers at Yale University Press who helped me refine the writing, arguments, and tone of the book in innumerable ways. Two excellent editors at Yale, first Jennifer Banks and then Heather Gold, have done much to shepherd the project along. I am very grateful also to Jessie Dolch, who copyedited the manuscript with a keen eye and saved me from numerous errors, and to Derek Gottlieb, who prepared the General Index.

Discussions with friends and family often helped me to think about the material in new ways, and with lightness and fun. I especially thank Sharika Thiranagama, Nat Levtow, Karen Stern, Lori Allan, Jenny Labendz, Jon Bialecki, Steve Thomas, Mike Arvan, Peter Woodford, and Danny Steinmetz-Jenkins.

Abbreviations

CTA   *Corpus des tablettes en cunéiformes alphabétiques découvertes à Ras Shamra-Ugarit de 1929 à 1939.* Edited by Andrée Herdner. Paris: Guethner, 1963

KTU   *Die keilalphabetischen Texte aus Ugarit.* Edited by Manfried Dietrich, Oswald Loretz, and Joaquín Sanmartín. Münster: Ugarit-Verlag, 2013

LXX   Septuagint

MT   Masoretic Text

NETS   *A New English Translation of the Septuagint.* Edited by Albert Pietersma and Benjamin G. Wright. New York: Oxford University Press, 2007

NRSV   New Revised Standard Version

RINAP   Royal Inscriptions of the Neo-Assyrian Period

SVF   *Stoicorum veterum fragmenta.* Hans von Arnim. Leipzig: Teubner, 1903–1905

Introduction:
The Politics of Heaven

Apocalyptic prophecies lie at the heart of Christian origins. Our earliest sources for the Christian movement, the letters of Paul, expect the return of Christ in the near future, together with material transformation of the Christ-followers and a conflict and judgment of cataclysmic proportions. So the letters imagine Christ's return as imminent; as bringing about the full transformation of the Christ-followers into heavenly, pneumatic bodies (1 Cor 15:12–57; cf. 1 Thess 4:15–17); and as a time when they will somehow assume their true heavenly home (Phil 3:14–21, 2 Cor 4:16–5:5; cf. Gal 4:26).[1] Texts like 1 Thess 1:10 speak of an impending day of wrath, while Romans 1–2 warns of a coming judgment against impiety and wickedness, with rewards of glory, honor, peace, and eternal life and punishments of wrath, anguish, distress, and fury (cf. Rom 6:23, 2 Cor 5:10, Rom 14:10). First Corinthians 6 claims that the Christ-followers will themselves judge the cosmos. While 1 Thess 4:16 includes language about a trumpet and battle cry, 1 Cor 15:23–28 briefly describes a conflict with "rulers, powers, and authorities" (*archai, dunameis,* and *exousiai*), construed as enemies that Christ will defeat before handing the kingdom back to the father. Though the surviving letters provide little detail about this time of wrath and reward, the horizon of expectation proves foundational for Paul's numerous arguments about human and cosmic history; about Christ's death, resurrection, and divine *pneuma* (breath or airy substance); about the Christ-followers' expectations of reward and perfection; and about the values, ethics, and goals of his idealized Christ-followers.

A broad scholarly consensus agrees on these basic points but not on how they might be understood in historical terms. To a significant extent,

1

this is due to certain tensions and contradictions that characterize the study of Paul and of Christian apocalypticism generally. The vast majority of interpreters agree that critical historical interpretation requires that we go beyond simply describing or paraphrasing Paul's ideas. Typically, this means that interpreters make arguments about comparisons and contexts that might plausibly illuminate them. Scholars also agree that the substantial body of material known as Jewish apocalyptic literature provides an obvious starting point for analysis of this kind. Somewhat paradoxically, however, they have tended to treat this literature in uncritical ways, particularly with a view to establishing that there is something new, unique, or at least highly distinctive about Christian apocalyptic thinking. As a result, many approaches to Paul's apocalypticism tacitly work to undermine the project of critical historical analysis and contextualization. Another, often related, set of problems concerns identifying the apocalyptic features of the literature in question. Interpreters often differ, for instance, on whether apocalypses are to be defined by certain generic literary features, by shared worldviews, or by strong internal claims about dualism, conflict, and evil. This study argues that much of the relevant literature can be more helpfully understood as myths about political relationships in the divine world. Reconceived in this way, I argue, a great deal more literature sheds light on Paul's apocalyptic thought, and it does so in more precise and clear ways.

Framing certain Jewish apocalyptic texts as myths about divine politics has a number of advantages for the historical project. First and foremost among them is that it broadens the field of possible comparisons and allows different patterns of continuity and discontinuity to emerge. Understood in this way, for instance, the diverse apocalyptic texts collected in 1 Enoch, the biblical apocalypse contained in Daniel 7–12, and a number of important texts preserved at Qumran are primarily of interest insofar as they illustrate some interesting features of their writers' political imaginations. Understood in this way, the category of apocalypses or an apocalyptic "perspective" need not control or delimit the field of possible comparisons relevant for understanding any one text. Furthermore, to the extent that some apocalyptic texts do show patterns of similarity, these often rise only to the level of taken-for-granted premises and assumptions that particular writers play with and adapt in creative ways. Thus, contrary to much of the scholarship on Christian apocalypticism, the largely unknown scribes who wrote, rewrote, and edited these texts do not seem to share a single coherent worldview, theological system, cosmology, or vision of evil and rebellion.[2] More constructively, however, they do tend to share certain premises, working assumptions, and strategies of argument.

One of the central arguments advanced here is that attention to these rather modest, taken for granted premises and strategies of argument brings out some illuminating patterns in the evidence. Most prominently, the writers considered here tend to assume that the world is constituted as a single, unified political hierarchy that requires a plurality of divine beings who organize, shape, and rule it.[3] The writers of texts such as 1 Enoch, Daniel 7–12, Jubilees, the War Scroll, and the Community Rule also share a marked ambivalence about the possibility of conflict and rebellion within this kingdom. In particular, they show a distinctive tendency to imagine political relationships in ways that suppress the possibility of conflict or competition, especially in relation to the upper tiers of the divine order. The texts are quite diverse, but six strategies for suppressing rivalry and rebellion prove common. First, writers frequently appeal to images of a supremely powerful heavenly king envisioned as ruling the entire created order, its variegated history, and all lower-level divinities. This ruler thus reigns supreme over a multitiered but characteristically submissive cosmic kingdom. Second, they avoid intimations of rivalry with the supreme God by imagining misguided insubordination (not rivalry or rebellion) as generally characteristic of disfavored humans and, in exceptional cases, some lower-ranking deities. Third, they depict harmful divinities as lower-level subordinates, instruments, and obedient henchmen of the high God but sometimes construe them as given to excess, overzealousness, and ignorance. Fourth, they deny rivalry and competition between the Jewish high God and the gods of other peoples by insisting that other gods do not have comparable rank, power, and status and/or by reclassifying them as relatively powerless subordinates of the Jewish God. Fifth, they affirm the providential management of world affairs by identifying consistent patterns of just reward and punishment in the past, present, and future, especially as it relates to a favored elect. And sixth, they envision climactic battles and culminating wars as serving to fully disclose, complete, and perfect the existing religious, political, and historical order. These patterns shed much needed light on a number of difficult issues with Paul's thought, especially his claims about divine enemies, the gods of other peoples, and the role of imminent war in fully disclosing or revealing the existing scheme of divine power, rule, and election that has been there all along.

Dualism and Powers of Evil in the Study of Jewish and Christian Apocalypticism

This study undertakes a critical reappraisal of the evidence for early Christian apocalypticism with a particular view to understanding Paul. Both the texts under review and the subject matter remain very controversial in the field, so I pause here to sketch a picture of the most prominent traditions of interpretation with which I am in dialogue. The aim is to provide a helpful simplification of the scholarship, one that will help to clarify the arguments advanced here and anticipate possible objections.

As noted already, historical analysis of Christian apocalypticism has often been frustrated by uncritical concepts and categories. Two problems have especially frustrated analysis. First, scholars often emphasize the seemingly radical aspects of Paul's thought and so construe his apocalypticism as centrally concerned with liberating transformation and opposition to the current political and social order. Interpreters find support for such views in dramatic discussions of persecution, freedom, and political confrontation in apocalyptic literature but often give inadequate attention to the images of violence, vengeance, and divine kingship that frequently appear alongside them.[4] Second, scholars of Paul have tended to operate with a rhetorical framework that obscures some of the most illuminating patterns in the evidence. In some cases, interpreters uncritically accept the normative perspective and values of their sources, but in other cases, they impose various sorts of interpretative models where they hardly seem to fit. For instance, many scholars hold that the idea of conflict or struggle between so-called dualistic forces or opponents is right at the core of apocalyptic thought. Some texts do evoke strong contrasts, such as those between a prince (*śar*) of light and a messenger (*mal'āk*) of darkness (1QS 3) or between Christ and Beliar (2 Cor 6:15), but taking such language as evidence of a dualistic struggle between good and evil opponents tends to accept and reproduce the normative claims of the texts. Such interpretations also tend to focus on moments of rhetorical climax and not on the quite varied and ambiguous roles these figures generally play in the literature. Despite these problems, much of the scholarship treats diverse traditions about harmful spirits, wayward divinities, and testing figures like Satan, Belial, and Mastema as if they all attest to the central importance of rebellious "powers of evil" in Jewish and Christian thought. According to many critics, in fact, Christian apocalypticism most centrally concerns Christ's triumph over rebellious powers of evil.

Myths about Christ's victory over rebel powers emerges relatively early in the study of apocalypticism. At the end of the nineteenth century, the German scholar Johannes Weiss inaugurated the study of early Christian apocalypticism with a short monograph titled *Jesus' Proclamation of the Kingdom of God*.[5] In Weiss's reading, Jesus's language about the kingdom conveys quite literal, immanent expectations, and Satan plays a central role in this apocalyptic drama.[6] In fact, Satan emerges as one of the main justifications for Christ's life, death, resurrection, and exaltation.[7] As Weiss formulated it, Christian apocalypticism has three basic tenets: first, the kingdom of God stands in opposition to the kingdom of Satan (hence, strict dualism); second, Christ's first coming marks the initial deathblow to Satan's rule, but the full triumph still awaits in the future (hence, the end of strict dualism); third, despite Christ's triumph, opponents like Satan and even "the flesh" still threaten until the final victory, so there is a modified dualistic struggle at work in the texts.[8] Such a scheme plausibly fits with certain discussions in the gospels and with the roles ascribed to "principalities and powers" in Colossians and Ephesians. Yet Weiss's theory reproduces the rhetorical claims of some (though not all) of the texts and requires tortured arguments that deny the relevance of more ambiguous and contradictory statements, especially about the relative power and independence of Satan. Nevertheless, after World War II Oscar Cullmann would popularize this scheme to imagine Christ's coming as the D-Day that presages the V-Day of the parousia.[9] Though many theories of apocalypticism develop similar ideas, like Weiss's theory of the satanic rule broken by Christ, claims about the enemies that Christ defeated at "D-Day" serve to legitimize Christ's victory as a past event while ignoring the prophecies about Christ's return, which appear right on the horizon in the earliest literature. In a number of ways, then, such approaches trade on shifting, ambiguous claims about the unfolding of time and the nature of Christ's victory.

Despite these problems, Weiss's criticisms of his contemporaries would largely succeed at establishing the "concrete" character of early Christian apocalypticism. Whereas Weiss mainly argued for a literal interpretation of certain New Testament prophecies, Albert Schweitzer also drew illuminating historical comparisons with Jewish literature in his monumental *The Quest for the Historical Jesus* and *The Mysticism of the Apostle Paul*. In *The Mysticism of the Apostle Paul*, for instance, he construes eschatological redemption—at least largely—as a pastiche of imagery and ideas found in certain biblical prophetic texts and Hellenistic apocalypses. Though he relies on a limited range of apocalyptic literature, his work shows a remarkable disinterest in positing Christian apocalypticism as sui generis or as a unique development of Jewish thought.[10] Unlike many interpreters before and after him, Schweitzer also refuses to characterize Jewish apocalypticism as dualistic. He writes:

> The Jewish eschatology does not recognize a real dualism, although it was strongly influenced by Zoroastrianism. The angels who in Gen 6:1–4 revolt against God are, according to the Book of Enoch, immediately overcome and kept in durance against their final punishment at the Judgment. But their progeny, begotten of the daughters of men, are the demons, who trouble the world until the end (1 Enoch 15:8–16:4). Their leader bears various names, and is often identified with Satan (the Accuser), who was originally not an enemy of God, but only the Accuser of men, whom God permits to act as such. In general, the view of Jewish eschatology is that the evil of the world comes from the demons, and that angelic beings have, with God's permission, established themselves between Him and mankind. In its simplest form the conception of redemption is that the Messianic Kingdom puts an end to this condition.[11]

Though this analysis relies on a limited subset of literature and treats angels and demons as unproblematic terms for critical analysis, Schweitzer imagines a hierarchical divine arrangement where intermediaries have complex and somewhat ambiguous roles and relationships. These subtle distinctions would be lost on many later interpreters.

Weiss and Schweitzer both found apocalypticism untenable for modern thought, but much of the subsequent scholarship would struggle to depict Christian apocalypticism as both unique and as enduringly relevant. For instance, the existentialist theologian Rudolf Bultmann sought to dispense with the apocalyptic dimensions of the early literature but also to identify a profound and enduringly relevant existentialist view of the human condition in Paul's anthropology.[12] Though largely derived from a few chapters in Romans, Paul's anthropology looms so large for Bultmann that it occupies nearly two hundred pages of his two-volume masterwork *The Theology of the New Testament*. By contrast, his student Ernst Käsemann would claim to reestablish the very links between self and cosmos that Bultmann had tried to sever. So Käsemann famously countered that "apocalypticism is the mother of Christian theology" and "anthropology is the projection of cosmology."[13] Though he conceived of Christian apocalypticism (or cosmology) in terms of Weiss's dualism of kingdoms and rulers, Käsemann expanded this idea by drawing on then-prominent theories that Jewish apocalypticism was centrally concerned with so-called two-age dualism.[14] Where Weiss had found dualism in Jesus's proclamations about the kingdom, Käsemann argued that a dualism of the ages is also foundational for Jewish apocalypticism. On this basis, however, he argued that Christian thought modifies this schema so that the future age/kingdom breaks into the present (evil) age. He also expanded the emphasis on struggle with evil powers by adding sin and death as evil "cosmic powers" alongside Satan. The result was a much more expansive view of dualistic struggle that, largely due to certain ambiguities in the language about sin and death in chapters 5–8 of Romans, appeals to notions of invasion, possession, and powers of a so-called personal and cosmic nature. Many other interpreters had taken the language about sin and death in Romans as instances of metaphor and personification, but Käsemann would construe this as referring to evil divine beings of some kind, albeit of a largely unspecified type. So he argues: "Because the world is not finally a neutral place but the field of contending powers, mankind both individually and socially becomes the object of the struggle and an exponent of the powers that rule it."[15] Thus construed, Paul's language about sin and death in Romans 5–8 conveys a worldview where anthropomorphic beings and cosmic powers attack and invade the person from all sides.

Käsemann passionately embraced apocalyptic theology, but critics have undermined the historical foundations of his theory. Not only is his language about cosmic powers often vague and ill-defined, but Käsemann's specific contentions about aeons, powers, and cosmic conflict also lack serious historical contextualization.[16] In particular, the theory requires strict dualisms and opponent figures that do not fit easily with much of the evidence. As scholars of Jewish apocalypticism have shown, for instance, careful analysis of the literature reveals a more consistent understanding of kingdoms and periods of history that are already intermingling, not starkly opposed.[17] Rather than two ages or realms, the texts more consistently imagine a single cosmic order, albeit one that involves anxious interactions and ongoing threats in the present and that requires restoration, perfection, and renewal in the future.

Despite these problems, much contemporary historical and theological scholarship continues to appropriate Käsemann's work, especially his theory of Christian apocalypticism, Jewish two-age dualism, and his claims that sin, death, and other powers function as major players in the Christian apocalyptic drama.[18] In fact, discussion of Paul's apocalypticism, even as an historical matter, has largely unfolded within the framework Käsemann articulated. To a significant extent, this is because interpreters embrace the D-Day/V-Day schema as an explanation for the evils of their own time, whether they construe these evils as political oppression in Latin American (as Walter Wink does) or as the satanic influences of New Age religion and heavy metal (as Clinton Arnold does).[19] So figures like Johann Christiaan Beker, J. Louis Martyn, and Beverley Roberts Gaventa embraced Käsemann's project by appealing to a dualism of the ages, a cosmic conflict with sin and death, and the inextricable relations between apocalypticism and various other features of Christian thought and construe apocalypticism as community oriented and universalistic.[20] Though they often make tendentious and problematic historical claims, such voices have tended to dominate, or just drown out, those of more disinterested historical critics.[21]

The idea of dualistic ages and rulers continues to play an outsized role in the discussion about Christian apocalyptic thought, especially as it relates to Paul. For instance, Beker argued that Paul transforms Jewish apocalypticism in profound ways, especially in modifying a supposedly traditional paradigm of two-age dualism.[22] By this he means, like many before him, that the organizing logic of Jewish apocalypticism involves sharply distinct, antagonistic ages and kingdoms. Arranged in this way, the Christian apocalypticists can then be claimed to innovate by understanding the two ages as already intermingled so as to create a tense expectation about the world to come. As Loren Stuckenbruck and others have shown, however, few Jewish texts suggest that such formulations of two-age dualism have merit.[23] Likewise, Beker envisions Paul as replacing more typical Jewish opponents and eschatological enemies with Käsemann's powers of sin and death, so that once again, Jewish traditions serve mainly as foils that are useful for establishing Christian difference.[24] In another study, Martinus de Boer attempts to take Jewish traditions seriously but is hampered by a similar apologetic framework.[25] The results are predictable. For instance, de Boer relies on the highly tendentious claim of Philipp Vielhauer to the effect that "there can be 'no continuity' between the two ages" in Jewish apocalyptic thought.[26] On this basis, he claims to establish the unique contribution of the Christian view that the end has already dawned, thus reentrenching a resilient apologetic formulation of two-age dualism. De Boer also tends to arrive at conclusions so saturated with normative language about righteousness, salvation, and Christian victory that it proves difficult to evaluate whether or not meaningful illumination has taken place. So in one instance, he claims, "Paul does not preach apocalyptic eschatology, not even Christian apocalyptic eschatology; he preaches the crucified Christ whom Christ raised from the dead, nothing else (cf. 1 Cor 1:23; 2:2)."[27] Though de Boer hardly means to claim more than that the "Christ event" organizes Paul's thought, he evokes critical categories that quickly shade into normative confessional claims.

Scholarly work on Jewish apocalypticism has greatly advanced since the time of Weiss, Schweitzer, and Käsemann. Especially influenced by the mid-twentieth-century discovery of the Dead Sea Scrolls, generations of scholars have shown renewed interest in noncanonical literature such 1 Enoch and Jubilees, as well as Daniel, which contains the only apocalypse preserved in the Hebrew Bible. They have also worked to undermine traditions of biblical theology that conceived of apocalyptic theology, literature, and movements as holistic, synthetic, or unified complexes of thought. Work on the so-called apocalyptic genre underscores these points. In the late 1970s, the Society of Biblical Literature Genre Project charged a group of scholars with critically defining apocalyptic texts as a distinct literary genre. This group treated a very wide range of texts and produced a definition that resisted simplistic, unifying theological paradigms as well as speculative theorizing about historical developments that had been in vogue earlier. The preliminary results were published in a 1979 special issue of *Semeia* that included an introduction justifying this methodology and a collection of essays on Greek, Latin, Persian, gnostic, and rabbinic apocalypses as well as Jewish and Christian ones. So John J. Collins famously defined the apocalyptic genre as "a genre of revelatory literature with a narrative framework, in which revelation is mediated by an otherworldly being to a human recipient, disclosing a transcendent reality which is both temporal, insofar as it envisages eschatological salvation, and spatial insofar as it involves another, supernatural world."[28]

Critics may take issue with the language of supernatural and otherworldly beings, but by defining the apocalyptic genre as a subspecies of revelatory literature, Collins avoids apologetic formulations of this literature as being uniquely Jewish or Christian. Collins's formulation also points to a distinctive temporal and spatial framework but does not offer an overly specific discussion of other constituent features, interests, or motifs.[29] This open-endedness appears as a necessary outcome of a close analysis of the sources. As Collins showed, for instance, once specific images, ideas, and motifs are taken as constituting apocalypticism, the commonalities among the texts in question often prove strikingly minimal. His essay on Jewish traditions includes a chart showing the distribution of twenty-seven specific elements and motifs, including categories like cosmogony, primordial events, resurrection, and "other forms of afterlife."[30] Though most of the texts share an interest in a spatial axis, visions, and otherworldly beings, none of them individually contains all of these so-called temporal and eschatological elements aside from that of "judgment/ destruction of the wicked." Though some critics found this a weakness of the theory, this result helps to bring attention to the diversity that characterizes the literature.[31]

This study builds on three major findings of the genre project. First, the group produced a view of apocalyptic literature as constituted by a constellation of imagery, ideas, and motifs that appear in diverse patterns in apocalyptic and nonapocalyptic literature. By emphasizing the non-uniqueness of virtually every constituent feature, such approaches allow for the potential relevance of a wide variety of other texts and traditions of ancient Mediterranean and West Asian provenance.[32] Second, these results undermine notions of apocalypticism as a unified set of ideas or patterns of thought that constitute identifiable theological, historical, or social movements. So Collins convincingly argues that even once a genre emerges in the late-first-century CE, the common features and motifs prove far too minimal to illuminate particular texts in and of themselves, and they are of even less help for chronicling precise developments of supposed schools of thought or historical movements.[33] At best, the genre may point to some interesting and fruitful avenues for comparison and contextualization of particular cases, but it does not supply all the relevant materials for understanding them. Close analysis of particular texts thus becomes the test of relevant comparison and illumination, not categories like Jewish apocalypticism conceived of as having some independent or hypostatic cultural or religious identity. Third, while the genre identifies certain minimal shared features of the literature, Collins also allows that some basic worldview or symbolic universe may inform them. He defines an apocalyptic worldview as follows: "The world is mysterious and revelation must be transmitted from a supernatural source, through the mediation of angels; there is a hidden world of angels and demons that is directly relevant to human destiny; and this destiny is finally determined by a definitive eschatological judgment. In short, human life is bounded in the present by the supernatural world of angels and demons and in the future by the inevitability of a final judgment."[34] While insisting that texts comprise the primary data for establishing the relevance of such a "symbolic universe," this definition correlates the common features of the genre with an underlying framework of thought that lends the texts some minimal continuity and coherence. Like the shared features of the genre, however, these characteristics do not serve up robust theological or literary content but rather offer a very basic framework for considering the diverse, creative, and context-specific elaborations of images, language, and argument. Furthermore, the evidence does not suggest that apocalyptic myths were central to or inevitable preoccupations of Jewish thought. Instead, they seem to be relatively esoteric works that probably circulated among networks of highly literate scribes.

Building on Collins's minimalistic approach, this study conceives of Paul as holding certain basic apocalyptic commitments but also as drawing on an open-ended intellectual repertoire. Without altogether dispensing with the rubric of Judaism or Jewish apocalypticism, imagining Paul as drawing creatively on an open-ended repertoire can help to avoid conceiving of traditions, worldviews, or symbolic universes as well-defined, rigid, or closed frameworks of thought. This approach allows for the possibility of creative synthesis and adaptation across many traditions and discourses, including but not limited to certain Greek traditions about the soul, the cosmos, and the nature of the gods.

Building on this work, this study finds that literature such as 1 Enoch, Jubilees, Daniel 7–12, and the letters of Paul do not share a particular Jewish apocalyptic theology or system of thought; that their cosmologies are not aptly characterized as dualistic; and that they show little agreement about allegedly "evil" characters, conflicts with said characters, or the precise causes and consequences of waywardness, disarray, and ambiguity characteristic of the past, present, and future worlds. To the extent that they do show similarities, these more often rise to the level of shared premises and assumptions about the cosmos, the gods, and political relationships in the world of divinity. The comparisons do show some points of continuity, then, but these are largely at the level of common working assumptions and premises, not worldviews or traditions conceived of as some "package deal" of language, culture, or ideology that we can easily characterize as Jewish, apocalyptic, Greek, or Christian.

Overview of the Arguments

The first two chapters develop a critical reappraisal of the evidence for Jewish traditions central to an analysis of early Christian apocalypticism. Here I pay particular attention to the divine political order imagined in

Jewish literature and to traditions of so-called conflict myth. A central goal is to clarify a number of difficult issues with alleged dualisms, conflict, and divine opponents, as well as with "angels" and "demons," that are often understood as central to apocalyptic texts. Chapters 3, 4, and 5 then shift to a series of case studies that show how this reappraisal can shed light on some difficult issues in the letters of Paul. Thus, chapters 1 and 2 are not conceived of as providing the background or foundation for understanding Paul's thought. Rather, I argue that some (though not all) of this literature can help us to understand Paul's intellectual repertoire and to make better sense of some of the difficult images and arguments that appear in the letters.

Chapter 1 treats the Enuma Elish, the Baal Cycle, the Epic of Anzu, and the *Theogony*, paying particular attention to portrayals of wars and conflicts that lead to more settled hierarchies under the gods Marduk, Zeus, Enlil, and El/Baal. Though these texts do not exhibit a totally distinctive and unified way of thinking about the gods or the cosmos, they do share certain assumptions about the cosmic order, namely, that it functions more or less like a human political arrangement where a supremely powerful divine being rules together with lower ranks of subordinates. Further, dramatic myths about rebellion, opposition, and matched battle often serve to legitimate the power of certain ruling gods by imagining those gods as heroically defeating enemies. As a consequence of these heroics, other divinities often acclaim their power, status, and right to rule others, sometimes in ways that legitimate institutions or rulers in the earthly realm. Attention to these rather basic points helps to illuminate patterns of continuity and discontinuity in the mythic narratives that survive from Babylon, Ugarit, and Greece and the distinctive appropriation of similar images and ideas in Israelite and Jewish traditions.

As has been well-established by scholars of ancient Judaism, longer mythic narratives such as those about Marduk and Baal prove illuminating for a number of biblical texts, particularly those where Yahweh is envisioned as defeating or ruling over the sea or a sea dragon and as participating in battles as a warrior and/or as a general who leads heavenly armies. In contrast to the extended mythic narratives, however, the biblical discussions typically deny the coming-to-be of Yahweh's rule and tend to omit or suppress the possibility of true conflict and competition with other gods, humans, or lower-level divine beings. As a result, the battles of the Jewish high God tend to be portrayed as highly asymmetrical affairs, whether these involve past conflicts with the Reed Sea, the wars of conquest, or future ones predicted in oracles about the day of Yahweh in the prophets. In contrast to Mesopotamian and Babylonian myths about heroic battles with the sea or a sea dragon, for instance, the biblical texts tend to appropriate these motifs as minor skirmishes rather than as great battles between matched powers, rebels, and rivals.

Chapter 2 treats 1 Enoch, Jubilees, Daniel 7–12, and writings from Qumran like the War Scroll and the Community Rule. This chapter argues that like many biblical writings, these myths tend to strategically suppress the possibility of rivalry in the divine world, often by affirming the incomparable power and justice of the true rulers in heaven. The texts show varying levels of interest in the lower ranks, but they typically construe lesser deities as obedient subordinates of the high god, not as extremely powerful, rebellious, evil agents gone rogue. With the possible (and partial) exceptions of the War Scroll and 1QS 3, writers more commonly use images of a vast, well-regulated, and generally obedient heavenly kingdom and of the just unfolding of history in ways that marginalize rebellion and conflict (cf. Rev 12:7–9). Such myths serve to exemplify the power and might of supreme gods while also offering plausible explanations for the complexity and ambiguity characteristic of the present world order, at least in the lower earthly domains. Further, such formulations can also accommodate gentile gods as lower-ranking subordinates of Israel's deity. In many cases, gentile gods have an ambiguous status as both operatives of the supreme deity and (mistaken) objects of worship, a tension that explains language about the future destruction of "idols," harmful spirits, and intermediaries that sometimes appears in eschatological war contexts and in polemics about idolatry.

Chapter 3 treats Paul's language about Christ as warrior in the context of Jewish traditions about holy war and the battle of the gods. Such traditions especially illuminate the role of eschatological war in organizing Paul's thought about stability and change in the historical and cosmic orders. I contend that, like a range of discussions about the "day of Yahweh" in prophetic texts and eschatological war in apocalyptic literature, Paul imagines a coming battle that will more fully reveal the divine rule already inherent in the cosmic and political orders. This approach especially sheds light on certain vexed issues with the so-called principalities and powers in 1 Cor 15:23–28 and on tensions and ambiguities surrounding issues of rule and rebellion in the heavenly ranks. In particular, I argue that Paul's "principalities and powers" are the gods of others that have been polemically reclassified as subordinates and operatives of the God of Israel. While *archai, exousiai,* and *dunameis* have sometimes been understood as hostile, rebellious forces of evil, Paul's language makes more sense as of a piece with the varied, vague, and typically anthropomorphic terms used to elaborate the lower ranks of divinity in Jewish tradition. Like these traditions, Paul treats these deities as having somewhat ambiguous roles because they are objects of (mistaken) gentile worship. In addition, he imagines their destruction as bringing about a time when all alike will worship the Jewish high God, consistent with texts such as Second Zechariah, the Animal Apocalypse of Enoch, and other literature.[35] This approach also casts new light on some difficult features of Phil 2:6–11. Unlike the rich traditions of myth about conflict and competition explored in chapter 1, the Philippians hymn imagines Christ as elevated to uniquely high status in return for his heroic obedience and lack of rivalry. While Phil 2:9–11 could allude to Christ's future role as divine warrior, this text more explicitly imagines Christ's being elevated to a rank of exceptionally high status as a reward for noncompetition and heroic submission.

Chapter 4 extends the treatment of divine subordinates and "other gods" to Gal 4:3–10, 1 Cor 8:1–11:1, and Rom 1:18–32. I argue that conceiving of Paul's *stoicheia* (elements) and *daimonia* (divinities) as divine subordinates, like the so-called principalities and powers in 1 Cor 15:23–28, resolves certain longstanding issues with interpreting these texts. Like the *archai, exousiai,* and *dunameis* elsewhere in the letters, Paul's *stoicheia* and *daimonia* refer to an ambiguous class of beings who are conceived of both as subordinates of the high God and as (mistaken) objects of worship among the gentiles. This approach brings attention to Jewish traditions of polemic that deny the existence and power of other peoples' gods and reclassify them as servants of the Jewish God. These patterns make good sense of Paul's claims about *stoicheia* in Galatians 4 and of his vacillation about the precise status of "other gods and lords" in 1 Cor 8:1–11:1. While in some cases Paul's discussion reflects the influence of philosophical cosmology—such as the language about prepositional metaphysics in 1 Cor 8:6—he generally adapts this language to fit relatively straightforward polemical arguments that satirize, demote, and polemically reclassify the gods of others.

Chapter 5 focuses attention on Paul's representations of the Christ-elect as a unified, victimized, and righteously alienated elite. Somewhat like the images of a righteous remnant in texts such as 1 Enoch, Daniel 11–12, and 1QS, Paul imagines the Christ-elect as having access to heavenly secrets, true interpretations, divine *pneuma,* and the power and protection of the supreme deity through Christ. At the same time, the letters frequently imagine this elect as beset by anxiety and threat, whether from hostile outsiders; inauthentic insiders; their own penchants for factionalism, rivalry, and self-interest; or the passions, desires, and flesh that threaten from their own bodies. In fact, I argue that Paul appropriates from Platonic and Stoic traditions in ways that expand the discourse about righteous alienation and threat that is already prominent in apocalyptic literature. As adapted by Paul, Platonic premises about inner conflict become the basis for an influential discourse about an ongoing struggle to resist the passions of the flesh, the aim of which is to achieve some level of self-mastery and (importantly) also submission to God (so Rom 6–8, 2 Cor 4–5, and Gal 5). The letters also appropriate Stoic teaching to characterize the ethics and goals of this Christ-elect. This is particularly clear in Romans 12–15, where Paul evokes an imagined community that is a discrete, unified social formation built on love, solidarity, and mutual up-building. At the same time, Paul continuously appeals to ongoing threats, whether from inauthentic teachers or the readers' own bad habits (so Phil 1–3, Rom 12–15, and 1 Cor 1–4). So, whether they are portrayed as beset by persecuting outsiders, wayward insiders, or corrosive factionalism and self-interest or as struggling to subdue their own passions and desires, Paul's Christ-elect emerge as an anxious elite engaged in a life-and-death struggle to submit to one another, as well as to God, Christ, and Paul. I contend that this approach greatly clarifies the complex interrelation between self, cosmos, and community in the letters and offers an historically grounded context for making sense of some of Paul's most opaque texts.

The conclusion summarizes these findings and their implications for scholarship on Paul and early Christianity. In contrast to theories that make a battle between good and evil foundational for apocalyptic thought, I find that Paul's letters are centrally preoccupied with the ongoing and just rule of supreme powers in heaven; that "angels," "demons," and "powers" are in fact divine beings of different ranks; and that Paul's end-time scenario envisions the purification and perfection of the existing social and political order rather than its complete reversal or revolutionary overturning. At the same time, the letters also develop a powerful discourse about inner struggle, heroic submission, and ethical solidarity that proves to be one of the most enduring and influential features of Pauline Christianity.

One contribution of this study is to reevaluate the roles of lesser divine beings, spirits, and variously construed "powers" in one subset of literature because their roles in these texts have often been misunderstood. To this end, I emphasize that mythmakers tend to imagine insubordination and conflict in ways that serve their claims about divinities of greater power. This should not be taken to mean, however, that I take beliefs about harmful spirits or misleading divinities as somehow being insignificant. The exorcisms in the gospels and the evidence of amulets, curse tablets, and binding spells suggest that such agents played central roles in everyday beliefs and practices, especially in relation to practical concerns with health and disease.[36] Further, though invasion and possession are important, they are not the only, or always the most dominant, ways of conceiving of divine influence or threat. Without excluding invasion and possession, much of the literature considered here also imagines beings like Mastema and Belial as anthropomorphic agents who interact with others, often in a dialogical way. These imagined interactions often allude to scheming, persuading, and influencing, but they typically leave room for human actors to resist, respond to, and negotiate with them. Without appealing to modern notions of a Kantian autonomous self (or its opposite, the possessed self), such discussions imply that human beings actively participate in a complex web of relationships, including other people and types of divine beings.

Because so much scholarly discussion has swirled around the idea of evil beings and opponents, it is important to clarify the nature and scope of the arguments advanced here. In particular, I imagine that readers or hearers of much of this literature—perhaps especially the War Scroll or the book of Revelation—might indeed conclude that much of the world around them is the domain of dangerous powers and divinities of immediate practical relevance for their associations, practices, and identifications. I maintain, however, that such ideas are features of the texts' ideologies and that their rhetorical effectiveness depends on their claims to supply privilege, protection, and access to more powerful beings. In other words, claims to the effect that forces of "good" are to be arrayed against the forces of "evil" might adequately describe important patterns in some of the literature (though not all of it), but they do not constitute critical analysis of these patterns. We can more productively conceive of such images as developing binary categories—like insiders/outsiders, angels/demons, or Christ/Beliar—that serve broader taxonomies about the hierarchical world order. This approach sheds light on the many different roles, characters, and relationships these divinities have in the literature, and it allows us to treat specific claims about confrontation and threat—such as when the forces of light meet the forces of darkness in certain Qumran texts—as moments of rhetorical flourish that overstate the power of illegitimate gods, angels, or humans. In other words, these binaries are not free-floating metaphysical realities but strategic contrasts that generate and reinforce broader (and generally hierarchical) claims about order, classification, and rule. Such an approach offers a more productive way to identify the supposed continuities and discontinuities in the surviving literature, and it brings attention to the asymmetrical relationships of power that generally characterize the world of divinity. Further, important traditions of ancient myth do explore the possibility of full-scale divine rebellion and coups. As discussed in chapter 1, texts like the Enuma Elish, the Epic of Anzu, and the *Theogony* present rivalry and competition among the gods in colorful, high-pitched battles fought to establish, defend, and renegotiate divine rule. Because these battles are typically set in the hoary primordial past, the current world order generally emerges as stable, inevitable, natural, and good. This study argues, however, that the literature most relevant for understanding Paul's letters tends rather to suppress the possibility of rivalry and competition in the world of divinity, whether conceived of as set in the past, present, or future.

1 Creation, Battle, and Cosmic Intrigue

Since the pioneering work of Hermann Gunkel in the late nineteenth century, scholars of the Hebrew Bible and ancient Judaism have shown great interest in Babylonian and Ugaritic writings that depict rivalry, conflict, and battle among the gods.[1] Interpreters have especially drawn on second- and first-millennium BCE texts like the Enuma Elish and the Baal Cycle, where great battles prove central to mythic dramas about the creation of the world and the deities that shape, organize, and rule it. Following Gunkel's lead, numerous studies have shown that Mesopotamian, Babylonian, and Syrian traditions shed light on biblical literature, especially in contexts where Yahweh acts as divine warrior on behalf of Israel. Such comparisons prove especially illuminating for images of military victory that appear in prophetic and apocalyptic texts.[2] Many biblical writers imagine Yahweh's triumphs as set in the past or as being right on the horizon of the expected future; some combine both motifs.[3] Understood in this way, the future orientation that characterizes many prophetic and apocalyptic texts constitutes an adaptation of more foundational premises, namely, that Yahweh serves as divine warrior and benefactor of Israel.

According to Gunkel, a myth about combat is to be found embodied in the Enuma Elish and appropriated in biblical writings from Genesis to Revelation. At its core, this myth is fundamentally about the struggle between chaos and order (the *Chaoskampf*). Though Gunkel's work remains generative and influential, critics have also challenged key elements of the *Chaoskampf* theory. From one angle of approach, the discovery of a more expansive set of Ugaritic, Assyrian, and Babylonian traditions has

18

done much to undermine his claim that combat traditions share an essential cosmogonic core. For instance, works like the Epic of Anzu and the Baal Cycle show little interest in world creation, and even in the supposed paradigm, the Enuma Elish, opponent gods threaten primarily as political rivals, not as cosmogonic entities like the sea or sky.[4] From another perspective, Gunkel's *Chaoskampf* works with theories of myth that have since been discredited. Like Gunkel, early theorists such as Georges Dumézil, Claude Lévi-Strauss, and Mircea Eliade understood myths as involving special, transcendental aspects of human activity. These theorists tended, therefore, to posit broad or quasi-universal symbolic referents for certain core myths.[5] Eliade, for instance, theorized a set of categories like order versus chaos and sacred (or primal) time, and others linked certain types of myth to supposed racial phenotypes such as the Aryans and Indo-Europeans.[6] Such theories allow the meanings of myth to float free from the complex, local, and mutable contexts in which they are produced. Whether they arise from some characteristically human yearning, psychic habit, or racial phenotype, myths are not primarily to be understood by appealing to the interests, skills, and ambitions of the people who sang, wrote, and edited them. Instead, they reflect underlying symbolic patterns that derive from broad, perhaps universal categories of meaning.

Though scholars have labored to correct the excesses and blind spots of Gunkel's famous study, many interpreters continue to employ some of his most problematic concepts and categories. In fact, the scholarly literature abounds with language about threatening "chaos-monsters," battles between order and chaos, and wars where good fights against evil.[7] As Debra Scoggins Ballentine argues, such formulations tend to reproduce the moralizing rhetoric and normative claims of the texts rather than subjecting them to critical analysis and second-order redescription.[8] Of course, some of the ancient scribes and mythmakers do correlate threats of disorder with defeated opponents, as when the writer of the Enuma Elish imagines Marduk fighting Tiamat's monstrous army or the author of Revelation 12 pictures a terrible beast that rises from the sea to wreak havoc on earth. Such episodes imply that parts of the natural world harbor threatening anthropomorphic deities of some kind. Nevertheless, the implicit assumption that the cosmos has a stable order, has had one in the past, or will have one in the future presupposes a complex array of ideological assumptions and normative commitments, commitments that should themselves become objects of critical scrutiny. Myths make all sorts of implicit and explicit claims about what is natural, universal, true, legitimate, and good, but these claims must become objects of analysis and second-order explanation.[9]

In what follows, I treat myths about divine war drawn from the extant literature of ancient Babylonia, Assyria, Ugarit, and Greece and from the biblical anthology.[10] Rather than consider these myths as inevitably about cosmogony, order/chaos, or good/evil, I find that the people who wrote and redacted them share certain anthropomorphic sensibilities, especially when it comes to the characters of the gods and their humanlike political arrangements. Consistent with numerous other traditions, biblical writers and editors show an intense preoccupation with relationships of military and political domination. In many cases, however, the biblical writers show a distinctive tendency to create myths about conflict that suppress the possibility of rivalry and competition with Israel's deity. Unlike the more complex narratives in Babylonian, Ugaritic, and Greek literature that involve stronger and weaker gods, negotiated partnerships and schemes, or matched battles and insurrections, the biblical traditions tend to represent conflicts as highly asymmetrical affairs so that victory appears inevitable.[11] As Ballentine argues persuasively, however, many of these distinctions relate to different literary forms and modes of appropriation rather than to some imagined divide between biblical and nonbiblical traditions of myth.[12] Thus, the longer mythic narratives, such as the Baal Cycle or the Epic of Anzu, constitute what she terms "whole narrative articulations" of the conflict topos, whereas the biblical anthology generally preserves shorter epitomes, references, and motifs related to this topos.

Before proceeding, it is important to clarify that the arguments presented in this chapter do not typically posit straightforward cultural or linguistic contacts between texts, cultures, or traditions. To the extent that I focus on common patterns of anthropomorphism, for instance, Greek texts such as the *Iliad* and the *Theogony* prove as relevant as the Enuma Elish and the Baal Cycle.[13] There are many instances, however, where scholars have identified shared patterns of language and imagery, especially among Ugaritic and biblical texts of a similar North-West Semitic provenance. Such findings offer rich insights into the interests, ambitions, and repertoires of the specialists who produced the biblical texts, and they also help to undermine apologetic tendencies to construe biblical traditions as unique, isolated, or exceptional. Nevertheless, it is important to stress that even the most illuminating and direct literary comparisons do not suggest some simplistic unity or straightforward agreement among ancient minds, traditions, and cultures. The people who wrote and redacted these myths do not seem to act as slavish imitators of a static body of given cultural codes or literary forms. Rather, particular writers seem to adapt a complex repertoire of stories, images, motifs, language, and assumptions to suit particular interests and ambitions.[14] Understood in this way, these extant literary creations allow us insight into the complex and largely indeterminate intellectual repertoires of the people who wrote, sang, and edited them.

The Enuma Elish

At the beginning of the nineteenth century, archeologists unearthed Sumerian and Babylonian tablets that greatly expanded our knowledge of ancient Mesopotamia.[15] The Babylonian creation myth known as the Enuma Elish is one of the most important of these finds. The text survives on seven clay tablets that preserve 1,091 lines of Akkadian cuneiform in relatively complete form.[16] As extant, the Enuma Elish presents a story about creation and combat that celebrates the elevation of Marduk as king of the gods. Because Marduk is identified as the patron god of Babylon, it is likely that some version of the Marduk-centered myth circulated during the eighteenth-century BCE reign of Hammurabi, a time of military expansion. Political control of the Babylonian Empire later fluctuated between local tribes and dynasts, but the reign of Nebuchadnezzar I (1126–1104 BCE) marks the rise of a native Babylonian king and the beginning of a campaign for religious renewal focused around Marduk's cult statue.[17] This period thus constitutes the most plausible setting for the creation of this form of the Enuma Elish, though its writer or editor seems to rework earlier traditions.[18] Most scholars consider the text as the product of a single literary hand, most likely that of a scribe working to promote an ideology favorable to the king, namely, the promotion of Marduk to reign over earlier high gods such as Enlil and Anu.[19]

In the Babylonian version, the Enuma Elish opens on a time of primordial unity where Apsu and Tiamat, fresh and salt waters, harmoniously intermingle. In this primeval period, the cosmos lacks gods, land, and firm destinies. These watery gods soon beget children who compete with each other and incite conflicts between their parents. Problems first arise when the young gods become so rambunctious and noisy that they disturb the sleep of Apsu and Tiamat. Desperate for rest, Apsu plots to kill his rowdy offspring, though without Tiamat's consent. One of these children (Ea) discovers the plot and acts defensively to kill his father Apsu. As victorious warrior, Ea then builds a dwelling on Apsu's body and goes on to father Marduk, the mightiest of all the gods.[20] A second cycle of conflict then ensues, one that results in a more fully formed cosmic and divine order. By the end of this battle, the writer of the Enuma Elish installs Marduk as the unrivaled ruler of all the gods, and Marduk goes on to finish the work of creation by organizing the cosmos into a more complex and well-regulated political order. Thus, in a seemingly natural and necessary way, the finished world arrives in the Enuma Elish as one where heavenly bodies, earth, and the heavens all obey Marduk, their heroic benefactor, arbiter, and king.

In a variety of ways, the writer uses Marduk's victory in battle to legitimate a view of the cosmos as a single, unified kingdom under the command of its supreme divine king.[21] Most centrally, the author portrays Marduk both as an unwitting instigator of conflict and as the heroic conqueror and benefactor who frees others from threat. At his birth, Marduk already appears as the most physically powerful, perfect, and wise of all the gods, and he shows early creative potential by fashioning winds as a plaything. Problems arise, however, when these winds stir up Tiamat's waters and irritate some of the other gods. Unable to rest, these deities campaign to persuade the powerful mother-goddess Tiamat to rise against Marduk, urging her to defeat Marduk to avenge Apsu's murder. Still feeling the sting of Apsu's demise, Tiamat agrees and gives birth to a terrifying army composed of eleven monstrous creatures. Playing the role of an adept political leader, Tiamat persuades her consort Qingu to serve as commander of the army, promising him the prize of kingship over the assembly of gods. Responding again in self-defense, Ea and Marduk negotiate an alliance intended to defeat Tiamat and take political power for themselves. As the martial drama unfolds, the writer offers detailed descriptions of Tiamat's battle array and of her tremulous opponents struggling to find a suitable warrior. After two other would-be warriors decline, Marduk arrives on the scene as the valiant, unmatched hero who alone deigns to fight this terrifying foe. In return, however, he also demands supreme political power.[22]

When the rival forces finally meet in battle, Marduk crushes and dismembers Tiamat, binds and imprisons her monstrous offspring, and then uses her body as part of an elaborate building project.[23] Splitting Tiamat in half, he uses one part to create a barrier in the heavens to contain her waters and the other part to shape the earth. Marduk's creative acts also include building a replica of Esagil in the heavens with shrines in it for Ea, Enlil, and Anu as well as fashioning the stars, constellations, moon, years, months, and days, which all work together in a complex and carefully guarded cyclical order (V, 1–46).[24] The writer emphasizes the fixed, well-regulated movements of the heavenly bodies with statements such as, "He established the heavenly station of Nēberu to fix the stars' intervals. That none should transgress or be slothful" (V, 6–7), and elsewhere takes pains to insist that the sun and moon are subordinates of the new high god (V, 11–26).[25] Like the heavenly bodies, other substances and domains (e.g., the waters of heaven, IV, 139–140) also have guards or watchers set over them. Marduk's building projects also include the winds, waters, and mountains (V, 46–64), but in tablet 6 it is the lesser gods who take charge of creating human beings, ostensibly motivated by a desire to avoid the hard work of growing their own food. These gods act collectively to identify Qingu as the instigator of the battle, condemn him to death, and then use his blood to create humankind. Like the heavens, humankind must be fashioned out of the body of another. Near the close of the Enuma Elish, Marduk commands that the divine council build the city of Babylon. This city, located at the very center of the universe, marks a divine political space where the gods will meet and hold council. The work closes with the lower gods singing a series of hymns, each of which celebrates the incomparable power of Marduk and his unrivaled status as supreme ruler, benefactor, and king.

The writer of the Enuma Elish presents a highly anthropomorphic account of creation, one in which the irritations, attachments, and resentments of the gods motivate the unfolding drama and lend it narrative tension. These gods have distinctively nonhuman characteristics—they are, after all, clearly distinguished as deities—but they also have sex, burn with rage, tremble with fear, and in a variety of ways compete, conspire, and cooperate on common political projects. In fact, embedded in this tale of Marduk's awesome military feats and cosmic building projects, we find a not-so-subtle celebration of the stable, well-regulated, and hierarchical political system that emerges to replace the fractious, unpredictable world of the primordial period. These patterns are especially clear in the many scenes where the council acclaims Marduk as their rightful king.[26] To give only one salient example, consider the actions of the assembly in tablet 6:

> The great gods assembled,
> They exalted the destiny of Marduk and did obeisance.

They invoked a curse on themselves
> And took an oath with water and oil, and put their hands to their
> > throats.

They granted him the right to exercise kingship over the gods,
> They confirmed him as lord of the gods of heaven and netherworld.

Anšar gave him his exalted name, Asalluḫi:
> "At the mention of his name, let us show submission!" (VI, 95–102;
> > trans. Lambert)

Similar to the unanimous cry in line 102, the following lines go on to heap acclamation on acclamation in an extended meditation on political justice and obeisance. The story told in the Enuma Elish also reinforces the unstated assumption that martial conquests are the most important qualification for kingship, though these conquests are carefully qualified as feats of a beneficent champion who acts heroically on behalf of others.

By the end of the Enuma Elish, the writer presents the reader with a celebratory picture of a complex, multitiered, and well-ruled cosmos. An organizing conceit is that the world achieves its complete, final, and recognizable form only once it is organized as a fixed hierarchy of substances, realms, and types of being. Though Marduk's rise to power marks a newly stable phase in world history, it is important to stress that the author does not treat the earlier primordial period as a time of unqualified threat, disorder, chaos, or evil. For instance, there is the primordial time of unity and harmony before Apsu and Tiamat have children; problems arise only when Tiamat gives birth to the younger gods, a narrative turn that appears natural and inevitable. Motivations also prove complex, whether the precise issue involves Ea's patricide or Tiamat's vengeful rage, stirred up as it is by other deities. The gods of the Enuma Elish are certainly imbued with positive and negative characteristics, but this is not only, or even primarily, a myth about good or legitimate gods defeating evil, illegitimate ones.

The Epic of Anzu

The Babylonian text known as the Epic of Anzu tells of the heroic military exploits of the god Ninurta and his subsequent rise to kingship.[27] Somewhat like the story of Marduk and Tiamat, the victorious Ninurta defeats a terrifying military-political opponent and wins an elevated position in the assembly. The Standard Babylonian version survives only in fragmentary form but still provides some illuminating points of contrast and continuity with the Enuma Elish and other traditions.[28] This version is preserved on clay tablets that likely date to the first millennium BCE, perhaps the ninth or eighth century.[29] The myth portrays Ninurta's victory as unfolding on a universal, worldwide stage, but the story also includes allusions to the city of Nippur that suggest an association with this particular city.[30]

The unknown author/editor of Anzu opens by celebrating Ninurta's heroic feats. He is portrayed as "Ekur's child, leader of the Anunnaki, focus of Eninnu, who waters cattle-pens, irrigated gardens, ponds (?), in country and town. Flood-wave of battles, who darkens the sash, warrior . . . Strong warrior who slays with his weapon, powerful one who is quick to form a battle array" (I, 5–14).[31] After this preview, the writer then turns to the past to tell of an intermediate stage in creation, a time when the riverbeds of the Tigris and Euphrates had been formed but the world still lacked springs, clouds, and firm destinies for the gods.[32] Even in this period, however, Enlil clearly reigns as supreme ruler, and this status seems secure because he possesses the Tablets of Destiny.[33] Enlil also presides over Anzu's birth, which itself seems to become an occasion for the release of waters that allow Enlil to bathe (I, 65, 79).[34] Enlil appoints Anzu as doorkeeper to his throne room, but this would-be servant instead plots a coup: "I shall take the gods' Tablets of Destinies for myself and control the orders of all the gods, and shall possess the throne and be master of rites! I shall direct every one of the Igigi!" (I, 72–76). In short order Anzu tricks Enlil, steals the Tablets of Destiny, seizes supreme power, and controls "all the rites."

In response to Anzu's coup, a group of shocked and terrified gods assemble and plot to retake kingship by force (I, 87). Enlil attempts to find a champion to fight on their behalf, plying them with promises of unrivaled power among the gods as well as cult centers. Three would-be warriors decline this offer, citing Anzu's power to command and curse, his unequaled status in the assembly, and his total command of cult centers and rites (I, 98–157). Stymied, Enlil schemes to flatter the mother of the gods so that she will persuade her son Ninurta to fight Anzu. As part of this project, Enlil names her mistress of all the gods, the assembly worships her, and she gives a long speech, charging that Anzu has violated the established political order: "Anzu has disrupted the kingship that I designated!" (I, 207). She also offers key advice about the coming battle, suggesting that Ninurta use "evil winds," terrifying thunder, whirlwinds, fog, and the sun and moon, and that he slit Anzu's throat and shoot him with poisoned arrows.

Whereas Anzu stole the tablets by trickery, Ninurta wins them back in a protracted battle involving the heavenly bodies, winds, and waters. So the sun turns dark, Ninurta amasses waters as a flood weapon, and the clouds burst with lightning. After an initial cycle of defeats, the warrior is given additional advice from the other gods, and he uses this to tire and kill Anzu, sometimes portrayed as "slaying the mountain." In thanks, the gods repay their hero by granting him secret lore (*pirishtu*) and names of honor among them, along with the rites and cult centers already promised.[35] The end of tablet 3 is fragmentary, but the lines that do survive contain a long scene of acclamation, as other deities praise Ninurta in the assembly with cries such as "you have won complete dominion, every single rite" and a series of honorific titles that include a uniquely high "name" among the gods. Despite this elevated status, the precise nature of Ninurta's relationship to Enlil remains ambiguous. Amar Annus suggests that he remains the obedient warrior and son of the supreme god, as evident in epithets like "son of the king of habitations" and in language that celebrates Ninurta's dutiful service to Enlil.[36] Whether Ninurta becomes ultimate ruler or simply gains an elevated status in the council of lesser gods, the writer/editor emphasizes both his privileged standing and the unanimous agreement of the council about this new arrangement. Not only do these other gods celebrate his hard-won victory, but they also affirm, repeatedly, that they freely submit to their exalted champion and king.

The weapons involved in the battle between Anzu and Ninurta deserve further comment. The writer tells of a single usurper figure who seizes the Tablets of Destiny, tablets that somehow concentrate an array of distinctive powers in such a way that Anzu is instantly transformed from servant of the high god to king in his place. Though lacking the powers associated with these tablets, Ninurta can manipulate the forces of nature and marches into battle with waters, heavenly bodies, lightning, hail, and whirlwinds at his side. Though Ninurta ultimately kills Anzu with an arrow, these other weapons imply that the heavenly bodies, winds, and storms are quasi-independent beings or instruments; they are gods or can somehow cooperate with and obey gods. In context, however, they primarily serve to illustrate something about the scope of Ninurta's military prowess. In this form of the myth, the writer evokes an intermediate, quasi-primordial phase of world creation but shows little concern with connecting the battle fought and won with a transition to some new stage of creation. Nevertheless, the opening hymn alludes to the idea that Ninurta's victories are a prelude to the creation of springs and irrigating waters, and in other parts of the text the writer associates Ninurta's victory with recovering or freeing waters in some way. As some scholars have argued, this could imply an association between Ninurta's victory and the spring overflow of the Tigris and Euphrates rivers, a seasonal flooding that was enormously important for agricultural productivity.[37] In the extant form of the text, however, these connections remain allusive.

The Baal Cycle

The work known as the Baal Cycle collects a number of myths about conflicts, threat, and rivalry within the Syrian or Ugaritic pantheon. Dating to the fourteenth century BCE, the text survives on six tablets that preserve roughly 1,830 lines of text from a much longer original.[38] The title suggests a single complete text, but the work is better understood as a collection or compilation, albeit one focused on the intrigues and exploits of Baal.[39] Though virtually nothing is known about the original compositions, it seems clear that the writers, editors, or compilers responsible for this form of the text have taken pains to string together tales about the military exploits of Baal, exploits that justify his rise to rule over expansive cosmic domains.[40] Thus in the first cycle of conflict, Baal battles Yamm/Sea (tablets 7–8), in the second he wins a palace (tablets 9–10), and in the third he conquers Mot/Death (tablets 11–12).

The myths contained in the Baal Cycle are disparate and episodic, but each of them plays out on a similar cosmo-political stage. The basic political structure is straightforward: a single high god (El) presides over a crowded, multitiered pantheon of lesser gods. Many of these gods play relatively anonymous, supporting roles, but the main characters tend to have distinctive personalities, powers, relationships, and ambitions.[41] Just beneath El is the assembly or council where the power players meet together to dine, debate actions, instigate conflicts, and settle disputes. Indeed, the individual stories typically open with council-level disputes about issues of decorum, privilege, or perceived slights.[42] While these dramatic tales of intrigue unfold in the assembly and the world below, the figure of El consistently looms over them serving as father, arbiter, and unchallenged master. In a remarkably consistent way, then, this single supreme deity functions to stabilize the vicissitudes of the narratives and lend plausible consistency and coherence to the mythic worlds imagined in each one of them.

In the first cycle of conflict, El conspires with his favored son Yamm (Sea) against Baal. The precise origins of the conflict remain murky, but in the surviving portions of the text Yamm sends his messengers to El's court and brashly demands that El give him Baal as a servant. Following Yamm's instruction, these messengers also refuse to prostrate themselves before El. Instead, they impudently demand, "Give up, O Gods, the one you obey, the one you obey, [O Multitu]de; give up Baal that I may humble him, the son of Dagan, that I may possess his gold" (*KTU* 1.2 I, 34–35; cf. 1.2 I, 18–19; 1 Kgs 20:2–4). These lines imply that Baal is already a ruler of considerable standing, but the writer/editor quickly goes on to describe Baal as an attendant who serves El at the banquet of the gods. El proves agreeable, and in the midst of the court or assembly, he declares to Yamm's messengers, "He will bring tribute to you, like the Gods, [a gift to you] he will bring, like the Holy Ones, offerings to you" (*KTU* 1.2 I, 38). Following this, the goddess Astarte proclaims Baal's demise (*KTU* 1.2 IV, 6–7) but a craftsman god (Kothar-wa-Hasis) instigates resistance. The craftsman urges Baal to fight Yamm and win kingship ("May you take your eternal kingship, your everlasting dominion" [*KTU* 1.2 IV, 10]) and happily supplies him with weapons of war. In quick succession, Baal then defeats Yamm and is acclaimed king in his place. The gods declare, "Yamm surely is dead! [Baal reigns (?)], he indeed rules!" (*KTU* 1.2 IV, 34–35; cf. 32–33, 36–37).[43] The assembly plays a number of important roles, particularly in scenes where they collectively prostrate themselves before their superiors. For instance, they lower their heads to their knees before Yamm's messengers (*KTU* 1.2 II, 23–24), and when Baal rebukes them, they raise their heads again (II, 29) at his command (*KTU* 1.2 II, 24–25, 27–28). Toward the end of the conflict with Baal, two gods celebrate by acclaiming his victory and hymning his rightful rule (*KTU* 1.2 IV, 32–37). Though the text is fragmentary, this acclamation may have been conceived of as addressed to the assembly.

The next set of conflicts center on Baal's ambitions for a palace. In these stories, the goddess Anat plays a starring role both as an emissary on Baal's behalf and as a warrior who rescues Baal from the underworld. Anat's warrior status, personality, and affinity for Baal become pivotal and lend the story much of its dramatic tension. For instance, when she first attempts to persuade El to grant Baal a palace, she offends him by threatening to kill him. Quick to see the error of this challenge to the supreme god, she then attempts a softer approach:

Your decree, O El, is wise,
Your wisdom is eternal,
A fortunate life[44] is your decree.
Our king is Mightiest Baal,
Our ruler, with none above him.[45]
All of us will bring him a chalice,
All of us will bring him a cup.
In lament,
Indeed he cries to Bull El, his Father,
To El, the King who created/established him.
He cries to Athirat and her children,
The goddess and the band of her brood. (*KTU* 1.3 V, 30–37; cf. 1.4 IV,
    41–46)

Here the goddess celebrates the supreme, unrivaled status of father El and
pleads with him to redress the disgrace that now falls on his beloved son.
Her speech portrays Baal as king of the assembly and therefore as entitled
to a palace where he can receive supplication and honors commensurate
with this standing. Though at first aggravated, El eventually plays the role
of an agreeable diplomat and father concerned to settle disputes among his
sometimes difficult children. In the end, then, Anat will succeed and Baal
will have his palace.

The third cycle of conflict involves multiple battles fought between rivals. In the first phase, Mot (Death) captures and "kills" Baal, but in the
next Anat herself kills Mot and returns Baal to his heavenly home.[46] Finally, however, Baal himself defeats Mot again, this time without the help
of the goddess. These dramas begin with the gods assembled at a banquet
meant to celebrate Baal's new temple. When Baal attempts to proclaim
his kingship to Mot, Mot threatens to kill and then take him captive. Remarkably, Baal agrees. Without protest, he simply declares, "Greetings,
O Divine Mot: your servant I am, and yours forever" (*KTU* 1.5 II, 11–12,
19–20), and then he takes his winds, thunderbolts, and rains with him to
become an inmate of the underworld.[47] The other gods mourn him, "Per-
ished the Prince, the Lord of the Earth" (*KTU* 1.5 VI, 8–10), while a deeply
aggrieved Anat sets off on her own to perform an elaborate set of burial
rites. Meanwhile, the council meets to find a successor, but three would-be
replacements come up short. Eventually, however, Anat goes searching for
Baal, kills Mot, and then burns, grinds, and scatters his body over the earth
and sea. When Baal returns to his throne, Mot soon reappears in a brash

and vengeful state, complaining of Anat's harsh treatment. In the end, there is a climactic scene where Baal finally meets Mot in hand-to-hand combat. In a quite distinctive way, this conflict is portrayed as a matched battle between rivals, as each of them trade blows: "They gore each other like buffalo, Mot is fierce, Baal is fierce" (*KTU* 1.6 VI, 17–19); "they drag each other like runners, Mot falls, Baal falls" (*KTU* 1.6 VI, 20–22). The struggle continues until El intervenes to favor Baal. So the goddess Shapsh reports El's decree:

> "Hear now, Divine Mot:
> How can you fi[gh]t with
>   Mightiest Baal?
> How will Bull El, your Father,
>   hea[r] you?
>
> Surely he will remove the sup-
>   port of your throne,
> Surely he will overturn the
>   seat of your kingship,
> Surely he will break the
>   scepter of your rule." (*KTU* 1.6 VI, 23–29)

This decree reaffirms El's kingship by threatening to crush Mot. Though clearly favoring Baal, this settlement allows Mot to keep his own particular domain, together with the scepter and throne so important for rule. Trembling fearfully before El, Mot acquiesces (*KTU* 1.6 VI, 33–35).

Though the evidence is often difficult and fragmentary, most scholars understand the Baal Cycle as a collection with a teleological structure. Understood in this way, each episode serves to justify the extension of Baal's rule, first from the sky (the fitting domain of the storm god), then to the sea (Yamm), and finally to the underworld (Mot).[48] El remains supreme throughout, but it is Baal who comes to rule over the second tier, an expansive domain that extends from the sky down to the earth, sea, and underworld below. A distinctive strand of scholarship has also sought to link these myths with specific festivals or seasonal changes.[49] I agree with Mark Smith and others, however, that these traditions have no necessary relation to particular seasons or cultic contexts, even though Baal's association with winds, storms, and rains certainly proves intriguing, as does his descent to, and return from, the underworld. It is certainly possible that Baal's death and resurrection are in some way envisioned as correlating with the lack of rain in the hot, dry summer and the return of the rains in the fall. Less speculatively, however, these myths show us that certain elite scribes, editors, and collectors took an interest in mythmaking about Baal's kingship. Though in many ways disparate, their literary creations do show certain overarching points of continuity. For instance, they consistently imagine powerful, anthropomorphic agents who do battle, compete with one another, and cooperate to settle disputes or negotiate political domains; once nested together, these territories describe a single, all-encompassing cosmic order.[50] The worlds that emerge, then, are singular, unified, and finite political arrangements; they may be more or less harmonious, but they are consistently hierarchical.[51]

The Battle of the Gods in Hesiod and Homer

Since at least the sixth century BCE, commentators have attached the name Hesiod to the *Works and Days* and the *Theogony*.[52] Both works preserve myths about the primordial past, but the *Theogony* contains a relatively complete creation story, one that begins with a formless, undifferentiated mass and then moves teleologically toward a more recognizable world order under the righteous command of Zeus. It is important to stress, however, that neither of these traditions embodies a widely agreed-upon canon of lore about the gods or the worlds they create, inhabit, and rule. Not only do the myths they preserve appear idiosyncratic when compared with other Greek traditions, but a strong scholarly consensus also holds that they are not the product of a single writer or author.[53] Instead, they are literary artifacts that compile a body of archaic or archaizing Greek poetry that likely dates to the eighth or seventh century BCE.[54] In the *Works and Days*, for instance, an authorial persona emerges that describes itself as a poor shepherd from Boeotia. Though colorful, this persona is best understood as a literary artifice rather than an autobiographical self-description, a conventional trope rather than reliable data about a singular author or worldview.[55] Furthermore, framing the *Theogony* as a composite or amalgamated text helps to account for its complex, sometimes incongruous texture as well as for the editorial or compositional work that, at some point, must have created the stunningly clear, Olympian-centric arc that shapes the surviving form of the narrative.[56]

The *Theogony* tells an elaborate series of myths about sex, reproduction, intrigue, rivalry, and violence. In addition to major players such as Chronos,

Zeus, and Hera, the writer(s) lingers over multistage divine couplings and the riotous broods they produce. Against the backdrop of ongoing couplings and births of new gods, the Titans and Olympians emerge to fight one another for survival and preeminence. As announced in the prologue, this work tells of how the gods "divided wealth and allotted honors, and first possessed deep-ridged Olympos (ἄφενος δάσσαντο καὶ ὡς τιμὰς διέλοντο)" (112–113).[57] Zeus also comes into focus here at the beginning: "King in the sky, he holds the vajra thunder and flashing lightning. He defeated his father Kronos by force, and he ordained laws for the gods and assigned them their rights (κάρτεϊ νικήσας πατέρα Κρόνον· εὖ δὲ ἕκαστα ἀθανάτοις διέταξεν ὁμῶς καὶ ἐπέφραδε τιμάς)" (73–75).[58] In keeping with this framing mandate, the subsequent tales focus on a succession of three high gods: Uranos, Chronos (154–210), and Zeus (453–506, recapitulated in 617–885).

Following an extended, framing preamble (1–115), the cosmogony opens on an abyss (Κάεος, 123).[59] Out of this unformed or empty space emerge Erebos and Night, who go on to bear Aether and Day.[60] At line 126, Earth (Gaia) appears and gives birth to Ouranos, Mountains, Sea, and Ocean, and then through sex with Ouranos, a range of named demigods. Up to this point, divine births appear as neutral or celebratory affairs, but when Gaia gives birth to the Titans, the writer lingers over their monstrous appearances and vicious characters.[61] The firstborn, Chronos, emerges as the most terrible of all, followed quickly by other hideous offspring; cruelty and violence ensue. In the first cycle of conflict, the Titan children provoke hatred, deviousness, and violence in both parents. In a tale of radical dysfunction, Ouranos learns of prophecies about his violent overthrow and attempts to stymie the birth of his Titan children; eventually, an agonizingly pregnant Gaia conspires to help Chronos emasculate his father and finally give birth to these malevolent children (154–172).[62] The victorious Chronos goes on to free many of his Titan brethren, though he drives others under the earth where they await their revenge.

The demise of Ouranos also allows for the birth of more gods, as his spilt blood gives birth to furies and giants, his genitals to Aphrodite (163–206); divine sex and reproduction also continue, breeding many more deities. Some of them appear to be personifications or abstractions such as doom, black fate, death, sleep, dreams, destinies, deception, friendship, and old age; others seem to maintain law and order, such as the fates, which "prosecute transgressions (παραιβασίας) of mortals and gods" (220). Still others correlate with an increasingly complex natural landscape. So Tethys and Ocean generate a series of rivers, and Theia and Sun bear Selene and Dawn, while Dawn and Astraios bear winds, and Erigneia gives birth to the Dawnstar and the other stars.

At line 453, Hesiod's Olympians finally appear on the scene and begin to instigate a second cycle of conflict. As with the first, Zeus prevails against the reigning high god, another bad parent who tries (and fails) to suppress the birth of his Olympian children. In all of this, Zeus's beneficence and power loom large, distinguishing this young god and forecasting his future role as warrior and king. In this episode, for instance, his allies create his weapons (thunder and lightning) out of gratitude for their freedom (501–509); in subsequent tales the Olympians continue to appear as a united military and political alliance, led by a heroic military champion.

On the heels of this redemptive patricide, the writer lingers over Pandora and the evils women bring to men, a distinctive preoccupation that also characterizes the *Works and Days*.[63] Eventually, however, attention returns again to conflict in the divine world, this time with the so-called Titanomachy (621–725), a long, cataclysmic battle fought by Titans and Olympians. Unlike the nimble trickery involved in the overthrow of Chronos, here a full-scale war unfolds as twin allied powers fight for world domination, with the cosmos serving as the theater of war. So the earth quakes, and Zeus's thunderbolts burn forests, melt continents, and boil seas (693–696). Other sources attest to similar myths about a battle between Titans and Olympians, but in the *Theogony* Zeus comes to play a quite distinctive role. Here the battle is equally matched for ten years, but it is Zeus who breaks the stalemate by freeing the hundred-handed gods driven into the earth by Chronos; with these gods on their side, the Olympians finally win the war. A banquet scene set near the end of the war adds dramatic tension and emphasis. Here Zeus gives a rousing speech that recalls how he redeemed the hundred-handers from their "cruel dungeon," and they respond with acclamation: "Your thoughts are supreme, your mind surpassing, that you saved the immortals from the war's cold light . . . Our minds are bent therefore, and our wills fixed on preserving your power through the horror of war (ῥυσόμεθα κράτος ὑμὸν)" (660–666). To similar ends, the writer adds a long scene in which Zeus battles in single combat (687–712) just before the hundred-handers finally intervene to rout the Titans and end the war.[64]

The writer/editor might have ended with this Olympian victory and the settled political order that emerges with it. Instead, the writer adds yet one more scene of conflict, one that seems to definitively install Zeus and put an end to usurpation. So the Typhomachy (826–885) tells of how a single monstrous, hundred-headed Titan named Typhon attempts a coup that fails.[65] Remarkably, Typhon's prowess nearly matches that of Zeus. So the writer notes, He "would have ruled over immortals and men, had the father of both not taken quick notice" (844–845). The gods enter into hand-to-hand combat, and the heavens, earth, and underworld heave and quake as the gods hurl thunderbolts and winds (846–859); finally, Zeus manages to strike each of Typhon's heads with thunderbolts. These missiles melt the earth and cast Typhon down to the underworld (860–874), though remnants of the would-be usurper persist aboveground in the form of sudden, violent winds and capricious storms.[66] This last battle seems to put an end to threats of usurpation, rivalry, and coups, in part by definitively establishing the preeminence of Zeus.

After this last battle, Zeus distributes honors among the Olympians and then consolidates his power through a series of marriages. As in the Mesopotamian and Syrian myths considered already, Zeus's military prowess and benefaction come to justify his status as ruler and judge over all.[67] For all the culminating political and creative drama, however, it is important to note that Hesiod's new world order remains fraught with potential ambiguity. So in a brief addendum, for instance, Zeus swallows Athena so that "she would devise with him good and evil both" (905) and then himself fathers the seasons, as well as Eunomia, Dike, Eirene, the graces, and the fates who assign good and evil to humans.

While the *Theogony* takes every opportunity to celebrate the rule of Zeus, the Hesiodic *Works and Days* develops a succession myth that casts the rule of Chronos as a golden age characterized by leisure and abundance. Here the mythmaker or mythmakers explore the creation of gods, demi-gods, and humans as a series of experimental, often bungled attempts at creation.[68] The work opens with a dark characterization of the present, one where human life is torn by strife, toil, sickness, and pain, much of which is attributed to Pandora and her ilk (74–125). The narrator then turns back to tell of a degenerative primordial past with a succession story that involves five ages and types of humans (129–234). First there is a golden age under Chronos, a time of abundance and leisure when humans live like gods (109–201). Upon their death, the race of gold become *daimones* that roam the earth "tending to justice, repaying criminal acts and dispensing wealth. This is their royal honor" (146–147). Without further explanation (or hint of conflict), the next race simply appears onstage, as the Olympians create a second species—a race of degenerate morons. Though they bring harm to one another, Zeus destroys this race because they fail to carry out their principal duty: to honor the gods (160). Nevertheless, they continue to populate the underworld as "blessed underground mortals" (162). Zeus then creates a third, monstrous race of bronze, a savage brood with untamable spirits and weapons growing out of their shoulders where their arms should be. Fittingly, they destroy one another, without any divine intervention.[69] The writer/editor then disrupts the march of degeneracy by lingering over a race of heroes and demigods. These die fighting heroic battles at Thebes and Troy, and at their demise, Zeus ("the father of gods and men" [196]) sends them off to the ends of the earth, the Isles of the Blessed, where they dwell apart from other mortals under the rule of the august Chronos.[70]

Hesiod's fifth and final race is given again to depravity and decay; their age also encompasses the present. So with the final race of iron, the narrator laments, "I wish I had nothing to do with this fifth generation, wish I had died before or been born after" (201–203). In a long hymn predicting a climax of evils, the writer tells of a time of social and political collapse, as children turn against parents, cities break oaths and go to war, vicious people slay the good, and the natural order reverses course as babies are born with graying hair. At the culmination, the goddesses Shame (or Respect, *aidos*) and Nemesis (Decency) leave earth for heaven so that "horrible suffering will be left for mortal men, and no defense against evil" (233–234).[71]

For all the pessimism that characterizes the *Works and Days*, the narrator also presents images of a just heavenly world, one where Zeus presides over rulers, kings, and ordinary humans. So in the prologue, the judgments of Zeus can easily "straighten the crooked and wither the proud" (11–12), and a later paean celebrates Zeus for sending punishing disasters like famine, plague, and military defeat on account of even "one bad man and his damn fool schemes" (279). In a warning to unjust rulers, the narrator also insists that thirty thousand spirits walk the earth and attend to the courts, while a just and righteous council presides in heaven:

> And there's the Virgin Justice, Zeus' own daughter,
> Honored and revered among the Olympian gods.
> Whenever anyone hurts her by besmirching her name,
> She sits down by the Son of Kronos, her father,
> And speaks to him about men's unjust hearts
> Until the people pay for their foolhardy rulers'

Unjust verdicts and biased decisions.
Guard against this, you bribe eating lords.
Judge rightly. Forget your crooked deals. (296–304)

These lines offer a utopian picture of a divine political order: Zeus presides over all but also distributes rights and responsibilities among subordinates in the council or assembly of gods. Guardian deities also watch over mortals, as does the goddess Justice, who has the ear of Zeus and intervenes to aid the righteous in affairs below. For all the dark pessimism that enshrouds the *Work and Days,* the Hesiodic narrator also allows glimpses of a pristine and just divine world where an illustrious divine council, together with guards, couriers, and patrons all work to better the affairs of humans.

The tales of succession developed in the *Theogony* and the *Works and Days* contrast with other traditions about how the Olympians arrive at a settled political system. So Homer, Plato, and others appeal to myths where Zeus, Poseidon, and Hades agree to apportion the heavens, earth, and underworld by drawing lots.[72] Similarly, a later work by pseudo-Apollodorus recounts the familiar succession of gods (*Bibl.* 1.1.1–1.1.6) but presents the Titanomachy as a joint effort among Zeus, Poseidon, and Pluto fighting to free the Cyclopes (1.2.1). This cooperative effort sets up nicely for their agreement to cast lots (1.2.1), which results in their taking the sky, the sea, and Hades as their respective domains (ἀρχή and δυναστεία). In this kind of myth, the settled rule among the Olympians arises from mutual agreements among three victorious warriors, not from acts of heroism that legitimize a single ruler over all. Nevertheless, the texts share common visions of a settled hierarchy among the gods, one that is won through negotiation and cooperation, as well as through military triumphs.

Books 20–21 of the *Iliad* contain a brief but fascinating account of open conflict in the Olympian court.[73] Homer's gods participate in earthly politics in all sorts of ways, but they generally do so indirectly, such as by inciting passions, causing an arrow to miss its mark, offering counsel, or spiriting someone away shrouded in mist. Human beings, for their part, also remain important participants in their own victories and defeats. In book 20, however, Zeus calls a meeting in which he allows the other Olympians to enter the fray of battle in a much more direct way (20.1–30). This battle ultimately does little to alter the balance of power in heaven, but it does create a thunderous uproar from the heights of heavens to the depths of Tartarus (20.54–75) and adds a good deal of narrative tension. So the gods debate courses of actions, negotiate pull-backs, act as spectators, insult one another, rouse emotions, recall affections and old wounds, attempt to settle old scores, and create new ones. Issues of status and decorum figure prominently. For instance, when Apollo goads Aeneas into battle against Achilles, he insists that his divine mother actually ranks higher than Achilles's, a point that Aeneas himself repeats when they meet in battle (20.105, 199–241). Similarly, in book 21 the gods stand poised for confrontation, but after Athena crushes Ares and Aphrodite (21.400–415), the others negotiate a ceasefire (21.435–467). Soon after, Hera browbeats Athena (21.468–501), and she flees weeping to Zeus, the somewhat aloof patriarch who stands apart from these conflicts, sometimes guffawing with amusement.

"Yahweh Is a Man of War (*'îš milḥāmâ*)" (Exod 15:3): Divine Warriors in Biblical Literature

A rich literary corpus about divine war survives from the ancient Mediterranean and West Asia, and a long tradition of biblical scholarship has made use of this literature to understand the military roles played by Yahweh in the biblical anthology.[74] This comparative work has helped to undermine apologetic theories that claim an exceptional status for biblical traditions and has also helped to shed light on the language, imagery, and assumptions operative in many of the biblical texts. In particular, these comparisons help to normalize the premise that gods act as military and political patrons.[75] For instance, consider the way the Neo-Assyrian king Sennacherib memorializes a successful campaign against Jerusalem: "With the support of the god Aššur, my lord, I fought with them and defeated them. In the thick of battle, I captured alive [the Egyptian charioteers (and) princes (lit., "the sons of the kings"), together with the char]ioteers of the king of the land of Meluḫḫa" (RINAP, no. 140, 8–9).[76] While the king takes these enemies, the support of Aššur is crucial in securing victory. Likewise, in a later campaign the annals recount Sennacherib's prayer: "I myself prayed to [the deities, Aššur, Sîn, Šamaš, Nergal, (. . .) Iš]tar of Nineveh, Ištar of Arbela, Bēl, Nabû, . . . [. . . the god]s who support me, for victory over the army of (my) enemy [and they immediately heeded my prayers (and) ca]me to my aid" (RINAP, no. 148, 6b–9a). In the next generation of Assyrian kings, Esarhaddon appeals to a similar cast of characters and affirms, "The king, who with the help of the gods Aššur, Sîn, Šamaš, Nabu,

Marduk, Ištar of Nineveh, (and) Ištar of Arbela, marched freely from the Upper Sea to the Lower Sea and made all of his enemies [and the] rulers who were unsubmissive to him bow down at his feet" (RINAP, no. 77, 12–14).[77] In these inscriptions, the gods achieve victory while the kings fight alongside them as trusting and obedient servants. Similar patterns emerge in traditions about Ninurta and in the surviving literature from Mari.[78]

An important subset of biblical literature presents Yahweh serving as Israel's military champion, whether in celebrations of past victories over the sea or sea dragon or predictions of a great battle still to come. Indeed, since Julius Wellhausen announced that the military camp was the cradle of the Israelite nation and even its "primitive sanctuary," scholars have generally agreed that Yahweh plays a central role as a warrior throughout the biblical anthology.[79] As a sign of this consensus, much of the scholarly debate has focused on correlating this literature to specific historical, political, and religious realities.[80] The scholarship from the early to mid-twentieth century, for instance, evinces great optimism about reconstructing concrete practices and institutions. So the influential work of Gerhard von Rad famously distinguishes the development of holy war as an institution of the tribal confederacy (the amphictyony).[81] According to this theory, genuine holy war belongs to the period of the judges (not the wars of conquest) where it supposedly appears as a military/political institution with quite specific cultic practices. This institution falls into abeyance when the rise of the monarchy brings a standing army but prophets like Isaiah spiritualize the language of the earlier texts as a critique of the monarchy; the Deuteronomist subsequently reappropriates it to respond to external threats (e.g., Deut 20:1–20, 21:10–14, 24:5, 25:17–19).[82] Von Rad took pains to represent holy war traditions as complex and fluid, but scholars have challenged many aspects of his theory, typically on the grounds that it misrepresents the diversity and ambiguities of the material in service of fairly speculative reconstructions.[83]

Von Rad's reconstructive optimism now appears dated, but Frank Moore Cross published two very significant essays in the late-1960s that remain influential. In "The Divine Warrior in Israel's Early Cult" and "The Song of the Sea in Canaanite Myth," Cross draws on Gunkel's theory of *Chaoskampf* to argue that texts such as the Baal Cycle and the Enuma Elish shed light on the earliest poetic traditions, especially Exodus 15, Judges 5, Deuteronomy 33, and Psalm 68.[84] In a book-length study, *The Divine Warrior in Early Israel*, Patrick Miller further develops these comparisons while also avoiding the kinds of speculative reconstructions that had been so popular in earlier scholarship.[85] Miller also stresses the shifting, often ambiguous roles played by divine assemblies in the literature, whether drawn from inside or outside the biblical corpus.[86]

Building on the work of Cross and Miller, the following analysis treats exemplary texts in which Yahweh appears as a military champion. I focus especially on Exodus 15, Deuteronomy 32–33, a number of the psalms, and prophetic literature that speaks of an impending "day of Yahweh." These examples show biblical mythmakers rather freely adapting images of military triumph, rule, and restoration in idiosyncratic and interesting ways. Despite their many differences, the scribes who wrote and redacted these texts also seem to share a distinctive political agenda, especially when it comes to representing would-be political rivals and military opponents. That is, in a fairly consistent way, they represent Israel's God as battling relatively powerless enemies and nonthreatening opponents. Thus, somewhat different from the longer narrative literature that survives from Syria, Mesopotamia, and Greece, the wars of Yahweh tend to emerge as highly asymmetrical affairs in which victory is certain. To be sure, if all that survived of the Baal Cycle and the Enuma Elish were small bits of text that celebrate the victorious warrior as an unrivaled, fearsome warrior and king, the distinctive attributes of the biblical myths would disappear. As edited in the biblical anthology, however, the enemies of Yahweh tend to appear as more diminutive, even instrumental opponents. In these relatively brief snippets of myth, the scribes and editors do not build narrative tension over competition and conflict in the divine world but rather tend to suppress it.

Though images of Yahweh as warrior abound in the biblical anthology, it is important to note that many discussions of war do not envision Israel's God as actively engaged in the fighting. So in many cases, the scribes prefer to imagine a patron who directs the hearts and minds of favored individuals or communicates through divination. In Judges 20, for instance, Yahweh provides decisive counsel about the unfolding battle against the tribe of Benjamin. Though the Israelites do the fighting, it is later claimed that "The Lord (YHWH) defeated Benjamin before Israel" (20:35 NRSV). In other cases, the divine patron intercedes in different ways, such as by inciting Saul's destructive outrage with the "spirit of God (*rûaḥ ʾĕlōhîm*)" (1 Sam 11:6; cf. Judg 6:34, 11:29, 16:20; 1 Sam 16:14). Elsewhere in 1 Samuel (16:4), the *rûaḥ* of Yahweh departs from Saul while an evil *rûaḥ* comes to terrorize him, though it is explicitly sent by Yahweh for this very purpose.

The Song of the Sea in Exodus 15 and Related Literature

The earliest biblical poetry attests to strong interests in divine military exploits, especially the mythic topos of Yahweh's victory over the sea.[87] Like the Song of Deborah in Judges 5, the so-called Song of the Sea in Exod 15:1b–18 portrays the crushing defeat of Pharaoh at the Reed Sea.[88] In this case, the biblical editors are careful to cast would-be opponents as human enemies (cf. Judg 5:8). So Pharaoh's scheming mind is made to say: "I will pursue, I will overtake, I will divide the spoil, my desire shall have its fill of them (*timlā'ēmô napšî*).[89] I will draw my sword, my hand shall destroy them" (Exod 15:9 NRSV).[90] In works like the Enuma Elish and the Epic of Anzu, desires frequently incite conflict, rivalry, and coups in the divine world. Here, the upstart appears in the form of a human king.[91] The writers and redactors heavily emphasize this asymmetry, in part by portraying Israel's God using the sea as a weapon in poetic images such as "You blew with your wind, the sea covered them" (15:10 NRSV) and "You stretched out your right hand, the earth swallowed them" (15:12 NRSV).[92] Presented in this way, Yahweh's power appears incomparable, his victory inevitable.[93]

The biblical scribes frequently return to images of Yahweh manipulating the sea (15:1, 4, 5, 8, 10, 12, 19), an event so awe-inspiring that the inhabitants of Edom, Moab, and Philistia simply melt with terror and dread (15:14–17). As its enemies recede, Israel safely marches on to Yahweh's mountain (cf. Josh 2:9–11, 24).[94] The asymmetrical relationships of military power come out in repeated appeals to the docility of the sea, the easy fall of Pharaoh, and the trembling weakness of the inhabitants of Canaan, who cower in fear at Yahweh's approach.[95] In all of this, there is little hint that the Egyptians and the inhabitants of Canaan have their own gods, even though a plurality of divinities is required for incomparability hymns such as "Who is like you, O Lord, among the gods (*mî-kāmōkâ bā'ēlim* YHWH)? Who is like you, feared among the holy ones,[96] awesome in splendor, doing wonders?" (15:11). Such acclamations resonate with the cries of the assemblies in the Enuma Elish, the Baal Cycle, and other literature, but here they are set in the mouths of the Israelites. Thus, claims such as "Who is like you, O Yahweh, among the gods (*bā'ēlim*)?" intimate the existence of an assembly of gods, but they serve as foils for hymning the exceptional status Israel's deity, not as allies and co-conspirators with developed personalities, roles, and relationships.

Similar imagery appears in Psalm 114, which treats the lands of Israel and Judah as the sanctuary of Yahweh. So the psalmist tells of Yahweh's easy domination of the sea, imagines the river Jordan turning to flee, and has the mountains and hills "skip like rams" while the earth trembles. Like the writer of Exodus 15, the psalmist recalls a past where Yahweh intervened on Israel's behalf (and inevitably triumphed). So the earth becomes a fearful servant: "Tremble, O earth, at the presence of the Lord (*'ādôn*),[97] at the presence of the God of Jacob (*'ĕlôah ya 'ăqōb*), who turns the rock into a pool of water, the flint into a spring of water" (114:7–8 NRSV; cf. Judg 5:4–5, Ps 29:6). The personifications of the earth, water, and mountains may hint at their status as independent gods, but here they tremble fearfully, perhaps implying that they are cowardly subordinates or lesser beings that are easily manipulated, transformed, and rendered obedient to Yahweh's whim.[98] As with the Song of the Sea in Exodus and other literature, Yahweh's victory also serves as a prelude to establishing a sanctuary for the king. A similar constellation of images and ideas appears in Psalm 24. The psalmist opens with a hymn to Yahweh's creative and kingly powers, noting specifically that "he has founded it" on the waters in v. 2 and then connecting this to a sanctuary or holy place, which only those with "pure hearts" may enter (v. 4). Then beginning in v. 7, the scribe adds a series of acclamations that are nearly identical to a celebratory hymn about Baal's kingship. So the psalmist cries: "Lift up your heads, O gates! and be lifted up, O ancient doors (*śĕ'û śĕ 'ārîm rā 'śêkem wĕhinnāśĕ'û pitḥê 'ôlām*)! that the King of glory may come in" (24:7, 9 NRSV), and "Who is the King of glory? The Lord (YHWH), strong and mighty, the Lord (YHWH), mighty in battle" (24:8 NRSV; cf. YHWH *ṣĕbā'ôt* in v. 10). As Cross showed more than half a century ago, the language about "gates (*śĕ 'ārîm*)" in vv. 7–8 glosses divine beings, as evident in a near word-for-word parallel in an acclamation of Baal.[99] In this way, the writer/redactor appropriates the language of Baal's acclaiming assembly (or reuses a previous appropriation) so that it celebrates Yahweh's privilege instead of Baal's. The "gates" raising their heads remains a somewhat awkward and ill-fitting image, but this gloss proves ideologically elegant in that it erases all other deities, even those occupying the lesser ranks, such as the council that submits to Baal.

A number of other psalms tell of Yahweh battling the sea, often in connection with the Reed Sea (e.g., Ps 78:11–13; Neh 9:11; Pss 66:6, 78:13, 106:7–10, and 136:12–15).[100] Such literature has provided rich subject matter for comparative analysis, especially the topos of Yahweh's defeat of the sea or sea dragon.[101] For our purposes, however, it suffices to treat examples that show biblical writers negotiating a place for other deities in diverse, changing political imaginaries. In some cases, lesser divine beings serve as an adoring host whose acclamations illustrate the incomparable power of the high God, as in Exod 15:11 ("who is like you, O Lord, among the gods?" (NRSV).[102] In these brief snippets, it often remains unclear whether or not the lesser gods choose this submissive status. In other cases, the created order tends to be personified as trembling subordinates or instruments of the high God, not as independent gods with distinct powers and personalities. In yet other cases, monstrous deities, dragons, and waters appear as Yahweh's defeated foes. All three patterns come together in Psalm 77. So in v. 13, the psalmist evokes other gods to underscore the incomparable status of Yahweh—"Your way, O God, is holy. What god is so great as our God?" (77:13 NRSV)—and then goes on to valorize Yahweh's past deeds.[103] In this context, however, the Reed Sea myth comes to involve a battle with the waters, not with Pharaoh:[104]

> When the waters saw you, O God ('ĕlōhîm),
> > when the waters saw you, they were afraid [lit., "writhed," yāḥîlû];[105]
> > the very deep trembled (yirgĕzû tĕhōmôt).
> The clouds poured out water;
> > the skies [lit., clouds, 'ābôt] thundered;
> > your arrows flashed on every side.
> The crash of your thunder was in the whirlwind;[106]
> > your lightnings lit up the world;
> > the earth trembled and shook (rāgĕzâ wattir'aš hā'āreṣ). (77:16–18
> > NRSV; cf. Isa 51:9–11)

Yahweh appears thunderously as the conquering warrior deity and, as in the exodus myth, makes a path through the waters for Moses, Aaron, and their flocks (vv. 19–20). Yet instead of the sea and earth fighting as powerful, threatening opponents, we find them only trembling with fear before the deity with his mighty storm weapon. The precise opponents and relationships of power thus change significantly while the picture of Yahweh as irresistible warrior and benefactor remains largely the same.

Like Psalm 77, Psalm 106 celebrates Israel's God as a supreme creator and commander who manipulates the earth, sea, and storms. This psalm also develops a distinctive representation of the past as the out-workings of a divine plan for just punishment and reward.[107] So Yahweh rebukes the sea (vv. 9–11), sends disease as punishment in the wilderness (vv. 14–15; cf. Num 11:18–24a, 31–34; Ps 78:17–31), has the earth swallow Dathan and Abiram's faction (v. 17; Num 16), sends a punishing fire that burns the wicked (v. 18; cf. Lev 10:2), and unleashes a severe plague (v. 30; Num 13–14,

25; Deut 1:24–27). After the Israelites refuse to obliterate every native of Canaan (v. 34)—preferring to join them in extravagant acts of "idolatry" (vv. 35–39)—Yahweh hands them over to be ruled by their enemies (vv. 41–42).[108] Though language about the rebuke of the sea suggests conflict ("He rebuked the Red Sea, and it became dry; he led them through the deep as through a desert" [v. 9 NRSV; cf. v. 22]), the scribe here represents the domination of the sea as one in a string of episodes where Yahweh metes out righteous divine punishment and reward, whether by using the earth, sea, fire, or disease. The language about the rebuke of the sea in v. 9 probably alludes to a myth of battle, but in general Israel's God appears not to battle other gods in this context but instead to wreak righteous, punishing violence against Israel and its human enemies. Similar patterns appear in Psalm 74, which presents a seemingly intimate lament of despair, loss, and defeat. So the writer imagines "enemies" destroying the sanctuary and burning the meeting places (as Ps 106:41; cf. Pss 44, 77, 80, 83, 89) but never alludes to other gods. The subsequent verses turn back to a heroic past:

> Yet God my King is from of old (*wĕ'lōhîm malkî miqqedem*),
>> accomplishing victories (*yĕšû'ōt*) in the midst of the earth.[109]
> You divided the sea by your might;
>> you broke the heads of the dragons in the waters (*rā'šê tannînim 'al-hammāyim*)
> You crushed the heads of Leviathan;
>> you gave him as food for the creatures of the wilderness.[110]
> You cut openings for springs and torrents;
>> you dried up ever-flowing streams.
> Yours is the day, yours also the night;
>> you established the luminaries and the sun.
> You have fixed all the bounds of the earth (*gĕbûlôt 'āreṣ*);
>> you made summer and winter.
>
> Remember this, O Lord (YHWH), how the enemy scoffs,
>> and an impious people reviles your name. (74:12–18 NRSV; cf. Pss 104:5, 96:10, 33:6–7)

Unlike the very brief discussions in Psalms 77 and 106, this text repeatedly evokes a victory over the sea, which is here construed as a monstrous dragon or Leviathan. Like Marduk's victory over Tiamat, this victory precedes Yahweh's creation of the luminaries, night and day, springs, dry land, the boundaries of the earth, and the seasons.[111] In startling ways, the writer illustrates Yahweh's awesome power by imagining a great battle with the sea followed by a (seemingly) peaceful command thereafter. Other gods thus make brief appearances here but principally as past defeated enemies who move quickly offstage.

As we have noted already, other gods appear rather frequently in rhetorical crescendos about the exceptionalism of Yahweh. Typically, they serve to illustrate something about Yahweh's unmatched, irresistible power. In some cases, however, the host, sons of God, or assemblies become objects of more sustained attention. So in Psalm 96, the psalmist opens by calling the whole world to worship Yahweh and then insists: "He is to be revered above all gods (*kol-'ĕlōhîm*). For all the gods of the peoples (*kol-'ĕlōhê hā'ammîm*) are idols [or "nothings," *'ĕlîlîm*], but the Lord (YHWH) made the heavens. Honor and majesty are before him; strength and beauty are in his sanctuary" (vv. 4–6 NRSV).[112] These statements imply that other gods exist in some form but only as lesser powers, "nothings," and probably subjects of Yahweh's rule. Their precise identifications remain ambiguous, but the psalmist is unequivocal about their lesser status. Similar claims about Yahweh's right to rule abound in the exhortations that follow:

> Worship the Lord (YHWH) in holy splendor;
>> tremble before him, all the earth.
>
> Say among the nations, "The Lord is king (YHWH *mālāk*)![113]
>> The world is firmly established; it shall never be moved.
>> He will judge the peoples with equity."
> Let the heavens be glad, and let the earth rejoice;
>> let the sea roar, and all that fills it;
>> let the field exult, and everything in it.
> Then shall all the trees of the forest sing for joy
>> before the Lord (YHWH); for he is coming,
>> for he is coming to judge the earth. (Ps 96:9–13 NRSV; cf. 29:1–2)[114]

Here the cosmos appears as a stable, well-regulated kingdom that is ruled by its unrivaled divine creator and king. The earth and its peoples are called to joyously celebrate (and submit to) the high God. This may also be implied for the lesser gods evoked in vv. 4–6 (cf. Ps 93) and the heavens in v. 11.[115] The writer of Psalm 89 imagines a similar system of rule but puts even more emphasis on the divine council:

> Let the heavens praise your wonders, O Lord (YHWH),
>> your faithfulness in the assembly of the holy ones (*'ĕmûnātĕkā biqhal qĕdōšîm*).

For who in the skies can be compared to the Lord (*mî baššaḥaq ya ʿărōk la*-YHWH)?

>Who among the heavenly beings[116] is like the Lord (*yidmeh la*-YHWH *bibnê ʾēlîm*),

a God feared in the council of the holy ones (*ʾēl naʿărāṣ bĕsôd qĕdōšîm*),

>great and awesome above all that are around him?

O Lord God of hosts (YHWH *ʾĕlōhê ṣĕbāʾôt*),

>who is as mighty as you?

>Your faithfulness surrounds you.[117]

You rule the raging of the sea;

>when its waves rise, you still them.

You crushed Rahab like a carcass;

>you scattered your enemies with your mighty arm.[118]

The heavens are yours, the earth also is yours;

>the world and all that is in it—you have founded them. (Ps 89:5–11 NRSV; cf. Ps 74:12–17)[119]

The incomparable Yahweh has crushed Rahab and the sea, founded the earth and heaven, and thus fittingly rules as an eternal benefactor, landlord, and king. There are other gods in heaven, but these clearly are of lesser power and rank (v. 6); they assume a submissive posture as the "assembly of holy ones" that acclaims Yahweh (v. 5); and in v. 7 they tremble in fear before their rightful ruler and king. The assembly thus comes to illustrate something about the grandeur and glory of the one set over them.[120] Set in the past, however, there is also the violent image of Yahweh annihilating Rahab (and perhaps other enemies in v. 11) and taking rightful command over the sea. Rahab appears as a divine opponent but one that comes onstage briefly, soon to become a carcass. Thus, as a past defeated foe, Rahab becomes but one more illustration of the exceptional powers of this one-time warrior and now king. In ways that are similar and different, Psalm 29 evokes both the "sons of God" and Yahweh triumphant over the waters: "Ascribe to the Lord, O heavenly beings (*hābû la*-YHWH *bĕnê ʾēlîm*), ascribe to the Lord (YHWH) glory and strength. Ascribe to the Lord the glory of his name; worship the Lord in holy splendor. The voice of the Lord is over the waters; the God of glory thunders, the Lord, over mighty waters (*ʾēl-hakkābôd hirʿîm* YHWH *ʿal mayim*)" (29:1–3 NRSV). These lines suggest an acclaiming assembly of lesser gods and a supreme God who is now dominant over the sea. Though the psalm offers only a "snapshot" and lacks an extended narrative about a battle with the sea, the waters become emphatic subjects of Yahweh.[121] Fittingly, the hymn closes with an image of Yahweh as a king enthroned on the flood (29:10).

In many of the psalms treated so far, other gods appear as members of a council or assembly that explicitly serve as subordinates and subjects of Yahweh. In these cases, the psalmists also tend to personify the earth, sea, winds, and weather as obedient subordinates, even if some have become so only by force.[122] Similar patterns appear in other texts, such as the Song of Deborah in Judges 5, where the earth and heavens are personified as trembling at Yahweh's theophany (5:4–5). Psalm 18 (also 2 Sam 22) likewise pictures the earth quaking and a submissive heaven that bows as the supreme deity descends from above. Upon arrival, this deity then uses the storm as a weapon against the sea.[123] We find yet more images of a trembling earth and fearful host in Psalm 68, but here the psalmist also imagines lesser gods as warriors in a triumphant military march.[124] The writer hymns: "With mighty chariotry, twice ten thousand, thousands upon thousands,[125] the Lord (*'ădōnāy*) came from Sinai into the holy place. You ascended the high mount,[126] leading captives in your train[127] and receiving gifts from people" (68:17–18 NRSV; cf. Pss 50:2, 47:5). In keeping with this triumphal picture, it is soon affirmed that Yahweh will "shatter the heads of his enemies" so that "you may bathe your feet in blood, so that the tongues of your dogs may have their share from the foe" (68:21, 23 NRSV).[128] A quite remarkable image also appears in Judg 5:20, where stars fight as warriors of Yahweh against Sisera. This implies that the heavenly bodies serve as part of the divine military retinue, a notion that may also inform the imagery of texts such as Josh 10:12–13, where Joshua asks a divine patron to make the sun and moon stand still (cf. Hab 3:11; Isa 14:12; Ps 148:2–3; 1 Kgs 22:19; Deut 4:19). In this case, Yahweh accedes to Joshua's request and freezes the heavens while the Israelites take the Amorites in battle. The implication is that Yahweh (and Joshua) has the power to halt the movements of the sun and moon, not that the heavenly bodies themselves are involved in the fighting. As if to qualify these relationships, Yahweh is later said to have fought on behalf of Israel (v. 14).

The Song of Moses in Deuteronomy 32–33

At the beginning of the so-called Song of Moses, a voice emerges that calls the heavens and earth to witness the grandeur of Yahweh (Deut 32:1). With the stage thus set, the writer then presents a compressed overview of

Yahweh's relationship with his favored people and, in this context, also describes the origins of this relationship in a curious way. In a remarkable passage (32:8–9), the nations of the world are said to be divided up among the "sons of god" (*bĕnê 'ĕlōhîm;* LXX υἱῶν θεοῦ), one of which is identified as Yahweh (cf. Deut 4:19; Sir 17:17; Jub. 15:31; Acts 7:42–43).[129] As Mark Smith has argued, these verses could preserve a form of the myth that distinguishes a supreme deity, El, from a set of lesser gods. Though other translations elide possible distinctions between El and Yahweh, Smith treats them as different:

> When the Most High (*'elyôn*) gave to the nations their inheritance,
> when he separated humanity,
> he fixed the boundaries of the peoples
> according to the number of divine beings.
> For Yahweh's portion is his people,
> Jacob his allotted heritage. (32:8–9)[130]

Smith's reading lends support to the theory that Yahweh and El were originally distinct gods, as El distributes the rule of the nations among the "sons of God" (cf. 32:6–7) and Yahweh rules but one of many nations.[131] Further, Yahweh seems to serve in the assembly or council beneath El, the presiding supreme God. Of course, it is also possible that Elyon should be taken as an epithet of Yahweh.[132] In Smith's interpretation, however, Israel's deity has a privileged rank that is, in theory at least, comparable to that of others.

Following the intriguing claims about the "sons of God" in vv. 8–9, the writer/redactor telescopes to focus on Yahweh's relationship with Israel. As a result, the gods of the nations largely fade into the background, only to come onstage again in affirmations of exceptionalism (e.g., "The Lord [YHWH] alone guided him; no foreign god [*'ēl nēkār*] was with him" [Deut 32:12 NRSV]) or in high-pitched rhetoric about the powerlessness of other gods. In some cases, however, other deities appear as a host of heavenly warriors.[133] So in Deut 33:2, Yahweh appears on Sinai with "myriads of holy ones; at his right, a host of his own,"[134] and v. 3 stresses the obedience of this host, which "marched at your heels, accepted direction from you." Here a pliant, obedient band of lesser deities comes to illustrate the commanding, irresistible nature of Yahweh's battle array. In significant contrast, the subject of foreign gods surfaces repeatedly in Deuteronomy 32, but the precise relationships of those gods with Yahweh prove more ambiguous. For instance, in a lengthy tirade about Israel's waywardness, the gods of the nations reappear as non-gods, strange gods, and *šēdîm*, often misleadingly translated as "demons."[135] So the writer harangues Israel:

> He abandoned God (*'ĕlôha*) who made him,
>   and scoffed at the Rock of his salvation.
> They made him jealous with strange gods (*yaqni'uhû bĕzārîm*),
>   with abhorrent things they provoked him (*bĕtô'ēbōt yak'îsuhû*).
> They sacrificed to demons, not God (*yizbĕhû laššēdîm lō' 'ĕlōha*),
>   to deities they had never known (*'ĕlōhîm lō' yĕdā'ûm*),
> to new ones recently arrived (*hădāšîm miqqārōb bā'û*),
>   whom your ancestors had not feared (*lō' śĕ'ārûm 'ăbōtêkem*).
> You were unmindful of the Rock that bore you;
>   you forgot the God who gave you birth (*wattiškah 'ēl mĕhōlēlekā*).[136]
>   (32:15–18 NRSV)

The main emphasis here is on Israel's foolhardy, disastrously disloyal ways. In this context, however, the writer/redactor imagines Jacob prostrate before strange gods, foreign gods, and the mysteriously termed *šēdîm*. The changing language used to designate these gods can be explained by appealing to the common use of parallelism in biblical poetry. It is important to stress, however, that though the writers seem content to mark these gods as illegitimate, at least for Israel, the context everywhere implies that they are competitors of Yahweh. This complex of issues also comes to the fore when the writers imagine the eventual restoration of Israel and evoke the taunts of enemies: "Our hand is triumphant; it was not the Lord who did all of this" (32:27 NRSV). However much the writers/redactors may extol the incomparable powers of Israel's God, other gods remain implicitly (and in these cases, explicitly) on the scene. Indeed, the rhetoric of exceptionalism proves nonsensical without them.

The writers and redactors of Deuteronomy 32 take pains to insist that Israel's deity cannot be defeated. To this end, they depict Yahweh as motivated by love, care, jealousy, anger, and concern with standing vis-à-vis other gods. So the writers inveigh: "How could one have routed a thousand, and two put a myriad to flight, unless their Rock had sold them, the Lord (YHWH) had given them up? Indeed their rock is not like our Rock; our enemies are fools" (32:30–31 NRSV). The driving conceit here is that Yahweh, though of towering military might, nevertheless allows the nations to dominate Israel as just punishment for disobedience. Relatedly, grand plans are in the works to restore Israel, though primarily to display Yahweh's exceptional military and political prowess. So the voice of Yahweh is made to declare:

> See now that I, even I, am he (*'anî 'anî hû'*);
>> there is no god besides me (*wĕ'ên 'ĕlōhîm 'immādî 'ănî*).
> I kill and I make alive;
>> I wound and I heal;
>> and no one can deliver from my hand.
> For I lift up my hand to heaven,
>> and swear: As I live forever,
> when I whet my flashing sword,
>> and my hand takes hold on judgment;
> I will take vengeance on my adversaries,
>> and will repay those who hate me.
> I will make my arrows drunk with blood,
>> and my sword shall devour flesh—
> with the blood of the slain and the captives,
>> from the long-haired enemy.
>
> Praise, O heavens, his people,
>> worship him, all you gods (*kol-'ĕlōhîm*)![137]
> For he will avenge the blood of his children,
>> and take vengeance on his adversaries;
> he will repay those who hate him,
>> and cleanse the land for his people. (32:39–43 NRSV)

Here the writer plays with the language of divinity to depict Yahweh as the triumphant, irresistible, and incomparable military hero. In some contrast to the strange, recent, and foreign gods in vv. 15–18, other gods appear only to be acclaimed as nonexistent (v. 39) or as an anonymous group that is commanded to celebrate the grandeur of Israel's deity. Though there are other gods and peoples, they are utterly powerless to resist the might of Israel's deity. Such a scheme neatly avoids implying that other gods might oppose, fight, or overcome Yahweh, despite Israel's changing political fortunes. To this end, the writers hymn Yahweh's military triumphs but curiously, and consistently, avoid developing myths about the battles supposedly fought and won. Lacking military drama or divine opponents, these triumphs primarily serve to display the awesome, towering nature of Israel's deity. These ideological tensions explain both the absence of divine opponents in this text and the evocation of other gods, which make a brief, anonymous appearance in v. 42, only to be ordered to do obeisance.

The Day of Yahweh in the Prophets

Many prophetic texts appeal to language about a specific day or time when Israel's deity will bring about a great war.[138] Such events are often set on the horizon of the future, but in some contexts "day of Yahweh" motifs are used retrospectively to characterize wars already fought and won.[139] Though examples could be multiplied, texts drawn from Habakkuk 3, Isaiah 13, Joel 3, and Zechariah 14 will suffice to illustrate some especially interesting and illuminating patterns.

As preserved in the MT, Habakkuk 1–3 presents a dialogue between the prophet and God (1:1–2:4), a series of woes or oracles in 2:5–20, and a plea for divine intervention that recalls past victories of Yahweh in chapter 3.[140] As extant, Habakkuk 3 provides evidence of writers and editors rather freely adapting myths about victories over rivers, the sea, and death.[141] In this case, such victories are treated as evidence of overwhelming military might, and they are set alongside a general, nonspecific triumph over the nations. So Yahweh is portrayed as having power that is "like the sun" and marching in a thunderous military procession: "Before him went Deber, and Reshep[142] followed close behind. He stopped and shook the earth; he looked and made the nations tremble. The eternal mountains were shattered; along his ancient pathways the everlasting hills sank low"[143] (vv. 5–6). Yahweh's military retinue includes plague gods like Reshep and Deber (cf. Isa 51), and their march causes the earth to collapse tremulously, a motif that is common to other divine war traditions.[144] Other feats add luster to Yahweh's military might:

> Was your wrath against the rivers, O Lord (YHWH)?
>> Or your anger against the rivers,
>> or your rage against the sea,
> when you drove your horses,
>> your chariots to victory?
> You brandished your naked bow,
>> sated were the arrows at your command.[145] (Selah)
>> You split the earth with rivers.
> The mountains saw you, and writhed;
>> a torrent of water swept by;[146]

the deep gave forth its voice.
>   The sun raised high its hands;
the moon stood still in its exalted place,
>   at the light of your arrows speeding by,
>   at the gleam of your flashing spear.
In fury you trod the earth,
>   in anger you trampled nations.
You came forth to save your people,
>   to save your anointed (*lĕyēšā' 'et-mĕšîḥekā*).[147] (Hab 3:8–13 NRSV)

The precise reconstruction of the text proves difficult, but the MT of these verses recalls a past victory over the sea. Much of the created order also seems to participate in, or at least to respond to, this display of divine dominance. So the writhing of the mountains and the stillness of the sun and moon attest to the shock and awe inspired by Yahweh's military deeds, similar to texts like 2 Sam 22:8, Ps 18:7–8, and Joel 2:10.[148] Importantly, Yahweh's past defeated enemies also include the nations in v. 12, which seems to provide an analogy for the present and looming future. So the writer insists, "I wait quietly for the day of calamity to come upon the people who attack us" (3:16 NRSV) and thus aligns past victories with future ones.

The writers or redactors of Isaiah 13 present a lengthy tale of impending military calamity.[149] Because the extant form of the text shifts temporal perspectives frequently and alternates between the first and third person, some scholars speculate that it combines originally distinct oracles.[150] Whatever the case, the surviving form of the text makes broad use of divine warrior motifs to imagine Yahweh as a mighty cosmic puppeteer. As with Habakkuk 3, the writers/editors of Isaiah 13 imagine a particular enemy (Babylon) or set of enemies, but they also portray this conflict as key to a much larger, all-encompassing world drama. Thus construed, vengeance against Babylon becomes a war of heaven "to destroy the whole earth." In this light, consider language about a mustering of heavenly armies:

> Listen, a tumult on the mountains
>   as of a great multitude!
> Listen, an uproar of kingdoms,
>   of nations gathering together!
> The Lord of hosts is mustering (YHWH *ṣĕbā'ôt mĕpaqqēd*)
>   an army for battle (*ṣĕbā' milḥāmâ*).
> They come from a distant land,
>   from the end of the heavens,

The Lord and the weapons[151] of his indignation (YHWH *ûkělê za ʿmô*),[152]
 to destroy the whole earth (*lĕḥabbēl kol-hāʾāreṣ*).[153] (Isa 13:4–5 NRSV)

Here a towering army of divine and human warriors will lay waste to the earth.[154] Though in context the enemy is clearly Babylon, the writers/editors stage this as a battle between heavenly and earthly powers so that it comes to have worldwide scope and significance.[155] In the subsequent lines, the writers paint these enemies as religiously depraved and wicked, consistent with moralizing rhetoric found in other literature about enemies and opponents. For instance, in v. 9 the writers/editors appeal to language about the "day of Yahweh," insisting, "See, the day of the Lord (*yôm-*YHWH) comes, cruel, with wrath and fierce anger, to make the earth a desolation, and to destroy its sinners from it (*wĕḥaṭṭāʾehā yašmîd mimmennâ*)" (13:9 NRSV). Changes in the luminaries, earth, and waters at Yahweh's arrival likewise signal the broad, cosmic staging of these events, as "the stars of the heavens and their constellations[156] will not give their light; the sun will be dark at its rising, and the moon will not shed its light" (13:10 NRSV). In the following verses, images of violence and vengeance escalate:

> I will punish the world for its evil,
> and the wicked for their iniquity;
> I will put an end to the pride of the arrogant,
> and lay low the insolence of tyrants.
> I will make mortals more rare than fine gold,
> and humans than the gold of Ophir.
> Therefore I will make the heavens tremble,
> and the earth will be shaken out of its place,
> at the wrath of the Lord of hosts (*bĕ ʿebrat* YHWH *ṣĕbāʾôt*)
> in the day of his fierce anger (*ûbĕyôm ḥārôn ʾappô*).
> Like a hunted gazelle,
> or like sheep with no one to gather them,
> all will turn to their own people,
> and all will flee to their own lands.
> Whoever is found will be thrust through,
> and whoever is caught will fall by the sword.
> Their infants will be dashed to pieces
> before their eyes;
> their houses will be plundered,
> and their wives ravished. (Isa 13:11–16 NRSV)

Like the promised destruction of "the whole earth" in 13:5, God's wrath
is directed against the evil of "the world (*tēbēl rā'â*)" (v. 11) writ large. The
characterization of the luminaries in v. 10 and of the earth and heavens in
v. 13 could suggest that they are deities of some kind, but they do not seem
to be targets of the military campaign. Instead, Yahweh's enemies are more
clearly pictured as humans whose wickedness justifies their savage, pitiless
torture and death.[157] In keeping with this general picture, the writers go on
to depict the enemy as arrogant, sinful, and wicked and in v. 19 promise to
make Babylon like Sodom and Gemorrah.[158] Similar oracles appear in texts
like Isaiah 34, where the target is Edom, and in Zeph 2:13–14, where it is
Ninevah. Likewise, Ezekiel 30 tells of how Yahweh uses Babylon to desolate Egypt and its allies (cf. Ezek 7, Jer 46). Somewhat like Babylon in Ezekiel 30, the writers of Isaiah 13 go on to construe the Medes as instruments
of punishment.[159] According to the picture drawn here, a single heavenly
power manages earthly affairs, whether by making war against diminutive
human kingdoms or by using some of these kingdoms to punish others of
them. It is also notable that Yahweh is not pictured as fighting against other
gods, at least in this case. Indeed, other deities hardly appear here, and the
cosmos serves as little more than a framing panorama that helps to portray
Yahweh as universal ruler and righteous divine puppeteer. Typical of other
divine war traditions found in the biblical anthology, Yahweh also appears
with an army and achieves military defeat in a highly asymmetrical war.[160]

The writers of Joel and Zechariah 14 develop images of battle that some
scholars construe as full-blown eschatological wars.[161] In Joel 1:1–2:17, for
instance, Yahweh rouses the nations against Israel as a judgment for its
misdeeds, but then in 2:18–4:17 the heavenly armies summarily defeat the
nations and Yahweh takes up residence in a newly restored Israel.[162] So in
Joel 2:1, a war trumpet signals the arrival of the "day of Yahweh" and of an
army, "their like has never been from of old, nor will be again after them in
ages to come" (2:2 NRSV).[163] This irresistible force advances with a destructive fire and with divine beings that have the appearance of war horses; its
chariots and warriors scale walls, leap upon cities, and desolate the land
(2:2–9). For all the mayhem and devastation, comments such as "each keeps
to its own course, they do not swerve from their paths (*wě'îš bidrākāyw
yēlēkûn wělō' yě'abbēṭûn 'ōrĕḥôtām*)" (2:7 NRSV) affirm that these armies
are organized and obedient.[164] In keeping with this picture of an organized assault, their commander soon emerges: "The Lord utters his voice at

the head of his army (YHWH *nātan qôlô lipnê ḥêlô*); how vast is his host! Numberless are those[165] who obey his command (*kî rab mĕ'ōd maḥănēhû kî 'āṣûm 'ōśēh dĕbārô*). Truly the day of the Lord is great (*gādôl yôm*-YHWH); terrible indeed—who can endure it?" (2:11 NRSV; cf. Mal 3:2–4; Jer 10:10). In chapter 3, the writers shift to war imagery that targets the nations:

> Proclaim this among the nations:
> Prepare war (*qaddĕšû milḥāmâ*),
>> stir up the warriors (*hā'îrû haggibbôrîm*).
> Let all the soldiers draw near (*kōl 'anšê hammilḥāmâ*),
>> let them come up.
> Beat your plowshares into swords,
>> and your pruning hooks into spears;
>> let the weakling say, "I am a warrior (*gibbôr 'ānî*)."
>
> Come quickly,
>> all you nations all around,
>> gather yourselves there.
> Bring down your warriors, O Lord (*ḥanḥat* YHWH *gibbôrêkā*).[166]
> Let the nations rouse themselves,
>> and come up to the valley of Jehoshaphat;
> for there I will sit to judge
>> all the neighboring nations. (Joel 3:9–12 NRSV; Heb 4:9–12)[167]

As Patrick Miller notes, the writers call on Yahweh to appear with an army of heavenly warriors (*gibbôrîm*) while the nations are gathered below and brought to the valley of Jehoshaphat.[168] In the subsequent lines, the heavenly bodies darken (as in Isa 13:10, Judg 5:20, Hab 3:11, and Josh 10:12–13) and the earth quakes at Yahweh's arrival (cf. Judg 5, Ps 68, Deut 33, 2 Sam 22 = Ps 18, Hab 3):

> Multitudes, multitudes,[169]
>> in the valley of decision!
> For the day of the Lord is near (*qārôb yôm* YHWH)
>> in the valley of decision.
> The sun and the moon are darkened,
>> and the stars withdraw their shining.
>
> The Lord roars from Zion (YHWH *miṣṣiyôn yiš'āg*),
>> and utters his voice from Jerusalem,
>> and the heavens and the earth shake.
> But the Lord is a refuge for his people,
>> a stronghold for the people of Israel.

So you shall know that I, the Lord your God (*'ănî* YHWH *'ĕlōhêkem*),
> dwell in Zion, my holy mountain.
And Jerusalem shall be holy,
> and strangers (*wĕzārîm*) shall never again pass through it. (Joel
> 3:14–17; Heb 4:14–17 NRSV; cf. Zech 14:21, Isa 52:1)[170]

The idea that Israel will be restored by violence is common enough in other
literature, but the geographic details and the gathering of the nations here
prove distinctive. As the context makes clear, however, these enemies are
roused and gathered together to fight by the will of heaven. Then, following
a terrible but definitive war, Yahweh will dwell in Zion, perhaps guarantee-
ing its purity, integrity, and impermeability. The work closes (3:18–21 NRSV;
Heb 4:18–21) with the image of a restored Jerusalem flowing with milk and
honey.

Zechariah 14 also tells a quite developed drama about a "day of Yahweh" and a culminating war against the nations (cf. Ezek 37–38). Jerusalem
itself first becomes a target of divine wrath and is defeated, at least in part.
Just after this, however, comes a great, vengeance-exacting war against the
nations. So Yahweh is made to proclaim: "I will gather[171] all the nations
to Jerusalem, for war. Then the city will be captured, the houses will be
plundered, and the women will be ravished; half the city will go into exile, but the rest of the people will not be cut off from the city.[172] Yahweh
will go forth[173] and fight against those nations as when he fights on the
day of battle (*wĕyāṣā* YHWH *wĕnilḥam baggôyim hāhēm kĕyôm hillāḥămô
bĕyôm qĕrāb*) (14:2–3).[174] Consistent with other imagined wars against the
gentile nations, especially those in Jeremiah (e.g., 4:5–8, 25:1–21), the writ-
ers/editors here evoke a broad, all-encompassing punishment of "all the
nations" (cf. Jer 25:26, Zech 1:20–21).[175] The appearance of the divine army
causes dramatic changes in the heavens and on earth, as the heavenly bodies change their courses and Yahweh stands on the Mount of Olives, splitting the earth:

> Then Yahweh my God will come; and all the holy ones will be with you (*ûbā*
> YHWH *'ĕlōhay kol-qĕdōšîm 'immāk*).[176]
>
> It will be on that day: there will no longer be cold or frost. One day, that
> will be known to Yahweh, there will be neither day nor night, for at evening
> time it will be light.
>
> On that day, the living waters will go forth from Jerusalem, half of
> them to the eastern sea and half of them to the western sea. This will be so
> in summer and in winter.

Yahweh will be king over all the earth (*wĕhāyāh* YHWH *lĕmelek 'al-kol-hā 'āreṣ*);[177] and on that day Yahweh will be one, and his name one (*bayyôm hahû' yihyeh* YHWH *'eḥād ûšĕmô 'eḥād*). (Zech 14:5–9)[178]

The deity arrives with a host of divine beings and radically transforms the earth, the heavenly bodies, and the cycles of the seasons, all of which underscore the power of the high God.[179] Likewise, language about a set "day" reaffirms the divine plan for history, and the focus on Jerusalem organizes world political space so that Israel's God appears at its center.[180] Yahweh's arrival as king and commander also serves as a prelude to a culminating war against the nations. So in subsequent verses Yahweh's army sends flesh-eating plagues and panic, and they seize the wealth of the nations as booty (vv. 12–19). After such devastation, Zechariah 14 adds a vision of the surviving nations coming to Jerusalem to worship at the festival of booths, on pain of plague and famine (vv. 18–19).

The above texts from Habakkuk, Isaiah, Joel, and Zechariah adapt language, images, and assumptions about divine battle to imagine wars of Yahweh set in the future. In a number of cases, these wars are conceived of as culminating battles against the nations as well as against the wayward of Israel. In these texts, we find images of Yahweh as a towering warrior from on high, at whose arrival the earth trembles, shakes, and changes its form, sometimes radically, as in Zechariah 14. Language about the heavenly bodies and divine military hosts underscores the cosmic scope of Yahweh's military power, consistent with images of the divine assembly and the host elsewhere as a faceless group of subordinates.[181] In fact, in this literature, the host, the heavens, the earth, and the heavenly bodies are typically imagined as serving as Yahweh's minions and subordinates (cf. Isa 34). This picture of heavenly order avoids intimations that Yahweh might fight against divine opponents, the gods of the conquering (and soon to be conquered) nations. Instead, there are only highly asymmetrical wars where pitiful human armies are foolishly arrayed against heaven. Consistent with texts such as Exodus 15, Deuteronomy 32–33, and many of the psalms, discussions of the day of Yahweh also strategically suppress intimations that Yahweh could have divine opponents or rivals who could pose significant threats.[182]

Conclusion

Because "conflict myths" are so often used to understand biblical discussions of war, it is important to be clear about just what points of continuity can be plausibly discerned in the literature. As argued here, the mythmakers who wrote and edited texts such as the Baal Cycle, the Epic of Anzu, the Enuma Elish, and the *Theogony* do not share a single, widely agreed-upon set of beliefs, frameworks, or worldviews. Rather, they seem to play with or improvise on some basic premises and assumptions, the most widely shared of which is that powerful anthropomorphic beings create, sustain, and rule the cosmos. Sex, rivalry, and competition among the gods—particularly over issues of status or standing—seem to follow from this shared anthropomorphic habit, in a seemingly inevitable and natural way. In cases where rivalries lead to open conflict, mythmakers often build narrative tension by stressing the awesome power of opponents and the uncertain nature of the conflict's outcome. So warrior gods sometimes tremble in fear, lose battles, fail in their initial attempts, and can even be killed, at least temporarily. Warriors such as Ninurta, Marduk, and Baal also tend to work together with other gods to forms alliances and coalitions. In Hesiod's *Theogony*, for instance, the battles fought by Chronos and Zeus become (at least in part) heroic battles to free others from tyranny, feats that also serve to justify their acclamation and elevation within an assembly of other gods.

The biblical mythmakers work with similar assumptions about the nature of divinity, but whereas myths from Ugarit, Babylon, and Greece distribute domains and responsibilities within a relatively crowded pantheon, biblical writers and editors tend to centralize many of these roles in a single deity. Despite much rhetoric about the nonexistence of others gods, however, most of the biblical writers and redactors continue to imagine lesser beings that serve Yahweh, whether they constitute a military retinue, a divine council, heavenly bodies, or an anonymous heavenly host. Thus, the comparisons suggest that the biblical mythmakers work with distinctive interests and strategies, none of which are aptly characterized as monotheistic.[183] Instead, they attest to a common centralizing strategy, one that has important implications for myths about divine conflict and war.

The biblical texts treated here do not reveal a single set of ideas, language, or images about conflict and battle, but they do show a marked tendency to suppress the idea that Israel's God has enemies and opponents in the divine realm. One of the most important results is that Yahweh tends to defeat relatively powerless enemies and instrumental opponents. Writers and redactors use a variety of literary strategies for suppressing conflict, but four are particularly common: they omit or edit out other gods; they demote or reclassify other gods and potential competitors to ranks of docile or relatively powerless subordinates; they defer Yahweh's direct military activity to the past and the future; and they reinterpret military defeat and conquest as acts of righteous chastisement and punishment by the supreme deity.[184] Most of these strategies are also evident in Mesopotamian, Ugaritic, and Greek myths, where gods regularly displace and expropriate the powers of other gods, and military defeats are often claimed to be punishment for sin and impiety. The biblical discussions attest to the ongoing usefulness of these strategies in new and changing contexts.

2 Assemblies, Councils, and Ranks of Divinity

The previous chapter treated myths about conflict and combat in the Enuma Elish, the Epic of Anzu, the Baal Cycle, and the *t* as well as in a number of shorter discussions drawn from the biblical anthology. Though these traditions are of diverse provenance, I argued that they share common anthropomorphic premises about the nature of the cosmos and the gods, especially insofar as they envision the world as a single, organized political system ruled by a supreme god acting together with lesser-ranking deities. The writers of the longer Mesopotamian, Syrian, and Greek narratives make these roles and relationships central as they create highly anthropomorphic characters that fight to establish, defend, or renegotiate their places within the divine political order. The biblical writers work with similar anthropomorphic assumptions but tend to explore divine conflicts in quite distinctive ways. In particular, their innovative myths about political power tend to suppress the possibility of rivalry, conflict, and coups in the world of divinity. Whereas the longer narratives involve stronger and weaker gods, negotiated partnerships and schemes, matched battles, and even death and dismemberment, the biblical traditions tend to portray military victories won by a god without rival. Despite these differences, many of the biblical writers continue to envision the cosmos as an organized political system with a plurality of gods. Rather than disappear, then, lesser gods frequently appear at the sidelines, whether in brief evocations of defeated foes, as attendants crowding the heavenly court, or as anonymous hosts of armies and heavenly bodies whose dutiful service reflects the glory of their divine creator, commander, and king.

In this chapter, I extend this analysis to the later Hellenistic traditions of 1 Enoch, Jubilees, Daniel 7–12, and texts from Qumran such as the War

Scroll and the Community Rule. With the partial exception of Jubilees, these works have been at the center of scholarly debate about the nature of Jewish and Christian apocalypticism. An especially resilient tradition of interpretation has sought to frame this literature, and apocalypticism generally, as concerned with cosmic rebellion, a battle to defeat evil, and various kinds of struggle against supposed demonic beings and evil powers.[1] Among other problems, such frameworks of analysis reflect normative interests and apologetics, and they often lead to tendentious conclusions about the meaning or function of these conflict motifs across a wide array of literary settings. Many of the texts considered here, for instance, work to locate conflict and struggle on the periphery rather than at the center of the world stage so as to avoid intimations of full-scale rebellion, competition, and coups. Furthermore, proponents of the powers theories place heavy emphasis on opponent figures—whether construed as demonic powers, rebel angels, or more nondescript "evil powers"—in ways that confuse normative categories of analysis with second-order critical ones.[2] As with claims about world rebellion and cosmic war, such approaches often lead to superficial amalgamations of the evidence that obscure some of the most interesting patterns in the literature.

The conceptual framework of a cosmic polity offers a more helpful way to understand the diverse interests, motifs, and assumptions that inform works such as 1 Enoch, Daniel 7–12, Jubilees, and the War Scroll. Understood in this way, the people who wrote and edited these works share only a limited set of interests in mythmaking about divine politics and some familiar conceptual resources for doing so. That is, they adapt a shared model of a humanlike political kingdom where power is centralized in a single ruler. This model easily accommodates different levels and types of agents, from the supreme deity to subservient messengers and generals, worshippers in the heavenly court, disobedient divinities, leaders of the heavenly bodies, functionaries controlling winds and weather, evil spirits accidentally unleashed on the earth, and named figures like Mastema and Belial. Though the lower ranks are generally characterized as docile and submissive, some writers also develop myths about foolish insubordinates, overzealous divine managers, and harassing hosts. Understood in context, however, these characters typically serve as foils in a cosmic drama that is more fundamentally about the irresistible, providential, and just center of political power high above in the heavens.

Ranks of Divine Beings and Divine Councils in Biblical Literature

The Hellenistic texts treated here show distinctive interests in myth-making about lesser deities, but they operate with conceptions of divine hierarchy that stand in continuity with much biblical and other literature. As scholars such as Frank Moore Cross, Theodore Mullen, Patrick Miller, and Mark Smith have demonstrated, notions of a heavenly political order familiar from the Enuma Elish, the Baal Cycle, and the Epic of Anzu prove resilient in biblical texts.[3] For instance, while some texts imagine other deities acclaiming the God of Israel (e.g., Pss 29:1 and 96:7), Psalm 82 imagines Yahweh standing in a council of gods and judging the others worthy of death, thus preserving a vestige of the very assembly it claims to obliterate.[4] To quite different ends, the writer of Deuteronomy 32 imagines a supreme god allocating rule of the nations to each of the sons of god and identifies Israel as "Yahweh's portion" (32:9). Whereas in Psalm 82 Yahweh destroys divine peers and competitors, Deuteronomy 32 preserves the idea of a second-tier council of considerable rank and importance, one of whom is identified as the God of Israel. Much later, the editors of the MT change the "sons of god" to "sons of Israel," but the Aramaic fragments from Qumran support the reconstruction "sons of god (*běnê 'ĕlōhîm*)." Taking the earlier text as "sons of god" also explains the *huiôn* or *aggelôn theou* (sons or messengers of God) of the LXX Greek translations.[5] Such examples show that biblical scribes worked with concepts of a divine assembly familiar from other West Asian and Mediterranean religions where gods such as Baal and Mot serve in the court of El, or Poseidon and Hades work together as co-regents with Zeus. At the same time, the polemic in Psalm 82 and the redaction history of the "sons of god" in Deuteronomy 32 also suggest an interest in shifting and reclassifying members of the heavenly entourage in ways that centralize powers in Israel's God.[6]

As Mark Smith argues, the conceptual framework of a pantheon persists in biblical texts but has undergone "a process of collapse and telescoping."[7] Some biblical writers adapt images of divine assemblies and councils, but they tend to imagine a single high God who presides over a less active, usually nameless group of lesser beings who lack independence and personality. Though more peripheral, these beings continue to function as messengers, attendants, worshippers, fighters, generals, and overseers of the heavenly bodies and various cosmic subregions, just as they do in much other West Asian and Mediterranean literature.[8] For instance, Reshep,

Deber, and Astarte appear in Mesopotamian traditions as gods of considerable interest and intrigue, but the writer of Habakkuk renders them as mere subordinates who duly serve Yahweh in battle (Hab 3:5), just as the sea obeys Yahweh's command in Exodus 15 and other literature.[9] In Habakkuk 3, Reshep and Deber also appear briefly and with little intimation that they have personalities, independence, or volition. Images of a deliberative council also appear in 1 Kings 22 and Job 1–2 but they mainly serve to illustrate the greater glory of the heavenly king. In 1 Kings (22:19b–22), for instance, Micaiah reports a vision of Yahweh enthroned with the hosts of heaven (*ṣĕbā' haššāmayim*) on each side, and in v. 21 the seer overhears a discussion among unnamed members of the assembly. Similarly, the writer of Isa 6:1–11 portrays a supreme deity on a lofty throne with seraphs as attendants, and in Job 1, sons of God (*bĕnê hā'ĕlōhîm*) present themselves before Yahweh, including an accuser figure (*haśśāṭān;* cf. Zech 3:5) who deliberates with the high God (Job 1:6–12, 2:1–7a).[10] Though typically minor actors, these docile crowds, intermediary figures, and attendants serve myths about heavenly power where all lesser beings happily submit to their supreme ruler, arbiter, and king.[11]

Much of the biblical literature evokes faceless subordinates and anonymous hosts, but the writers of Ezekiel and Zechariah share a marked interest in mythmaking about the lesser ranks. Though sometimes treated as evidence for Jewish traditions of angelology, these divine operatives are better understood as members of the lesser ranks, councils, or hosts that prove resilient in biblical and nonbiblical literature. Instead of introducing some new category of beings, then, the writers and editors of Ezekiel and Zechariah elaborate on the idea of a cosmic polity in innovative and interesting ways.

The unknown author of Ezekiel lays out a divine plan for punishing Israel for impurity, idolatry, and deception, with a particular focus on indicting Jerusalem's priests and prophets.[12] In chapters 5–6, the writer charges Israel with abandoning its favored status, following the ways of the outsiders, and outdoing the nations in wickedness. Repeated first-person statements such as "I will bring the worst of the nations to take possession of their houses" (7:24 NRSV) affirm God's direct control of these acts of righteous retribution, whether they take the form of famines, plagues, mass death, or deportation. Chapters 8–11 shift the focus to visions of the heavenly court where a glorious king parcels out righteous judgments to divine delegates and subordinates. Framed in this way, the destruction of Jerusalem is brought about by divine servants who dutifully obey their orders (8:5–6). Whether in marking the repentant city dwellers (9:4) or executing all the others (9:5–6), these servants of heaven carry out acts of righteous violence exactly as commanded by the supreme deity (9:6–11). Though maintaining a focus on Israel's crimes throughout, the writer also warns the "arrogant" princes of Tyre, Edom, and Assyria that a coming destruction awaits them and predicts an ominous, punishing war against the nations in chapters 28 and 36. So chapters 12–37 labor to represent heavenly powers pulling the strings in these earthly dramas, but chapter 38 predicts a time when the supreme God will rouse an army from the north to come against Israel in order to "display my greatness and my holiness and make myself known in the eyes of many nations" (38:23 NRSV). Instead of building narrative tension with tales of combat and political intrigue, Ezekiel envisions a battle where enemies are instrumental and victory is assured. Chapters 40–48 also look to the future with elaborate visions of a restored temple, land, and people, promising that the high God will again live inside the temple and the people will no longer defile it.

The writer of Ezekiel shows an intense preoccupation with mythmaking about heavenly and earthly politics. Among other uses, these myths avoid intimations that Israel's God could suffer loss, weakness, or defeat at the hands of others. To this end, the writer creates a picture of heavenly rule in which the gods of other peoples simply disappear, leaving Israel's God alone as a heavy-handed ruler and omniscient judge. According to this picture of things, the divine world consists of a single political order in which obedient operatives and subordinates carry out the just commands of heaven. Thus construed, extravagant levels of violence, warfare, and death become righteous acts of divine punishment. Nevertheless, after a punishing war against the nations, a restored Israel will reemerge in which a purified, obedient people will finally behave just as they should have done all along.[13]

In ways that are similar and different, the unknown author of Zechariah 1–8 frequently appeals to the lesser ranks to explore rule, punishment, and restoration.[14] In chapter 1, for instance, a divine being converses with the chief deity on matters of political justice (1:12) while others serve as messengers (*hammal'āk,* 1:9) or roam the earth on patrol (1:10; cf. 1:11, 6:7; Job 2:2; Gen 3:8). In this and other scenes, the writer represents a single, unified political system where the gentile nations serve the interests of heaven. Though Israel's political subjection generally serves these interests, in some cases the writer allows that the nations may overstep their punishing mandate. So in chapter 1, the supreme God voices concern and dissatisfaction: "I feel great wrath against the nations which rest securely[15] with whom I felt but little wrath although they fostered evil" (1:15).[16] The deity also promises to restore Israel and crush the conquering kingdoms with four divine "blacksmiths" (or "smiths," ḥārāšîm, 1:20).[17] Though ambiguous, these lines suggest that the nations have exceeded their punishing mandate and, like Israel, will be objects of punishing justice from above. Numerous other scenes give prominent roles to divine servants, such as the seven patrolling eyes of God in 4:10, the anointed ones at the side of Yahweh in 4:14, and the chariots of the four winds in 6:1–8 (cf. Ps 104:4).[18] In other cases, these lesser deities take on more developed political roles in the divine court, such as when two divine beings (an accuser figure and a mal'āk of Yahweh) present Joshua before the throne of God (Zech 3; cf. Job 1–2, 1 Kgs 22:19–22, 1 Sam 28:4, Ps 109:4).[19] Despite much dour news from above, the writer also promises respite, restoration, and judgment. So chapter 8, for instance, promises a time of restoration and return when ten people will grasp hold of every Jew, begging, "Let us go with you, for we have heard that God is with you ('ĕlōhîm 'immākem)" (8:23; cf. 2:11; 14:9, 16–19).

Later Jewish and Christian writers develop similar representations of heavenly politics, often portraying Yahweh enthroned and surrounded by attendants, receiving messengers within the heavenly court, and directing subordinate generals and fighters such as Michael or Melchizedek. The writers of 1 Enoch, Daniel 7–12, and many texts from Qumran build images of a glorious political system in heaven that is singular, just, unified, and uniquely tied to Israel (cf. Rev 4–5). For instance, in 1 En. 14, the narrator beholds a magnificent heavenly palace of hailstones, fire, snow, and shooting stars that encloses the throne room of God. Though the throne is surrounded by thousands and thousands of holy ones and watchers, the writer takes pains to clarify that these beings do not approach it and that the supreme God "needed no counselor" (14:22).[20] Fittingly, the narrator himself falls prostrate and receives a long message about the divine plan for history (15:1–16:4). Similarly, the writer/editor of Daniel 7 presents a political myth about four kingdoms, each of which is punished in a heavenly court. Here in the heavens, thrones are set up for the council and the Ancient of Days takes his seat on a resplendent throne surrounded by "a thousand thousands" who serve him and "ten thousand times ten thousand" who stand before him (7:10 NRSV). By imagining exalted powers in heaven managing the affairs of history, these writers exploit the unseen heavenly realms and the creative abstraction of time itself to depict divine rule as self-evident, unified, and providential. While each of these heavenly dramas proves innovative and distinctive, they share certain interests and conceptual resources with numerous other traditions, including writings drawn from the biblical anthology and Mesopotamian, Syrian, and Greek myths that develop more robust tales of political intrigue.

The Traditions of 1 Enoch

First Enoch preserves at least five distinct compositions of differing provenance: the Astronomical Book, the Book of the Watchers, the Book of Dreams or Dream Visions, the Epistle of Enoch, and the Similitudes or Parables of Enoch. The figure of Enoch plays prominent roles in each of these works, as do myths about heavenly rulers and apocalyptic judgments. A number of these traditions also include myths about divine insubordinates.[21] Though often construed as myths about rebellious, controlling powers of evil, the Enochic writers labor to portray these moments of divine disobedience as relatively minor eruptions within a settled, unified, and well-ordered political kingdom. Thus, myths about overzealous divine managers and adventurous watchers work to suppress the possibility of rebellion, usurpation, and coups.

The Astronomical Book of Enoch

The Astronomical Book presents a detailed set of expositions about the ranks and movements of the heavenly bodies. The most basic premise of the Astronomical Book is that the regular movements of the luminaries reflect a militaristic chain of command in the world of divinity.[22] So an opening summary characterizes the work as a whole: "The book about the motion of the heavenly luminaries (*berhānāta samāy*), all as they are in their kinds, their jurisdiction, their time, their name, their origins, and their months which Uriel, the holy angel (*mal'ak qeddus*) who was with me (and) who is their leader, showed me. The entire book about them, as it is, he showed me and how every year of the world will be forever, until a new creation lasting forever is made" (72:1). In much of the following text, the unknown writer/redactor explains the somewhat abstruse mechanics of a system where each of the ranks obeys Uriel and Uriel in turn serves God. In this presentation, the movements of the heavenly bodies and the alterations in the winds and

weather are inextricably bound together in a single, well-organized cosmo-
political system.[23] These patterns are summarized in chapter 82:

> These are the names of those who lead them (*yemarrexewwomu*), who keep
> watch so that they enter at their times (*wa-'aqqebu wa-yebawwe'u ba-
> 'azmāna*), who lead them in their places, in their orders, in their times, in their
> months, in their jurisdictions, and in their positions (*'ella yemarrexewwomu
> ba-makānātihomu wa-ba-šer'ātātihomu wa-ba-gizeyātihomu wa-ba-'awrā-
> xihomu wa-ba-šelṭānātihomu wa-ba-meqwāmātihomu*). Their four leaders
> (*marāḥeyānihomu*) who divide the four parts of the year enter first, and after
> them (come) the twelve leaders (*marāḥeyān*) of the orders who divide the
> months, and the 360 heads (*'ar'est*) of the thousands who separate the days,
> and the four additional ones with them who are their leaders (*marāḥeyān*)
> who separate its four parts. (82:10–12)

Here a centrally organized, hierarchical system accounts for the movements
of the heavenly bodies, changing weather patterns, and cycles of days, seasons, months, and years entailed in the solar calendar.

Though the work elsewhere teaches about order and regularity, chapters 80–82 also envision a time of disruption in the heavenly ranks.[24] The
tale of disarray and confusion among the stars is likely to be a later addition, one that was composed sometime during the early phases of the
Maccabean uprising. Considered within its literary context, however, this
disruption comes to exemplify the system of order that looms large elsewhere in the text. Whereas chapters 72–79 only hint at the possibility of a
"new creation" (72:1), chapter 80 predicts turmoil: "In the days of the sinners
the years will grow shorter, their seed will be late on their land and in their
fields. Everything on the earth will change and will not appear at their
times" (80:2). This breakdown in command seems to throw seasonal patterns into disarray, thus building on the premise of the earlier chapters that
the movements of the luminaries determine seasonal changes and weather
patterns. The result is confusion, mass disorder, and wickedness:

> Many heads of the stars will stray from the command (*wa-yešeḥḥetu
> bezuxān'ar'estihomu la-kawâkebt ta'zāza*)[25]
> > and will change their ways and actions (*wa-'ellu yemayyeṭu
> > fenāwihomu wa-gebromu*)
> > and will not appear at the times prescribed for them.
> The entire law of the stars will be closed to the sinners (*wa-kwellu šer'āta
> kawâkebt yet'addaw lā'la xāṭe'ān*)
> > and the thoughts (*wa-ḥellināhomu*) of those on the earth will err
> > regarding them.

They will turn back from all their ways,
    will err, and will take them to be gods (*wa-yemasselewwomu 'amālekt*)
Evil will multiply against them
    and punishment will come upon them to destroy all. (80:6–8; cf. Jub.
    6:32–37)

The writer seems to play on the idea of disobedient stars or watchers known from other literature, but to distinctive ends. Here disorder among the luminaries provokes a cascading series of problems below.[26] Though seemingly minor, these disruptions trickle down to cause confusion, error, and distress in the lower spheres, the main issue being that people mistake the luminaries for gods. The idea that gentiles mistakenly worship lesser-ranking deities—such as the heavenly bodies or hosts—constitutes a well-worn polemic about gentile religion (e.g., 2 Kgs 21:5; Deut 4:19, 17:3; Wis 13:1–2). In this case, however, the writer also offers a fairly elaborate myth about the origins of gentile worship, one where a temporary breakdown in the command among the stars provokes illegitimate worship below. The writer thus makes creative use of a distinctive body of astronomical lore to develop a polemical tradition that is well-attested elsewhere in Jewish tradition.

The calamity explored in chapter 82 leads ultimately to a time of judgment and restoration, one that involves heavenly tablets that record "all the actions of people and of all humans who will be on the earth for the generations of the world" (81:2). In these myths about judgment, punishment, and just reward, the writer works to distinguish a privileged elect and to integrate them within an all-encompassing vision of a timeless, universal, and self-evident world political order. Predictions of punishment also lend themselves to this agenda by imagining a time when this cosmic polity will be purified, perfected, or refined, often by violence ("the sinner will die with the sinner and the apostate will drown with the apostate" [81:8]). The writer evokes the elect in rather vague terms earlier in the work, but here they appear as a more circumscribed group that is defined, to a significant extent, by their access to astrological truths. Presumably, these truths are those contained in the Astronomical Book. Fittingly, the writer concludes that these revelations are to be passed on to Enoch's offspring and their heirs in subsequent generations.

Though chapters 80–82 explore a time of catastrophic disarray, it is important to emphasize that the writer/redactor (at least of this form of the text) does little to clarify whether the stars are to be conceived of as actively rebelling against their superiors or merely as making mistakes about their orders.[27] If these acts are deliberate, the writer does virtually nothing to explain their actions, motivations, or consequences in the heavenly realm. Instead, the wayward luminaries remain high above in the heavens; there is no hint of stars falling or stealing away for sexual adventures on earth. Rather, this disruption causes a cascading series of problems, most crucially, their worship by those who (mistakenly) take them as gods. In the earthly realms, however, this time of mass iniquity and religious perversion also sets up for the emergence of a righteous elect. Because this elect gain access to the true heavenly plan—at least in part, through the astronomical teachings of the Astronomical Book—they are assured of remaining loyal to the kingdom of heaven, rightly understood, and gaining a place of great privilege in the new or more perfect creation.

The Book of the Watchers

The Book of the Watchers has often been understood as a myth about angelic rebellion and the origins of evil.[28] Given these interests, interpreters have lavished attention on chapters 6–16, where a troupe of heavenly beings abandon their lofty station to have sex with the "daughters of men." Though unintended, mayhem ensues. Understood within the larger literary context of the Book of the Watchers as a whole, however, these tales of intrigue and disaster serve to illustrate the unlimited and inexorable power of the true king of heaven. So the Book of the Watchers opens with a grand vision of the supreme God descending to mete out punishing justice to all: "He will appear with his army, he will appear with his mighty host from the heaven of heavens. All the watchers will fear and [quake],[29] and those who are hiding in all the ends of the earth will sing" (1:4–5).[30] At this point the adventurous watchers are bound beneath the earth, where they await this, their second punishment. Images of them trembling in fear thus serve to underscore the terrible and all-encompassing nature of the impending judgment. In the warnings that follow (1 En. 1–5), the writer draws sharply contrasting portraits of favored versus disfavored peoples but does not suggest, at least in this context, that the adventurous watchers or evil spirits play any role in distinguishing them. Most basically, these dire exhortations express a fundamental reality about the world, namely, that it functions as a single, vast, well-organized, and ultimately just political system. So a long series of exhortations in chapter 2 appeal to the regular cycle of the seasons, the movements of the sun, and the growth and death of trees as proof of this grand cosmic design. The writer then concludes:

> Contemplate all these works, and understand that he who
>> lives for all the ages made all these works. And his works
>> take place from year to year, and they all carry out their
>> works for him, and their works do not alter, but they all
>> carry out his word.
> Observe how, in like manner, the sea and the rivers carry out
>> and do not alter their works from his words.
> But you have not stood firm nor acted according to his commandments;
>> but you have turned aside, you have spoken proud and hard words
>> with your unclean mouth against his majesty.
> Hard of heart! There will be no peace for you! (5:1–4)[31]

Here patterns of regularity observed in the natural world express God's awesome power over the entire creation. Though wickedness and disobedience abound in the human realm, images of an idealized political order in heaven work to counterbalance and relativize it. In this way, the seething mass of evils is confined to a present time of wickedness, the human sphere in general, and the nonelect in particular.

Following these warnings of judgment in chapters 1–5, the writer shifts to tell a story about divine disobedience staged in a distant, semiprimordial era (1 En. 6–16). Here a troupe of heavenly beings steals away to earth to sate their desires for women. The results are disastrous. Not only do they teach the women secret skills, but they also produce terrible hybrid children, a monstrous race of giants. These offspring are massive in size and have enormous appetites; having exhausted every other source of food, they finally turn to eating humans. As they do so, however, the souls of the dying humans cry out to heaven and at last provoke the divine court to action. The heavenly king quickly intervenes by sending two henchmen (Michael and Gabriel) with instructions that they punish the watchers and kill the giants. The supreme deity also gives a long decree about the watchers' misdeeds: "You were holy ones and spirits, living forever (*qeddusān manfasāwiyān heyāwāna heywat za-la-ʿālam*). With the blood of women you have defiled yourselves, and with the blood of flesh you have begotten, and with the blood of men you have lusted, and you have done as they do—flesh and blood, who die and perish" (15:4). Though the watchers and giants are sentenced to punishment and destruction, a special class of harmful spirits survives:

> The spirits of heaven (*manfasāwiyān samāy;* τὰ πνεύμα[τα] τοῦ οὐρανοῦ),
>> in heaven is their dwelling;

But now the giants who were begotten by the spirits and flesh (*tawaldu*
'*em-manāfest wa-šeḡa*; ἀπὸ τῶν πνευμάτων καὶ σαρκὸς)—
  they will call them evil spirits (*manfasāta 'ekuyāna*; πνεύμα[τα]
  ἰσχυρὰ/πνεύματα πονηρὰ) on the earth,
  for their dwelling will be on earth.[32]
The spirits that have gone forth from the body of their flesh are evil spirits
(*wa-nafsāt 'ekuyān*),[33]
  for from humans they came into being, and from the holy watchers
  was the origin of their creation.
  Evil spirits they will be on the earth, and evil spirits they will be called
  (*manfasa 'ekuya yekawwenu ba-diba medr wa-manfasa 'ekuyān yes-
  sammayus*; πνεύματα πονηρὰ κληθήσεται).[34] (15:7–9)

Here, divine-human interbreeding violates the natural order and produces
dangerous and displaced monstrosities; their descendants remain harmful
but are of much diminished power and influence:

  And the spirits of the giants [lead astray],[35] do violence, make
  desolate, and attack and wrestle and hurl ('*ella yegaffe 'u wa-
  yāmāssenu wa-yewaddequ wa-yetba''asu wa-yedaqqequ*; ἀδικοῦντα,
  ἀφανίζοντα καὶ ἐνπίπτοντα καὶ συνπαλαίοντα καὶ συνρίπτοντα)
  upon the earth and [cause illnesses].[36] They eat nothing, but abstain
  from food and are thirsty and smite. These spirits (will) rise up
  against the sons of men and against the women, for they have come
  forth from them.
  From the day of the slaughter and destruction and death of the
  giants, from the soul of whose flesh the spirits are proceeding (*manāfest 'em-nafsāta šegāhomu*; ἀφ' ὧν τὰ πνεύματα
  ἐκπορευόμενα ἐκ τῆς ψυχῆς τῆς σαρκὸς), they are making
  desolate without (incurring) judgment. Thus they will make desolate
  until the day of the consummation of the great judgment, when
  the great age will be consummated.[37] It will be consummated all
  at once. (15:11–16:1)[38]

Rather than envisioning a highly specific set of roles for these spirits, the
writer offers a hodge-podge of harmful effects that seem connected to the
spirits' mixed origins. They cause a variety of nondescript evils, with ill-
nesses and perhaps leading astray as the most concrete and specific. The
writer also emphasizes that they rise up against men and women and that
they will be subject to judgment. Whereas the watchers directed their desires downward, these spirits occupy a sphere at even greater remove from

the heavenly court. Some two generations removed from their restless grandfathers, these divine leftovers haunt the earthly realms where they rage against men and women. They thus threaten in a distant earthly sphere but pose no threat to heaven above.

Though many scholars construe 1 Enoch 16 as an etiology for evil demons, there is little in the text to encourage this interpretation. Instead of singular origins and essential causes, the spirits take their place in a variegated array of other problems, including those created by illicit teachings about metallurgy, astrology, and cosmetology (8:1–3, 9:6–9). They thus appear as one element (or set of elements) in an increasingly complex postflood world. Fittingly, the spirits that emerge from the slain giants in 1 Enoch 16 play little role elsewhere in the Book of the Watchers, aside from a few lines in chapter 19 where they are blamed for idolatry.[39]

Whereas chapters 6–16 focus on the wayward watchers, the second half of the work (1 En. 17–36) turns to Uriel, who takes Enoch on a series of grand cosmic tours. Among other sites, they visit the heights, depths, and foundations of the earth; the storehouses of the winds, waters, and precious stones; and the gates and set courses of the stars in the firmament. They also explore numerous spaces that have been prepared in advance for punishment, including dungeonlike chambers, valleys, and burning pillars of fire at the edge of the earth (1 En. 19, 21–22; cf. 27:2–4). Though these punishing spaces will hold human and divine criminals, Uriel repeatedly points to the watchers (and/or stars) being tortured for their crimes (19:1, 18:13–16, 21:1–10). The effect is to dramatically underscore the dangers involved in straying from the will of heaven, even for the heavenly elite. As Uriel explains in one of these episodes: "And Uriel said to me, 'There stand the angels (*malā'ekt*; ἄγγελοι) who mingled with the women. And their spirits (*wa-manāfestihomu*; πνεύματα)—having assumed many forms—bring destruction on men and lead them astray to sacrifice to demons as to gods (*bezuxa rā'eya kawinomu 'arkwasewwomu la-sab' wa-yāshetewwomu kama yešu'u la-'agānent kama 'amālekt*; τὰ πνεύματα αὐτῶν πολύμορφα γενόμενα λυμαίνεται τοὺς ἀνθρώπους καὶ πλανήσει αὐτοὺς ἐπιθύειν τοῖς δαιμονίοις) until the day of the great judgment, in which they will be judged with finality. And the wives of the transgressing angels will become sirens (*kama salamāwiyāt*; εἰς σειρῆνας)'" (19:1–2).[40] It remains unclear whether "their spirits" refers to the watchers themselves or the evil spirits of their offspring, the giants, discussed earlier in Book of the Watchers 15. Nevertheless, the main issues appear straightforward: some people misunderstand the relationships of power operative in the divine world, so disastrously, that they become allies of harmful lesser spirits that are unworthy of sacrifice. Though the writer characterizes the spirits as destructive, here they are primarily blamed for grievous errors about the divine world.

The first half of the Book of the Watchers focuses on mythmaking about the watchers' misdeeds, with repeated scenes that emphasize the evils of violating their station in heaven, whether by interbreeding with women or by disclosing heavenly secrets. These divine characters desire women, plot adventures, have sex, reproduce, disclose secrets, and, when affairs get away from them, lament their punishment, tremble in fear, and beg for reprieve. The story takes a different turn in chapters 17–36, as Enoch explores the limits and structure of the world. These tours give special attention to the suffering of the watchers, who reappear frequently as stars tortured in pillars of fire at the ends of the earth or held captive in deep chasms beneath it. As construed by the writer/editor, these punishments come to exemplify the workings of a just divine polity. In chapter 20, the author pauses to add more definition and shape to this political world by naming its constituent leaders, which are here construed as "holy angels," "angels of power," and "holy angels who watch" (*yetaggehu qeddusān malā'ekt;* ἄγγελοι τῶν δυνάμεων). Here it is explained that Uriel rules over the world and over Tartarus; Raphael oversees the spirits of humans (*za-manāfest sab';* ἐπὶ τῶν πνευμάτων τῶν ἀνθρώπων); Reuel presides over the punishment of the luminaries; Michael over the "good ones" of the people; Sariel over the spirits who sin against the spirit (*za-diba manāfest ['egwāla 'emmaḥeyāw] za-manāfesta yaxāṭṭe'u;* ἐπὶ τῶν πνευμάτων οἵτινες ἐπὶ τῷ πνεύματι ἁμαρτάνουσιν); Gabriel over paradise, serpents, and the cherubim; and Remiel over "all of them that rise" (1 En. 20:1–8). As in numerous other contexts, the writer creates a picture of a vast hierarchical order that extends from the king high above in the heavens down to the depths of Tartarus below.

The Book of Dreams or the Dream Visions of Enoch

The Book of Dreams contains two distinct myths about an apocalyptic time of reckoning.[41] The first presents a brief dream vision about total world annihilation. The second is known as the Animal Apocalypse of Enoch and tells a much longer and more involved story about the changing political fortunes of Israel (85:1–90:42).[42] Despite its brevity, the first vision provides an instructive counterpoint to the more extended political myths of the Animal Apocalypse. In the first dream vision, the young Enoch reports a terrible dream in which the heavens collapse, the earth is torn asunder, and the whole mass dissolves into a great abyss. He tells his grandfather, who interprets the nightmare as containing "the secrets of all the sin of the earth" (83:7). He advises Enoch to plead with the God of heaven to leave a remnant on earth and not utterly destroy the world (83:8; cf. 84:5–6). Obediently, Enoch turns his gaze heavenward and begins a long hymn that celebrates the current world order. In doing so, he makes dramatic appeals to the cyclical movements of the sun, moon, stars, "and everything as he [made] it from the beginning" (83:11), noting that each of the heavenly bodies is made to go forth, rise, and traverse the path "that it was shown" (8:11). The hymn builds toward an even more expansive celebration of a cosmic theocracy:

> Blessed are you, O Lord, King,
>> great and mighty is your majesty,
>> Lord of all the creation of the heaven,
>> King of kings and God of all eternity.
> Your power and your reign and your majesty abide forever and forever and
>> ever,
>> and to all generations, your dominion.
> All the heavens are your throne forever,
>> and all the earth is your footstool forever and forever and ever.
> For you have made and you rule all things,
>> and nothing is too difficult for you;
> Wisdom does not escape you,
>> [and it does not turn away from your throne,] nor from your presence.
> You know and see and hear all things,
>> and there is nothing that is hidden from you.[43]
> And now the angels of your heavens are doing wrong (*wa-ye'ezēni*
>> *malā'ekt samāyātika*),
>> and upon human flesh (*wa-diba šegā sab'*) is your wrath until the great
>> day of judgment. (84:2–4)[44]

In a seemingly inevitable and natural way, the cosmos appears here as a finite and well-organized political system that is subservient to a single creator, ruler, and king. Though the language about the heavenly bodies, angels of heaven, and perhaps even "wisdom (*ṭebab*)" alludes to lesser ranks of beings, the writer telescopes to focus on the main character, the supreme deity, who becomes the object of sustained celebration. One effect is to portray all members of the lesser ranks as playing diminutive roles. So Enoch draws attention to his lowly status, and the brief comments about misdeeds among the "angels of heaven" likewise serve to underscore the awesome powers of their ruler, who responds by plotting world annihilation.

The author of the first dream vision makes grand assertions about the unlimited creative and destructive powers of the reigning world sovereign. Though working with a similar conception of a cosmic polity, the unknown author of the Animal Apocalypse (85:1–90:42) tells a compressed series of allegorical tales about Israel's political fortunes. In these stories, animals like bulls, sheep, and wolves stand in for characters and groups such as Adam, the watchers, Noah, the patriarchs, King David, and conquering nations such as the Assyrians, Babylonians, and Greeks. As Patrick Tiller notes, the work is structured around three ages, each of which is inaugurated by a patriarchal figure. There is the past (Adam), the present (Noah), and an ideal future with an unidentified eschatological figure.[45] The first age more or less traces the biblical outline from Adam to Noah, though it adds a myth about wayward deities known as the watchers in other traditions. The second age follows much of the story known from Genesis to 2 Kings but pauses to develop a remarkable story about seventy divine shepherds who rule Israel beginning with the exile. The end of the second age brings quite radical change and transformation, including an eschatological judgment, the emergence of a new Jerusalem, and an ingathering of surviving Israelites who are then worshipped by the gentile nations.[46] Though this might seem resolution enough, the writer also adds a brief exploration of a third age in which a remarkable figure emerges that transforms all the species of the earth into white bulls, the form originally associated with Adam.[47]

Though framed as an all-encompassing myth about the history of the world, the Animal Apocalypse more basically concerns the political subjection of Israel. To a significant extent, this reflects the writer's interests in portraying Israel's return from exile and rebuilding of the temple as a failed restoration. So the temple remains polluted in 89:72–73, and evils continue to escalate up to the time of the Maccabean uprising.[48] Initially, the writer tells this as yet another allegory involving the "sheep" of Israel (89:54–58). So the sheep abandon the "house of the Lord," degenerate, and become blind, and the "Lord of the sheep" responds by allowing wild animals to slaughter them as punishment for their crimes. Though they cry out in anguish, the

Lord of the sheep stands by silently and rejoices "because they were being devoured and swallowed up and carried off, and he abandoned them into the hands of all the wild beasts as fodder" (89:58). Subsequently, however, the writer pauses to retell this story so that it comes to exemplify the punishing, but ultimately just, workings of a multitiered heavenly bureaucracy. Whereas in the earlier allegories, deities appear only in clipped allusions, such as to the fallen stars or the Lord of the sheep, here the writer presents a dramatic picture of heavenly mediators who manage all the earth's political affairs (89:59–90:1). Instead of rejoicing as Israel is overrun by its enemies, here the supreme sovereign hands over Israel to a set of the punishing mediators ("shepherds [*nolāweyān*]") with careful instructions that they kill and persecute a deserving Israel. This story lacks clear precedents in biblical literature, but the seventy shepherds seems to play off language in Jeremiah 25 about seventy years of exile, as do the analogies relating to animal husbandry that are so prominent throughout (cf. Isa 56:11, Jer 23:2, Zech 10:3, Ezek 34).[49] These relationships also involve the idea of allocating political resources that is familiar from texts such as Deuteronomy 32 and much other literature.[50] In quite remarkable ways, however, the writer construes gentile gods as divine intermediaries and functionaries who serve at the behest of Israel's deity.

The myth of the shepherd-managers transforms gentile gods into servants and intermediaries, but the writer also labors to portray them as submissive operatives who carry out the plans of their superior. So the ultimate ruler commissions the shepherds (*nolāweyān*): "Every one of you from now on shall pasture the sheep, and everything that I command you, do. I am handing them over to you duly numbered, and I will tell you which of them are to be destroyed. Destroy them" (89:60). Even while commissioning the shepherds, however, the supreme God foresees that they will become overzealous in inflicting this righteous, punishing violence (cf. Isa 40:2 and Ps 79). Thus, another divine being is introduced, an accounting figure who is charged with writing down these misdeeds. This figure also receives careful instructions:

> Observe and see everything that the shepherds do against these sheep, for they will destroy more of them than I have commanded them. Every excess and destruction that is done by the shepherds, write down—how many they destroy at my command, and how many they destroy on their own. Every destruction by each individual shepherd, write down against them. And by number read them in my presence—how many they destroy and

> how many they hand over to destruction, so that I may have this testimony against them, that I may know every deed of the shepherds, that I may [measure] them and see what they are doing—whether they are acting according to the command (*ba-te'ezāzeya*) that I gave them or not.[51] And do not let them know it, and do not show them or rebuke them. But write down every destruction by the shepherds, one by one, in his own time, and bring it all up to me. (89:61–64)

Though the seventy managers will overreach their mandate, a towering heavenly bureaucracy is in place that will hold them to account. These precise roles and relationships are illustrated again on three more occasions (89:65–72a, 89:74–90:1, and 90:2–5), each of which imagines punishing excesses by the shepherd-managers that are duly recorded by the accounting deity and presented in the heavenly courtroom. In the final episode (90:2–5), heavenly favor turns to the Maccabean rebels after the accountant intercedes on their behalf.[52]

This myth about overzealous shepherds allows for some level of heavenly impropriety but quite radically circumscribes the possibility of divine disobedience or dissent.[53] Thus, we find relatively minor, unintended moments of overreach that somehow serve a larger scheme of righteous condemnation and reward. This agenda especially informs the visions of eschatological transformation that appear toward the end of the work. During the rule of the last twelve shepherds, evils escalate until the supreme sovereign finally intervenes to reward the sheep and punish their enemies. In one scene, a throne is built for the high God in the "pleasant land" (90:20), the seven stars/watchers are judged, and then the seventy shepherds and blinded sheep are all thrown into a fiery abyss.[54] After this, a new Jerusalem comes down from heaven to house the remaining sheep, who are then worshipped by the nations: "And all the animals upon the earth and all the birds of heaven were falling down and worshipping those sheep and making petition to them and obeying them in every thing" (90:30).[55] Thus construed, restoration requires not only a winnowing of Israel (so the blinded sheep are destroyed), but also that the survivors themselves become objects of veneration and worship. The writer concludes by predicting an end to violence, the perfection of the scattered sheep, and the birth of a white bull who transforms the gentile nations into its own form. This suggests a paradigmatic figure that somehow transforms the gentile nature, as if undoing the long history of flux, conflict, and decline since the appearance of the first white bull, Adam. The difference and diversity of the world's peoples are implicitly construed as negative, since the perfection of the whole involves a return to sameness and continuity in substance and identity. The future restoration thus serves to purify the world of difference, ambiguity, imperfection, and complexity.

The Epistle of Enoch

The unknown authors/editors of the Epistle of Enoch make remarkable claims about the providential unfolding of history and the violent, purifying consummation of time.[56] In a part of the work known as the Apocalypse of Weeks, human history is organized into a compressed series of ages or "weeks."[57] On the whole, the weeks tend to oscillate between degeneration, punishment, and restoration.[58] The first week is portrayed as a time of righteousness, followed by a second age of "deceit and violence" (93:4) that culminates with the election of Noah and the restorative, purifying violence brought on by the flood. Similarly, the sixth week is a time of horror when "the hearts of all will stray from wisdom (*lebbomu la-kwellomu 'em-ṭebab*)," a catastrophe that results in the destruction of the temple and the dispersal of the chosen (93:8). Both disasters constitute just punishments from on high.[59] In a different way, the writer stages an eschatological surge in the ninth and tenth ages, as the righteous slaughter the wicked (e.g., 91:12), the temple is rebuilt (91:13), and a righteous law is revealed. This new and righteous law serves to root out all wickedness so that "all humankind will look to the path of everlasting righteousness" (91:14). The tenth week also brings a judgment against the watchers, a great war, a new heaven and earth, and a new age of "many weeks without number forever, in which they[60] will do piety and righteousness, and from then on sin will never again be mentioned" (91:17). Rather than arrive at an end or culmination, then, time will march onward again in a much improved, utopian world order. On the whole, the past and present alike reveal a coherent, rational, and just plan that expresses the will of heaven. The eschatological future also involves a kind of perfection of the world order, not a radical refounding or overturning of the existing system of rule.

Scholars have tended to focus on the shorter Apocalypse of Weeks, but the bulk of the Epistle of Enoch is structured as a long series of exhortations or "woes" (1 En. 94–108). Predictably, these exhortations draw sharp contrasts between chosen and unchosen peoples, but the writers/editors map their contours in interesting and variegated ways. So the woes evoke a great morass of wicked, lying witnesses and persecutors of the righteous who glut themselves on ill-gotten wealth and secret murders, unaware that their misdeeds have already been revealed to (and recorded by) the political powers in heaven (96:4). Among other crimes, they consume blood (98:11), write deceitful words (98:15), alter true words (99:2; cf. 104:9–11), and worship mere statuary and "evil spirits" (99:7–9).[61] In one instance, they also impugn slavery as a human institution and affirm that "evil" is a resolutely human creation: "Lawlessness was not sent upon the earth; but men created it by themselves" (98:4). When it finally arrives, the resolution to these evils will entail extraordinary violence. So these lawless hordes will be righteously murdered, fall by the sword (100:1–2), burn (100:9; cf. 102:1), suffer drought and cold (100:12–13), and be led to Sheol for punishment (103:7). Indeed, the world will tremble at the manifestation of the heavenly sovereign, and the "angels will fulfill what was commanded them" (102:3).

In sharp contrast to the alleged criminals, the elect—both living and dead—are imagined by the writer to win respite in the future, be healed (e.g., 96:3), and gleefully slaughter their former oppressors (e.g., 96:1 and 98:12). In a number of cases, they are also explicitly said to move upward toward heaven. So they will "ascend like eagles, and higher than the vultures will be your nests" (96:2), and the portals of heaven will stand open to them (104:2). They will have joy like the luminaries of heaven (104:2, 4; cf. Dan 12:3), be companions of the host (104:6), and listen to the words of the Most High (99:10).[62] In the present, however, the righteous suffer terribly, whether they are refused respite by harsh slave masters or are victims of those who devour, disperse, murder, and "make us few" (103:15).

The idea of a just heavenly court also appears prominently throughout the work. So the writer frequently imagines an august heavenly court where a righteous judge presides, hears the testimony of witnesses, and considers petitions and where crowds of intermediaries record all good and evil deeds in written form.[63] To give only a few examples, the writer insists that the hearts of the lawless sinners will convict them (96:4); the "angels" of heaven record their deeds (97:7) and so ensure their destruction by the "Most High"; and the prayers of the righteous will be heard in the future (97:5–6) when "all the words of your lawless deeds will be read out before the Holy One" (97:6). In many other instances (e.g., 98:6–8; 104:1, 3, 7–8), heavenly justice involves formal petitions and testimony, as when the righteous are encouraged to "present your petitions as a reminder, offer them as a testimony before the angels, that they may bring in the sins of the unrighteous before the Most High as a reminder" (99:3). Frequently, this also involves writing down, archiving, and revealing documents in court (e.g., 104:1). In another set of exhortations, the narrator addresses the wicked and thunderously announces that the luminaries, clouds, and dews will testify against them (102:10–13), affirming "all your sins are being written down day by day. And now I show you that light and darkness, day and night, observe all your sins" (104:7–8). These motifs come together again as the narrator assures: "I know this mystery. For I have read the tablets of heaven, and I have seen the writing of what must be,[64] and I know the things that are written in them and inscribed concerning you" (103:2). Fittingly, the work concludes with warnings against altering the text or adding deceitful words but promises to pass on "my books" to the righteous in a pure and unadulterated form (104:9–105:1).

Throughout the Epistle of Enoch, lesser deities appear as dutiful attendants who populate the heavenly court and archive and "make disclosure" about affairs on earth (e.g., 97:2 and 99:3). In other cases, they also play supporting roles in dispensing just decrees and judgments. So the writer envisions a time of punishment when the nonelect will suffer terribly as women abort, sell, and abandon their infants and families are murdered one and all. At the climax of violence:

> A horse will wade up to its breast through the blood of the sinners,
>> and the chariot will sink to its axles.
> The angels will descend, going down into the hidden places on that day;
>> and those who aided iniquity will be gathered into one place.[65]
> And the Most High will be aroused on that day
>> to execute great judgment on all.
> He will set a guard of the holy angels (*'em-malā'ekt qeddusān*) over all the righteous and holy;
>> and they will be kept as the apple of the eye
>> until evil and sin come to an end. (1 En. 100:3–5)

Here the political program for judgment involves crowds of lesser deities and a heavenly retinue that will protect the chosen from harm. Aroused to action at last, the king of heaven will also take pleasure in dispensing this punishing justice. So the narrator warns that "he who created you will overturn you; and for your fall there will be no compassion, and your Creator will rejoice at your destruction" (94:10). In numerous other portrayals of cataclysm and doom, intermediary "angels" appear as instruments or extensions of a single, unified, and consistent heavenly rationale who work to "fulfill what was commanded to them" (102:3).

The subject of idolatry does not appear prominently in the Epistle, but in one passage the writer/editor excoriates the worship of statues and also connects this to evil spirits and phantoms. So the writer impugns the worship of statues and mundane images as well as the alleged rank and status of these "false" or illegitimate gods:

> Those who worship stones—
> and who carve images of silver and gold and wood and stone and clay
>> and worship phantoms and demons and abominations and evil
>>> spirits[66] and all errors, not according to knowledge;
>> no help will you find from them.
> They will be led astray by the folly of their hearts,
>> and their eyes will be blinded by the fear of their hearts,
>> and the visions of (your) dreams will lead you astray[67]—
> You and the false works that you have made and constructed of stone,
>> you will be destroyed together. (99:7–9; cf. 91:8)

Unlike the crowds of heavenly attendants elsewhere in the text, here the writer evokes evil spirits and phantoms in oblique and allusive ways. These beings offer no benefits ("no help will you find from them") and serve only to deceive those hapless dupes who are foolish enough to worship them. In fact, it is human misunderstanding, misperception, and delusion that comes into sharpest focus here, whether in language about foolish hearts, misread dreams, or the blind worship of stones and statues. Further emphasizing the diminutive status of these phantoms, stones, and "evil spirits," the writer insists that they are doomed to perish together in the furnace of heavenly justice.

Daniel 7–12

The writer/editor of Daniel 7 presents a remarkable myth about four monstrous beings that rise from the sea and are quickly identified with four kingdoms that ruled over Israel.[68] The first three kingdoms set up for the fourth, whose last king—a thinly veiled stand-in for the Greek-Seleucid ruler Antiochus IV Epiphanes—becomes the object of sustained myth-making in chapters 7–12.[69] Daniel 7 also predicts the coming of a fifth and final empire, albeit on drastically different terms. Unlike the monsters that rise from the sea, this last empire involves a heavenly ruler from above who presides over an eternal, matchless kingdom that will rule all other nations.

The narrator of Daniel 7 reports a dream vision in which four winds stir up "the great sea" and provoke the rise of four terrible beasts (7:4). The writer portrays the first three beasts as manipulated and commissioned, presumably by the divine agents that remain offstage until 7:9. So the first beast is "lifted up" and "made to stand on two feet like a human being" (7:4); the second is "raised up" and obeys orders to "arise, devour much flesh" (7:5); and the third has "dominion given to it (*wĕ-šolṭān yĕhîb lah*)" (7:6).[70] In some contrast, the fourth beast is not said to follow orders and proves stronger and more destructive ("it ate and crushed and trampled what was left with its feet" [7:7]). Ten horns (or "rulers") also emerge from this fourth beast, and the last horn "roots out" the preceding three and speaks "great" or "arrogant things" (7:8; cf. Dan 7:25, 11:36; Isa 14:12–14, 37:23; Ps 12:3). This offense seems finally to provoke heavenly action, as the narrator turns to lavish attention on a heavenly scene where thrones are "set up" and a court is "seated." A figure designated as the "Ancient of Days" seems to preside over these affairs from a flaming throne, and "a thousand thousands served him and ten thousand times ten thousand stood before him" (7:10). Acting together, the court as a whole sits in judgment, opens the books, slays the last beast, and takes away "dominion (*šolṭānĕhôn*)" from the other three ("an extension of life was given to them for a time and a season" [7:12]). Then a curious figure appears before the Ancient of Days who is described as "one like a human being (*kĕbar ʾĕnāš*)" (7:13). This figure is promised rule of an eternal kingdom where "all peoples, nations, and languages will serve him. His dominion is everlasting dominion, which will not pass away, and his kingdom is indestructible (*šolṭānēh šolṭān ʿālam dî lā ʾ yeʿdēh ûmalkûtēh dî lā tithabbal)*" (7:14). The heavens thus become the stage for a mythic drama about a just and providential political system located high above in the heavens.

The story told in 7:1–14 ends with a vision of political harmony, but vv. 15–24 turn back again to revisit the terrible fourth beast. Still perched in heaven, the narrator approaches one of the attendants and asks for clarification about what he has just seen (7:16). The attendant responds by explaining that the beasts are stand-ins for four kings but assures that eventually "the holy ones of the Most High (*qaddîšê ʿelyônîn*)" will rise to power (7:18). This character then goes on to retell the tale of the final tyrant two more times, each in rather different ways. The story now emerges as involving an open conflict between the last king and the "holy ones" as "[the horn] waged war · on the holy ones and prevailed over them" (7:21).[71] The second retelling also gives a more precise context for these political events: this will be the last of ten kings, and he will "speak words against the Most High and will afflict the holy ones of the Most High. He will think to change times and law, and he will have power over them for a time" (7:25; cf. 1 Macc 1:45 and 2 Macc 6:6).[72] The attendant affirms that these ravages will be allowed only "for a time" (a point that is repeated in 8:14; 9:27; and 12:11, 12) and insists that, after this, the court will be seated, its dominion will be taken away, and political power will then pass to the eternal kingdom: "Kingdom and dominion and the greatness of the kingdoms under all heaven (*malakûtāh wĕšolṭānā' ûrĕbûtā' dî malkĕwāt tĕḥôt kol-šĕmayyā'*) were given to the people of the holy ones of the Most High. Its kingdom is an everlasting kingdom, and all the dominions shall serve and obey it (*malkûtēh malkût 'ālam wĕkōl šolṭānayyā lēh yiplĕḥûn wĕyištammĕ'ûn*)" (7:27).[73]

The myth of the tyrant king in Daniel 7 allows for some sort of war against heaven, at least in the second and third repetitions of the story where the king "wages war on" and "prevails against" the holy ones. As retold again in chapter 8, this conflict more explicitly comes to involve the lesser ranks of divinity. Reporting yet another dream vision, the seer describes a ram, a he-goat, and a terrible horn that rises against heaven: "It threw down some of the host and some of the stars (*min-haṣṣābā' ûminhakkôkābîm*) to the earth and trampled on them. He grew great even up to the prince of the host (*wĕ'ad śar-haṣṣābā'*), from whom the daily offering was taken away and whose sanctuary place was cast down. A host was given over (*wĕṣābā' tinnātēn*)[74] together with the daily offering, in the course of transgression" (8:10–12). Here the alleged desecration of the temple appears as a successful campaign against a subset of the stars and/or the host (cf. Rev 12 and Isa 24). Remarkably, the writer pictures stars (or the host) descending to earth—presumably against their will—where Antiochus tramples them underfoot.[75] This language could suggest that the temple itself has its own ranks of heavenly orderlies and that these make up a subset or portion of the host. A mere earthly king also defeats this host, at least temporarily, while the ultimate sovereign or "prince of princes" remains firmly ensconced in the heights above, even if largely offstage (8:11, 25).

Antiochus's defeat of the host in Dan 8:10–12 proves quite remarkable, but the writer also maintains that this serves a providential function. So in 8:13, Daniel overhears a conversation among heavenly attendants (cf. Zech 2:7–8), one of whom asks the other: "For how long is the vision of the daily offering and the desolating transgression (*hattāmîd wĕhappeša' šōmēm*), and his giving over of sanctuary and host to be trampled?" (8:13).

The answer given is that this will last for twenty-three hundred days (8:14), one of several temporal containment schemes that appear elsewhere in the work (7:25; 9:27; 12:7, 11, 12). Likewise, in the second half of chapter 8 Gabriel appears in the likeness of a human, only to explain (yet again) that the plan for world political history involves a series of ruling empires and rulers (here Media, Persia, Greece, and the Diadochoi) and affirms that Antiochus himself plays a key role in the "end time" (8:17) and "in the latter time of the wrath ... the appointed time of the end" (8:19; cf. 11:40). So Gabriel explains, "When their sins are complete, a bold-faced king will arise, adept in duplicity" (8:23). This figure will plot against "the holy ones," "grow great in his own mind," and "oppose the prince of princes ($śar śārîm$), but he will be broken without human hand" (8:25). The language about opposition to the "prince of princes" suggests that Antiochus directs his ire against the supreme God, but this insolence appears as an act of reckless, perhaps even suicidal grandiosity, not unlike the arrogant kings who are brought low in texts such as Isaiah 14 and 37 and Ezekiel 28.[76] Similar charges appear again in chapter 11, where Antiochus is said to "magnify himself against every god ($kāl 'ēl$)," to speak "wondrous things against the God of gods ('$al 'ēl 'ēlîm$)" (11:36), and to dishonor his own ancestral deities—"a god ('$al 'ĕlōhê 'ăbōtāyw$) whom his fathers did not know he will honor" (11:37).

In at least one instance, the writer/editor construes these events as forms of righteous retribution from heaven.[77] So in Daniel 9, Daniel gives a long speech describing a vast gulf that separates the august heavenly ruler from the sinful people below and construes these upheavals as fitting punishment for the law-breaking rebellion of Israel (9:11–16). The seer offers a dramatic supplication that accepts the punishment as just, replete with exclamations such as "you scattered them for the treachery with which they betrayed you" (9:7), you "poured out on us" righteous curses (9:11), and "the Lord (YHWH) watched and brought it upon us" (9:14). Acting as an emissary who merely reads the decree of his master, Gabriel responds by assuring Daniel that this punishment will last for only a limited timespan (here seventy weeks, 9:24–27). The supreme deity thus acts as righteous puppeteer of political affairs and so guarantees that there is a unified, rational, and ultimately just plan for world management.[78]

At the beginning of chapter 10, Gabriel appears and offers a series of *ex eventu* political prophecies spanning from the rise of the Persian Empire to the outrages of Antiochus.[79] Though somewhat similar to the earlier tales about the four kingdoms, these predictions generally focus on campaigns, alliances, and political instability in the earthly sphere without much concern with the world of divinity. In one important scene, however, attention turns to the lesser ranks where Gabriel and Michael fight against the "princes" (*śārîm*) of Persia and Greece. Here the writer creates an elaborate scene where Gabriel appears to Daniel and explains, "The prince of the kingdom of Persia opposed me for twenty-one days, and behold, Michael, one of the chief princes, came to help me, and I left him there with the prince of the kingdom of Persia" (10:13).[80] Gabriel soon continues: "Do you know why I have come to you? And now I will return to fight with the prince of Persia, and behold, when I go out the prince of Greece will come. But I will tell you what is written in the book of truth. There is no one who supports me against these except Michael your prince" (10:20–21; cf. 1 En. 20:5). In contrast to earlier discussions where the kingdom beasts seem to obey their heavenly handlers (with the exception of Antiochus, at least), the writer here suggests that each empire has its own heavenly prince and that they go to war against one another. Thus construed, the rise of Persia and Greece involves the defeat of Michael and Gabriel, who seem to fight a weak or ineffective campaign, at least for a time.[81] Whereas other biblical traditions typically understand Yahweh as supreme commander and warrior, here Michael and Gabriel take on leading military roles, as do Michael and Melchizedek in other writings (e.g., 1QM 17.6–7 and Rev 12:7–9).[82] Likewise, whereas much other literature prefers to ignore the gods of the conquering nations, here the princes of Persia and Greece are recategorized as subordinate princes of the empire of heaven. The members of the lower ranks thus turn out to be highly constructive characters for military and political reassignments.[83]

Like the rise and fall of ruling empires so prominent elsewhere in Daniel 7–12, the temporary defeat of Michael and Gabriel in Daniel 10 strongly implies that something is not quite right in the earthly political sphere. In general, however, the writer/editor maintains that there is an ongoing, just political order in heaven, one that unifies and stabilizes the world as it is, has been, and will be. In this case, the writer touches on the weakness and failure of Michael and Gabriel very briefly and quickly moves to affirm that this expresses the divine plan "written in the book of truth" (10:21).

In further dream visions that make up the substance of 11:2–12:4, the narrator traces a long series of campaigns, alliances, and political reversals among Persian, Greek, Seleucid, and Ptolemaic rulers. Attention again comes to settle on the Seleucids, especially the last king (Antiochus), who profanes the sanctuary and works to "remove the daily offerings, and set up the desolating abomination" (11:31). This mad rule is also marked by religious impropriety of other kinds, as Antiochus abandons his ancestral gods, introduces new ones, and dishonors the supreme God of gods (11:24, 37, 38). Whereas the extended political allegories in chapter 11 generally treat political intrigues as earthly affairs, Antiochus's outrage comes in for special treatment. Thus, the writer returns to the image of a tyrant king who will "exalt and magnify himself against every god, and he will speak wondrous things against the God of gods, and he will succeed until the wrath is finished, for that which is decreed will happen" (11:36). Though these events are scandalous, the writer depicts them as determined in advance (e.g., 11:27, 36) and explores the election of a righteous but alienated group of wise *maśkîlîm* (11:33) who will teach others but otherwise seem to remain politically quietistic. So the writer predicts that Antiochus will fall and then "Michael will arise, the great prince (*haśśar haggādôl*) who stands over your people" (12:1). Michael's arrival brings yet further disasters, but those found "written in the book" will be delivered from it and go on to "shine like the splendor of the firmament (*yazhirû kĕzōhar hārāqîʿa*), and those who lead the common people to righteousness like the stars (*kakkôkābîm*) forever and ever" (12:3). Consistent with this picture, 12:5–13 offers a concluding summary that again affirms the vindication of the *maśkîlîm*, a band of heroic teachers that seems to allude to the circle in which Daniel 7–12 was written, edited, and reworked.

Scholars frequently understand figures such as Michael, Gabriel, and the princes of Persia and Greece in Daniel 10 by drawing on traditions about the divine council or assembly.[84] It is important to emphasize, however, that these characters do not appear in some isolated stratum of the heavenly world but rather serve as operatives of a unified heavenly polity where power is centralized in a supreme deity.[85] Throughout Daniel 7–12, this conceptual framework allows the writer/editor to maintain that there is consistency and coherence in the political order while at the same time presenting new personalities, roles, and relationships on the conceit that they had always been there, whether this involves characters such as the "one like a human being," Gabriel, or the victimized *maśkîlîm* who appear in Daniel 11 and 12.

Jubilees

Jubilees is dated to the mid-second century BCE, and its writer shows a marked interest in mythmaking about lesser deities such as watchers, "angels," princes, various spirits, and named figures such as Mastema and Belial.[86] The work as a whole rewrites much of the biblical storyline that runs from Genesis to Exodus 12, with lesser deities often playing important roles. In many cases, the writer takes care to emphasize that these lesser deities serve as operatives of the supreme God, even when they play harassing and misleading roles.[87]

The opening chapters of Jubilees report a dialogue between Moses and God that takes place on Mt. Sinai and serves as a kind of framing prologue to the work as a whole. The substance concerns the impending disobedience, punishment, and eventual restoration of Israel. Thus construed, Israel's fortunes express the providential rule of its powerful divine patron, a God who also serves as the unrivaled king of the universe (1:6). Lesser deities and spirits consistently serve this larger agenda. So in Jubilees 1, the writer presents an extensive list of Israel's crimes but gives special attention to the worship of other gods; failure to keep the law (especially as related to the temple); and the practices of idolatry, sacrificing children to "demons (*'agānent*)," killing God's witnesses, and persecuting those who study the law. In one instance, the writer adds, "When they eat and are full [having gained the land of milk and honey], they will turn to foreign gods (*'amlāk nakir*)— to ones which will not save them from any of their afflictions" (1:7–8).[88] A similar issue appears again just a few lines later. After predicting a series of catastrophes that include military losses, abandoning the law, impurities, and serving the gods of the nations, the writer adds: "They will sacrifice their children to demons (*'agānent*) and to every product (conceived by) their erring minds (*wa-la-kwellu gebra sehtata lebbomu*)" (1:11). The roles ascribed to "foreign gods" and "demons" in vv. 8 and 11 imply that gentile gods are diminutive and ineffective so that the wayward Israelites err by misdirection; they worship beings who are powerless to help them. Despite these delinquencies, the deity assures that a brighter future awaits the people: "I will gather them from among all the nations, and they will search for me so that I may be found by them when they have searched for me with all their minds and with all their souls (*ba-kwellu lebbomu wa-ba-kwellu nafsomu*). I will rightly disclose to them abundant peace. I will transform them into a righteous plant with all my mind and all my soul (*ba-kwellu lebbeya wa-ba-kwellu nafseya*)" (1:15–16). Here the writer focuses on knowledge, minds, and souls to illustrate Israel's wicked ways and to explain the eventual return and restoration that the supreme deity will one day instigate. In this case, the deity also has a mind and soul, a point that lends further emphasis to the centrality of mind, thought, and understanding.

The writer of Jubilees often depicts lesser deities and harassing princes as important characters while also maintaining a marked preoccupation with the disposition of human hearts and minds. For instance, Moses pleads in chapter 1:

> Lord my God, do not allow your people and your heritage to go along in the error of their minds, and do not deliver them into the control of the nations with the result that they rule over them lest they make them sin against you. May your mercy, Lord, be lifted over your people. Create for them a just spirit (*manfasa retu'a*). May the spirit of Belial not rule them (*manfasa bēleḥor*) so as to bring charges against them before you and to trap them away from every proper path so that they may be destroyed from your presence. They are your people and your heritage whom you have rescued from Egyptian control by your great power. Create for them a pure mind and a holy spirit (*lebba neṣuḥa wa-manfasa qeddusa*). May they not be trapped in their sins from now to eternity. (1:19–21)

Here the writer connects the rule of the nations to Israel's disobedience, perhaps suggesting that the people will be seduced by gentile practices. Belial appears to instigate this dereliction in some way but acts as an accusing or harassing figure who serves in the court of Israel's deity. In this case, waywardness and error are also problems that involve the hearts, minds, and souls of the Israelites. This point is emphasized again in God's reply:

> I know their contrary nature, their way of thinking, and their stubbornness. They will not listen until they acknowledge their sins and the sins of their ancestors. After this they will return to me in a fully upright manner and with all (their) minds and all (their) souls (*wa-ba-kwellu lebb wa-ba-kwellu nafs*). I will cut away the foreskins of their minds (*qwelfata lebbomu*) and the foreskins of their descendants' minds (*wa-qwelfata lebb zar'omu*). I will create a holy spirit (*manfasa qeddusa*) for them and will purify them in order that they may not turn away from me from that time forever. Their souls (*nafsomu*) will adhere to me and to all my commandments (*te'ezāzeya*). They will perform my commandments. I will become their father and they will become my children. All of them will be called children of the living God (*kwellomu weluda 'amlāk ḥeyāw*). Every angel and every spirit (*kwellu mal'ak wa-kwellu manfas*) will know them.[89] They will know that they are my children and that I am their father in a just and proper way and that I love them. (1:22–25)

After finally acknowledging its past crimes, Israel will renew its relationship with the supreme deity; the deity, in turn, will intervene in quasi-surgical ways to strengthen, reform, and remake the minds and souls of the people.

Issues of mind and understanding also intersect with the world of divinity in interesting ways in chapter 12. The writer imagines Abraham first coming to discern the existence of a supreme God by observing the movements of the heavenly bodies. As he ponders the heavens, a voice suddenly announces: "All the signs of the stars and signs of the moon and the sun—all are under the Lord's control. Why should I be investigating (them)?" (12:17).[90] That very night, Abraham responds with a dramatic supplication that requests divine aid to ward off "evil spirits." So he cries: "Save me from the power of the evil spirits who rule the thoughts of people's minds. May they not mislead me from following you, my God" (12:20). Other gods now appear (by implication, at least) as "evil spirits" who can lead Abraham and his posterity astray. The divinities evoked here are conceived of as agents who can pressure, influence, meddle, and intervene in a variety of ways, but perhaps most characteristically they influence human thought. Fittingly, Abraham implores, "May I not proceed in the error of my mind, my God?" (12:21).[91]

Harmful spirits are prominent in Jubilees 5, 7, and 10–11, but they are strikingly absent from the account of creation.[92] In Jubilees 2, God creates the heavens, the earth, and the waters, as well as "all the spirits (*manfas*) who serve before him." These include

> the angels of the presence; the angels of holiness; the angels of the spirits of fire; the angels of the spirits of the winds; the angels of the spirits of the clouds, of darkness, *snow*, hail, and frost; the angels of the sounds, the thunders, and the lightnings; and the angels of the spirits of cold and heat, of winter, spring, autumn, and summer, and of all the spirits of his creatures which are in the heavens, on earth, and in every (place).[93] [There were also] the depths, darkness and light, dawn and evening which he prepared through the knowledge of his mind (*ba-'a'mero lebbu*). Then we saw his works and blessed him. (2:2–3)

The precise relationship between "angels" (*malā'ekt*) and "spirits" (*manfas*) here proves unclear, but the language suggests humanlike beings who are charged with ministering particular regions and territories. The writer could envision the spirits serving as lower-ranking deities who serve angelic leaders above them, not unlike some of the ranks in the Enochic Astronomical Book. However the writer imagines the precise roles of these spirits, it seems to be assumed that the created order functions as a multitiered political system. Appropriately, these lesser ranks serve as obedient subordinates and henchmen who bless, praise, and do the bidding of their creator deity and king.[94]

In chapters 5 and 7 of Jubilees, the writer tells of disobedient "watchers" who are familiar from Enochic traditions. Yet whereas the watchers sneak away to earth in the Book of the Watchers, in Jubilees the supreme deity deliberately sends them with orders to teach justice to humankind (4:15, 5:6). When they enter into illicit unions and father disastrous monster children, the deity sends another set of henchmen to strip them of their positions and bind them beneath the earth. The supreme deity also displays extraordinary powers by creating a "new and righteous nature (*feṭrata*) for all his creatures so that they would not sin with their whole nature (*ba-kwellu feṭratomu*) until eternity" (5:12).[95] Chapter 7 again tells of the watchers who acted "apart from the mandate of their authority" (7:21) in having sex with women. In this context, Noah gives a long speech that draws an analogy between the watchers' misdeeds (and their eventual annihilation) and the evils now rampant among his children (7:26–39). This speech characterizes the interbreeding of the watchers as "the first (acts) of uncleanness. They fathered (as their) sons the Nephilim. They were all dissimilar (from one another) and would devour one another" (7:21–22; cf. 5:1, 6–11). The watchers pervert the natural order by mixing different substances, ranks, and types of beings; the result is, in a seemingly inevitable way, monstrous dissimilarity, ethical mayhem, and righteous punishments that rain down from above (7:22–24).[96] So Noah warns his children that "demons (*'agānent*)" (7:27) have begun to lead them astray, especially to commit acts of rivalry, jealousy, inappropriate sex, homicide, injustice, and impurity associated with blood (7:27–39).

Further tales of waywardness and woe also relate how "evil spirits" come to afflict Noah's offspring. In an important scene in chapter 10, "impure demons (*'axazu 'agānent*)" (10:1) again begin to lead Noah's grandchildren astray, but these troubles are now resolved through a courtlike proceeding.[97] So Noah pleads that the "God of the spirits (*'amlāka manāfest*)" (10:3) take action against these "wicked spirits (*manāfest 'ekuyān*)":

> You know how your Watchers, the fathers of these spirits (*'abawihomu la-'ellu manfas*), have acted during my lifetime. As for these spirits who have remained alive (*manāfest 'ella hallawu*), imprison them and hold them captive in the place of judgment. May they not cause destruction among your servant's sons, my God, for they are savage and were created for the

purpose of destroying. May they not rule the spirits of the living (*wa-'i-yemabbelu ba-manfasa ḥeyāwān*) for you alone know their punishment; and may they not have power over the sons of the righteous from now and forevermore. (10:5–6)[98]

Corrupting spirits bring destruction and harm, but they were created for just this purpose. Noah also seems to argue that the supreme God is a more appropriate disciplinarian ("you alone know their punishment"). The character of Mastema, the "the leader of the spirits (*mal'aka manāfest*)," then emerges and voices his own concerns: the spirits are essential because they allow Mastema to "exercise the authority of my will (*'i-yekel gabira selṭana faqādeya*) among mankind. For they are meant (for the purpose of) destroying and misleading before my punishment because the evil of mankind is great" (10:8). Seeming to agree with both parties, the ruling deity soon arrives at a compromise: most of the spirits will be bound beneath the earth, but one-tenth of them will remain aboveground to serve as the punishing minions of Mastema. Some protection is also guaranteed to Noah's descendants because the supreme deity foresees "that they would neither conduct themselves properly nor fight fairly" (10:10). To this end, divine intermediaries reveal secrets about medicines and herbs that can fight "their diseases and deceptions" (10:12), and Noah dutifully writes these secrets down in a book and hands them on to Shem, his favorite son. This myth about the political and ethical order thus casts the evil spirits as operatives within the divine kingdom even while allowing that they may sometimes overreach. Helpfully, this allows the writer to differentiate Noah's offspring as those who possess written secrets that can ward off "their diseases and their deceptions." Ultimately, "the evil spirits were precluded from pursuing Noah's children" (10:13), at least for a time.

Chapter 11 presents the last major discussion of Mastema and his minions. Here Ur begins to make "statues, and images, and unclean things; the spirits (*manāfest*) of the savage ones[99] were helping and misleading (them) so that they would commit sins, impurities, and transgression" (11:4). Though callous and cruel, these spirits nevertheless function as servants of the high God. The association with idolatry also suggests that gentile gods are being polemically recategorized as lesser spirits and specifically as agents of punishment. So it is explained: "Prince Mastema was exerting his power in effecting all these actions and, by means of the spirits, he was sending to those who were placed under his control (the ability) to commit every (kind of) error and sin and every (kind of) transgression; to corrupt, to destroy, and to shed blood on the earth" (11:5). Mastema brings a panoply of ills, but only for "those who were placed under his control." The identification of gentile gods with evil spirits again becomes explicit in chapter 15 where lower-ranking spirits lead all other nations astray, though in full accord with the divine plan for world management:

> He sanctified them and gathered (them) from all mankind. For there are many nations and many peoples and all belong to him. He made spirits rule over all in order to lead them astray from following him (*wa-diba kwellu 'aslaṭa manāfesta kama yāsḥetomu 'em-dexrēhu*). But over Israel he made no angel or spirit (*mal'aka wa-manfasa*) rule because he alone is their ruler. He will guard them and require them for himself from his angels, his spirits, and everyone, and all his powers (*malā'ektihu wa-'emmena manāfestihu wa-'em-'eda kwellu wa-kwellu te'ezāzātihu*) so that he may guard them and bless them and so that they may be his and he theirs from now and forever. (15:31–32; cf. 19:28)[100]

In a play on Deuteronomy 32, the writer imagines Israel as having a privileged, unmediated relationship to the supreme God. In sharp contrast, the nations are alienated from the ultimate sovereign and ruled instead by lesser, misleading operatives of that God. Somehow, this is all in accord with a single, unified, and consistent rationale that has been fixed by the ultimate ruler of all.[101]

In a number of other instances, the writer of Jubilees uses lesser deities and misleading spirits to explain the threats posed by other gods. So chapter 19 evokes the possibility that Mastema and his spirits may rule over the people of God and keep them from "following the Lord" (19:28). In a different way, Abraham's blessing of Jacob in chapter 22 also admonishes that he separate from the nations with their abominable practices such as sacrificing to the dead, worshipping demons, eating in tombs, and worshipping mere statues (22:16–18).[102] As in other cases, gentile gods are implicitly demoted and recast as misleading spirits who populate the lesser ranks of the divine kingdom. Gentiles perversely worship these spirits (while presumably ignoring the supreme God) and commit a range of other crimes that involve misdirection and misunderstanding. In these cases, oppositions between God and "demons" or true and false religious beliefs do not reflect some uniquely dualistic worldview, as some scholars maintain.[103] Rather, these oppositions work to generate and reproduce a hierarchical conception of the cosmo-political order, one that incites certain loyalties, associations, and obligations. In Jubilees, "demons" and wicked spirits typically threaten in ways that serve the author's claims about of the true, the legitimate, and the good, whether this means worshipping the wrong sorts of gods, eating meat with blood in it, or entering into mixed marriages.

For all its mythmaking about the lesser ranks, Jubilees also tells of human misdeeds that do not involve these intermediaries. To give only a few examples, in chapter 10 the supreme God descends from heaven together with a band of attendants and intervenes by confusing the tongues of the Tower of Babel builders, "so that one plan no longer remains with them until the day of judgment" (10:22). Acting in a very direct way, the high God disperses the people and sends a wind that fells the tower (10:26). In other cases, blinded hearts and foolish minds also become central preoccupations (as, e.g., 1:19–25 and 12:21), even though divine beings may also take some of the praise or blame. In chapter 16, for instance, the writer depicts the punishment of Sodom without reference to evil spirits or Belial (as also 20:5), but in Jubilees 21 Isaac will be "kept from every evil one (*'em-kwellu 'ekuy*) ... that he may save you from every (kind of) death" (21:20), provided that he keeps the commands of God. Similarly, chapter 21 also discourses on the depravity of humankind but makes little mention of harmful spirits; and in 23:12 human life is shortened because of escalating dereliction, but evil spirits do not appear on the scene. In general, the divine world that emerges in Jubilees appears as a variegated, multitiered whole where people participate in a complex (but well-defined) web of relationships, including with other people and divine beings of varying natures, powers, and domains.

Divine Enemies and Heavenly Ranks at Qumran

Many scholars of early Judaism and Christianity look to Qumran writings (the so-called Dead Sea Scrolls) for evidence of apocalyptic dualism, especially the so-called Treatise on the Two Spirits (1QS 3.13–4.26) and the War Scroll. In doing so, they follow a substantial tradition of scholarship that characterizes Qumran sectarian literature as dualistic, with the Treatise on the Two Spirits exemplifying the most thoroughgoing or complete form of this dualism. Indeed, the Treatise is frequently trotted out as evidence for a form of dualism that is at once cosmological, ontological, metaphysical, ethical, and anthropological (or psychological).[104] Though such characterizations pepper the scholarly literature, interpreters show little consensus about the precise meanings, definition, and significance of this dualism or about the language of ontology, metaphysics, and cosmology that so often appears alongside it. For instance, the majority of scholars seem to hold that dualism in 1QS 3.13–4.26 involves dueling metaphysical principles and/or deities, but they do not distinguish clearly between concepts of deities and metaphysical principles, to say nothing of the general significance that should be attributed to them in the immediate literary context of 1QS 3–4, in relation to other sectarian and nonsectarian literature, or the much-disputed question of Iranian or Babylonian influence. Perhaps relatedly, many scholars introduce Zoroastrian traditions as paradigmatic of a dualistic metaphysical system (or a particular type of religious worldview) whether or not they are convinced that such traditions have a direct literary relationship with any of the Qumran texts.[105] As a result, Zoroastrianism (and language about metaphysics) tends to hover in the background as an exemplary case.[106] To raise yet another constellation of issues, some scholars extend the idea of conflict between twin deities in 1QS (where the prince of light and the *mal'āk* of darkness explicitly do battle) so that dualistic conflict characterizes other sectarian literature as well. According to many of these approaches, dualism appears virtually everywhere that interpreters plausibly identify characters like Belial or something like a "demonic realm."[107]

Finally, scholars commonly connect language about dualistic oppositions and struggle between competing princes, peoples, and realms in 1QS 3–4 to ethical and to anthropological or psychological dualism. Understood in this way, the whole of the Treatise seems to turn on a single axis. Notions of ethical dualisms typically pick out strong moralizing statements that pit truth against injustice and envision the sons of light and darkness walking on incommensurable "paths." For instance, a number of texts describe a vast gulf separating positive qualities (a spirit of meekness, patience, and understanding, etc.) from its opposite (a spirit of deceit, greed, insincerity, and so on) (4.9). Along the same lines, language about multiple "spirits" within the human heart (esp. 4.20–26) can be aligned along the same dualistic axis, yielding evidence for so-called anthropological dualisms. On the whole, then, claims to the effect that the Treatise contains a "thoroughgoing dualism" typically envision this pattern extending from the inner regions of the human being all the way to the outer reaches of the cosmos.

Despite its popularity, a number of critics have challenged the consensus that dualism plays an organizing role in the Treatise on the Two Spirits and in sectarian literature generally.[108] Among other problems, they note that the language of the Treatise is notoriously ambiguous on a number of key points, and even if given the most strongly dualistic interpretations, the allegedly dualistic views they express seem out of step with other sectarian literature.[109] Furthermore, the Treatise itself seems to vacillate between claims that appear sharply dualistic and language that describes a more integrated space, within both the self and the cosmos writ large. So in some instances we find assertions about two incommensurable types and domains—such as spirits, lots, or the prince of light and "angel" of darkness—but these appear right alongside arguments that integrate them, whether by envisioning a competing morass of spirits in the heart of each human being (4.20–26) or a current world order in which the spirits of the disfavored lot act to "cause the sons of light to fall" (3.24). This vacillation has not gone unnoticed by both champions and critics of dualism theories, but proponents tend to understand this as an unproblematic extension of the dualistic core of 1QS 3–4 while critics have tended to propose multiple layers of redaction.[110] Few seem to entertain the possibility that such dualisms might be better understood as forms of simplistic overstatement or as rhetorical generalizations, rather than as straightforward descriptions about the structure of the cosmos, the nature of reality, or the nature of the human person.

The Treatise on the Two Spirits survives in complete form in a single text from Cave 1 that is known as the Community Rule.[111] This short work presents a string of intriguing, beguiling, and inconsistent ruminations about the origins, roles, and destinies of twin lots of spirits, divinities, and types of people. Set within the longer Community Rule, the Treatise follows a lengthy set of rules proscribed for ranks of priests, Levites, and Israelites in a covenant renewal ceremony. Following a break in the text at 1QS 3.13, the subject matter shifts to a general set of claims about the divine plan for creation:[112]

> The instructor should instruct and teach all the sons of light about the generations of all the sons of man (*bětôlĕdôt kôl bĕnê 'îš*),[113] concerning all the ranks of their spirits (*lěko(w)l mînê rûḥôtām*),[114] in accordance with their signs (*bĕ'ôtôtām*) concerning their deeds in their generations (*lěma'ăśêhem bĕdôrôtām*), and concerning the visitation of their punishments and the times of their peace (*wělipqu(w)ddat nĕgî'êhem 'im qiṣṣê šělômām*). From the God of knowledge stems all there is and all there shall be. Before they existed he established their entire design. And when they have come into being, at their appointed time, they will execute all their works according to his glorious design, without altering anything (*wě'ên lěhašnôt*). In his hand are the laws of all things and he supports them in all their affairs. (1QS 3.13–17)[115]

The "generations of all the sons of man" provides an occasion for mythmaking that ties together ranks of spirits and human beings with the providential shape of world history.[116] Here the past, present, and future express the rationale of a deity who stands supreme over creation, ensuring that all marches forward "according to his glorious design, without altering anything." This immutable, unified, and rational heavenly plan sets up for a series of meditations about different classes or types of spirits (*rûḥôt*):

> He created man[117] to rule the world and placed before him two spirits[118] so that he would walk with them until the moment of his visitation: they are the spirits of truth and deceit (*wĕhû'â bārā' 'ĕnôš lĕmemšelet tēbēl wayyāśem lô šĕtê rûḥôt lĕhithallēk bām 'ad mô'ēd pĕqu(w)ddātô ḥēnnāh rûḥôt hā'ĕmet wĕhā'āwel*). From the spring of light stem the generations of truth, and from the source of darkness the generations of deceit. And in the hand of the Prince of Lights is dominion over all the sons of justice (*bĕyad śar 'ôrîm memšelet ko(w)l bĕnê ṣedeq*); they walk on paths of light. And in the hand of the Angel of Darkness is total dominion over the sons of deceit (*ûbĕyad mal'ak ḥôšek ko(w)l memšelet bĕnê 'āwel*); they walk on paths of darkness. From the Angel of Darkness stems the corruption of all the sons of justice (*ûbĕmal'ak ḥôšek tā'ût ko(w)l bĕnê ṣedeq*), and all their sins, their iniquities, their guilts and their offensive deeds are under his dominion in compliance with the mysteries of God until his moment (*bĕmemšaltô lĕpî rāzê 'ēl 'ad qiṣṣô*); and all their afflictions and their periods of grief are caused by the dominion of his enmity (*wĕko(w)l nĕgî'ēhem ûmô'ādê ṣārôtām bĕmemšelet maśtēmātô*); and all the spirits of his lot cause the sons of light to fall (*wĕko(w)l rûḥê gôrālô lĕhakšîl bĕnê 'ôr*). However, the God of Israel and the angel of his truth assist all the sons of light. He created the spirits of light and darkness and on them established every deed, [o]n their [path]s every labor [and on their paths [eve]ry [labo]ur]. God loves one of them for all eternal [a]ges and in all his deeds he takes pleasure for ever; the other one he detests, his counsel and all his paths he hates forever. (1QS 3.17–4.1)

These lines evoke a necessary and inevitable conflict between light and darkness, truth and deceit, love and hate. Such oppositions also seem to play out in terms of twin dominions (*memšelet*) or spheres that are ruled by distinctive deities: a *śar* (prince) and a *mal'āk* (messenger or intermediary). Though the writer/editor first posits a sharp antithesis between these paths, spirits, and divine administrators, it soon becomes clear that they overlap, intermingle, and interact at many levels. So in vv. 21–24, the dark leader and his spirits cause the sons of light to stumble and err; the result is that they suffer from "periods of grief" but are helped by the supreme God and his "angel of truth."

Despite the prominent roles given to "spirits" (*rûḥôt*) in the above text, it is extremely difficult to distinguish the precise valence of this language.[119] In particular, it remains unclear whether *rûḥôt* should be construed as something like the souls/hearts of human beings (perhaps approximating something like the "generations of men") or as divine subordinates of some kind (perhaps stand-ins for the prince of light or the *mal'āk* of darkness) or some admixture of both. In the above passage, however, there is no suggestion of interior or so-called psychological dualism, unless we just assume that two lots of spirits occupy the human heart in some unspecified way. Certainly, the writer/redactor does speak elsewhere of multiple spirits within humans (as 4.20–22) or of singular spirits with many characteristics (as 4.3–11).[120] For many proponents of dualism theories, however, the idea of psychological dualism requires a substantial ontological core of some kind, so that people have two parts/impulses/inclinations warring within them, one good and one evil. Typically, this imagined inner bifurcation is then correlated with the broader lots of individuals, administrative deities, and ethical paths that appear elsewhere in the Treatise as "dualistic pairs," and perhaps also with later rabbinic discussions about good and evil inclinations of a *yēṣer*.[121] The translation of García Martínez and Tigchelaar, especially of 3.17, is consistent with this line of interpretation. Against most other translators, for instance, their popular *Dead Sea Scrolls Study Edition* renders v. 17 as, "He created man to rule the world and placed within him two spirits [*rûḥôt*]." If the writer/editor had wished to locate these two spirits inside of humans, then *wayyāśem lô* proves an odd choice because this use of the verb *śm* more typically connotes something like "to establish for" or "place before." Such an interiorizing translation thus risks imposing a greater level of coherence than is warranted by the textual evidence. Likewise, common proposals to the effect that the *rûḥôt* are simultaneously both interior dispositions and external deities of some kind do not so much resolve these difficulties as compound them because they, too, paper over the lack of evidence for the idea of a self torn in two (and only in two).

Though the case for anthropological or psychological dualism in 1QS 3 proves weak, the repeated appeals to God having created a world rent in two prove distinctive, even if they are ultimately idiosyncratic to the Treatise. Other writings develop analogous language about different paths and divine intermediaries, but the writer/editor of the Treatise, at least in the form preserved in 1QS, makes repeated declarations that the supreme deity created them in just this way and frequently insists on their innate conflict or enmity. So we learn that, for certain mysterious ends, God created spirits of two distinct types; that the sovereign loves the sons of light and hates their counterparts; and that both the supreme God and his designated "angel" assist the favored sons of light. These statements could allude to a distinctive myth of origins, but the writer focuses quite intently on the power, intentionality, and disposition of the supreme deity and provides little more than allusive suggestions about creation as a whole. As repeatedly hammered home, everything hinges on the rational design and inclinations of the supreme God, from the respective habits, natures, and value assigned to the sons of light and darkness to the organization of history, the interactions between these lots, and the deeds (and misdeeds) of each. Quite remarkably, the deity almost compulsively sorts things into two symmetrical lots or types, but it remains unclear what conclusions might reasonably be drawn from this.

Though scholars frequently characterize the Treatise as dualistic, in 1QS 3 the elect sons of light are given to "afflictions" and "periods of grief" caused by the agents of the opposed camp. This implies that the domains of these twin deities and peoples interact and intertwine, at least in the normative present.[122] This more entangled, complex reality seems clearly in view elsewhere in the Community Rule, as in column 2, which refers to a period of "testing" within the community that takes place "during the dominion of Belial" (see also 1.18, 2.19, and 2.23–24). Here the writer/editor opens with a generalizing statement about Belial's reign but then quickly moves to explain this as a period of punishment wrought from on high. So the speaker evokes a furious but just judge who exacts punishment through intermediaries, with exhortations such as "may he hand you over to terror by the hands of all those carrying out acts of vengeance" and "may he not forgive by purifying your iniquities. May he lift the countenance of his anger to avenge himself on you, and may there be no peace for you by the mouth of those who intercede" (2.4). Here punishment rests on the disposition of the supreme sovereign, though intercessors may plead their case. Other curses target one who is "stubborn in his heart," imploring: "May God separate him for evil, and may he be cut off from the midst of all the sons of light because of his straying from following God on account of his idols and obstacle of his iniquity. May he assign his lot with the accursed ones forever" (2.16–17). Despite the antithetical rhetoric about types and lots, people are here envisioned as moving between them, not as belonging only to one or the other (see also 1QS 2.7–9 and 2.20). Here again, the rule of Belial, the opposed "lots," and the people torn between them do not appear in isolation. Rather, they serve certain distinctive roles within a rational world order, one in which a single supreme deity acts as righteous commander and judge. This rather basic point makes good sense of why the character, mind, rationale, inclinations, and creative mastery of a supreme sovereign appear much more central than characters like Belial, the *mal'āk* of darkness, or the evil spirits.

In column 4, the writer/editor addresses a range of interior human states and dispositions, but here again, there is little hint of ontological or anthropological "dualism." Like the complex but hierarchical relationships between lots, rulers, and characters in 1QS 2 and 3.21–24, some parts of column 4 suggest that the sons of light have a mixed inheritance within them while others speak again of sorting them into two equal lots.[123] The first half of column 4 consists of a series of admonitions about virtues, vices, and dispositions of the "spirit." Here the "spirit" emerges as an organizing center of thought, emotion, desire, and inclination, perhaps not unlike other ancient conceptions of mind or soul. The habits of the good spirit are "respect for the precepts of God. It is a spirit of meekness, of patience, generous compassion, eternal goodness, intelligence, understanding, potent wisdom which trusts in all the deeds of God" (4.3–4). After an extended catalogue, the writer/editor summarizes these as "the foundations of the spirits of the sons of truth (in) the world" (4.6) and promises them rewards that include eternal life, a crown of glory, and majestic clothing (4.4, 6–7). The only alternative is a singular "spirit of deceit," from which derive multiform vices ranging from wickedness, cruelty, and impatience to "sluggishness in the service of justice" (4.9), "filthy paths in the service of impurity" (4.10), and enthusiasm for acts done with "lustful passion (*zĕnôt*)" (4.10). Those on this track are destined for destruction in accordance with the wrath of a mighty God, though their punishment will be realized by "the hands of the angels of destruction" and involves a permanent fire "in the dark regions" (4.12–14).

Building to a rhetorical crescendo, the writer again characterizes the whole morass: "In these (lies) the history of all men; in their (two) divisions (*bĕmiplagêhen*) all their armies have a share for their generations; in their paths they walk; every deed they do (falls) into their divisions, dependent on what might be the birthright of man. For God has sorted them into equal parts until the last time, and he has put everlasting loathing between [their] divisions" (4.15–17). The language about sorting into equal parts proves distinctive, but the picture of the twin armies in v. 15 soon gives way to a messier picture: there are two classes of deeds, and the fate of each person is determined along a spectrum of possible types, not a simple binary. The strong binary oppositions structure the language and imagery here, but they seem to serve as constructive generalizations, not as straightforward descriptions of the ethical landscape. In other words, these antitheses can be understood as attempts to incite certain associations, loyalties, values, and ideals, not as absolute designations for incommensurable spheres, domains, or species of human. Such binaries make good sense as generalizing rhetoric or simplistic overstatements that create and reinforce certain normative claims, especially ideological categories about identity, difference, nature, value, and the order of power that extends—in a seemingly inevitable way—from the heights of heavens down to the earthly world of humankind below.[124]

In keeping with this picture, the subsequent lines in column 4 then shift to a lengthy meditation on an eschatological refinement, one that involves a violent interior renovation. Here we find multiple spirits within as well as imperfection and ambiguity even among the elect. So the writer/editor inveighs:

> Then God will refine (*yĕbārēr ʾēl*), with his truth, all man's deeds, and he will purify for himself the structure of man, ripping out all the spirits of injustice from the innermost part of his flesh (*ziqqaq lô mibbĕnê ʾiš lĕhātēn ko(w)l rûaḥ ʿawlāh mitakmê bĕśārô*), and cleansing him with the spirit of holiness from every wicked deed. He will sprinkle over him the spirit of truth like lustral water (in order to cleanse him) from all the abhorrences of deceit and (from) the defilement of the unclean spirit, in order to instruct the upright ones with knowledge of the Most High, and to make understand the wisdom of the sons of heaven to those of perfect behavior. (1QS 4.20–22)

Here the righteous have multiple malevolent spirits within them, but these must be violently excised to achieve eschatological perfection. The language of purity and pollution requires a more mixed, ambiguous character even for the favored "sons of light," even though the sharp rhetoric elsewhere evokes hostility, enmity, and incommensurability. In keeping with this more ambivalent or mixed characterization, column 4 concludes: "Until now the spirits of truth and injustice feud in the heart of man (*yārîbû rûḥê ʾĕmet wĕʿāwel bilbab geber*): they walk in wisdom or in folly. In agreement with man's inheritance in the truth, he shall be righteous and so abhor injustice; and according to his share in the lot of injustice, he shall act wickedly in it, and so abhor the truth. For God has sorted them into equal parts until the appointed end and the new creation" (1QS 4.23–25). The sharp polarization between the spirits of truth and deceit captures something of great importance to the writer's thinking, but "dualism" is not adequate as a characterization of the writer's worldview, cosmology, or metaphysical world picture. An appreciation for this more complex and hierarchical texture also explains why people are envisioned as being on a spectrum and therefore also as being capable of backsliding, improvement, and reform.

Other Qumran literature appeals to figures such as Michael, Belial, and the prince of lights (e.g., 4Q177 and 4Q286), but the dueling deities and lots of spirits do not appear elsewhere.[125] As John Collins notes, for instance, the Damascus Document (CD) lacks such formulations, even though language about a prince of lights and Belial frequently appears in the work.[126] So CD 4 imagines a period when "Belial will be sent against Israel" (4.13) and describes Israel's errors in terms of the three "nets of Belial" (4.15). In CD 5, the prince of lights "raises up" Moses and Aaron while "Belial, with his cunning, raised up Jannes and his brother during the first deliverance of Israel" (5.18–19).[127] In a different way, the spirit of Belial dominates wayward sinners in CD 8.2 and 12.2, and in 19.14 covenant violators will be handed over to Belial for destruction, which implies some remedial or punishing function. It is telling, however, that Belial is absent from column 2, which contains a lengthy meditation on God's plan for creation. So the writer/editor of CD 2 explains:

> God loves knowledge; he has established wisdom and counsel before him; prudence and knowledge are at his service; patience is his and abundance of pardon, to atone for those who repent from sin; however, strength and power and a great anger with flames of fire by the [hand] of all the angels of destruction (*mal'ăkê ḥebel*) against those turning aside from the path and abominating the precept, without there being for them either a remnant or survivor. For God did not choose them at the beginning of the world, and before they were established he knew their deeds, and abominated the generations on account of blood and hid his face from the land, from [Israel], until their extinction. And he knew the years of existence, and the number and detail of their ages, of all those who exist over the centuries [and of those who will exist], until it occurs in their ages throughout all the everlasting years. (2.3–10)[128]

Rather than twin lots and divine princes, the supreme deity instead sorts favored from disfavored peoples as part of an elaborate plan for punishment and reward. The favored are characterized as wise, patient, prudent, and given to repentance, but the writer emphasizes that it is God who fashioned these characters and causes them to choose the correct path or to stray. In the subsequent lines, the plan for the ages also comes to includes a series of divine rescues that preserves an elect, "a remnant for the land and in order to fill the face of the world with their offspring. And he taught them by the hand of [the anointed ones] with his holy spirit and through seers of the truth, and their names were established with precision. But those he hates, he causes to stray" (CD 2.11–13). Here the spirit of God plays an instrumental role, as do seers who teach and instruct the chosen righteous. Thus conceived, a divine ruler and creator God works to distinguish favored individuals in each period in history so that a series of elect remnants always rise above the fray; "angels of destruction" serve similar ends. These myths about ages and righteous remnants serve as fitting preludes to exhortations to "choose what he is pleased with and repudiate what he hates" (2.15) and a moralizing myth about wayward watchers in 2.17–21, which further illustrates the dangers of disobedience.

The War Scroll tells of a climactic battle between favored and disfavored peoples, sometimes using imagery that echoes 1QS 3.13–4.26, at least faintly.[129] The idea of a great, culminating war against the nations fits with the conceptual expansion and agglomeration of Israel's enemies that is attested in other literature, especially in many of the biblical prophets (e.g., Isa 36:18, 37:12; Ezek 39; and Joel 3), psalms (e.g., Ps 2), and apocalyptic texts such as the Animal Apocalypse of Enoch (e.g., 90) and Daniel 7–12 (e.g., 7:14).[130] The writer/editor of the War Scroll also presents a quite idiosyncratic battle plan, one that involves a very precise, ritualized sequence and that has priests serving as military leaders. The prominent role of both priests and divine beings who intermingle with the armies may help to explain the intense focus on rules for maintaining purity in the camps, particularly in columns 2–9.[131]

The War Scroll lays out a very precise scenario in which the forces of "light" and "darkness" trade dominance for set periods during an extended forty-year war.[132] Though this seesaw may appear dualistic, the writer/editor of the text preserved in 1QM quite steadfastly maintains that the true powers of heaven are never threatened by the skirmishes below. The conceit of a preordained plan for battle and of a ritualistic series of reversals in this battle does much to further this agenda. For instance, column 1 contains a summary overview of the war that emphasizes the ultimate victory of God. Here the opponents are "the lot of the sons of darkness, against the army of Belial (*běgôral běnê ḥôšek běḥêl běliyaʿal*)" (1.1), and they are to be utterly destroyed (1.6–7).[133] Their opponents are the "[sons of jus]tice," and, by contrast, they "shall shine to all the edges of the earth, they shall go on shining, up to the end of all the periods of darkness; and in the time of God, his exalted greatness will shine for all the et[ernal] times, for peace and blessing, glory and joy, and length of days for all the sons of light" (1.8–9). The "sons of justice" stand off sharply from the lot of Belial, but the supreme powers of heaven also stand behind them and assure their vindication. Similarly, the writer inveighs:

> For this will be the day determined by him since ancient times for the war of extermination (*lěmilḥemet kālâ*) against the sons of darkness. On this (day), the assembly of the gods (*ʿădat ʾēlîm*) and the congregation of men shall confront each other for great destruction. The sons of light and the lot of darkness shall battle together for God's might, between the roar of a huge multitude and the shouts of gods (*ʾēlîm*) and of men, on the day of calamity. It will be a time of suffering fo[r al]l the nations redeemed by God. (1QM 1.10–12)

Recalling biblical "day of Yahweh" motifs, the writer here paints a picture of a thunderous clash between higher and lower ranks, as heaven and earth meet each other in battle. Though elsewhere in 1QM this struggle is described as involving princes of light and darkness (as in 13.10–13), the story told here evokes heavenly forces descending from on high and turning the battle decisively in favor of the sons of light. After lingering over the inevitable victory at the end, the writer/redactor turns back to explore earlier periods of the war and predicts six periods during which the armies will trade dominance. Thus, the sons of light will first vanquish the wicked and then retreat before the armies of Belial, only to be strengthened again by God in preparation for the next round (1.13–14). At the end, the supreme sovereign will descend from heaven to engage Belial directly: "God's great hand will subdue [Belial, and al]l the angels of his dominion (*malʾăkê memšaltô*) and all the men of [his lot]" (1.14–15).

Throughout the War Scroll, the writer/editor appeals to the exceptional status of the supreme deity in ways that affirm that this seemingly matched battle is really not so matched after all. One result is that the battle emerges as the outworking of a hidden or mysterious plan for history. So the prayers in columns 10–14 heavily emphasize the unrivaled power of the high God, imploring: "Who (is) like you, God of Israel (*mî' kāmôkâ 'ēl yiśrā'ēl*), in the hea[ven]s or on earth, to do great deeds like your deeds, marvels like your feats? And who (is) like your nation, Israel, whom you chose for yourself from among all the nations of the earth?" (10.8–9). Echoing incomparability claims familiar from other literature, the writer/editor imagines a divine political order in which ranks, powers, and destinies are all duly subordinate to the supreme power above (10.11). Consistent with this picture of divine politics, the subsequent lines evoke a single cosmic ruler who stands supreme over the entire created order (10.12–17). Building again toward images of an inevitable triumph, the writer then goes on to celebrate military victories against past defeated foes and to predict a future time when a "scepter and star" (11.6) will finally appear. This figure will lead a war against the hordes of Belial and achieve a victory that is just as inevitable as the defeat of Pharaoh's army and of Gog in Ezekiel. With language somewhat reminiscent of 1QS 3–4, the writer goes on to explain: "From of old you appointed the Prince of light to assist us, and in [his] ha[nd are all the angels of just]ice, and all the spirits of truth are under his dominion. You made Belial for the pit, angel of enmity; in dark[ness] is his [dom]ain, his counsel is to bring about wickedness and guilt. All the spirits of his lot are angels of destruction, they walk in the laws of darkness; towards it goes their only [de]sire" (1QM 13.10–12). Despite the strong contrasts between the prince of light and the *mal'āk* of darkness, the war here involves an asymmetrical alignment of heavenly powers against lesser ones below (as also in 16.1). Like the fixed nature of history, the expanses of the heavens, the earth, and "the pit" also serve to represent this order as necessary, universal, and inevitable. Similarly, the subsequent lines again hymn the incomparable status of the high God—"Which angel or prince (*mî' mal'āk wĕśar*) is an aid like [you]?" (13.14)—and reaffirm the magisterial, righteous, and fixed plan for world history (13.14–18; cf. 15.13–17). In these and other cases, the writer/redactor of the War Scroll uses binary oppositions between favored and disfavored peoples in ways that generate and reinforce its claims about the unfolding plan for world history and the privileged place of a righteous remnant within it.

One important function of this ritualistic, preordained battle plan is that it serves to suppress any possible intimations of powerlessness and defeat. For instance, in column 16, the priests and the armies of light are tested by the war with Belial as "the slain of the infantry start to fall in accordance with God's mysteries" (16.11; cf. 17.1). The writer/editor also affirms that following this period of testing "in the crucible" (17.1), there will be an "appointed time to humiliate and abase the prince of the dominion of evil" (17.5–6). At this time, the supreme God will send aid to his favored people, "by the power of the majestic angel for the sway of Michael in everlasting light, to illuminate with joy the covenant of Israel, peace and blessing to God's lot, to exalt the sway of Michael above all the gods, and the dominion of Israel over all flesh (lĕhārîm bā'ēlîm miśrat mîkā'ēl ûmemśelet yiśrā'ēl bĕko(w)l bāśār)" (17.6–7). Here a powerful divine being assumes the role of divine warrior, as does Melchizedek in other literature. The more direct clashes between God and Belial in other parts of 1QM (so 18.1–3 pits "the mighty hand of God" against Belial; cf. 18.6–8 and 19.1–7) suggest that divine warrior figures like Michael have been inconsistently integrated into the War Scroll.

The War Scroll and the Community Rule sometimes tell of conflicts between dueling, binary forces, but they quite consistently integrate the opposing armies, lots, and divine beings into a broader picture of a cosmos that is hierarchically organized. Understood in this way, visions of a broad cosmic and historical order construe the sons of darkness and the lot of Belial as subordinates whose presence is temporary, conditional, and under the thumb of the supreme powers in heaven. Other visions of the divine political order similarly accommodate figures such as Belial and malevolent spirits. To give only a few examples, similar images of the ranks of divinity are found in the Thanksgiving Psalms, the Songs of the Sabbath Sacrifice, and the Songs of the Maskil.[134] For instance, the writer/redactor of 4Q510 (the Songs of the Maskil or Songs of the Sage) presents a dramatic appeal for protection from various classes of spirits and "angels" (4Q510 1; cf. 4Q511 10).[135] In the opening hymn, however, relationships of power in the divine world appear unambiguous:

> To the God of knowledge, the glory of the po[werful] ones, God of gods, Lord of all the holy ones. [His] rea[lm] is above the powerful mighty, and before the might of his powe[r] all are terrified and scatter; they flee before the radiance of his glorious majestic strong[hold]. And I, a Sage, declare the splendor of his radiance in order to frighten and terr[ify] all the spirits of the ravaging angels (rûḥê mal'ăkê ḥebel) and the bastard spirits (rûḥôt mamzērîm), demons (śēd'îm),[136] Lilith (lîlît), owls, and [jackals . . .][137] and those who strike unexpectedly to lead astray the spirit of knowledge, to make their hearts forlorn. And you have been placed in the era of the rul[e

of] wickedness and in the periods of humiliation of the sons of lig[ht], in the guilty periods of [those defiled by] iniquities; not for an everlasting destruction [but ra]ther for the era of the humiliation of sin. (4Q510 1 2–8; cf. 4Q511 10)

Here a supreme sovereign presides over a myriad of lesser ranks, including powerful ones, gods, holy ones, and various harmful spirits, among others. Though harmful beings figure prominently, the "splendor of his [the supreme God's] radiance" is called on to protect against their onslaught. More basically, however, the ravaging angels, bastard spirits, Lilith, howlers, and those led astray appear to be confined to the earthly sphere where they serve the plans of the high God for a period of punishment and humiliation.[138] Thus, the scheme presented here entails a hierarchical system of rule that extends into the lower realms to distinguish different ranks of deities, people, and groups.

Finally, it should be noted that 1QS 3–4 and 1QM may reflect ideas of an originally Babylonian or Iranian provenance.[139] Though evidence for early Zoroastrian thought is scarce, it is certainly possible that Babylonian traditions can explain some of the idiosyncratic features of these texts. The strongest arguments for influence, however, do not focus so much on the idea of dueling deities or so-called metaphysical dualisms but rather on certain peculiar features of the battle plan, particularly the distinctive patterns of symmetry in the scheme for the war in 1QM, with its seesawing periods of victory and defeat.[140] Of course, it is possible to atomize some lines from these works and to construe these as evidence for a strong form of dualism that involves twin divine beings locked in opposition.[141] I maintain, however, that the texts preserved in 1QS and 1QM do not encourage such an interpretation. For in keeping with much other literature, the Community Rule and the War Scroll quite consistently appeal to binary categories such as the princes of light/darkness in ways that generate and reinforce a more complex and hierarchical taxonomy. Like strong rhetorical contrasts between insiders/outsiders, true/false teachings, and true/false religious practices, these binaries serve ideological claims about an elect remnant that is elevated over all other peoples. As a guarantee of this exceptional status, they are aligned with the supreme powers of heaven. Though scholars sometimes appeal to notions of dualism to understand these antitheses, the model of a hierarchical divine polity accounts for the ideological functions of these binaries, especially in constructing an alienated but empowered elect.

Conclusion

According to many scholars of Christianity, apocalypticists envision a world that is ruled by tyrannical divine rebels and evil gods. A more careful consideration of works such as 1 Enoch, Daniel 7–12, the War Scroll, and the Treatise on the Two Spirits (1QS 3–4) undermines such views. In place of rebel empires, these traditions more consistently imagine a unified cosmic empire where a supreme deity rules as king. They also show a marked ambivalence about the possibility of conflict, disobedience, and rebellion within it. To this end, writers often take pains to avoid portraying lesser deities as divine rebels who threaten the order of heaven. For instance, in the much-discussed Book of the Watchers, the comely daughters of men lure a troupe of heavenly middlemen down from their station. Though these adventures prove disastrous, the myth naturalizes notions of heavenly hierarchy by imagining the punishment of lesser powers by greater ones.[142] The watchers leave harmful spirits on earth, but these mainly harass idolaters, a pattern consistent with texts like Jubilees 15. In a different way, the Astronomical Book of Enoch predicts that some of the heavenly luminaries will one day disobey or misunderstand their commands, straying from their paths. The results are catastrophic but mainly because disfavored human beings mistakenly take them to be gods; they do not rise in rebellion or coups against the powers above them. In ways that are similar and different, the writer of the Animal Apocalypse creates a long scene in which the supreme sovereign entrusts divine governors (the shepherd-managers) with the rule of Israel. Though these shepherd-managers sometimes go too far in executing their punishing mandate, the writer construes these as matters of overreach and excessive zeal (cf. Dan 10 and Rev 12), not resistance or rebellion, and their eventual punishment is assured. Daniel 10 briefly evokes a heavenly conflict between divine subordinates (Michael, Gabriel, and the princes of Persia and Greece), but this unfolds at some distance from the high God, as does the matched battle in the War Scroll. Thus, whatever conflicts may erupt in the lesser ranks, the all-powerful ruler above assures the order, stability, and justice of the political system as a whole.

Theories of apocalyptic dualism and heavenly rebellion continue to loom large in the study of Christian apocalypticism, particularly among interpreters of Paul.[143] In some cases, this serves as the basic explanatory frame for understanding apocalypticism generally, and in others, it is invoked rather casually to explain some aspect of Paul's Jewish background.

As I have argued here, however, much of the relevant literature labors to construe lower-ranking deities as relatively powerless noncompetitors who are foolishly arrayed against heaven, not as rebels or usurpers who threaten the established order. Such formulations helpfully avoid intimations that gentile gods—especially the gods of the Assyrians, Babylonians, Greeks, and Romans—could defeat Israel's patron deity. This reassessment throws much needed light on Paul's letters, especially his mythmaking about eschatological enemies, gentile gods, and Christ's dutiful submission to the supreme God of all.

3 Conflict, Competition, and Paul's "Principalities and Powers" Reconsidered

This chapter treats Paul's language about Christ as a warrior in the context of Jewish traditions about eschatological war. I develop two related arguments here: first, that much of the relevant literature, though quite varied and diverse, implicitly envisions the world as a kind of anthropomorphic political hierarchy; and second, that this literature tends to adapt this model in ways that suppress the possibility of rivalry, opposition, and matched battle in the world of divinity. This pattern is especially marked in cases that involve the upper ranks of divine power, and potential rivalry with the supreme God perhaps most of all. The conceptual framework of a single, hierarchical world polity especially facilitates tales of highly asymmetrical warfare, evocative celebrations of heavenly political and military power, and myths that assimilate gentile gods to the lesser ranks of the divine order. In eschatological contexts, this frequently plays out in military dramas in which the empire of heaven (or its deputy warriors) wins a crushing victory against relatively powerless opponents and instrumental enemies. With victory inevitable, these military triumphs become yet one more display of the irresistible nature of heavenly power. These patterns shed much-needed light on Christ's defeat of the "principalities and powers" in 1 Cor 15:23–28 and on the role of eschatological battle in organizing Paul's thought generally.

In what follows, I identify common assumptions, strategies, and motifs that are resilient in texts such as Ezekiel 37–38, Joel 3, Daniel 7–12, and the traditions of 1 Enoch. These motifs and strategies shed light on 1 Cor 15:23–28 and Phil 2:6–9, texts that have seemed to resist historical contextualization. First, they illuminate Paul's principalities and powers as

108

gentile gods who have been reclassified as lesser deities and servants of Israel's God. Conceiving of the *archai, exousiai,* and *dunameis* in 1 Cor 15:23–28 both as subordinates of the supreme God and as objects of (mistaken) gentile worship explains many difficult features of the text, especially their brief emergence as "enemies" here, only to be summarily defeated by Christ. On these terms, 1 Cor 15:23–28 can be fruitfully compared to other writings that conjoin the imagined defeat or punishment of gentile gods with the submission of the gentile peoples. Second, tendencies to suppress rivalry and competition in the world of divinity explain why texts such as Phil 2:6–11 and 1 Cor 15:27–28 heavily emphasize Christ's unqualified submission and obedience. Whereas other mythmakers innovate with tales of wayward divine fools, overzealous divine managers, or haunting but diminutive spirits, Paul develops a distinctive myth that celebrates Christ's noncompetition and heroic submission. This explains why Paul labors over Christ's submission in 1 Cor 15:26–28 and so heavily emphasizes obedience and lack of rivalry in Phil 2:6–9. Third, and more generally, these patterns illuminate Paul's thought about how election, change, and transformation are embedded within the existing world order. Despite the seemingly radical change envisioned as being right on the horizon of the apocalyptic future, the letters consistently maintain that the cosmo-political system—the world as it is, has been, and will be—everywhere displays the ongoing, just, and providential rule of its supreme commander and king. Like a great number of other writers, then, Paul expects a full transformation in the near future that will not so much overturn the current world order as purify, re-create, and perfect it. Rather than arriving at an "end" or culmination of history, this apocalyptic future will more fully display and perfect the system of rule already inherent in it.

Uncontested Power: Non-gods, Idols, and Instrumental Enemies

A wide range of biblical and Hellenistic Jewish writings develop elaborate polemics about the true nature of heavenly power. In many cases, these polemics suppress any potential threats posed by other deities, whether by recategorizing and assimilating them to the lower ranks, by satirically identifying them with their cult statues, by assailing their powerlessness and/or nonexistence, or simply by omitting and ignoring them altogether.[1] Some of these traditions were explored in chapter 2, but these and related polemics require a more sustained analysis here. Such strategies are especially key for understanding myths about future wars where Yahweh will defeat, subdue, destroy, and/or enlighten the gentile nations, myths that are particularly relevant to understanding Paul's texts.[2]

A number of biblical passages warn of impending doom for the gentiles or "the nations," a broad and largely unmarked category of outsiders and opponents.[3] So Psalm 2 extols the great power of Yahweh and promises, "I will make the nations your heritage, and the ends of the earth your possession. You shall break them with a rod of iron, and dash them to pieces like a potter's vessel" (2:8–9 NRSV).[4] This psalm probably dates to the monarchy, but many postexilic writings reproduce and expand on this motif, frequently in ways that scale up the battle. So in Ezekiel 38–39, Israel's deity rouses an enemy host led by Gog, destroys this enemy in a grand fashion (39:4; cf. Dan 11:45), and vindicates Israel in an ostentatious display of military prowess. The writer envisions armies descending on Israel from the north but everywhere affirms their subordinate status with claims like "I will bring you against my land, so that the nations may know me, when through you, O Gog, I display my holiness before their eyes" (38:16 NRSV; cf. 38:23; 39:7, 21–22, 27; Isa 13:3–5; Hab 3:16).[5] On these terms, Yahweh creates an enemy host solely for the purpose of destroying it in a showy exhibition of military might. This exhibition in turn forces the wayward nations to acknowledge their true divine master. In keeping with this agenda, images of display, recognition, reconciliation, and inevitable defeat tend to predominate. In Ezekiel 37, for instance, the writer evokes a utopian political future: "My dwelling place shall be with them; and I will be their God, and they shall be my people. Then the nations shall know that I the Lord (YHWH) sanctify Israel, when my sanctuary is among them forevermore" (37:27–28 NRSV). Similarly, in Joel 3:9–16, Yahweh brings the nations to the valley of Jehoshaphat: "Come quickly, all you nations all around, gather yourselves there. Bring down your warriors, O Lord (*hanhat* YHWH *gibbôrêkā*).[6] Let the nations rouse themselves, and come up to the valley of Jehoshaphat; for there I will sit to judge all the neighboring nations" (3:11–12 NRSV; Heb 4:11–12).

The nations play prominent roles in Joel 3 and Ezekiel 37–38, but their gods are conspicuously absent. Indeed, it is easy to ignore them altogether, because a central conceit of the texts is that Yahweh fights powerless opponents and instrumental enemies, not deities of comparable rank and power. To a significant extent, this reflects the postexilic political situation in which Israel serves as a subject people within large foreign empires, a practical reality that suggests the weakness and defeat of Israel's patron. Such concerns become explicit in Joel 2, where a speaker implores, "Spare your people, O Lord, and do not make your heritage a mockery, a byword among the nations. Why should it be said among the peoples, 'Where is their God (*'ayyēh 'ělōhêhem*)?'" (2:17 NRSV; cf. Mic 7:10). The query "Where is their God?" deftly evokes a deity who is absent, not weak or defeated, and the subsequent lines dramatically reaffirm Yahweh's standing by imagining a time in the near future when a numberless, irresistible host will sweep down from heaven to devour all in its path (Joel 2:1–11, 25–27) and signal a damning judgment against the nations (Joel 3 [Heb 4]).

Like the writer/editor of Ezekiel, Joel largely ignores gentile gods, but other writers prefer to engage in a strategy of reclassification and assimilation. For instance, in Isaiah 37 the Assyrian king Sennacherib celebrates his conquest of other peoples and the defeat of their gods. On this basis, Sennacherib warns, "Do not let your God on whom you rely (*'ělōhêkā 'ǎšer 'attā bōṭēaḥ*) deceive you by promising that Jerusalem will not be given into the hand of the king of Assyria" (37:10 NRSV). Hezekiah responds with a prayer:

> O Lord of hosts, God of Israel (YHWH *ṣěbā'ôt 'ělōhê yiśrā'ēl*), who are enthroned above the cherubim, you are God, you alone, of all the kingdoms of the earth (*'attâ-hû' hā'ělōhîm lěbadděkā lěkōl mamlěkôt hā'āreṣ*);[7] you have made heaven and earth. Incline your ear, O Lord (YHWH), and hear; open your eyes, O Lord (YHWH), and see; hear all the words of Sennacherib, which he has sent to mock the living God (*'ělōhîm ḥāy*). Truly, O Lord (YHWH), the kings of Assyria have laid waste all the nations and their lands,[8] and have hurled their gods[9] into the fire, though they were no gods (*wěnātōn 'et-ělōhêhem bā'ēš kî lō' 'ělōhîm hēmmâ*), but the work of human hands—wood and stone—and so they were destroyed. So now, O Lord our God (YHWH *'ělōhênû*), save us from his hand, so that all the kingdoms of the earth may know that you alone are the Lord (YHWH).[10] (37:16–20 NRSV)

Here Israel's God appears enthroned in heaven above the cherubim, and this image soon becomes the basis for dramatic assertions that all earthy kingdoms actually serve this true ruler (though without realizing it) and that gentile gods are powerless nonbeings and "idols" of dead wood. While the character of Sennacherib maintains that other peoples do have gods of their own, the voice of Hezekiah dramatically reimagines the political terrain in ways that diminish Sennacherib together with his divine patrons.[11] This reclassification scheme neatly obliterates gentile gods and leaves only

Yahweh, the sole divine ruler and puppeteer of history. Fittingly, the scribe goes on to picture Sennacherib as Yahweh's plaything and to insist on a divine plan to punish him, rescue a remnant of Judah (37:30–32), and defend Jerusalem (37:33–35). In other cases, arrogant rulers play similar roles.[12] So the Babylonian king in Isa 14:3–23 exalts himself to a throne "above the stars of God" and deigns to make himself like "the most high." In Ezek 28:8–10, the king of Tyre also has divine pretensions, as does Antiochus IV Epiphanes in Daniel 7–12.

Prophecies about the defeat, obliteration, and submission of the gentiles appear in numerous other writings that are preserved both in and outside of the biblical anthology. A few salient examples illustrate some of the most resilient patterns in the evidence. Zechariah 14 evokes a time when Yahweh will bring the nations to desolate Israel and then appear in Jerusalem so that "Yahweh will become king over all the earth; and on that day Yahweh will be one, and his name one (*bayyôm hahû' yihyeh* YHWH *'eḥād ûšěmô 'eḥād*)" (14:9).[13] In the following lines, Yahweh sends a flesh-eating plague and a panic that utterly destroys the enemy (14:12–13), and then all the surviving nations come to Jerusalem to celebrate the festival of booths (cf. 14:17). This divine appearance also provokes upheavals of many kinds, as the Mount of Olives splits, new waters begin to flow, and the heavenly bodies change their cycles so that there is no more night, but only day (cf. Hab 3:12; Isa 40–43, 60:19–20). Images of reconciliation, winnowing, and renovation predominate, but there is no explicit mention of gentile deities, save perhaps in intimations of a time when Yahweh's name will be "one" (14:9). In some contrast, the writer/editor elsewhere predicts a time when Yahweh will "cut off the names of the idols (*'akrît 'et-šěmôt hā'ăṣabbîm*)[14] from the land, so they shall not be mentioned again" (13:2). Similar motifs appear in other literature. The writer/editor of Jeremiah 10 develops extended parodies about the mundane qualities of cult status but adds, "at the time of their punishment they will perish" (10:15 NRSV); the writer of Micah (1:7, 5:13–14) also identifies gentile gods with their cult objects and predicts, "I will cut off your images and your pillars (*pěsîlêkā ûmaṣṣēbôtêkā*) from among you, and you shall bow down no more to the work of your hands" (5:13 NRSV); and the writer/editor of the Epistle of Enoch includes the destruction of idols (91:8) in its eschatological scenario, though this is mentioned only briefly, as if in passing.

The idea of putting an end to idolatry by destroying statues or cult objects reflects a robust tradition of polemic that satirically identifies gentile gods with their cult statues.[15] In some cases, the ingathering of the gentiles seems to require the explicit destruction of non-gods, false gods, or "idols." As in Jeremiah 10 and Zechariah 13, the writer of Tobit 13 argues that although Israel's God is punishing Jerusalem at present, a time of restoration lies just on the horizon, a time when the deity will again dwell in Jerusalem and receive gifts from the nations (13:11). In this context, the writer evokes a "turning" of the gentiles, who come to recognize the true nature of divinity and offer appropriate forms of worship and supplication. In chapter 14, this includes the burial of their idols: "All the Gentiles will turn to fear the Lord God in truth (πάντα τὰ ἔθνη ἐπιστρέψουσιν ἀληθινῶς φοβεῖσθαι κύριον τὸν θεὸν), and will bury their idols (τὰ εἴδωλα). All the Gentiles will praise the Lord (κύριον), and his people will give thanks to God (τῷ θεῷ), and the Lord (κύριος) will exalt his people" (14:6–7 RSV). In a somewhat different way, 3 Sibylline Oracle predicts a time when Israel's God will again provide peace and protection for a Jerusalem elect and will instigate an ingathering of the nations (703–731). Here gentiles will recognize Israel's deity ("since he alone is sovereign"), keep his law, supplicate their immortal king, and repent of their past when "with mindless spirit we revered things made by hand, idols and statues of dead men" (722–723).[16] Though this adapts well-worn polemics, the writer of 3 Sibylline Oracle seems to envision the gentiles' restoration as a matter of changed thinking and acting that does not require the wholesale obliteration of cult objects.

Many of the examples considered so far explicitly conjoin motifs of gentile submission and the end of so-called idolatry. In other literature, however, writers rather tend to skirt the issue of other gods, even though the premise that gentiles have failed to worship Israel's God—and continue to do so—may still stand in the background or the shadows, as the case may be. So the writer of Psalm 22 anticipates a time when all the peoples of the earth will just remember their true ruler: "For dominion belongs to the Lord (YHWH), and he rules over the nations. To him, indeed, shall all who sleep in the earth bow down; before him shall bow all who go down to the dust, and I shall live for him" (22:28–29 NRSV; LXX Ps 21). Similar patterns appear in the prophecies of Zechariah 8, as a restored remnant of Israel emerges and the nations come to Jerusalem to serve Yahweh of hosts (8:20–23). Likewise, Micah (esp. 4:1–2 and 7:16–17) has a looming war where Yahweh will rout enemies inside and outside of Israel (cf. 1QM 12.13–14) and imagines gentiles bringing tribute and Yahweh sitting as judge over them. In Micah 4, the subject of gentile worship becomes more explicit:

"For all the peoples walk, each in the name of its god (*'îš běšēm 'ělōhāyw*), but we will walk in the name of the Lord our God (*běšēm-YHWH 'ělōhênû*)" (4:5 NRSV).[17] This comment appears briefly and in passing, however, as if the writer is at pains to move on.[18] In Isaiah 2, the nations stream to a restored house of God set on the highest hill, and in the Septuagint translation of Isaiah 11 there will be a root from Jesse, "in him the nations shall trust" (11:10 LXX).[19] Likewise, Second Isaiah imagines the nations bringing their wealth as tribute and kneeling in submission at last: "They shall follow you; they shall come over in chains and bow down to you. They will make supplication to you, saying, 'God is with you alone, and there is no other; there is no god besides him (*'ēl wě'ên 'ōd 'epes 'ělōhîm*)'" (45:14 NRSV).[20] The writer goes on to celebrate the unrivaled status of Israel's God and to deny the standing of others with excoriating rhetoric such as, "Assemble yourselves and come together,[21] draw near, you survivors of the nations! They have no knowledge—those who carry about their wooden idols, and keep on praying to a god that cannot save (*'ēl lō' yôšîa'*)"[22] (45:20 NRSV); and, "Turn to me and be saved, all the ends of the earth! For I am God, and there is no other (*'ănî-'ēl wě'ên 'ôd*)" (45:22 NRSV). For all the labored rhetoric, statements such as "I am God, and there is no other" implicitly evoke the very pluralistic reality that they take pains to deny.

Reclassification and Assimilation: Gentile Gods in the Ranks of Divinity

Many writers and editors present triumphalist visions of world rule that either ignore gentile gods or work to reclassify them as mundane statues instead of immortal rulers, patrons, and warriors on par with Israel's God. An important subset of polemical literature also works to recast the gods of others as bit players in the lesser ranks of the divine kingdom. Such strategies are often implicit in biblical texts that portray gentiles worshipping the stars, the heavenly bodies, or the host (as Deut 4:19; 2 Kgs 21:5, 23:5; Job 31:26). These motifs are resilient in the writings of Philo of Alexandria, Flavius Josephus, and Pseudo-Solomon, as well as in other literature, though with no one consensus view emerging. In Deuteronomy 32, other gods appear alternately as foreign gods, recent gods, and *šēdîm*, but these threaten only in the qualified sense that they provoke Israel's God to jealousy. Remarkably, however, the writer of Isaiah 24 suggests that the host, or some portion of the host, may indeed have gone rogue. So Isaiah

24 predicts a time when Yahweh will punish "the host of heaven in heaven (YHWH *ʿal-ṣĕbāʾ hammārôm bammārôm*), and on earth the kings of the earth" (24:21; cf. Ps 82).[23] The parallels between the host of heaven and the kings on earth suggest that the wayward host is to be identified with the gods of the gentile nations. Instead of clarifying this point, the writer seems content to recast these gods (or would-be gods) as a host of subordinates and to affirm that they will suffer eventually at the hands of their master above. Wrongdoing or mismanagement of some kind is also suggested by the "shame" of the moon and sun in the subsequent lines (24:23), but the punishment of the host comes to the fore again in chapter 34. Here the writer/editor insists: "All the host of heaven shall rot away (*wĕnāmaqqû kol-ṣĕbāʾ haššāmayim*), and the skies roll up like a scroll. All their host shall wither like a leaf withering on a vine, or fruit withering on a fig tree. When my sword has drunk its fill in the heavens, lo, it will descend upon Edom, upon the people I have doomed to judgment" (34:4–5 NRSV).[24] Notions of a wayward or rogue host may also be implied in other literature in which heavenly bodies sometimes darken, fall from heaven, or are renewed, restored, or altered in some way. It is notable, however, that the stars, planets, sun, and moon rarely become the objects of sustained mythmaking, save for in Enochic traditions that often identify the rogue watchers as stars.[25]

The works collected in 1 Enoch are of varying provenance, but they show a distinctive interest in the lower tiers of the divine order. In the Book of the Watchers, a band of foolish, wayward insubordinates are justly punished and condemned by the powers above them. Chapter 16 also adds a story about the anomalous birth of harmful spirits, which emerge from the bodies of the slain giants. In this context, the writer/editor emphasizes that these spirits direct their fury against human beings on earth, their own quasi-cousins, and later on in the story they are explicitly identified with gentile gods. So in chapter 19, the spirits serve not only as generic causes of harm, but they also lead people "to sacrifice to demons as to gods (*wa-yāsḥetewwomu kama yešuʿu la-ʾagānent kama ʾamālekt;* καὶ πλανήσει αὐτοὺς ἐπιθύειν τοῖς δαιμονίοις) until the day of the great judgment" (19:1). Somewhat like the foreign gods maligned in Deut 32:15–18, this polemic deftly reclassifies gentile gods as wayward, misleading spirits of destruction rather than as divine competitors and potential threats. The Astronomical Book of Enoch tells a quite different story, though to similar ends. Here we encounter a well-oiled heavenly machine where the luminaries operate according to a complex, militaristic hierarchy of command. For all the stress on order, regularity, and obedience, the writer/editor also allows that some of the luminaries will mishear or stray from their commands at some vaguely specified time in the future. The result is mass confusion about the nature of the gods and about the astronomical order: "Those on the earth will err regarding them. They will turn back from all their ways, will err, and will take them to be gods (*wa-yemasselewwomu'amālekt*). Evil will multiply against them and punishment will come upon them to destroy all" (80:7–8). Though this episode proves relatively brief, the claim that people misidentify the luminaries as gods fits with other polemics that imagine gentiles mistaking lesser beings for deities worthy of worship and cult, as observed already for the "demons" of 1 Enoch 19 (cf. Rom 1:18–32).

Whereas the spirits of the Book of the Watchers have an ambivalent relationship with the larger divine political order, Jubilees strongly affirms the instrumental role of all lesser figures, including but not limited to the watchers and their descendants. To this end, Jubilees insists that the supreme deity originally sent the Watchers to earth on a mission to teach justice (Jub. 4–5) and also adds an elaborate scene in which their leader (Mastema) negotiates with the high God to keep a punishing host to chastise humankind (Jub. 7). According to Jubilees, then, these spirits function as punishing operatives of the supreme God (not as leftovers and accidents, as in the Book of the Watchers), and their leader Mastema also acts as dutiful punisher elsewhere in Jubilees. The spirits also reappear in a number of tales about idolatry. So in Jubilees 11, Ur begins to make "statues, and images, and unclean things; the spirits of the savage ones[26] were helping and misleading (them) so that they would commit sins, impurities, and transgression" (11:4; cf. 1:11). Here the misleading spirits explain the origins of idolatry and work to characterize the gentiles as wildly delinquent. Idolatry becomes central again in Jubilees 15, where the spirits lead the gentiles astray: "For there are many nations and many peoples and all belong to him. He made spirits rule over all in order to lead them astray from following him (*wa-diba kwellu 'aslaṭa manāfesta kama yāsḥetomu 'em-dexrēhu*). But over Israel he made no angel or spirit (*mal'aka wa-manfasa*) rule because he alone is their ruler" (15:31). Here other gods fall away, leaving only a single divine king with a host of subordinates. These spirits sometimes play leadership roles, as they do in 15:31, but in other cases they help to explain the failings of Israel. So Jubilees 1 predicts: "When they [Israel] eat and are full [having gained the land of milk and honey] they will turn to foreign gods ('amlāk nakir)—to ones which will not save them from any of their afflictions" (1:7–8). On these terms, other gods are really diminutive spirits with no ability to protect, aid, or assist. Like the multiform gentile delusion, Israel's betrayal involves a catastrophic whirl of misperception, error, and mistaken alliances.

The Animal Apocalypse of Enoch works with familiar strategies and motifs to tell of a single, unified, multitiered heavenly bureaucracy. The heavenly world presented in the Animal Apocalypse is generally harmonious, but the writer singles out a special class of divine managers who come in for special attention. These shepherd-managers (*nolāweyān*) are explicitly identified with gentile gods, albeit reconceived as punishing operatives of Israel's. Thus construed, the patron gods of the conquering Persian, Greek, and Seleucid Empires become mere functionaries who obey Yahweh. To this end, the writer appeals to celebratory descriptions of a heavenly political system and affirms the abject position of the shepherd-managers within it. The writer does allow that the shepherds sometimes overreach in fulfilling their punishing mandate, but they maintain throughout that this is a problems of overzealousness, not outright defiance or rebellion (89:61–64, 89:65–72a, 89:74–90:1). Fittingly, a central conceit of the Animal Apocalypse is that the punishing shepherds will answer for their acts of overreach, each of which is duly written down in heaven by an accounting figure set over them. This punishment appears briefly in chapter 90 as part of the run-up to a worldwide cataclysm: "The Lord of the sheep came to them and took in his hand the staff of his wrath and struck the earth, and the earth was split, and all the beasts and all the birds of heaven fell (away) from among those sheep and sank in the earth and it covered them" (90:18). Though this marks only the beginning of a long series of eschatological events, these lines suggest the destruction of intermediary divinities (and perhaps earthly rulers as well) as punishment for their crimes. The idea of delayed punishment also appears in connection with the evil spirits in Book of the Watchers 16 and is frequently associated with the wayward watchers, who often appear as a band of miscreants who are bound beneath the earth to await a consummating eschatological punishment. Fittingly, their reckoning in the Animal Apocalypse seems to clear the way for an ingathering of the nations that finally come to worship and obey the "sheep" in Jerusalem.

Somewhat like the arrogant ruler of Babylon who exalts himself to heaven in Isaiah 14, Daniel 7–8 supplies visions of a tyrant king (Antiochus IV Epiphanes) on a mad campaign against the host. For all the outrage and intrigue this episode comes to involve, the stories told in Daniel 7–8 nimbly strip Antiochus of his own gods, leaving only the true powers of heaven arrayed against a foolish king. Of course, in chapter 10 we find explicit discussion of competition and a matched battle within the ranks of divinity, but this conflict plays out in the lower realms where the "princes (śārîm)" of Persia and Greece fight God's deputy warriors, Michael and Gabriel. By representing these affairs as involving members of the lesser ranks, the writer avoids any suggestion that the gods of other peoples might compete with (and even defeat) the sovereign who reigns supreme over all. God's deputies fight a weak or ineffective campaign, at least for a time, but in context this amounts to one brief chapter within a much larger design for world political history.

More in line with Daniel 10 and the shepherd-managers of the Animal Apocalypse, 1QM and 1QS tell of lower-ranking divine subordinates but heavily stress that they serve at the behest of a single, all-powerful world ruler. For instance, the War Scroll tends to construe the chief military opponents as the prince of light (sometimes identified as Michael) and the prince of darkness (sometimes identified with Belial), though at times the prince of light seems absent from the ranks of the favored divine fighters.[27] In column 1, which may have been originally independent, we find grand predictions of an eschatological war against "the lot of the sons of darkness, against the army of Belial" (1.1; cf. Dan 11:40–12:1), albeit one that here encompasses specific nations such as Edom, Moab, Philistia (1.1–2), the kings of the north (1.4), and the more general category of Kittim.[28] The writer envisions a fairly elaborate battle against coalition forces, but ultimately this will result in the destruction of the Kittim (1.6–7), Belial and his minions (1.6–7, 14–15), and the sons of darkness (13.10–11). Here and at numerous points throughout the work, the writer/editor also stresses that this follows a fixed, providential, and coherent rational plan from on high. In fact, it is precisely the plan, timing, and will of the supreme deity that organizes the diverse portrayals of war in 1QM and lends them plausible coherence, purpose, and inevitability.[29] This proves especially important for understanding the distinctive picture of a matched battle between the forces of light and darkness. Like Gog in Ezekiel 37–38, the spirits of Mastema in Jubilees, and the princes of Persia and Greece in Daniel 10, Belial and his horde appear here as relatively powerless opponents and instrumental enemies created by God explicitly for this purpose (e.g., 1QM 13.10–11).

Though the opposing lots, forces, and deities arrayed in 1QM and 1QS appear superficially dualistic, these oppositions play out within a hierarchical framework that imbues them with substantially different meanings, powers, relationships, and values. So in columns 10–14 of the War Scroll, for instance, the writer/editor underscores the hierarchical distribution of divine power and the exceptional status of Israel's God: "Who (is) like you, God of Israel (*mî' kāmôkâ 'ēl yiśrā'ēl*), in the hea[ven]s or on earth, to do great deeds like your deeds, marvels like your feats? And who (is) like your nation, Israel, whom you chose for yourself from among all the nations of the earth?" (10.8–9). Consistent with other rhetoric about divine exceptionalism, these questions evoke an unequal distribution of divine power and align "true Israel" with the supreme power. In the subsequent discussion, the speaker likewise extols the unrivaled standing of Israel's God and illustrates this with assertions about the unrivaled command over the sky, the luminaries, and the "tasks of the spirits, the dominions of the holy ones (*ûmaśśā' rûhôt ûmemšelet qĕdôšîm*)" (10.12), as well as the clouds, waters, seasons, years, ages, and separation of the nations (10.12–17). Similarly, column 13 sets up a rhetorical comparison between Israel's God and the princes of the nations, asking, "Which angel or prince (*mî' mal'āk wĕśar*) is an aid like [you]?" (13.14); column 14 alludes to the climax of battle as serving to humble the gods (14.15); and column 17 conjoins images of Michael's ruling over all other gods with that of Israel ruling over all flesh (17.7–8; cf. Dan 7:14, 27). Though 1QM and 1QS show little interest in gentile deities, such comments could imply a conceptual assimilation of gentile gods to the ranks of divinity, even though the focus remains principally on wayward Israel rather than the nations. In this sense, the forces of Belial or the prince of darkness are not so different from the spirits that afflict Israel in Jubilees or the operatives that punish in the Animal Apocalypse, even though the subject of idolatry seems of little interest in these works.[30]

Though omitted or ignored in some cases, the gods of the gentiles appear variously in Jewish literature as would-be opponents, dead and dumb statues, and subordinates of Yahweh who serve the divine plan for history. Most basically, however, such discussions show that the idea of a single heavenly political system with highly centralized powers could accommodate a myriad of different interests, arguments, and types of myths. This conceptual framework lends itself particularly well to claims of stability and consistency at the upper levels of the divine hierarchy while also preserving the lower ranks as constructive sites for mythmaking about new characters and relationships of power on the conceit that they had always been there. Such a framework proves especially illuminating for polemics that recast the gentile gods as noncompetitors of Israel's deity as well as for myths that develop characters such as Michael, Melchizedek, and Christ.

Christ as Divine Warrior in 1 Cor 15:23–28

The return of Christ appears ever on the horizon in Paul's letters, though rarely with much qualifying detail. Though still somewhat brief, 1 Cor 15:23–28 stands out as the most developed statement about Christ's return, or parousia, that survives in the letters.[31] Here Paul maintains that the Christ-elect will be swept up (v. 23) and Christ will "defeat every prince, authority, and power" before handing the kingdom back to the father (v. 24), and then he lingers over the relationships of divine power in vv. 25–28. All of this fits within a much longer set of arguments about the future transformation of baptized Christ-followers that run for nearly fifty verses (15:12–58). Read in context, then, the Christ war serves as yet one more illustration of the privileges of election. So 1 Cor 15:23 tells of an impending conflict, but as in 1 Thess 5:9, it is emphasized that the Christ-followers will be removed from the stage of conflict: "But each in their own order: Christ is the first fruits, then those who are of Christ at his parousia, then comes the end, when he hands over the kingdom to God the father, when he has destroyed every rule and every authority and every power (ὅταν καταργήσῃ πᾶσαν ἀρχὴν καὶ πᾶσαν ἐξουσίαν καὶ δύναμιν)" (15:23–24; cf. Phil 3:20–21). Opponent figures emerge rather suddenly here as *archê, exousia,* and *dunamis* (the so-called principalities and powers) only to be defeated by Christ. The subsequent verses do little to clarify the nature of this conflict. Instead, Paul treats the reader to an extended series of affirmations about Christ's dutiful submission:

> For it is necessary that he rule until he has put all his enemies under his feet. The last enemy to be defeated is death, "For God has put all things under his feet." But when it says "all things have been subjected," it is clear that it excepts the one to whom all things are subjected. When all things are subjected to him, then the son himself will be subjected to the one who subjected all things to himself, in order that God may be all to all (ὅταν δὲ ὑποταγῇ αὐτῷ τὰ πάντα, τότε [καὶ] αὐτὸς ὁ υἱὸς ὑποταγήσεται τῷ ὑποτάξαντι αὐτῷ τὰ πάντα, ἵνα ᾖ ὁ θεὸς [τὰ] πάντα ἐν πᾶσιν). (15:25–28)

These verses heavily emphasize Christ's power, obedience, and submission to the father, but they do not much clarify how Paul conceives of Christ's enemies, especially the precise sense in which they come to oppose Christ or what is entailed in their defeat.

Writings of diverse provenance, from Zechariah and Ezekiel to Daniel 7–12, 1QM, 1 Enoch, and Jubilees show a distinctive interest in mythmaking that exploits the lower tiers of the divine order. Generally, the effect is to shift power and responsibility onto lower-level divine beings, which assume a multitude of roles as intermediaries, court officials, managers, and even generals. Michael and Gabriel appear in this capacity in Daniel 10, at least briefly, and Dan 12:1 predicts that Michael will appear as prince at a time of cataclysmic upheaval and vindication (cf. 1QM 17.7–8). Similarly, Melchizedek, Michael, and the prince of light appear in this capacity in some of the Qumran literature (perhaps designating the same figure). The precise names, roles, relations, and responsibility of these figures differ in each case, but they are rather consistently portrayed as passive instruments carrying out the will of their commander and king. In this sense, the lesser ranks become foils for illustrating the centralized nature of divine power and for imagining a divine kingdom where all march in lock step (or *almost* all do, at the very least). Lower-ranking operatives appear in various capacities in Ezekiel, Zechariah, and the traditions of 1 Enoch, whether they play roles that involve punishing, testing, and judging or roles as misleading harassers and agents of harm. For instance, Michael and his cohort bind the watchers and destroy their offspring in the Book of the Watchers, a divine host punishes unrepentant Israel in Ezekiel, and the Animal Apocalypse has a recording divinity involved in punishing other members of the heavenly ranks—the shepherd-managers—for overreaching (cf. Zech 1:20).[32] Michael also appears in Revelation 12 as a warrior who defeats the dragon and casts it down to earth.

Like these and other writers, Paul builds a picture of harmony, submission, and noncompetition in the upper levels of the divine hierarchy, and he relentlessly focuses attention on these upper ranks as well. So in 1 Cor 15:26–28, the supreme figure extends this power—though only for a limited time—to an intermediary who quite explicitly carries out the will of the supreme sovereign above. This political model allows Paul to maintain that there will be some sort of battle (or even battle-cum-judgment) that will set things aright in the world below while also strongly affirming the integrity, harmony, and inevitability of the political system as a whole. Such an approach makes good sense of why Paul emphasizes that Christ's work merely expresses the power and intentionality of the supreme ruler and adapts a quote from Psalm 110, "For God has put all things under his feet," as an occasion for clarifying these relationships in vv. 27–28.[33] So he writes: "But when it says 'all things have been subjected,' it is clear that it excepts the one to whom all things are subjected. When all things are subjected to him, then the son himself will be subjected to the one who subjected all things to himself." By telescoping to focus on the harmonious, uncontested upper levels of power, the potential mayhem below simply disappears from view, leaving images of political harmony, whether of Christ who duly hands the kingdom back to the father or the "all" that finally submits in v. 28. Indeed, Paul's explicit claims about the heavenly political order provide a rhetorical counterweight to intimations of cataclysm and conflict implied by Christ's war in vv. 24–26, however briefly and allusively this conflict comes and goes in these verses.

According to this interpretation, Paul's mythmaking in 1 Corinthians 15 proves innovative and creative because of the way that it plays on familiar strategies to make Christ a hero of submission and noncompetition. In some contrast to the parricides, coups, and conflicts familiar from other traditions of myth, but in keeping with an array of other Jewish literature, Paul depicts Christ in 1 Cor 15:23–28 as an obedient general who summarily defeats opponents and then dutifully hands the kingdom "back to the father."[34] Understood in this way, 1 Cor 15:23–28 does not capture or express some unified or stable core of well-defined beliefs and doctrines, and even less so a uniform and highly circumscribed tradition of myth. Instead, Paul's text innovates, elaborates, and plays on certain resilient assumptions, interests, and strategies that are ready at hand in his intellectual repertoire. The very nonuniqueness of these interests, skills, strategies, and working assumptions allows for illuminating historical comparisons and meaningful contextualization. In this light, Paul appears no more or less creative than the scribes who wrote and edited works such as the Animal Apocalypse, Jubilees, or Daniel, and with quite a free hand. This constructive reappropriation and elaboration also helps to explain why he and other early Christian writers imagine Christ in substantially different terms, whether as the firstborn of creation in the pseudo-Pauline text of Colossians 1, the word become flesh in John 1, or the high priest in heaven who stands above the "angels" in Hebrews, to give only three examples.

An Ambivalent Host of Gentile Gods: The "Principalities and Powers" Reconsidered

Much of the scholarly literature construes Paul's "principalities and powers" as divine rebels and evil powers, frequently in connection with the *šēdîm*/δαιμονία of Deuteronomy 32 (32:15–18), the princes of Daniel 10 (10:13–14, 20–21), and the spirits of Jubilees (15:31), 1 Enoch, 1QS, and 1QM (cf. Sir 17:17 and Acts 7:42–43).[35] Though this remains a strong consensus view, its proponents struggle to marshal critical arguments that would favor it.[36] Reconceiving of these texts as myths about the lower ranks resolves these difficulties and sheds much-needed light on Paul's text. In particular, this reframing allows Christ's enemies to reemerge as gentile gods who have been assimilated to the lesser ranks of divinity.

Many biblical and Hellenistic traditions rail against the worship of "idols" and other alleged non-gods and objects of ridicule. So Jeremiah 14 portrays divine powers as centralized in Israel's deity: "Can any idols of the nations (*bĕhablê haggôyim*) bring rain? Or can the heavens give showers? Is it not you, O Lord our God (YHWH *'ĕlōhênû*)? We set our hope on you, for it is you who do all this" (14:22 NRSV).[37] Similarly, Second Isaiah urges full submission, in part by representing other gods as impotent: "Assemble yourselves and come together,[38] draw near, you survivors of the nations! They have no knowledge—those who carry about their wooden idols, and keep on praying to a god that cannot save (*'ēl lō' yôšîa'*)" (45:20 NRSV).[39] Yet for all the writings that assail the powerlessness and nonexistence of gentile gods, a great many others identify them as members of the host, the heavenly bodies, or the lesser ranks of divinity. A number of biblical writers polemicize about the worship of the host and the heavenly bodies, as Deut 4:19: "And when you look up to the heavens and see the sun, the moon, and the stars, all the host of heaven (*kōl ṣĕbā' haššāmayim*),[40] do not be led astray and bow down to them and serve them, things that the Lord your God (YHWH *'ĕlōhêkā*) has allotted to all the peoples everywhere under heaven" (NRSV).[41] Working with similar assumptions, the writer/editor of the Astronomical Book of Enoch claims that the misidentification of the luminaries will signal a time of a catastrophic upheaval and judgment (80:6–8), and the more philosophically oriented writer of the Wisdom of Solomon chastises idolaters for ignoring their true creator while deifying the elements, heavens, and heavenly bodies (13:1–2; cf. 7:17–20). Likewise, in many polemical contexts Philo of Alexandria develops tenets of Middle Platonism to render the heavenly bodies and elements as divine subordinates, mere servants, and "satraps" foolishly worshipped in place of their master and true divine king.[42]

The assimilating polemics developed in texts such as Deuteronomy 4, the works of Philo, and the Wisdom of Solomon are crucial for making sense of the destruction or punishment of the host in eschatological contexts. Indeed, the ambivalent status of gentile gods as both members of the lesser ranks and mistaken objects of gentile worship explains why their future reckoning might be conceived of as necessary in the first place. So there is the host of heaven to be punished in Isaiah 24 and in the Book of the Watchers, and harmful spirits left on earth will be subject to judgment from above (1 En. 16). In Book of the Watchers 19, these spirits mislead outsiders so that they "sacrifice to demons as to gods until the day of the great judgment" (19:1), a time when they will be punished along with the wayward watchers. In other contexts, the Enochic elaborators return to images of the wayward watchers and/or "stars" bound in a place of punishment where they await their final sentencing (21:1–10; cf. 18:13–16; 86; 88; 102:2). In a different way, the Animal Apocalypse accommodates the gods of the nations as punishing operatives of the Jewish God (e.g., 89:61–64, 65–72a; and 89:74–90:1) but also affirms that they will be punished for overreaching just before an ingathering and transformation of the gentile peoples (90:18). In addition, a presumed link between gentile gods and the heavenly bodies probably informs language about the heavenly bodies falling or changing their movements in some eschatological scenes, as seems clear in Isa 24:21 and 34:4–5. Of course, in other cases the luminaries work for Yahweh, as in Judg 5:20, where the stars fight from heaven against Sisera, and in the Epistle of Enoch, which warns of an impending doomsday: "From the angels inquiry into your deeds will be made in heaven, and from the sun and from the moon and from the stars, concerning your sins" (1 En. 100:10–11; cf. 104:1; 1 En. 1–5).

Taking the "principalities and powers" of 1 Cor 15:24 as gentile gods makes sense of a number of difficult features of 15:23–28.[43] Like numerous other writers, Paul conceives of a divine hierarchy in which all other deities fit somewhere in the lesser ranks, whether as divine governors, harassing spirits, or mere statuary. This basic conceptual model explains why a reckoning of the lesser ranks might be appropriate, at least in this context (cf. Phil 2:5–15), as well as the particular way that this unfolds in v. 24. Like the unknown writers if Isaiah 24, the Book of the Watchers, and the Animal Apocalypse, Paul imagines an eschatological time of reckoning when the true powers of heaven will finally deal with gentile gods by punishing, destroying, or subduing them. This explains the function of the Christ war in v. 24, and it also explains why he gives the battle rather short shrift (v. 24) and then quickly moves to refocus attention on the upper ranks (vv. 25–28).

Like other mythmakers, Paul evokes an image of battle but passes over this point rather quickly, as if in a hurry to affirm the stability of the cosmo-political order and to suppress the possibility of rebellion and conflict in the world of divinity. In this sense, the image of the Christ war in v. 24 serves as a triumphal showpiece that finally unmasks the true world ruler and brings the gentiles to their knees. Taking the principalities and powers as gentile gods not only allows for illuminating comparisons with other literature but also rather elegantly explains the central political drama in vv. 23–28. Here Christ rules and does battle, "until he has put all his enemies under his feet," and then hands the kingdom back to the father so that "God can be all to all."[44] Like the destruction of every "ruler and authority and power," Christ's rule must come to an end so that the supreme deity can rule directly. Though the statement that "God will be all to all (ὁ θεὸς τὰ πάντα ἐν πᾶσιν)" proves ambiguous, taken together with Christ's appearance and disappearance as divine warrior, it most likely alludes to a time when the whole cosmic kingdom will come to worship its true creator and king.[45]

Finally, though I have argued that Paul's principalities and powers are best understood as gentile gods, it is also possible that Christ's defeat of these "enemies" entails the dissolution of the created order. That is, Paul could envision the *archai, dunameis,* and *exousiai* as divine functionaries charged with ministering the creation, perhaps as controlling winds, meteo-rological phenomena, and heavenly bodies or as somehow manipulating or overseeing the elements. The defeat of these "enemies" would then involve the destruction of the world in its current form, more like recalling admin-istrators from the field or pulling up the tent poles of creation than like the bloody battles of Revelation, the War Scroll, and the Epistle of Enoch. Such an approach could accommodate the language of military victory and the defeat of Christ's enemies as literary license inspired by Psalm 110, here applied to the transformation or dissolution of the current material world, perhaps even conceived of along the lines of a Stoic or other kind of cosmic re-creation (ἔκπυρωσις or ἀναστοιχείωσις) (cf. 3 Sib. Or. 75–96; Lucretius, *Rer. Nat.* 5.373–405).[46] This would explain why 15:26 construes death as the last enemy and vv. 51–57 apply similar language to the transformation of earthly bodies into fully pneumatic ones, replete with quotations from Isa-iah and Hosea that make heavy use of military metaphors. Relatedly, Paul could also identify the *archai, exousiai,* and *dunameis* with heavenly bodies and conceive of some form of astrological realignment associated with ca-tastrophe or conflagration (cf. Plato, *Pol.* 272d–274e).[47]

A range of third- and fourth-century Christian writers comment on and reinterpret Paul's language about Christ's impending judgment. A number of them vacillate between more and less philosophically imbued interpretations. For instance, Jerome interprets 1 Thessalonians 4 as concerned with a worldwide judgment but singles out Roman gods and philosophers for special attention: "The world shall howl at the lord who comes to judge it, and the tribes of the earth shall smite the breast. Once mighty kings shall tremble in their nakedness. Venus shall be exposed, and her son, too. Jupiter with his fiery bolts will be brought to trial. Plato, with his disciples will be but a fool. Aristotle's arguments shall be of no avail" (*Letters* 14.11). Here motifs of trial and judgment predominate rather than those of battle, though the looming punishments probably involve violence. By way of contrast, Prudentius evokes a parousia that is more in line with Stoic theories of cosmic conflagration: "When at the awful trumpet's sound the earth will be consumed by fire, and with a mighty rush the world unhinged, will crash in dreadful ruin" (*Hymn* 11.105–108); and Gregory of Nazianzus speaks of the rise of the soul: "I await the voice of the archangel, the last trumpet, the transformation of the heavens, the transfiguration of the earth, the liberation of the elements, the renovation of the universe" (*On His Brother Caesarius* 21). Though Paul could envision a conflagration, perhaps like those of Prudentius, Gregory, or the earlier 3 Sibylline Oracle (75–96), his language in 1 Corinthians 15 proves too brief and ambiguous to settle the issue definitively. Furthermore, his use of terms such as *archê, exousia,* and *dunamis* here and in other contexts suggests divine intermediaries of some kind. Taken together with the ingathering of the gentiles in v. 28, this suggests that Paul's conception of them here is probably more in line with that of Jerome.

This approach to Paul's political imagination also sheds light on the use of the terms *archê, exousia,* and *dunamis* in 1 Corinthians 15 and elsewhere in the letters. Understood in this way, such terms do not reflect any one tradition or set of influences; rather, they express an anthropomorphic habit that is alive and well in Jewish and non-Jewish literature. For instance, in the LXX version of Gen 1:16, the supreme deity creates the sun and moon "as rulers (εἰς ἀρχὰς)" over day and night; 2 Macc 3:24 refers to God as "the ruler of spirits and all powers (ὁ τῶν πνευμάτων καὶ πάσης ἐξουσίας δυνάστης)"; and a wide range of other texts similarly cast heavenly bodies as lesser political figures or officials of some kind.[48] Greek traditions as early as Hesiod have Zeus dividing the earth among ranks of subordinate spirits and guardians (or watchers) (*Works and Days* 292–295), and philosophical writers use similar language in discussions of cosmology, as does Plato in the *Laws* (10.903b–d), where he describes the cosmos as having active and passive parts, each of which is "under the control of ruling powers (ἄρχοντες)."[49] Plutarch writes of the elements as ἄρχοντες and the heavenly bodies as managers (διοικηταὶ) and rulers (πρυτάνεις) (*Mor.* 601A); Apuleius (*Met.* 11.5, 2) refers to Isis as the "ruler of all the elements (*elementorum omnium domina*)"; and Cicero refers to the sun as lord, chief, and ruler of the other lights (*Somn. Sc.* 6.17).[50] Though examples drawn from philosophical texts make this point well, similar observations could be made for the language about the lesser ranks in much other literature.[51]

These comparisons suggest that Paul uses the terms *archê, exousia,* and *dunamis* because they constitute well-worn terms for lesser political figures and are thus appropriate for describing analogous ranks in the divine kingdom.[52] Indeed, this anthropomorphic habit also explains why notions of a cosmic "kingdom" would have such appeal to begin with. Such an approach also sheds light on Paul's comments about the ignorance of the "rulers (*archontôn*) of this age" in 1 Cor 2:8 as well as the obedience of all rulers and authorities (*exousiai* and *archontes*) in Rom 13:1–7. As with myths about ignorant fools and overzealous managers familiar from Enochic tradition, Paul acknowledges the presence of gentile gods within the divine ranks but also affirms their status as subordinates, not as willful antagonists or competitors with the supreme God. The model of a single world polity allows him to maintain that the "*archontôn* of this age" are merely ignorant, not rebels gone rogue. Likewise, this explains his affirmations as to the just and providential nature of the cosmic political order in Rom 13:1–7 and elsewhere in the letters.

The triad of 1 Cor 15:24 never appears again in the letters, but Romans 8 pictures *aggeloi, archai,* and *dunameis* as possible impediments to the upward ascent of the Christ-believers (8:38). These characters appear as part of an extended rumination on transformation that seems to evoke the kind of cataclysm suggested in 1 Corinthians 15 and 1 Thessalonians 4 (cf. 1 Thess 3:13 and Gal 5:5). Here the creation (*ktisis*) is personified as eagerly awaiting the "revealing of the sons of God," which suggests some positive alignment between the creation and the transformation of Christ-followers, but vv. 20–22 portray the creation as "groaning in travail" and subjected to futility (τῇ γὰρ ματαιότητι ἡ κτίσις ὑπετάγη) as well as hope.[53] This cosmic panorama serves to integrate Paul's imagined Christ-elect, who, with their own inner turmoil, are explicitly aligned with that of the whole creation (vv. 22–23; cf. 2 Cor 5:1–4).[54] Chapter 5 will treat Paul's claims about the alleged struggle (and inner conflict) of believers in more substantive ways, but here it is important to linger over the scene of cosmic transformation and the language about *aggeloi, archai,* and *dunameis* (vv. 37–39).

Paul's imagery again suggests that these have an intermediate status as lower-ranking divinities and perhaps even some association with the heavenly bodies. In this context, Paul also takes pains to emphasize the relative powerlessness of *archai* and *dunameis* by portraying them as part of a whole range of things that cannot but fall before God, Christ, and those who possess Christ's *pneuma*.[55] Military language also features prominently: "In all these things we are conquering through the one who loves us. For I am persuaded that neither death nor life nor *aggeloi* nor *archai* nor things present nor things to come, nor *dunameis,* nor height nor depth nor anything else in creation is able to separate us from the love of God in Christ Jesus our Lord" (Rom 8:37–39).[56] Here any present struggle becomes part of a larger victory guaranteed by allegiance to Christ. Though the language about *archai* and *dunameis* proves ambiguous, their significance is minimized relative to the larger world of divine power. In the subsequent discussion about creation (*ktisis*) in Rom 8:19–23, Paul goes on to suggest that the "victory" of the Christ-followers involves their ascent from the lower created order into the immortal heavenly worlds above.[57] However Paul conceives of the *archai* and *dunameis* in Romans 8, a connection with the heavenly bodies seems obvious to interpreters like Origen, who takes the futility of creation as the toil of the heavenly bodies (*On First Principles* 1.7.5).

Cosmos, History, and Particularity in Paul's Apocalyptic Future

The idea of a single, great cosmic kingdom looms large in 1 Corinthians 15. Here Paul presents Adam and Christ as forerunners for a new kind of humanity and offers a detailed cosmic taxonomy that places different kinds of bodies within a multitiered hierarchy of types, substances, beings, and value. The effect is to represent some fairly radical claims about transformation as the natural, inevitable, and intentionally organized outcome of a single coherent rationale. Arguments about the order of the cosmos, the nature of divine rule, and the unfolding plan for history serve as convenient vehicles for this project. In this sense, Paul's thought resembles that of numerous other apocalyptic and prophetic mythmakers who likewise portray moments of apocalyptic violence, upheaval, and change as inevitable outcomes of the existing world order, not as radical reversals that upend the existing one. With a familiar sleight of hand, then, Paul's seemingly radical breaks and promised transformations come to have solid, even eternal foundations.

The war of Christ in 1 Cor 15:23–28 appears as one in a series of arguments centered on the privileges of election, arguments in which figures like Adam and Christ often play starring roles. So in 15:20–22, Christ's resurrection in a pneumatic body establishes a pattern for the legitimate Christ-followers, just as Adam set the pattern for those after him.[58] As Paul explains: "But in fact Christ has been raised from the dead, the first fruits of those who have fallen asleep. For as by a man came death, by a man has come also the resurrection of the dead. For as in Adam all die, so also in Christ shall all be made alive" (15:20–22). Here Paul makes generalizing claims about all people while also maintaining that only the Christ-elect will be promoted within the ranks, at least at this stage of the eschatological scenario. Thus, Adam and Christ both serve as paradigmatic figures for all humanity even while the focus remains on the rewards extended to a select few. In this sense, grand evocations of Adam, Christ, all people, and the world writ large serve mainly as staging for quite particular claims on the idealized Corinthians.

The grand cosmic design comes to the fore in the Christ war of vv. 23–28, but Paul's attention soon turns again to concerns of a specific, concrete, and local nature. So in vv. 29–36, he constructs an imagined audience with confused beliefs while his own authorial persona emerges as a tireless leader who struggles heroically against the "beasts of Ephesus" and is willing even to "die every day!" (v. 31). This authoritative stance becomes the basis for direct rebukes such as, "Come out of your stupor and stop sinning; for some have no knowledge of God, I say to their shame" (15:34). Then beginning in v. 37, Paul shifts to a series of arguments that seek to embed these particulars within a larger cosmic stage. In one especially important subargument, he evokes different kinds of bodies as a segue to the larger cosmic taxonomy:

> For not all flesh is the same flesh, but there is one for man, another for animals, another for birds, another for fish; there are heavenly bodies and earthly bodies, but the glory of the heavenly is one kind, and the glory of the earthly is another; there is one glory for the sun, and another glory for the

moon, and another for the stars, and stars differ from one another in glory. So it is also with the resurrection of the dead. It is sown corruptible and raised incorruptible; it is sown in dishonor and raised in glory; it is sown in weakness and raised in power; it is sown as a *psychikon* body and raised as a *pneumatic* body. (15:38–44)[59]

Binary oppositions such as heavenly/earthly and corruptible/incorruptible drive a portrayal of difference as an all-encompassing, singular, stratified hierarchy of ranks and types of being.[60] Ultimately, then, all types of bodies fit somewhere in this multitiered hierarchical system, one that organizes natures, substances, beings, ranks, and value into a single taxonomic program or *scala naturae*. This hierarchical taxonomy maps onto the elect in an especially intimate way because it establishes a place of great privilege for those who "bear the image" of Christ. This idealized elect are guaranteed transformation and protection in the present as well as perfection at Christ's return, an event that remains ever on the expectant horizon (15:42–53).[61] Continuing this generalizing frame, Paul returns again to the figure of Adam, who now stands for an inferior type of earthly human ("the first man comes from the dust of the earth," 15:47), in contrast to the second Adam, who comes from heaven and with a far superior pneumatic nature. In this way, the simplistic Adam-Christ schema merges rather seamlessly with the larger cosmic taxonomy because both play off of and reproduce the same basic *scala naturae*. So Paul fittingly concludes that since "flesh and blood cannot inherit the kingdom of God" (15:50), so too "the perishable body must put on imperishability, and the mortal body must put on immortality" (15:53).

In other contexts, Paul similarly emphasizes the separation and elevation of the Christ-elite within a glorious heavenly order. So in 1 Cor 6:3 Paul claims that they will judge *aggeloi*, and in 1 Cor 11:32 he says they will avoid being judged along with the cosmos.[62] Images of a glorious heavenly hierarchy also loom large in texts such as 1 Thessalonians 4, Philippians 3, and 2 Corinthians 4–5. In 1 Thessalonians, Christ will rescue the elect from a coming wrath (1:10; cf. 1 Thess 5:9, Rom 1:18, 2 Cor 6:2), and in 1 Thessalonians 4 there will be a time when Christ will appear from heaven and the elect will "be with the Lord forever" (4:14–16). The trumpet and battle cry in 4:14–16 evoke a martial Christ leading the armies of heaven, but this warrior imagery never becomes the object of sustained attention. In fact, it serves primarily to showcase the awesome powers of heaven and in turn to guarantee the elevation of Paul's Christ-elite. In a more elaborate way, Paul invokes the "upward call of God in Christ Jesus" in Phil 3:14 and then paints a picture of a glorious heavenly polity (*politeuma*), insisting, "from it we await a savior, who will change our lowly bodies to be like his glorious body, by the power which enables him to subject all things to himself" (3:20–21). As in 1 Corinthians 15, the elect occupy a distinct place within a singular, united, multitiered world polity. Here they move spatially upward and receive new or transformed bodies, all of which is made possible by the same indomitable power that enables Christ to "subject all things to himself." The language about Christ subjecting the "all" suggests that he will somehow subdue the lower ranks, as suggested already in Phil 2:9–11. Yet here again, Paul gives little attention to the particulars of this new political arrangement and instead telescopes to focus on the glorious heavenly future that awaits. To similar ends, in 2 Corinthians 4–5 he lingers over the heavenly destiny of the elect but shows little interest in affairs below. So broad category distinctions between the heavenly and earthly set up for a predictable spotlight on the world above: "We look not for the visible but for things invisible; for the visible are transient, but the invisible are eternal" (4:18). These contrasts also set up for celebratory evocations of the illustrious bodies that await the true Christ-elite in heaven (5:1–4) and of the extraordinary divine being who made them (5:5). Though 2 Corinthians 4–5 lacks the kind of warrior imagery that appears elsewhere in the letters (at least briefly), Paul presents a distinctive picture of Christ as a heavenly judge: "For we must all appear before the judgment seat of Christ, so that each one may receive good or evil, according to what they have done in the body" (5:10). This image of a serene, orderly judgment helpfully avoids intimations of political conflict, but the *scala naturae* upon which these claims are premised is consistent with what we find elsewhere in the letters.

Like other prophetic and apocalyptic writers, Paul makes fairly radical claims about the present and near future, especially in conceiving of God's intervention with Christ as marking a new phase of history that will culminate soon with an even more radical, worldwide series of upheavals. At the same time, he takes great pains to insist that all of this conforms to a stable, coherent, unified, and rational plan that expresses the will of a supreme world sovereign. A few examples drawn from Romans will reinforce this basic point about Paul's political thought. In Romans 1–2, he develops thunderous polemics about the origins of idolatry and establishes the inevitability of retribution in the near future; in Romans 4 he uses a figure from the distant past (Abraham) to tell of a plan to rescue the gentiles in the present; and in Romans 9–11 Paul insists that the intransigence of Israel in the present is fully consistent with God's plan for world history. In arguing this case, he appeals to figures such as Jacob, Esau, and Pharaoh, each of whom comes to exemplify the coherent rationale of their divine puppeteer. More intimately, in Rom 5:3–6 and 8:18, Paul insists that even the suffering of the elect in the present moment fits within this larger divine plan. Here he first argues that the timing of Christ's death was in full accord with the divine rationale ("at the right time Christ died for the impious," 5:6) and then builds a simplistic scheme for understanding "sin" in the past, present, and future that involves Adam, Moses, and Christ (5:12–21). Somewhat similarly, in Romans 8, Paul gives an extended argument about the Christ-elect (8:1–17), briefly alludes to a current time of suffering (8:18), and then quickly relates this to the world as a whole so that the elect assume a place of great privilege within the larger cosmo-political order (8:19–24). In these cases, Paul's conceptions of a *scala naturae* and of cosmic design generally prove to be foundational for myths that weave concrete, local, and particular situations into tales about the universe writ large.

Heroic Submission and Noncompetition in the "Christ Hymn" of Philippians 2

The comparative materials brought to bear on 1 Corinthians 15 also shed light on some vexing issues posed by Phil 2:6–11, especially the curious statement that Christ did not seek equality with God as "something to be grasped by force (οὐχ ἁρπαγμὸν ἡγήσατο τὸ εἶναι ἴσα θεῷ)" (2:6).[63] Somewhat like 1 Cor 15:26–28, these lines emphatically celebrate Christ's noncompetition and lack of rivalry with the supreme deity. Christ's promotion within the divine world (2:9–11) and the appearance of divine beings who worship and acclaim him (2:10–11) also fit with traditions about victorious warriors acclaimed by a counsel of lesser-ranking deities. Rather than military victory, however, Philippians 2 appropriates these motifs to celebrate Christ's heroic obedience and noncompetition with the supreme sovereign above.

The precise translation of Phil 2:6 has proved extremely controversial, and much of the debate has centered on the status that should be attributed to Christ. In v. 6, Paul seems to say that Christ was originally "in the form of a God (ὅς ἐν μορφῇ θεοῦ ὑπάρχων)," but then he adds, "He did not seek equality with God as something to be grasped by force (οὐχ ἁρπαγμὸν ἡγήσατο τὸ εἶναι ἴσα θεῷ)." In the subsequent lines, Christ humbly accepts a lesser status and is rewarded with a name "above every other name" (2:9). Despite the fluctuation of status this story seems to entail, a long line of interpreters argue that Christ's precise standing does not really change, in part by insisting that the language about "not seizing/grasping" refers to not holding tightly to the uniquely high status that Christ has from the very beginning (*res rapta*).[64] An alternative tradition of interpretation holds that Christ's standing does change. According to many such approaches, Paul construes Christ as a divine being in 2:6, and his comment about not seeking "equality with God as something to be grasped by force (or as 'booty')" means that Christ did not try to usurp the status of the supreme God (*res rapienda*).[65] Though the language in v. 6 remains difficult, such a reading makes much better sense of the drama of 2:6–11, which seems to require a move from a lower rank in the heavens to a higher one. Furthermore, though many writers ridicule the use of terms like *theos* (god) for any but the supreme God of Jewish lore, this amounts to a polemical overstatement that is not carried out consistently in practice (see, e.g., 11QMelchizedek ii.10). Thus, the statement that Christ was "in the form of a god" (2:6) need not suggest that Christ had some special identification with the supreme deity, though this idea has proved seductive for some.[66] Instead, and in a rather straightforward way, being in the "form of a god" conveys that Christ was originally a lesser divine being, probably a member of the council or heavenly entourage.[67] This interpretation also makes good sense of the term ἁρπαγμὸν in this context, a word typically associated with robbery and theft, as captured by standard Greek definitions of the verb as "to seize, grasp, snatch up, overmaster" (Liddell, Scott, and Jones, *A Greek-English Lexicon*). Though precise parallels are lacking, the related term ἁρπαγμή has a similarly negative valence in the LXX and in much other Greek literature.[68]

Recent essays by Adela Yarbro Collins and Samuel Vollenweider draw attention to polemics about rulers who lay claim to a godlike status, most notably the king of Babylon in Isaiah 14, the prince of Tyre in Ezekiel 28, and the figure of Antiochus IV Epiphanes in Daniel 7–11.[69] Though this literature illuminates Phil 2:6 to some extent, the comparisons prove even more rewarding once the texts are reframed as myths that suppress the possibility of competition and usurpation in the divine world. Understood in this way, Christ is the antitype of not only the usurping king as Vollenweider maintains but also of the rival deity who deigns to make a play for supreme rule of heaven. The acclamation of other gods in these verses is also suggestive of the kind of political imaginary found in a range of Jewish and non-Jewish texts in which some sort of council or group of gods is frequently called on to acclaim the superiority of the ruling god. A somewhat similar approach is developed by James Sanders, who identifies Christ as a member of the heavenly council and draws out an implicit contrast between Christ's humble submission in Philippians 2 and the actions of certain heavenly renegades.[70] To this end, Sanders focuses on tales about defiance in the heavenly world, especially drawing on 1 Enoch (6:2, 15:2, 39:5, 64:1–2), Slavonic Enoch (7:3, 18:3), and 4QAges (4Q181 A i.7–10, B ii.2–3). According to Sanders, these myths form an implicit counterpoint to Christ's dutiful submission, and they also fit well with Paul's moralizing about the dangers of self-conceit and rivalry among the Philippians in the preceding verses (2:1–5). The language about grasping at "equality with God" in 2:6 also leads him to spotlight a rather narrow subset of literature that seems to exhibit similar concerns. So in 1 En. 68:4, the watchers are said to "act as if they were like the Lord," and in the Life of Adam and Eve (12–17), a *diabolos* figure balks at worshipping Adam and is made to declare, "If he [God] be wrathful with me, I will set my throne above the stars of heaven and will be like the most high" (15.3)—a threat that clearly repurposes Isaiah 14.[71] By contrast, the version of this story found in Slavonic Vita has a devil figure who duly accepts his station and levels no challenge whatsoever to heavenly figures above (33.2). Though these texts are indeed illuminating, the approach taken here enlarges the frame for understanding these so-called dissenting deities. Like the usurping kings of Isaiah 14, Ezekiel 28, and Daniel 7–11, Sanders's wayward watchers and heavenly ingrates make more sense when considered as characters who help to establish the illustrious, stable, and unchallenged nature of the political order in heaven. Though such concerns are prominent in the texts Sanders cites, they also loom large in myths about the managed insubordination of the Enochic watchers, the dutiful toil of divine managers, and the punishing minions of Mastema in Jubilees, among many others. According to the interpretation advanced here, the diverse writers, editors, and mythmakers who created these texts are understood to be improvising on common interests and assumptions. One kind of interest shared by these writers is in representing divine politics in ways that suppress the possibility of conflict and coups. They do so in various ways, such as by developing myths about self-destructive heavenly fools, mere earthly kings foolishly arrayed against heaven, or evocative celebrations of the heavenly political order that is everywhere on display.

In Philippians 2, Paul offers an innovative myth that celebrates Christ's noncompetition with the supreme God and presents him as a hero through his unqualified submission. So Christ emerges in v. 6 as an intermediary being who does not "seek equality with God as something to be grasped by force" and then willingly assumes a much lower rank, remaining obedient to the point of death. The lowly nature of this rank is heavily stressed in vv. 7–8, where Christ assumes the form of a slave (μορφὴν δούλου λαβών) and the form of a lowly human being (ἐν ὁμοιώματι ἀνθρώπων; σχήματι εὑρεθεὶς ὡς ἄνθρωπος). This exceptional deference and humility soon become the basis for extraordinary rewards: "Therefore God has highly exalted him and bestowed on him the name which is above every name, that at the name of Jesus every knee should bend, in heaven and on earth and under the earth, and every tongue confess that Jesus Christ is Lord, to the glory of God the father" (2:9–11). For all the focus on Christ in these lines and in vv. 6–11 as a whole, the drama here strongly affirms that there is continuity and stability in the upper reaches of the political order. So in v. 6, Christ does not deign to challenge the sovereign above, and here in vv. 9–11 his elevation serves, "to the glory of God the father," in a seemingly inevitable way (cf. 1 Cor 15:27–28). These verses also exalt Christ to a distinctively high status, somewhat like Phil 3:20–21 and 1 Cor 15:23–28. Of course, in Phil 2:9–11 and 3:19–21, Paul emphasizes the submission of the lesser ranks, not Christ's military victory as in 1 Cor 15:23–28. It is important not to force undue coherence or harmony onto these texts; but nevertheless, Paul's basic political assumptions appear to be relatively consistent, even if many of the particulars are up for negotiation, improvisation, and change.

Traditions about acclaiming assemblies and councils also help to explain the sudden appearance of divine beings in Phil 2:9–11 who bow before Christ. As observed for works such as the Enuma Elish, the Epic of Anzu, and the *Theogony*, lower-ranking deities often appear together to celebrate victorious warriors and exalted divine kings. Such acclamations appear so frequently, in fact, that early traditions of scholarship often construed them—quite anachronistically—as having a "liturgical" function. Similar images recur in biblical texts where Yahweh is acclaimed by other deities, as exemplified in an exhortation found in Deuteronomy 32, "Praise, O heavens, his people, worship him, all you gods (*kol 'ĕlōhîm*)!"[72] (32:43; cf. Pss 96:4–6; 93; 89:5–8; 149:1–8), and in the elaborate court scenes of Daniel 7 and much Enochic literature. Playing on similar ideas, Wisdom acclaims herself before the host in Sir 24: "In the assembly of the most high (ἐν ἐκκλησίᾳ ὑψίστος) she opens her mouth, and in the presence of his hosts (ἔναντι δυνάμεως αὐτοῦ) she tells of her glory" (24:2 NRSV); and in Ezekiel the Tragedian, Moses is exalted to a throne in heaven as the stars bow before him.[73] Similar political models also inform some of Philo's allegories. So in *On the Confusion of Tongues*, a firstborn *logos* is raised up above the *aggeloi* to become their ruler (*Conf.* 146), and in the *Life of Moses* God exalts Moses as reward for giving up his high status as heir to the throne, in contrast to those who attempt to seize such positions by force (1.27–28).[74] In other cases, nations and peoples perform acclaiming or submitting roles as well. So in Daniel 7, the supreme God gives "one like the son of a man" rule of an eternal kingdom, promising that "all peoples, nations, and languages will serve him" (7:14); 1QM imagines a great battle that will "exalt the sway of Michael above all the gods and the dominion of Israel over all flesh (*lĕhārîm bā'ĕlim miśrat mikā'ēl ûmemśelet yiśrā'ēl bĕko(w)l bāśār*)" (17.7–8); and Jubilees predicts a time of restoration when the Israelites will be exalted and "every angel and every spirit will know them (*kwellu mal'ak wa-kwellu manfas*)" (1:25). As Sanders also notes, 4QAges (4Q181 B) seems to exalt special humans to a permanent place in the heavenly council, and 11QMelchizedek combines the high priest of Genesis 14 and Psalm 110 in the figure of a deity ('*ĕlōhîm*) who is in turn exalted to the heavenly court and set above all other '*ĕlōhîm*.[75] In most cases, these acclamations seem to convey submission, acceptance, and agreement on who should rule, as they do in the much longer mythic narratives that survive from Babylon, Syria, and Greece.

While not precise analogues, these scenes shed a good deal of light on Phil 2:9–11. In particular, the claim that at Christ's name "every knee should bend, in heaven and on earth and under the earth, and every tongue confess that Jesus Christ is Lord, to the glory of God the father" (2:10–11) conveys a newly promoted figure to whom the lesser ranks duly submit. The adaptation of these ideas in Philippians 2 is especially remarkable in light of the way that vv. 9–11 appropriate Isa 45:23. Though both texts develop a similar political scheme, the MT and LXX of Isaiah 45 deride other gods with harsh satires about gentiles worshipping mere statues and bowing in shame before Israel's deity. Here Yahweh cries: "Turn to me and be saved, all the ends of the earth! For I am God, and there is no other (*kî 'ănî-'ēl wĕ'ên 'ôd*)! By myself I have sworn, from my mouth has gone forth in righteousness a word that shall not return: 'To me every knee shall bow, every tongue shall swear'" (45:22–23 NRSV). For this writer, assertions of the nonexistence and powerlessness of other gods serve to illustrate the exceptional standing of Yahweh alone. By contrast, Paul appropriates this language to evoke a new set of relationships in Phil 2:11, but he also names the divine ranks that are suppressed in the MT and LXX of Isa 45:23. As a result, Christ now becomes the object of acclamation, reverence, and submission (not the supreme God), and the adoring hosts emerge as all those "in heaven and on earth and under the earth." Though the supreme deity clearly remains at the helm, the intermediary status of Christ proves quite remarkable here as it does also in Philippians 3, which predicts that Christ will transform the lowly human bodies of the elect into glorious heavenly ones "by the power which allows him to submit all things to himself" (3:21). Similar scenes of acclamation and elevation also appear in texts like Heb 1:3–4 and Col 1:18–19. Though these works adapt philosophical language in distinctive ways, they employ a familiar model of political hierarchy to construe Christ's power in still more expansive ways (cf. John 1:1–18).[76]

Aggeloi, Daimonia, and *ha satanas* in the Divine Assembly

Appreciating the way that notions of political hierarchy frame Paul's thought about the divine world helps to explain certain ambiguities in his language about beings such as *aggeloi* and *satanas*. Like *daimonia* in 1 Corinthians 10, the letters contain relatively few references to *aggeloi*, and where they do appear, they play relatively marginal and passive roles.[77] So in 1 Corinthians 4, the believers are a spectacle to *aggeloi* (4:9); in chapter 6 the elect are to judge *aggeloi* (6:3); in chapter 11 women must wear veils on their heads on account of them (11:10); and in 1 Corinthians 13, *aggeloi* speak their own language (13:1). In 2 Corinthians, Paul warns that *satanas* may disguise himself as an *aggelos* (11:14; cf. Gal 1:8) and speaks of his "thorn in the flesh" as an *aggelos* of *satanas* in chapter 12 (12:7). In Galatians, he warns against accepting a different gospel even as from an *aggelos* in chapter 1 (1:8), imagines that *aggeloi* mediate the giving of the law in chapter 3 (3:19), and claims that the Galatians themselves received him as one in chapter 4 (4:14). In some contrast, Rom 8:38 conceives of *aggeloi* as one possible obstacle separating the believers from Christ; if 2 Thess 1:7 is authentic, *aggeloi* make up God's vengeance-exacting army.

Like the language about principalities and powers, *stoicheia*, and *daimonia*, *aggeloi* play diverse roles in Paul's letters. In most cases, however, Paul envisions them as playing mediating roles as subordinates, whether their precise roles prove helpful, harmful, or ambiguous. So his comments that the Galatians received Paul as an *aggelos* or that *satanas* might disguise himself as one suggest more positive roles, but in other cases they clearly have more diverse and ambiguous functions. So Paul's comments that the elect will judge the *aggeloi* (and that women must veil themselves on account of them) suggest some ambivalence toward this class of beings, as does his evocation of them as potential obstacles between the believers and Christ (Rom 8:38; cf. 1 Cor 4:9). Like Enochic rebels or the harmful spirits that lead gentiles astray in Jubilees, the discussion of *aggeloi* in Rom 8:38 and 1 Cor 6:3 suggests that they have an indeterminate status, probably because they serve both as intermediaries and as mistaken objects of worship.

Paul's language about *satanas*, the destroyer (τοῦ ὀλοθρευτοῦ), and even Beliar in 2 Corinthians 6 suggests that he envisions them as punishing operatives of the supreme deity. So 1 Corinthians 5 refers to *satanas* as playing a disciplining role for the man living with his stepmother, so that "handing him over to *satanas*" (5:5) emerges as a positive outcome, somewhat like the "destroyer" (τοῦ ὀλοθρευτοῦ) who punishes grumbling Israelites in 1 Cor 10:10.[78] Such agents seem to play testing roles in 2 Cor 2:11, which notes concern with outwitting the malevolent designs of *satanas*, somewhat like 1 Cor 7:5 where *satanas* may tempt those who lack self-control. In some contrast, 2 Corinthians 6 warns of threats posed by Beliar.[79] Treating the possibility of intermingling with unbelievers, Paul evokes a series of binary oppositions: "What partnership has righteousness and lawlessness? What fellowship does light have with darkness? What harmony is there between Christ and Beliar? What does a believer have in common with an unbeliever? What agreement is there between the temple of God and idols? For we are the temple of the living God" (2 Cor 6:14–16). Here Paul draws a stark contrast between insiders and outsiders and strategically associates the authentic Christ-followers with unity, purity, harmony, and the protection of truly powerful beings. In this case, the figure of Beliar works to establish the idealized purity and perfection of the supposed righteous who are protected from harmful agents by their allegiance to helpful ones.[80] Even as Paul incites anxiety about Beliar, he also insists that resistance is easily within reach. This is consistent with Paul's basic teachings elsewhere, which build toward images of a compliant elect in league with the supreme powers of heaven and joyously embracing their servant Paul. So 2 Cor 2:11, 11:14, 12:7; and 1 Thess 2:18, 3:5 all depict *satanas* as a tempter who tests the purity, integrity, and loyalty of the idealized Christ-elect. As is especially clear with the "thorn in the flesh" in 2 Cor 12:7, Paul tends to envisions this as ultimately positive in the sense that it affirms the power of the supreme deity: "'My grace is enough for you, for power is completed in weakness.' I will even more gladly boast of my weakness, that the power of Christ may rest upon me" (2 Cor 12:9).

Neither purely good nor purely evil, Paul envisions lower-ranking deities as serving a variety of roles. Such an approach especially illuminates the role of *aggeloi* in Gal 3:19.[81] Exploring the past and present function of the law, Paul insists: "It was added because of transgressions,[82] until the offspring should come to whom the promise had been made; and it was ordained by *aggeloi*, through an intermediary. But there is not just one intermediary, but there is only one God" (3:19–20).[83] Although some later rabbinic and Christian writers imagine other divine beings on Sinai, only a few early texts do. So Jubilees preserves a tradition where the "angel of the presence" dictates the law to Moses (1:27–29), though it also stresses the commanding authority of the high God by twice evoking the command to dictate (1:27, 2:1). In a different way, a text from Qumran imagines that Moses's voice took on the authority of God's voice (4Q377 2 ii), and in Acts 7, Stephen charges that his persecutors "received the law as delivered by *aggeloi* (εἰς διαταγὰς ἀγγέλων) but you did not keep it" (7:53).[84] Yet, rather than just adding lesser divinities to the myth about law-giving, in Gal 3:19 Paul also ignores the two main figures: Moses and the supreme God.[85] The result is a polemic that is somewhat like what we find in Acts 7:53 or even v. 42, which charges that the supreme God handed Israel over to the worship of the host as punishment for the golden calf incident.

Considered in this way, Paul's *aggeloi* in Galatians 3 are not so different from the panoply of lower-ranking beings that appear in diverse and unpredictable ways in texts like Daniel 7–12, 1 Enoch, and Jubilees. Though these mediators appear briefly in Gal 3:19, they function to displace the role of the high God at Sinai and so allow for an imaginative reconsideration of the law's origins, relevance, and authority. By playing on a myth about divine mediators, Paul sharply qualifies the law's origins, purpose, and sphere of influence. His comment "but there is not just one intermediary, but there is only one God" also draws a contrast between an ambiguous, complex divine world and one that is unified, coherent, and simple. In Galatians 3, Paul evokes multiplicity, mediation, and lower ranks of divine beings to raise questions about the law's legitimacy, sphere of influence, and relative value.

Conclusion

A strong scholarly consensus treats divine rebellion as an essential characteristic of apocalyptic myths. Against such views, I have argued that the most relevant texts for understanding Paul's thought do not share a common set of essential characteristics, subject matter, characters, or motifs. Instead, they share a modest but identifiable set of working assumptions about the nature of the cosmos and relations of power in the divine political order. As a result, they tend to conceive of the cosmos as a single, well-ordered, stable, and righteously ruled empire. Rather than imagining Belial, Mastema, or the *mal'āk* of darkness as rebels and opponents of the supreme God, writers of diverse provenance rather consistently affirm their lesser status as functionaries and servants of a larger world polity. One important result is a tendency to imagine eschatological wars in highly asymmetrical terms so that the forces of heaven fight only relatively powerless opponents and instrumental enemies. Another is a tendency to envision future moments of political restoration, renewal, and reconciliation rather than revolutionary uprisings, upheavals, or political reversals. Indeed, even the violence-saturated book of Revelation rarely depicts opposition coming from within the divine kingdom, save for the war that breaks out in heaven only to be quashed by Michael within the space of two short verses (12:7–9). Instead, destruction generally rains down as punishment from above in a grand display of heavenly justice. A similar political agenda also accounts for the ambiguous roles played by gentile gods, who are alternately ignored, ridiculed, subjected, assimilated, and punished along with the rest of the cosmos. Thus, like many other writers, Paul looks to a dramatically changed future, but he relentlessly portrays this transformation as an outgrowth of the true order of power already inherent in the world as it is, has been, and will be. Though gentile gods pose something of a problem for this political program, Paul adapts well-worn strategies to recast them as diminutive, nonthreatening threats. The conceits of gentile ignorance, of Christ's inevitable victory, and of political harmony at the upper ranks of divine power all serve this larger agenda.

4 Idols and Other Gods in 1 Corinthians, Galatians, and Romans

The preceding chapters have focused on issues of rule and rebellion in Jewish apocalyptic traditions. One of the central arguments advanced was that much of the literature suppresses rivalry and competition in the world of divinity, a pattern that proves key for understanding depictions of military challenge, eschatological war, and gentiles (and gentile gods) coming to recognize and submit to Israel's deity. This work offers an important correction to the scholarly consensus that puts divine conflict and rebellion right at the heart of Jewish apocalypticism. If my arguments have substantial merit, they show that mythmakers work hard to deny, suppress, diminish, and push divine conflict to the periphery—not the center—of the world political stage. Rather than a mere shift of emphasis, this kind of reorientation or reframing of apocalypticism allows us to identify more interesting and illuminating patterns in the evidence, whether these concern images of culminating political perfection and military triumph or polemics about outsiders and others.

This chapter follows through on this reorientation by treating Paul's polemics about other gods, with particular attention to Galatians 4, 1 Cor 8–11:1, and Rom 1:18–25. Though these arguments sometimes appear convoluted and inconsistent, I argue that attention to the complex texture of idolatry discourses in Jewish literature allows us to better understand some of Paul's most difficult statements and claims. In particular, his vacillation about whether other gods exist and his habit of recategorizing gentile deities as non-gods, lesser deities, or henchmen of the supreme God fit with polemics that are abundant in other literature. In cases such as 1 Cor 8:6 and Rom 1:18–25, Paul also appropriates philosophically imbued critiques that can be fruitfully compared to those found in the Wisdom of Solomon and the treatises of Philo of Alexandria. These comparisons are important for understanding Paul's intellectual repertoire, but in these cases, philosophical language and ideas mainly add depth and breadth to fairly traditional polemics about the gods of other peoples.

Cosmology and Critique in Biblical and Hellenistic Traditions

Derisive attacks on the mundane qualities of cult statues (and their human craftsmen) abound in texts such as Jeremiah, Ezekiel, and Second Isaiah.[1] In such contexts, gentile gods frequently emerge as deaf, dumb, wooden statues of mere human artifice, not as powerful anthropomorphic beings who extend benefits to humankind.[2] In this light, consider the way Jeremiah 10 pits the god of Israel against the illegitimate gods of the nations:

> Thus shall you say to them: The gods (*'ĕlāheyyā'*) who did not make the heavens and the earth shall perish from the earth and from under the heavens.[3]

> It is he who made the earth by his power,
>> who established the world by his wisdom,
>> and by his understanding stretched out the heavens.
> When he utters his voice, there is a tumult of waters in the heavens,
>> and he makes the mist rise from the ends of the earth.
> He makes lightnings for the rain,
>> and he brings out the wind from his storehouses.
> Everyone is stupid and without knowledge;
>> goldsmiths are all put to shame by their idols (*mippāsel*);
> for their images are false (*šeqer niskô*),
>> and there is no breath in them (*wĕ lō'-rûaḥ bām*).
> They are worthless, a work of delusion;
>> at the time of their punishment they shall perish (*bĕ'ēt pĕquddātām yō'bēdû*). (Jer 10:11–15 NRSV; cf. Jer 51:15–18 and Isa 44:9–20)

> Thus shall you say to them: Let gods who did not make the sky and the earth perish from the earth and from under this sky.

> It is the Lord (κύριος) who made the earth by his strength,
>> who set upright the world by his wisdom,
>> and by his prudence he stretched out the sky,

and a quantity of water was in the sky,
　　and he brought up clouds from the end of the earth.
Lightnings he made into rain,
　　and he brought out light from his storehouses.
Every person was stupid, apart from knowledge (ἐμωράνθη πᾶς ἄνθρωπος
ἀπὸ γνώσεως),
　　every goldsmith was put to shame at his carved images (κατησχύνθη
　　πᾶς χρυσοχόος ἐπὶ τοῖς γλυπτοῖς αὐτοῦ),
because they cast lies (ὅτι ψευδῆ ἐχώνευσαν);
　　there is no breath in them (οὐκ ἔστι πνεῦμα ἐν αὐτοῖς).
Worthless they are, works of mockery (μάταιά ἐστιν, ἔργα ἐμπεπαιγμένα);
　　at the time of their visitation they shall perish (ἐν καιρῷ ἐπισκοπῆς
　　αὐτῶν ἀπολοῦνται). (Jer 10:11–15 LXX; cf. 28:15–18)[4]

Though the MT and the LXX texts differ, they both imagine a highly asymmetrical confrontation between a supreme God and other deities, and they envision this confrontation as playing out on a broad, all-encompassing world stage. The incomparable creator and ruler God contrasts dramatically with the would-be challengers, which first emerge in v. 12 as "the gods who did not make the heavens and the earth" and are soon identified with their cult statues in vv. 14–15. According to these writers/editors and translators, other gods exist in some form, but they are vilified as noncreators, nonrulers, and mere statues bound for destruction. Their worshippers, in turn, emerge as delusional. For all the emphatic denials that other gods threaten as rivals, these claims evoke the very notions of competition and comparability that they take pains to suppress.

Many other biblical polemicists deride the powerlessness of cult statues (and gentile gods generally), but they also tend to waver on their precise ontological status or standing within the divine kingdom, especially about whether they are to be conceived of as lesser deities or as mere statues. Even Jer 10:15 (cf. LXX 28:18; MT 51:18), where idol statues are condemned to death, seems to tacitly suggest that they have some standing as divine beings and are not merely statues of dead wood. In this light, consider the varied claims about gentile gods that appear in Deuteronomy 32–33. In Deuteronomy 32, the writers/editors first establish that Yahweh is Israel's God and then charge Israel with disloyalty:

He [Israel] abandoned God (*ʾĕlôha*) who made him,
　　and scoffed at the Rock of his salvation.
They made him jealous with strange gods (*yaqniʾuhû bĕzārîm*),

with abhorrent things they provoked him (*bĕtô ʿēbōt yakʿîsuhû*).
They sacrificed to demons, not God (*yizbĕḥû laššēdîm lōʾ ʾĕlōha*),
   to deities they had never known (*ʾĕlōhîm lōʾ yĕdāʿûm*),
to new ones recently arrived (*ḥădāšîm miqqārōb bāʾû*)
   whom your ancestors had not feared (*lōʾ śĕʿārûm ʾăbōtêkem*).
You were unmindful of the Rock that bore you;
     you forgot the God who gave you birth (*wattiškaḥ ʾēl mĕḥōlĕlekā*).[5]
      (Deut 32:15–18 NRSV)

And he abandoned God who made him,
   and he departed from God his savior (ἀπὸ θεοῦ σωτῆρος αὐτοῦ).
They provoked me with foreign things (ἐπ' ἀλλοτρίοις);
   by their abominations they embittered me (ἐν βδελύγμασιν αὐτῶν
     ἐξεπίκρανάν με).
They sacrificed to demons and not to God (ἔθυσαν δαιμονίοις καὶ οὐ θεῷ),
   to gods they did not know (θεοῖς, οἷς οὐκ ᾔδεισαν).
New, recent ones have come (καινοὶ πρόσφατοι ἥκασιν),
   whom their fathers did not know.
You abandoned God who bore you (θεὸν τὸν γεννήσαντά),
   and you forgot God who nurtures you (θεοῦ τοῦ τρέφοντός σε).
     (Deut 32:15–18 LXX)

Here gentile gods are addressed as strange, new, foreign things, abominations and as *daimonia/šēdîm*. In this case, however, it is clear that the substantive divine power and source of threat come from the God of Israel. The writers/editors/translators are vague about the precise names, status, and rank of these beings but are unambiguous about their standing relative to Israel's God.

This point becomes exceptionally clear again in 32:30–43, which puts Yahweh/*Kurios* in control of Israel's political fortunes and then builds to a dramatic prophecy about conquest. At the climax, it is proclaimed:

Then he will say: Where are their gods (*ʾĕlōhēmô*),
   the rock in which they took refuge,
who ate the fat of their sacrifices,
   and drank the wine of their libations?
Let them rise up and help you,
   let them be your protection!

See now that I, even I, am he (*ʾanî ʾanî hûʾ*);
   there is no god besides me (*wĕʾēn ʾĕlōhîm ʿimmādî ʾānî*).

I kill and I make alive;
    I wound and I heal;
    and no one can deliver from my hand.
For I lift up my hand to heaven,
    and swear: As I live forever,
when I whet my flashing sword,
    and my hand takes hold on judgment;
I will take vengeance on my adversaries,
    and will repay those who hate me.
I will make my arrows drunk with blood,
    and my sword shall devour flesh—
with the blood of the slain and the captives,
    from the long-haired enemy.

Praise, O heavens, his people,
    worship him, all you gods (*kol 'ĕlōhîm*)![6]
For he will avenge the blood of his children,
    and take vengeance on his adversaries;
he will repay those who hate him,
    and cleanse the land for his people. (Deut 32:37–43 NRSV)

And the Lord said: Where are their gods,
    they in whom they trusted,
the fat of whose sacrifices you were eating
    and were drinking the wine of their libations?
Let them rise up and help you,
    and let them be protectors for you!

See, see that I am (ἴδετε ἴδετε ὅτι ἐγώ εἰμι),
    and there is no god except me (καὶ οὐκ ἔστιν θεὸς πλὴν ἐμοῦ).
I will kill, and I will make alive;
    I will strike, and I will heal,
    and there is no one who will deliver from my hands.
For I will lift up my hand to the sky,
    and I will swear by my right hand,
    and I will say: I live forever,
because I will sharpen my dagger like lightning,
    and my hand will take hold on judgment,
and I will repay my enemies with a sentence,
    and those who hate me I will repay.
I will make my arrows drunk with blood—
    and my dagger shall devour flesh—

> with the blood of the wounded and of captives,
>> from the head of the commanders of the enemies.
> Be glad, O skies, with him (εὐφράνθητε, οὐρανοί, ἅμα αὐτῷ),
>> and let all the divine sons do obeisance to him (καὶ προσκυνησάτωσαν
>> αὐτῷ πάντες υἱοὶ θεοῦ).
> Be glad, O nations, with his people (εὐφράνθητε, ἔθνη, μετὰ τοῦ λαοῦ
> αὐτοῦ),
>> and let all the angels of God prevail for him (καὶ ἐνισχυσάτωσαν
>> αὐτῷ πάντες ἄγγελοι θεοῦ).
> For he will avenge the blood of his sons
>> and take revenge and repay the enemies with a sentence,
> and he will repay those who hate,
>> and the Lord shall cleanse the land of his people.
>> (Deut 32:37–43 LXX)

The question "where are their gods?" and the sneers about eating, drinking, and offering protection suggest relatively powerless, absent, and perhaps even nonexistent beings. Bald assertions of the military prowess of Yahweh/*Kurios* and taunts such as "there is no God besides me" set the stage of divine power. Though the MT and the LXX differ, when other gods emerge again in v. 43, they do so as diminutive lesser beings who are now called to acclaim their true commander and king. Whereas the best Hebrew text has simply "worship him, all you gods" (v. 43), the LXX supplies a number of different calls for praise and obedience. Thus we have divine sons called to obeisance, "heavens" called to praise the deity, and in what is perhaps an allusion to a martial host, also the "angels" of God. The LXX of v. 43 thus provides a densely populated, expansive image of acclamation, as all peoples, skies, divine sons, and an angelic host are called to celebrate their commander. Both texts seem to suggest that the gods of other peoples are powerless before the supreme deity kindled to anger. Nevertheless, the strong claims about God's jealousy and rage, Israel's exclusive religious obligations, and the future defeat of the nations that run throughout Deuteronomy 32–33 all prove nonsensical without rivals and competitors of some kind. Thus, a competitive framework drives the narrative even though the writers/editors seem concerned to suppress the possibility that Israel's God has rivals of comparable power.

Idol polemics are also very prominent in Second Isaiah. So in chapters 40–52, for instance, the writers labor over mocking critiques of other deities, hymns that celebrate Yahweh as victor over others gods (and nongods), and in a myriad of other ways play with language about understanding, truth, and divinity to satirize gentile beliefs. So chapter 40 imagines the entire cosmos as subordinate to its rightful king:

> Have you not known? Have you not heard?
>> Has it not been told you from the beginning?
>> Have you not understood from the foundations of the earth?
> It is he who sits above the circle of the earth,
>> and its inhabitants are like grasshoppers;
> who stretches out the heavens like a curtain,
>> and spreads them like a tent to live in;
> who brings princes to naught,
>> and makes the rulers of the earth as nothing . . .
>
> To whom then will you compare me,
>> or who is my equal? says the Holy One (*yō'mar qādôš*).
> Lift up your eyes on high and see:
>> Who created these?
> He who brings out their host and numbers them (*hammôṣî' bĕmispār ṣĕbā'ām*),
>> calling them all by name;
> because he is great in strength,
>> mighty in power,
>> not one is missing. (Isa 40:21–23, 25–26 NRSV)[7]

> Will you not know? Will you not hear?
>> Has it not been declared to you from the beginning?
>> Have you not known the foundations of the earth?
> It is he who holds the circle of the earth,
>> and those who dwell in it are like grasshoppers,
> who has set up heaven like a vault
>> and stretched it out like a tent to live in,
> who has appointed rulers to rule for naught (ὁ διδοὺς ἄρχοντας εἰς οὐδὲν ἄρχειν)
>> and has made the earth as nothing . . .
>
> Now therefore to whom did you liken me (νῦν οὖν τίνι με ὡμοιώσατε)
>> and will I be made equal? said the Holy One (καὶ ἰσωθήσομαι· εἶπεν ὁ ἅγιος).
> Look up on high with your eyes, and see:
>> Who has exhibited all these?
> He who brings out his host by number (κατὰ ἀριθμὸν τὸν κόσμον αὐτοῦ),[8]
>> he will call them all by name;
> because of abundant glory

and by might of strength,
nothing has escaped you. (Isa 40:21–23, 25–26 LXX)

Here claims about the gods, hosts, the order of the natural world, and the histories of the world's peoples appear seamlessly knit together in visions of a cosmic hierarchy and rule beneath a single all-powerful king. Though mentioned only in passing, the language about the host (*ṣābā'*; κόσμος) in v. 26 implies a lesser tier of subordinates, perhaps to be identified with the heavenly bodies. Like the analogy of grasshoppers far below, this image of a compliant and dutiful host serves to illustrate something about the magnificent, lofty, and centralized nature of divine power. Evocations of the unrivaled status of Yahweh/*Kurios* also set for derisive barbs about others gods such as "who is my equal?" and "who has counseled the lord?" Similar rhetoric appears in Isa 46:

> To whom will you liken me and make me equal (*lĕmî tĕdamyûnî wĕtaśwû*),
>> and compare me, as though we were alike (*wĕtamšilûnî wĕnidmeh*)?[9]
> Those who lavish gold from the purse,
>> and weigh out silver in the scales—
> they hire a goldsmith, who makes it into a god (*wĕya'ăśēhû 'ēl*);
>> then they fall down and worship!
> They lift it to their shoulders, they carry it,
>> they set it in its place, and it stands there;
>> it cannot move from its place.
> If one cries out to it, it does not answer
>> or save anyone from trouble.
>
> Remember this and consider,
>> recall it to mind, you transgressors,
>> remember the former things of old;
> for I am God, and there is no other (*kî 'ānōkî 'ēl wĕ'ên 'ôd*);
>> I am God, and there is no one like me (*'ĕlōhîm wĕ'epes kāmônî*).
>> (Isa 46:5–9 NRSV)

> To whom have you likened me?
>> See, act with cunning (ἴδετε, τεχνάσασθε),
>> you who are going astray (οἱ πλανώμενοι)!
> Those who contribute gold from a bag
>> and silver in a balance
>> will set it on a scale,
> and after hiring a goldsmith, they made handiwork [idols] (χειροποίητα),
>> and bowing down they do obeisance to them!

They carry it on their shoulders and go,
>   and if they set it up, it stays in its place;
>   it will not move.
And whoever cries out to him, he will not listen;
>   he will not save him from evils.
Remember these things and groan (στενάξατε);
>   repent, you who have gone astray (μετανοήσατε, οἱ πεπλανημένοι);
>   turn in your heart (ἐπιστρέψατε τῇ καρδίᾳ),
and remember the former things of old,
>   because I am God, and there is no other besides me (ὅτι ἐγώ εἰμι ὁ
>   θεός, καὶ οὐκ ἔστιν ἔτι πλὴν ἐμοῦ). (Isa 46:5–9 LXX)

In both texts, other gods are portrayed merely as iconodules or cult statues, not competing deities with their own cults, pantheons, relationships, and systems of patronage. By reclassifying would-be gods as dead and lifeless images, Israel's patron emerges as victor (somewhat absurdly) in a battle against statuary. Once again, these claims strategically subordinate, demote, and reclassify gentile gods, even though they everywhere implicate them as competitors for status, power, and honor. This tension is nowhere more evident than in the pronouncement "I am God, and there is no other." Similar patterns appear in Psalms 115 and 135, Hab 2:18–19, the Epistle of Jeremiah, and Jubilees 11–12, among many other texts.

The idolatry polemics found in Deuteronomy 32–33, Jeremiah 10, and Second Isaiah labor to reclassify gentile gods while also concentrating and centralizing divine power in a single ruler and creator God, albeit in diverse ways. In such contexts, the cosmos often serves both as a kind of dramatic backdrop that enhances the stature of its central character and as evidence of the exceptional powers of its creator and unrivaled divine puppeteer. Images of the vast reaches of the cosmic order also portray the world as a single continuum, an organized political expanse that is at once unified, hierarchical, and well-regulated. In this light, consider similar patterns in Psalm 96:

Declare his glory among the nations,
>   his marvelous works among all the peoples.
For great is the Lord (YHWH), and greatly to be praised;
>   he is to be revered above all gods (mĕ'ōd nôrā' hû' 'al-kol-'ĕlōhîm).
For all the gods of the peoples are idols (kî kol-'ĕlōhê hā'ammîm 'ĕlîlîm)
>   but the Lord (YHWH) made the heavens.
Honor and majesty are before him;
>   strength and beauty are in his sanctuary.

Ascribe to the Lord, O families of the peoples,
    ascribe to the Lord glory and strength.
Ascribe to the Lord the glory due his name;
    bring an offering, and come into his courts. (Ps 96:3–8 NRSV)

Declare his glory among the nations,
    among all the peoples his marvelous works,
because great is the Lord and very much praiseworthy;
    he is terrible to all the gods (φοβερός ἐστιν ἐπὶ πάντας τοὺς θεούς),
because all the gods of the nations are demons (ὅτι πάντες οἱ θεοὶ τῶν
    ἐθνῶν δαιμόνια),
        but the Lord made the heavens (ὁ δὲ κύριος τοὺς οὐρανοὺς
        ἐποίησεν). Acknowledgment and beauty are before him;
        holiness and magnificence comprise his sanctity [or sanctuary] (ἐν τῷ
        ἁγιάσματι αὐτοῦ).

Bring to the Lord, O paternal families of the nations (αἱ πατριαὶ τῶν
    ἐθνῶν);
    bring to the Lord glory and honor.
Bring to the Lord glory due his name;
    raise offerings, and enter into his courts. (Ps 95:3–8 LXX)

Consistent with much other literature, these texts envision Israel's God as
having a uniquely high status relative to other gods and call on all peoples
to offer appropriate worship, acclamation, and honor to their true divine
king. Here in v. 4 the lesser standing of others gods adds luster to the glorious superpower above, but in v. 5 these gods are glossed as "idols" (ʾĕlîlîm)
in the MT, and in the LXX they are *daimonia*. Texts such as Isa 2:8, Ezek
30:13, and Hab 2:18 associate the term ʾĕlîlîm with the worship of statuary,
but nothing in the context here requires such an association. The Greek
connotes lesser deities of some kind, which is more consistent with the
claims made in v. 4 to the effect that Yahweh reigns "above all the gods."
Whether or not the LXX preserves the earlier text, both the MT and the
Greek texts play with the category of others gods but are ambiguous about
their precise status or standing within the divine world. Whether construed
as other gods in v. 4 or as ʾĕlîlîm and *daimonia* in v. 5, these beings appear
as relatively minor characters that illustrate something important about the
nature of the divine political order. Fittingly, the cosmic stage also comes
clearly in view in vv. 10–12, which calls the heavens, earth, sea, fields, and
nations to acclaim Yahweh as king.

Prominent strands of biblical tradition satirize gentile beliefs and practices, but concerns with so-called idolatry seem to become even more common in Hellenistic literature. Scholars such as Wolfgang Roth conjecture that issues with idolatry were becoming increasingly prominent during this period, as suggested by the climactic pronouncement in the Wisdom of Solomon that "the worship of the unspeakable idols is the beginning, cause, and end of every evil" (Wis 14:27; cf. Josephus, *Ant.* 44.7).[10] As we will see, certain strategies and patterns of argument predominate in both biblical and Hellenistic sources. Though none of these polemics is exactly alike, writers very often ignore, suppress, and/or assimilate gentile gods to the court of Israel's deity, and they often identify them satirically with their cult statues. Whether gentile gods are construed as lesser gods or as mere statues, however, both strategies work to recategorize them by ignoring, demoting, or assimilating the gods of others to Israel's political imaginary. Without suggesting some kind of singular or linear trajectory, the evidence thus suggests that writers found reclassification strategies or polemics useful in a wide variety of literary contexts.

Subordinating Polemics in Galatians 4

Paul treats idolatry and gentile gods at some length in Gal 4:3–10, 1 Cor 8:1–11:1, and Rom 1:18–25. Consistent with many biblical and nonbiblical writings, these arguments involve varying, ambiguous, and sometimes contradictory claims about the precise status of other gods, but Paul quite consistently maintains that they pose no threat to Israel's deity. Also consistent with this literature, Paul lavishes attention on the upper levels of the divine hierarchy while reclassifying other gods as statues, lower-ranking divinities, ignorant subordinates, and mere components of the created order.

In Galatians 4, Paul develops a series of arguments about knowledge and moral development that ultimately recast gentile deities as lower-level gods. These arguments come as part of a critique and reappropriation of "the law" that runs throughout the letter. Here, however, Paul builds an analogy between the law as an intermediary and a temporary overseer and posits that his Galatian gentiles were formerly enslaved to this intermediary.[11] So Gal 4:1–2 associates the law with guardians or trustees who care for young children in accord with the wishes of their father. The guardian-child analogy soon becomes an occasion to reconsider gentile gods in vv. 3–10. So Paul announces the changed nature of these relationships: "When we were children, we were slaves to the elements of the cosmos (ὑπὸ τὰ στοιχεῖα τοῦ κόσμου ἤμεθα δεδουλωμένοι), but when the fullness of time had arrived, God sent his son, born of a woman and born under the law, to redeem those under the law, so we might receive sonship"[12] (4:3–5). In other contexts, Paul prefers to imagine gentile gods as false, nonexistent, or powerless relative to the supreme God (so 1 Thess 1:9, Rom 1:18–25, and 1 Cor 8:6), but in Galatians 4 he seems to take a more generous position, at least at first. Here gentile gods have a place in the world, albeit as "elements of the cosmos (*stoicheia tou kosmou*)" whose legitimate roles as overseers and helpers are inevitably due to expire. In the subsequent verses, Paul builds on these ideas by adding language about days, months, seasons, and years. He also develops a more barbed critique of these *stoicheia*: "Formerly, when you did not know God, you were enslaved to those that are by nature not gods (φύσει μὴ οὖσιν θεοῖς) but now that you know God, or rather have come to be known by God, how can you turn back all over again to the weak and impoverished *stoicheia* (τὰ ἀσθενῆ καὶ πτωχὰ στοιχεῖα) to which you again desire to be enslaved? You are carefully watching days and months and seasons and years" (Gal 4:8–10). Instead of guardians, the *stoicheia* now appear as gentile gods and, in turn, lesser beings who pale in comparison to the true God of all. Paul's language of "weak" *stoicheia* and non-gods (lit., "not gods by nature") is consistent with other discourses that vilify gentile gods while at the same time vacillating on their precise ontological status. In this case, Paul implicates worshippers in juvenile beliefs that ensnare them in relationships that are less intimately connected to the upper reaches of the divine ranks. By contrast, the new alliances offered to the Christ-elect come with pneumatic gifts and allow the elect greater maturity and intimacy so that they move from a slave status under intermediaries to that of sons ruled directly by their father. This entails a kind of elevation or promotion, but the relations of power remain otherwise unchanged. Thus, the Christ-followers may have transformed minds and pneumatic gifts, and they may have moved up in the divine ranks, but the order of power and priority as a whole appears generally stable and unchanged, at least in the anxious present just before Christ's return.[13]

Scholars of Paul have labored over the *stoicheia tou kosmou* of Galatians 4. They have worked especially hard to establish a plausible semantic range for the term *stoicheia* in Greek literature.[14] Their proposals vary, but all of them have something to do with components or parts of a larger whole.[15] So *stoicheia* may designate parts of speech (conceived of as subsets of language) or even letters of the alphabet (conceived of as subsets of the entire alphabet); in other cases the term designates the four elements of the created order (earth, water, air, and fire) or the heavenly bodies; and in others it refers to preliminary or elementary instruction, conceived of as a subset of a larger educational curriculum.[16] Given that a number of Jewish polemics charge others with deifying the elements, it is tempting to prefer the second alternative—that Paul means to designate the four elements (earth, water, air, and fire). Yet in Galatians 4, Paul goes on to connect "enslavement" to the *stoicheia* with observing "days, and months, and seasons, and years" (4:10). This would seem to point to the heavenly bodies, since it is their cyclical movements that produce night, day, and the calendar as a whole. Of course, it is possible to imagine charges of deifying elements and of worshipping heavenly bodies as on a continuum, not as different or antithetical. In this light, consider the typology of error developed in the Wisdom of Solomon 13: "Born to mindlessness were all those who were [inherently] ignorant of God, and unable to perceive the existent one from visible goods, nor recognize the artificer, though intent on his works. But either fire, or breath, or swift air, or starry heaven, or torrential water, or the celestial lights, cosmic lords, they accounted gods" (13:1–2). As in many of Philo's treatises, Pseudo-Solomon conjoins the deification of the elements and heavenly bodies along with a hodgepodge of other cosmological errors. In this case, however, Pseudo-Solomon distinguishes different species of error, so that divinizing the elements appears to be a different matter from taking "starry heaven" or "cosmic lights" to be divine. Philo of Alexandria (e.g., *Spec.* 2.255 and *Dec.* 54–55) and Philo of Byblos make similar distinctions (frag. 1 = *Praep. Ev.* 1.9.23–29, 1.10).

It is possible that Paul's statements about *stoicheia* in vv. 3 and 9 effectively intermingle two distinctive lines of argument—one that identifies gentile gods with the four elements, and another that identifies them with the heavenly bodies. A simpler alternative, however, is to take the *stoicheia tou kosmou* as parts or lesser components of the cosmos, which are soon identified with the heavenly bodies in v. 10. In other words, *stoicheia tou kosmou* carries the rather literal sense of "subordinate or lesser parts of the universe." In this reading, serving them amounts to worshipping some part of the created order, not unlike Paul's generalizing rhetoric about the worship of creation in Rom 1:25, instead of the true God who stands outside of it (Rom 1:19–25). Following this general characterization in Gal 4:3, 9,

Paul targets the heavenly bodies in v. 10, which are as much "components" or "parts" of the cosmos as anything else. Such a reading is consistent with the pervasive use of *stoicheia* for denoting subspecies, components, or parts of some larger whole, and it avoids implying that some obvious meaning follows everywhere the word *stoicheia* appears beside *tou kosmou*.[17] The claim that gentiles worship the heavenly bodies is well-attested in the biblical anthology (e.g., Deut 4:19; 2 Kgs 21:5, 23:5; Job 31:26–28) and in a number of nonbiblical sources such as Jubilees, the works of Philo of Alexandria, and the writings of Josephus. It also fits relatively easily with Greek and Roman traditions that connect the heavenly bodies with gods.

The charge of worshipping the lesser parts of the created order, and the heavenly bodies specifically, also fits rather neatly into Paul's invectives about the true meaning of the Mosaic law. In this interpretation, Galatians 4 starts with the law, then moves to the analogy of guardians and temporary intermediaries, then to *stoicheia* that are components or lesser intermediaries of the cosmos, then on to *stoicheia* as gentile gods cum intermediaries that are now obsolete. Next, Paul moves to a well-established polemic about the folly of worshipping powerless non-gods, which soon becomes an attack on the practice of observing festivals, presumably because attention to the calendar is somehow akin to worshipping the heavenly bodies. Thus, the whole vignette circles back again to the law.[18] In the process we learn a number of interesting things about gentile gods and the cosmos, or at least the kinds of ideas, images, and arguments that are ready at hand for Paul. For all the intricacies of these arguments, much of Paul's argument about other gods is relatively straightforward: Christ-followers must not submit to old, weak intermediaries but rather to strong, true, and loftier gods; likewise, they should not submit to laws that are, analogously, only instrumental relics of a bygone era.

It is important to emphasize that in Paul's thought, the recent and seemingly radical upheavals occasioned by Christ's life and death also fit seamlessly within an all-encompassing and fixed plan for the past, present, and future. This makes good sense of why he so heavily uses analogies relating to intimacy, maturity, progress, and perfection rather than complete reversal or radical change. It also accounts for the prominence of slavery/freedom analogies, since these lend themselves to arguments about the modification of existing rights and relationships, as do images of guardians, trustees, and parent-children relationships in Galatians 4. For instance, in Galatians 3, Paul charges that the wayward Galatians have reversed the order of progress, which ought to have culminated with the spirit, not a return to the flesh (3:3–4). He also offers multiple arguments about Abraham, each of which aims to establish that there is continuity and consistency over time, not radical breaks. The analogies of a ratified will in Gal 3:17 and of harvesting/maturity in 6:7–9 serve similar ends. Furthermore, when Paul does build toward ideas that entail breaks and disjunctures, he tends to envision relatively intimate moments of human transformation, not the reversal or collapse of the existing cosmo-political order. For instance, in Galatians 2 Paul dramatically compares his own transformation to dying to the world (2:19–20); in Gal 3:28 he famously announces the end of old distinctions between slave/free and male/female (at least for those "in Christ"); and in Galatians 6 he attacks his perceived opponents with the thunderous announcement of a "new creation" (6:15). In each case, these pronouncements serve as rhetorical climaxes that underscore certain pointed issues of dispute, namely, whether people should esteem his views over those of his competitors. Even Paul's strong language about freedom "from this present evil age" in Gal 1:4 comes alongside an expansive vision of a providential world order: all of this has been fixed by the supreme powers of heaven so that "this age" is but a temporary imposition.

First Corinthians 8–11:1

First Corinthians 8–11:1 contains some of the most sustained but seemingly convoluted of Paul's arguments about idolatry.[19] Here Paul first entertains the possibility of eating meat sacrificed to gentile gods, announces that these gods do not really exist, and then suggests some qualified terms on which eating meat sacrificed in their honor might still be inappropriate. When he returns to questions about eating idol meat in chapter 10, however, Paul seems to reverse these earlier practical recommendations and his claims about other gods. So in chapter 10, eating idol meat may anger the Judean God, but other gods also reemerge as *daimonia*.[20] This might plausibly be understood as a reversal or climax of the earlier arguments, but in the very next lines Paul adds that one may eat meat in the home of an unbeliever without pangs of conscience, though some restrictions apply. To some extent, Paul's changing arguments can be explained as addressing different kinds of practical settings for consuming said idol meat.[21] Indeed, an emerging scholarly consensus holds that 10:1–22 treats table fellowship in a temple but that 8:1–13 and 10:25–11:1 are about eating meat in less openly ritual contexts. Nevertheless, it remains unclear why Paul would view these contexts so differently.

As we have seen, an array of biblical and Hellenistic writers make vacillating and somewhat contradictory claims about the precise status of other gods, but they emphatically maintain that those gods are powerless and insignificant relative to the supreme God. Paul's changing arguments in 1 Corinthians 8 and 10 are actually quite consistent with this basic picture of the divine world. In this light, consider Paul's claims in chapter 8: "An idol has no real existence (οὐδὲν εἴδωλον ἐν κόσμῳ) and there is no God except the one God (οὐδεὶς θεὸς εἰ μὴ εἷς)" (8:4). While these claims appear straightforward, he then turns to address a more pluralistic reality: "There are those called gods and lords in heaven and earth (καὶ γὰρ εἴπερ εἰσὶν λεγόμενοι θεοὶ εἴτε ἐν οὐρανῷ εἴτε ἐπὶ γῆς), so in that sense there are many gods and lords (ὥσπερ εἰσὶν θεοὶ πολλοὶ καὶ κύριοι πολλοί)" (8:5).[22] Whereas outsiders imagine a more crowded cosmology, Paul distinguishes the singular, true beliefs that are supposedly held by his compatriots. So 8:6 goes on to emphasize: "For us, by contrast, there is one God, the father, from whom are all things and for whom we are, and one lord Jesus Christ, through whom are all things and through whom we are (ἀλλ᾽ ἡμῖν εἷς θεὸς ὁ πατὴρ ἐξ οὗ τὰ πάντα καὶ ἡμεῖς εἰς αὐτόν καὶ εἷς κύριος Ἰησοῦς Χριστὸς δι᾽ οὗ τὰ πάντα καὶ ἡμεῖς δι᾽ αὐτοῦ)." While others may have so-called gods and lords, the Christ-followers have access to the true divine powers that reign supreme over all.

In the context of 1 Corinthians 8, then, Paul introduces other gods and then strategically ignores them. Though "idols" may be "nothings," this need not imply that "other gods and lords" are strictly nonexistent. Indeed, the arguments that follow in chapter 8 strongly imply that such gods are powerless and ineffective. So Paul writes: "Food will not better our standing before God. We are no better off if we don't eat, or if we do (βρῶμα δὲ ἡμᾶς οὐ παραστήσει τῷ θεῷ. οὔτε ἐὰν μὴ φάγωμεν ὑστερούμεθα, οὔτε ἐὰν φάγωμεν περισσεύομεν)" (8:8).[23] Such claims deny one of the basic premises of traditional religions, namely, that sacrifices involve meaningful exchange with the gods.[24] Paul then goes on to evoke anxiety about the moral up-building of other Christ-followers, especially the possibility that those with "weaker" dispositions may misunderstand this eating and so be "destroyed" (8:11). Again, this might seem to imply that other gods do not really exist, but it actually only requires that they are not powerful anthropomorphic agents who can help or harm. The arguments that follow in 9:1–26 explore issues of freedom (ἐλευθερία) and authority (ἐξουσία) but do not address questions of eating food sacrificed to other gods, at least not directly.[25]

Whereas in 1 Corinthians 8, Paul seems content to deny the effective power of gentile gods, in chapter 10 his concerns about idols and other gods appear much more alarmist and expansive.[26] Consistent with other literature, however, he makes these arguments by appealing to the punishing wrath of the supreme God, not any imagined threats that come from others. So in 10:1–13 Paul introduces exemplary instances of Israel's disobedience, in verse 14 he demands "therefore, flee the worship/service of *eidôla* (φεύγετε ἀπὸ τῆς εἰδωλολατρίας)," and in vv. 15–22 he construes sacrifices as offered to *daimonia*.[27] Here in vv. 15–22, Paul posits direct parallels between sharing the body and blood of Christ and eating meat sacrificed on the Jewish altar (the case of "Israel according to the flesh" [10:18]). Though Paul's imagined Christ-followers lack a communal sacrificial meal in honor of the deity, he evokes their meatless meal in honor of Christ and God (10:16–17) and then compares it to the Israelite practices of sacrifice and meat distribution, asking, "Are not the people who eat sacrifices sharers in the sacrificial altar?" (10:18).[28] These rhetorical questions set up for the penultimate discussion of idol meat: "Am I saying that idol meat is something or that an idol is something? No, rather that the things they sacrifice are sacrificed to *daimonia* and not to God. I do not want you to be fellow sharers with *daimonia*. You cannot drink the cup of the lord and the cup of *daimonia* or partake of the table of the lord and the table of *daimonia*. Or shall we provoke the lord to jealousy? Are we stronger than he is?" (10:19–22). Though much attention has been lavished on the supposed language about "demons" here, it is important to stress that this argument triangulates to the austere demands of the supreme God and renders *daimonia* only as minor players. As in a host of other literature, there is no hint that these other gods are malevolent or even capable of action or influence. Instead, the argument pivots to the ruling God who threatens jealously from on high (cf. Deut 32:21; Exod 20:4–5, 34:14; Josh 24:19–24; Ps 78).

Paul's claims about *daimonia* in chapter 10 fit particularly well with polemical traditions that avoid attributing power, efficacy, or malevolence to gentile gods.[29] Of course, the powerlessness of gentile gods is a central premise of parodies that identify them with statuary. This premise is also implied in many polemical discourses that classify these gods as lesser deities and operatives of the true divine creator and king. For instance, other gods often come on and off the scene very quickly, such as in the LXX version of Psalm 96: "All the gods of the nations are *daimonia* but Yahweh made the heavens" (95:5 [96:5]). In this brief encounter, other gods have diminutive powers, but it remains unclear whether they are capable of malevolent design or even independent action. In other cases, writers more emphatically construe them as powerless. So the writer of Jubilees foretells a time when Israel will stray, writing, "When they eat and are full [having gained the land of milk and honey] they will turn to foreign gods (*'amlāk nakir*)—to ones which will not save them from any of their afflictions" (1:7–8).[30] The conceit of powerlessness allows the writer to imply that other gods exist in some form while also maintaining that they lack any capacity to help or harm. Pseudo-Solomon makes a similar point about the practice of swearing oaths to other gods: "For it is not the power of those by whom they swear, but the judgment of them that sin, that ever proceeds against the transgression of the wicked (οὐ γὰρ ἡ τῶν ὀμνυμένων δύναμις, ἀλλ' ἡ τῶν ἁμαρτανόντων δίκη ἐπεξέρχεται ἀεὶ τὴν τῶν ἀδίκων παράβασις)" (14:31). This pronouncement follows a long idol satire that derides the worship of dead and lifeless statues. Even in the context of a sustained parody about statuary, however, Pseudo-Solomon takes pains to emphasize the utter powerlessness of these would-be gods and to insist that just retribution falls from on high. Further, even where writers seem to suggest malevolent beings of some kind, they quite consistently construe the supreme God as the most dangerous of all. In this light, consider the varied ways that the Epistle of Enoch represents the gods of others:

> Those who worship stones—
> and who carve images of silver and gold and wood and stone and clay
>> and worship phantoms and demons and abominations and evil
>>> spirits[31] and all errors, not according to knowledge;
>> no help will you find from them.
> They will be led astray by the folly of their hearts,
>> and their eyes will be blinded by the fear of their hearts,
>> and the visions of (your) dreams will lead you astray[32]—
> You and the false works that you have made and constructed of stone,
>> you will be destroyed together. (99:7–9; cf. 91:8)

This tirade strings together a number of different objects of illegitimate worship, some of which appear sinister. So there are cult statues, "phantoms," "demons," "abominations," and "evil spirits," but the writer offers no further qualification as to their precise identifications, roles, or relationships. Instead, the writer warns, "no help will you find from them," and then quickly turns to excoriating rhetoric about knowledge and errors of mind. The writer also insists that both the worshippers and their statuary will be destroyed together (cf. Jer 10:15, 1 En. 91:9), thus affirming that the true God proves to be the most harmful and threatening of all.

Traditions of polemic that recategorize gentile gods as lesser deities shed light on Paul's *daimonia* in 1 Corinthians 10, particularly traditions that stress the powerlessness of gentile gods or would-be gods. It is important to emphasize, however, that Paul's more basic claims about relationships of power are consistent with what we find in an array of other literature. For instance, in the midst of a sustained celebration of Yahweh's supremacy in Jeremiah 10, we find an Aramaic addition: "Thus shall you say to them: The gods (*'ĕlāhayyā'*) who did not make the heavens and the earth shall perish from the earth and from under the heavens" (10:11, NRSV). The "other gods" here allow the redactor to accommodate the gods of others while relegating them to a subordinate status; their diminutive standing also magnifies the glory of the true world creator who towers over them. In ways that are similar and different, the writer/editor of Deuteronomy 32 pillories strange gods, recent gods, and *šēdîm* but avoids attributing them powers or efficacy. Instead, the central threat comes from the wrath of Israel's God. This becomes especially clear as the writer/editor predicts a time of restoration and has Yahweh cry: "Where are their gods (*'ĕlōhêmô*), the rock in which they took refuge, who ate the fat of their sacrifices, and drank the wine of their libations? Let them rise up and help you, let them be your protection! See now that I, even I, am he; there is no god besides me (*'anî 'anî hû' wĕ'ên 'ĕlōhîm 'immādî 'ānî)*" (32:37–39, NRSV). Here anger, jealousy, and preeminence all figure prominently, as they do also in 1 Corinthians 10. As with other writings, we find language about other gods but virtually no sustained mythmaking that might explain their precise standing, powers, roles, and relationships. This vagueness and inconsistency are not incidental but rather are key polemical strategies.

Paul's seeming vacillations about "idol" meat and other gods are consistent with other traditions that vilify gentile religious beliefs and practices.[33] Thus construed, the arguments of 1 Corinthians 8 largely ignore gentile gods and suppress intimations that they have powers or standing comparable to those of Israel's deity. This does not require, however, that Paul deny them some kind of standing in the divine world, however vague and

nonspecific such formulations prove to be. Comparisons with other literature shed light both on the rather extended arguments in 1 Corinthians 8
to the effect that gentile gods do not really exist "for us" and on the more
alarmist warnings in 1 Corinthians 10 which seem to claim that they actually do. Malevolent forces may be at work in the divine world, then, but
they come from the jealous demands of the supreme deity who dispenses
judgment from on high. Though Paul may seem to walk something of an
ideological "tightrope" here, these basic arguments and strategies are well-
represented in polemical traditions of diverse provenance.

Philosophical Epithets in 1 Corinthians 8

For all the attention lavished on illegitimate gods in 1 Cor 8–11:1, Paul
also characterizes his true and legitimate ones in curious ways, especially
in 8:6. Here he insists: "For us, by contrast, there is one God, the father,
from whom are all things and for whom we are, and one lord Jesus Christ,
through whom are all things and through whom we are (ἀλλ' ἡμῖν εἷς θεὸς
ὁ πατὴρ ἐξ οὗ τὰ πάντα καὶ ἡμεῖς εἰς αὐτόν καὶ εἷς κύριος Ἰησοῦς Χριστὸς
δι' οὗ τὰ πάντα καὶ ἡμεῖς δι'αὐτοῦ)" (8:6). In one sense, this reflects a traditional strategy: Paul first allows for the possibility in v. 4 that there might
be other gods but then telescopes to focus on the upper ranks of divine
power. In this case, he creates a picture of a universal cosmic stage on which
the only real actors appear to be God, Christ, some abstract "all," and an
intimate elect addressed with first-person language. Yet in another sense,
his use of prepositions reflects philosophical shorthand for exploring issues
of causality.[34] This shows that certain philosophical images, language, and
assumptions were part of Paul's intellectual repertoire, ready at hand for
creative reuse and improvisation.

Debates about a first cause (or causes) are already robust among the
Pre-Socratics, and they continue among philosophers after them. Among
Platonists, Peripatetics, and Stoics, these discussions come to involve
prepositional phrases such as "from which," "through which," "by which,"
and "for which."[35] For instance, consider the helpful simplification offered
by the Middle Platonist Alcinous, writing in the second century CE.
Summarizing some of Plato's lengthier arguments, Alcinous writes: "It is
necessary that the most beautiful of constructions, the world, should have
been fashioned by (ὑπὸ) God looking to (πρὸς) a form of World, that being
the model of our world, which is only copied from it, and it is by assimila-

tion to it that it is fashioned by the creator, who proceeds through a most admirable providence and administrative care to create the world, because (διότι) 'he was good' (*Tim.* 29e). He created it, then, out of (ἐκ) the totality of matter" (*Did.* 12.1–2).[36] Here each preposition designates a particular type of cause, and taken together, these causes explain certain fundamental features of the Middle-Platonic cosmos. Though the use of terminology sometimes varies, these are typically distinguished as efficient, formal, instrumental, and material causes. In Alcinous's summary, then, God becomes the efficient cause (ὑπὸ), matter the material cause (ἐκ), God's goodness the formal cause (διότι), and the pattern the instrumental cause, the model that God looks to (πρὸς) in fashioning the world.

Predictably, philosophers disagree on the number of causes and the precise nature of any one of them, even within identifiably Platonic or Stoic traditions.[37] Though Philo is no systematic philosopher, his readings of biblical traditions as philosophical allegory show how one interpreter constructively adapts and plays on Platonic theories of causality as suits his changing interest and aims.[38] For instance, in *On the Cherubim* (124–130), he begins a long excursus on causality by evoking the "oracles which Moses wrote in the sacred books" (124) and then turns to Eve's statement in Gen 4:1: "I have gotten a man through God (διὰ τοῦ θεοῦ)." Whereas the literal sense of the text has Eve reflecting on bearing Cain, in Philo's hands this becomes the voice of mind that mistakenly considers the "offspring engendered by union with sense his own possession" (124). The prepositional phrase "through God (διὰ τοῦ θεοῦ)," in turn, becomes emblematic of a mistaken view of causality, one that confuses supreme with instrumental causes. As Philo will go on to argue at length, the finer points of these distinctions actually matter a great deal. For him, at least two causes are involved here, one of which has priority: "That which comes into being is brought into being through an instrument but [also] by a cause (τὸ δὲ γινόμενον δι᾽ ὀργάνου μὲν ὑπὸ δὲ αἰτίου)" (125). It is this "by (διά)" cause that is of the utmost importance, since it is identified with Philo's Platonic God, the first and primary principle. Philo then trots out an infamous arrangement of four causes: by which (ὑφ᾽ οὗ), from which (ἐξ οὗ), through which (δι᾽ οὗ), and for which (δι᾽ ὅ) (125–126). Like Alcinous, he equates these with the ultimate cause, the material cause, the instrument, and the end or object (126). He then turns to the commonplace analogies of cities and houses so that the cosmos itself becomes "the greatest of houses or cities" (127). Understood along Platonic lines, this cosmos reveals God as the first/ultimate cause, the elements as the material cause, God's logos as the instrument "through which it was framed," and the fourth or final cause as the goodness of the architect (God).

Thus far Philo's analysis is recognizably Platonic, even if he plays up the instrumental cause in some novel ways. Some illuminating variations also appear in his excurses on the figure of Joseph in Genesis 40 (*Cher.* 128). Here he adds that Joseph makes a similar mistake when, in Gen 40:8, he claims that the true meaning of dreams would come "through God (διὰ τοῦ θεοῦ)." As Philo lingers over this case, he allows that although God is the true cause (here designated with ὑπό), nevertheless "we are the instruments (ὄργανα γὰρ ἡμεῖς)." In this way, a philosophical position on issues of metaphysics and cosmology comes to have relevance for a more specific, local audience in the human world. So he continues: "We are the instruments, wielded in varying degrees of force, through which each particular form of action is produced (δι' ὧν αἱ κατὰ μέρος ἐνέργειαι, ἐπιτεινόμενα καὶ ἀνιέμενα); the craftsman it is who brings to bear on the material the impact of our forces, whether of soul or body (τεχνίτης δὲ ὁ τὴν πλῆξιν ἐργαζόμενος τῶν σώματός τε καὶ ψυχῆς δυνάμεων), even he by whom all things are moved (ὑφ' οὗ πάντα κινεῖται)" (*Cher.* 128). Here the quite intimate "we" become instruments of God, and this deity appears in some way to generate all "our" actions. As the discussion continues, Philo again plays with prepositions in ways that diverge from the standard designations he has presented already. In a characteristic polemic, he first derides the ignorant masses for making mistakes similar to those of Joseph (129), jabs at contentious "lovers of strife" (presumably other philosophers), and then closes the whole treatise by praising those who adhere to the true and consistent philosophy and have Moses as their foundation. Finally, Philo insists that this true philosophy is exemplified in Exod 14:3, where "salvation is from the Lord (τὴν παρὰ τοῦ κυρίου)." In Philo's hands this shows that "not through God (διὰ τοῦ θεοῦ), but from him as cause (παρ' αὐτοῦ ὡς αἰτίου) does salvation come" (130). Though elsewhere Philo has insisted that ὑπό designates the supreme, ultimate cause of all, here the prepositional phrase παρ' αὐτοῦ stands in just as well.

As Gregory Sterling has shown, Paul's "prepositional metaphysics" in 1 Cor 8:6 is not quite in line with either Stoic or Platonic uses of these terms.[39] As is well-known, the Stoics typically allow only two causes but emphasize the role of the active cause that is at once material, immanent, and instrumental.[40] Though such views allow for both active and passive causes (so Seneca, *Ep.* 58, 65), the organizing role of the active, dynamic, rational, and providential cause (Zeus or *pneuma*) in Stoic thought can lead easily to the kind of monism hymned by Marcus Aurelius: "All things come from you, subsist in you, go back to you (ἐκ σοῦ πάντα, ἐν σοὶ πάντα, εἰς σὲ πάντα)" (*Med.* 4:23). Remarkably, a similar formulation appears in Romans 11, where Paul first hymns the inscrutable ways of God in 11:34–35 and then adds "from him (ἐξ αὐτοῦ) and through him (δι᾽ αὐτοῦ) and to him are all things (εἰς αὐτὸν τὰ πάντα)" (11:36; cf. Heb 2:10). Yet in 1 Cor 8:6 we find distinctive language about Christ and the elect and an appeal to causal prepositions that seems of a more mixed philosophical heritage. Read in light of Platonic formulations, Paul's statements might construe God as the supreme principle and Christ as the instrumental one: "For us, by contrast, there is one God, the father, from whom are all things and for whom we are, and one lord Jesus Christ, through whom are all things and through whom we are (ἀλλ᾽ ἡμῖν εἷς θεὸς ὁ πατὴρ ἐξ οὗ τὰ πάντα καὶ ἡμεῖς εἰς αὐτόν καὶ εἷς κύριος Ἰησοῦς Χριστὸς δι᾽ οὗ τὰ πάντα καὶ ἡμεῖς δι᾽ αὐτοῦ)" (8:6). The language about ἐξ and εἰς, however, fits better with Stoic schemas, unless Paul means here to make a rather general statement about God as the first cause of "the all" (cf. *Tim.* 29e). At the same time, the use of διά with the genitive to designate Christ's role fits well with Platonic schemas that would make Christ the instrument, and Paul's later allegory of Christ as the pneumatic "rock" in 10:5 could also fit with this interpretation.[41] In addition, Philo's play on these prepositions to describe an intimate relationship between God and "us" also proves suggestive for understanding Paul's integration of the elect into the grand picture of cosmic causality in 1 Corinthians 8. So in 8:6, he invokes "the all" and then focuses attention on distinguishing the ἡμεῖς (us), who are εἰς αὐτόν (for God) and δι᾽ αὐτοῦ (through Christ).

Though it is difficult to be sure just what Paul means by asserting that all things are from, through, and for God and Christ, this statement can be best understood as a philosophically imbued epithet or saying that Paul uses to illustrate something about the nature of divine power. The use of philosophical language shows that Paul, like other mythmakers, rather freely borrows and adapts multiple traditions and discourses as it suits his literary aims. In one sense, this is not so different from the way Yahweh comes to acquire epithets of Baal or that Ninurta takes over the mighty deeds of other gods and claims them for his own. In another sense, Paul tends to represent God and Christ in ways that seem a far cry from the gods of the philosophers, whether imagined as an active divine *pneuma* that suffuses the cosmos or as first, instrumental, material, or final causes. Nevertheless, Paul's use of philosophical images is an important clue to the complex texture of his intellectual repertoire. Though few of Paul's readers or hearers might have appreciated these philosophical resonances, he probably writes with particular concern for those who would have heard them.[42] For those who would not, his basic claims about relationships of power would probably have seemed relatively straightforward and could be easily assimilated to more traditional claims about the divine ranks. That is, Paul imagines God as all-powerful, distinguishes Christ as having a similar but slightly different status, and affirms that, by virtue of their relationships with God and Christ, the elect attain a place of great privilege in this sweeping, all-encompassing cosmic totality.

Greek Cosmology and Ethics in Romans 1:18–32

In Galatians 4 and 1 Cor 8–11:1, Paul uses "so-called gods and lords," *stoicheia, eidôla,* and *daimonia,* largely as foils for exploring the exceptional status of Israel's deity. In some contrast, Rom 1:18–25 reviles gentiles for misapprehending the created order, failing to perceive the true divine power that stands supreme over that order, and perversely worshipping the creation in place of its creator. In this remarkable turn, Paul thus neatly avoids other gods by explaining the origins of idolatry as a form of intellectual error or confusion about the nature of reality. So in Rom 1:18, Paul announces a wrathful punishment against impiety (ἀσέβεια) and wickedness (ἀδικία) and then explains that these alleged evils all derive ultimately from a single cause: the failure to worship the supreme divine creator. After this thunderous condemnation of the wicked, Paul explains: "In fact, knowledge of God was clearly displayed to them (διότι τὸ γνωστὸν τοῦ θεοῦ φανερόν ἐστιν ἐν αὐτοῖς). God displayed it to them. For his invisible attributes are intellectually discerned in the created order, ever since the creation of the cosmos (ὁ θεὸς γὰρ αὐτοῖς ἐφανέρωσεν. τὰ γὰρ ἀόρατα αὐτοῦ ἀπὸ κτίσεως κόσμου τοῖς ποιήμασιν νοούμενα καθορᾶται), namely, his eternal power and godliness (ἥ τε ἀΐδιος αὐτοῦ δύναμις καὶ θειότης), therefore they are without excuse" (1:19–20). In this line of argument, gentiles should have observed the world around them and come to intuit an unseen creator outside of it.[43] These claims become foundational for a satirical representation of gentile religious practices in vv. 21–23, and they come to justify punishment on a grand scale in vv. 24–32. So Paul emphasizes three times that they are "without excuse" because they failed to honor and glorify God (1:21); they "exchanged the glory of the incorruptible God for the likeness of an image of a corruptible man (ἐν ὁμοιώματι εἰκόνος φθαρτοῦ ἀνθρώπου) and of birds and of four-footed animals and reptiles" (1:23; cf. Ps 106 [LXX 105] and Wis 11:15); and they exchanged "the truth about God for a lie and worshiped and served the creation instead of the creator, who is blessed for ever, amen" (1:25).

The charge that gentiles mistakenly worship the creation also appears in many of the works of Philo of Alexandria and in the Wisdom of Solomon.[44] As we have observed, however, biblical polemics often evoke the grandeur of the heavens as proof that Israel's God reigns supreme. So the writer/editor of Second Isaiah charges others with ignorance and inveighs, "It is he who sits above the circle of the earth and its inhabitants are like grasshoppers" (40:22 NRSV). Here and in subsequent verses the writer creates a picture of a supreme God who towers over creation and acts as its righteous divine puppeteer. In ways that are similar and different, the writers/editors of Jeremiah 10 appeal to creative and sustaining heroics: "It is the Lord (κύριος) who made the earth by his strength, who set upright the world by his wisdom, and by his prudence he stretched out the sky, and a quantity of water was in the sky, and he brought up clouds from the end of the earth" (Jer 10:12–13 LXX). Such celebratory evocations of a towering cosmic ruler hint at the creative and ideological potential of these ideas for intellectuals of many stripes, including figures such as Pseudo-Solomon and Philo of Alexandria, who appropriate as suits their polemical interests.

In quite substantial ways, both Philo and Pseudo-Solomon adapt robust traditions of philosophical argument about the true nature of the cosmos. Of particular relevance here is their creative repurposing of so-called arguments from design. Socrates and Plato generate a distinctive and enduring line of argument that appeals to the design of the creation as proof of an intelligent, providential creator. As originally developed, these arguments often took explicit aim at Pre-Socratic philosophers. Even though most of the Pre-Socratics retained a role for divine agents and principles in their cosmologies, Socrates and Plato treat them as de facto atheists and attempt to reassert more traditional notions of providence and teleology. According to Xenophon, for instance, Socrates heroically takes down shameless, iconoclastic atheists (other philosophers and scientists) by arguing that the cosmos itself demonstrates the providential design and care of the gods (*Mem.* 4.3.2–18, 1.1.11–16).[45] In his *Memorabilia*, Socrates does so by working systematically through the hierarchy of nature. First he appeals to the evidence of light (4.3.2); then the heavenly bodies (4.3.4), the seasons (4.3.5), water (4.3.6), fire (4.3.7), the sun (4.3.8–9), and animals (4.3.10); and finally to humankind's capacities for perception, reason, and language (4.3.11–12).[46] Xenophon shows particular concern to argue that this demonstrates the workings of a supreme deity who "co-ordinates and holds together the universe, wherein all things are fair and good" and exhibits his presence "in his supreme works, and yet is unseen by us in the ordering of them" (4.3.13). To this end, he turns to lower-level "ministers" who invisibly govern thunderbolts, winds, and even human souls (4.3.14) and, on this basis, argues for participation in local religious customs (4.3.15). Similar appeals to the created order appear variously in the works of Plato, Aristotle, the Stoics, and many philosophers after them, though particular exempla and forms of the argument vary.[47] To give only one further example, Cicero's *On the Nature of the Gods* preserves a Stoic argument to the effect that even if humans were at first confused by the creation, upon observing its uniformity they should "infer the presence not merely of an inhabitant of this celestial and divine abode, but also of a ruler and governor, the architect as it were of this mighty and monumental structure" (*De nat.* 2.35.90).

In numerous cases, Philo charges that others misunderstand the true nature of the cosmos, and he often adapts arguments from design to serve these polemical ends. In the *Special Laws* and the *Decalogue,* for instance, we find attacks on those who allegedly divinize the elements of nature, the whole created order, and the heavenly bodies. In the *Special Laws,* Philo even goes so far as to justify the death sentence for idol worshippers:

> How great a punishment does he deserve who denies the truly existing God and honors created beings before their maker (τοὺς γεγονότας πρὸ τοῦ πεποιηκότος) and thinks fit to revere, not only earth or water or air or fire, the elements of the all (τὰ στοιχεῖα τοῦ παντός), or again the sun and moon and planets and fixed stars, or the whole heaven and universe, but also the works of mortal craftsmen, sticks and stones, which they have fashioned into human shape? And therefore let him too himself be made like unto these works of men's hands. For it is right that he who honors lifeless things should have no part in life, especially if he has become a disciple of Moses. (*Spec.* 2.255–256)

Philo's language about the creation, the elements, the heavenly bodies, and the whole heavens reflects arguments from design familiar from Xenophon. Somewhat like the example of Xenophon, Philo also twists the visible creation to polemical ends, though the targets in view are those who supposedly divinize this creation, not Socrates's alleged atheists. As a result, idolaters not only worship dead and lifeless statues but also the visible world, whether the creation as a whole or one or another of its parts.[48] To this basic set of arguments he also adds quite traditional claims about standing, power, and appropriate worship. Thus, Philo rather seamlessly combines a quite developed picture of philosophical cosmology with traditional satires about the worship of statuary and about standing, relationships of power, and appropriate worship.[49]

A similar constellation of claims appears in *On the Decalogue* (esp. 52–81), where Philo charges that the misattribution of divinity gives rise to virtually every species of error. In this case, he opens with a derisive portrayal of artisans who fashion cult statues, set them before altars, and demonstrate that they "have assigned celestial and divine honors to idols of stone and wood and suchlike images, all of them lifeless [soulless] things" (*Dec.* 7–8). This is a fairly standard idol parody, but Philo then turns to the delusions that characterize the "larger part of mankind": "For some have deified the four elements (ἐκτεθειώκασι γὰρ οἱ μὲν τὰς τέσσαρας ἀρχάς), earth, water, air and fire, others the sun, moon, planets and fixed stars, others again the heaven by itself, others the whole world. But the highest and the most august, the begetter, the ruler of the great world-city, the commander-in-chief of the invincible host, the pilot who ever steers all things in safety, him they have hidden from sight by the misleading titles assigned to the objects of worship mentioned above" (*Dec.* 53–54). Philo insists that other people hold mistaken views about philosophical cosmology, a view he maintains, in large part, by astutely ignoring the supreme gods, mindlike causes, and organizing principles native to virtually all other traditions. As the excursus continues, he also draws heavy-handed analogies that relate the creator's standing over the created order to the priority of a master over servants and that of a king over subjects. Portraying both cosmic and social hierarchies as self-evidently natural, inevitable, and good, he charges that idolaters honor "the subordinate satraps (ὑπάρχοις σατράπαις)" with honors rightfully due their king; that they give to "servants what belonged to their master (τὰ δεσπότου δούλοις)"; and that they fail to submit to their superiors as they should (*Dec.* 61). In other instances, Philo rages against those who hold "any of the parts of the universe to be the omnipotent god (τοῦ κόσμου μερῶν αὐτοκρατῆ θεὸν ὑπολαμβάνειν)" (*Dec.* 58) and who fail to move beyond the realm of the senses, even though this should properly serve as a "natural stepping stone to the conception of the uncreated and eternal, the invisible charioteer who guides in safety the whole universe" (*Dec.* 60; cf. *Ebr.* 110).[50] Thus, Platonic arguments about intellectual progress and the intelligible realm appear right alongside idol parodies and traditional arguments about the obligations that inferior beings owe to their superiors.

Similar lines of argument appear in Wisdom 13, though Stoic language, images, and ideas predominate in this text much more than do Platonic ones. Here Pseudo-Solomon charges that idolaters fail to infer an "existent one" or "artificer" from the visible works of creation.[51] Drawing on Stoic language, Pseudo-Solomon calls the Jewish God "the existent one," the "artificer," and the "primal author of beauty." This philosophically imbued vision of cosmic hierarchy also includes "fire, or breath, or swift air, or starry heaven, or torrential water, or the celestial lights, cosmic lords, they accounted gods" (13:2).[52] As with Philo's polemics, Pseudo-Solomon simply ignores the gods of other traditions and depicts the created order as self-evidently composed of elements, heavenly bodies, or the whole "starry heavens." Further, these crass idolaters delighted "in the beauty of these things" but failed to discern "how much superior is the master of these things, for it was the primal author of beauty who created them" (13:3). Likewise, v. 4 allows that the dynamic operations (δύναμιν καὶ ἐνέργειαν) of creation are indeed beautiful but rails against those who fail to "apprehend from these how much more powerful is he who shaped them"; v. 5 contends that the "greatness and beauty" of creation ought to have led gentiles to posit a still more powerful and more beautiful author; and in the lengthy series of idol polemics in chapters 13–16, it is repeatedly claimed that attributing life to mundane statues involves strikingly obvious errors in judgment about the true nature of the cosmos, especially as it pertains to the priority of the creator over the created, that of the artisan over dead wood, and that of ensouled beings over soulless matter (13:17–19).

Scholars often draw comparisons between Romans 1 and the idolatry discourses found in Wisdom.[53] Though Wisdom could be a plausible conduit for Paul's imagery and argument, the polemical arguments found in it are themselves part of a broader tradition of idol parody that uses philosophical cosmology in important ways. More broadly conceived, multiple polemical discourses shed light on Paul's distinctive claims about the cosmos, reason, mind, and the duties owed to the supreme God in Romans 1. Here Paul argues that the cosmos requires a divine creator who providentially sustains it and that God has "invisible attributes" that are "intellectually discerned in the created order, ever since the creation of the cosmos (ἀπὸ κτίσεως κόσμου τοῖς ποιήμασιν νοούμενα καθορᾶται)" (v. 20). In Romans 1, Paul does not appeal to other levels of the heavenly hierarchy, such as elements and heavenly bodies, but his emphasis on the grave intellectual error of worshipping the creation in place of the creator reflects the foundational premise of these critiques. So there is Philo's barbed critique in the *Opificio mundi* that others are "amazed at the cosmos more than the creator of the cosmos (κοσμοποιὸν)" (*Opif.* 7) and his argument that anyone who denies "the truly existing God and honors created beings before their maker (τοὺς γεγονότας πρὸ τοῦ πεποιηκότος)" (*Spec.* 2.255) deserves death. Pseudo-Solomon also counsels that idolaters delight "in the beauty of these things" but fail to understand "how much superior is the master of these things, for it is the primal author of beauty who created them" (13:3). Such arguments shed light on Paul's insistence that "God displayed to them (ὁ θεὸς γὰρ αὐτοῖς ἐφανέρωσεν) his invisible attributes (τὰ γὰρ ἀόρατα αὐτοῦ)" as well as the strong distinctions drawn between the creator/created order. His claims about the creator/created, the seen/unseen worlds, and the central roles of intellectual discernment, mind, and wisdom make much more sense when placed alongside these polemics. In fact, to the extent that vv. 20–22 suggest that all people had this knowledge before turning to idolatry, Paul's arguments also fit with certain philosophical arguments about the origins of traditional religion (so Seneca, *Ep.* 90.28; Pseudo-Heraclitus, *Ep.* 4.10–15).[54]

Whereas other polemicists happily charge that other peoples worship images of stone and wood instead of the true ruler who reigns supreme, Paul's arguments here resemble the philosophically imbued polemics found in Wisdom and the writings of Philo, particularly those that turn arguments from design into polemics about the supposed deification of the cosmos (or its parts). Like these writers, he also makes very strong claims about honors due the supreme God and about relationships of divine power. So Paul argues in Rom 1:18–25 that gentile delusion leads to grave religious errors, namely, the failure to render appropriate honor and service to Israel's God. Like masters over slaves, rulers over subjects, and the creator over the created order, Rom 1:18–25 represents obedient submission to the true heavenly powers as natural, just, and good.

It should also be emphasized that Paul could have chosen to represent gentiles as handed over to other gods, spirits, or *aggeloi*, as do texts such as Deuteronomy 32 and Jubilees 15. Instead, he insists that the supreme deity handed gentiles over to passions and desires, stating three times that

God intervened directly to give them over to the "desires of their hearts (ἐπιθυμίαις τῶν καρδιῶν)" (1:24), "dishonorable passions (πάθη ἀτιμίας)" (1:26), and "a base mind (ἀδόκιμον νοῦν)" (1:28). As others have argued, this distinctive argument adapts traditions of ethical thought that understand passions and desires to be the root causes of error and immorality.[55] Thus, it makes good sense that the unleashing of passions and desires here causes a cascading series of evils, from exchanging natural for unnatural relationships to gossip, slander, and murder (1:24–32). In the context of Romans 1, however, the turn inward to gentile passions, hearts, and minds also helpfully avoids intimating that gentile gods might wield political-religious power. Indeed, even their alleged "idols" appear here in passing, as examples of a larger intellectual perversion leading to a righteous punishment at the hands of an angry God. On these terms, God's righteous retribution—unleashing a seething morass of desires and giving the gentiles up to a "debased mind (ἀδόκιμον νοῦν)"—also becomes a punishment that fits the crime.

Conclusion

Paul's language about other gods and lesser divine beings presents a number of difficulties for interpretation. Indeed, extracted from their immediate contexts, his words are quite mysterious. So in Galatians 4, Paul attacks those who would "turn back" again to weak and lowly *stoicheia* but never uses this language again in the surviving letters, though the unknown writers of Colossians and Ephesians play with the term in interesting ways. In 1 Corinthians 8, Paul allows for the existence of beings called "other gods and lords" and construes eating meat sacrificed in their honor as a matter of indifference, and then in 1 Corinthians 10 excoriates participation in sacrificial meals as dishonoring the true God by sacrificing to *daimonia* (10:20–21). Like the word *stoicheia*, however, this language does not appear again in the letters. Similarly, 1 Cor 15:24 mentions *archai, exousiai,* and *dunameis* as enemies that Christ will defeat before handing the kingdom back to the father but does not linger over them or provide developed mythmaking about their precise identification. In Romans 8, *archai* and *dunameis* appear alongside *aggeloi* as possible obstacles to the upward ascent of Christ-believers, but in 13:1–7 Paul takes pains to insist on obeying *archai* and *exousiai* because they function as servants appointed by God for punishment and rebuke. In 1 Cor 2:8 he briefly mentions the "rulers of the present age (ἀρχόντων τοῦ αἰῶνος τούτου)," only to emphasize that they were ignorant of Christ's true identity. The figure of *satanas* appears briefly as a tempting or testing figure in a number of contexts (1 Cor 5:5, 7:5; 2 Cor 2:11, 11:14, 12:7; 1 Thess 2:18, 3:5), but though in 2 Corinthians Paul pauses to portray Beliar and Christ as antithetical (2 Cor 6:14–16), even here he does not make Beliar into an object of sustained attention.

The preceding analysis explains two difficult features of this language and argument. First, Paul's vacillating, ambiguous, and brief appeals to these figures gains coherence when understood as an outgrowth of a certain type of political imagination. Most centrally, this type of political thinking implicitly reclassifies other gods so that they are imagined as subordinates of the Jewish God. Like other traditions of polemic, Paul's extant letters exhibit little consistency when it comes to the precise names, roles, and personalities of such agents, but they quite consistently work to suppress intimations of the power, independence, and potential rivalry of these figures. As in other reclassification schemes, Paul's lesser divine agents become foils for exhibiting something about the exceptional nature of Israel's deity. To be sure, these similarities do not imply that there are strong and explicit "parallels" among the texts in question. Instead, they show that the scribes, editors, and mythmakers who produced them work with implicit common assumptions and strategies of argument.

Second, I have found that certain philosophically imbued traditions of polemic shed light on some of Paul's most curious imagery, especially in 1 Cor 8:6, where Paul describes the relationship between God, Christ, and the elect using distinctively philosophical prepositions; and in Rom 1:18–25, where he charges gentiles with misapprehending the cosmos, especially the hierarchy of power and priority within it. Though Paul's language is often brief and allusive, the polemics of Philo and Pseudo-Solomon provide a helpful context for considering Paul's intellectual practices, appropriative interests, and habits. In one sense, these polemics are suggestive insofar as they furnish evidence of other Jewish intellectuals appropriating from philosophical cosmology in ways that expand their polemical arsenals. They show that philosophical arguments about cosmology, first principles, and causality were being productively expropriated and applied to the God of Jewish ethnic tradition. In a basic way, then, some of the idolatry critiques presented in the works of Philo and Pseudo-Solomon provide a context for understanding Paul's practices, interests, and aims. In another sense, some of Paul's claims about the true nature of the cosmos, understanding, and category mistakes about the created order strongly resemble the sorts of arguments presented in the Wisdom of Solomon and in many of the treatises of Philo. Like Paul's claims about unleashing gentile passions and desires in Rom 1:24 and 26, his statements about the cosmos and the gods require robust comparison and contextualization. I am keen to avoid speculating about Paul's precise intellectual influences or contacts, but if these arguments have substantial merit, they show that certain philosophical discourses and traditions of argument were part of his intellectual repertoire, ready at hand for the kind of distinctive, creative synthesis of multiple traditions that we find in Romans 1 and elsewhere in the letters.

5 Victimization, Alienation, and Privilege Among the Christ-Elect

In the preceding chapters, I have worked to build a nuanced account of Jewish traditions about conflict in the divine world, particularly with a view to understanding the culminating violence that appears on the horizon in so much of Paul's thought. Here I shift to focus on the communities, minds, and bodies that are also central to Paul's mythmaking.[1] In a number of ways, the model of a hierarchical cosmos or *scala naturae* sets up well for just this kind of project. For one, the conceptual model of a multitiered continuum offers an alternative to some common anachronistic habits, such as conceiving of distinctions between human/divine, natural/supernatural, and self/cosmos in terms of sharply drawn, oppositional categories. Conversely, the *scala naturae* also provides an alternative to scholarly approaches that just "smash together" the human and divine worlds, as if taking down the conceptual divide between them leads inevitably to mayhem, a kind of primordial substrate out of which virtually any theology might be fashioned.[2] By imagining apocalyptic cosmology as the fluid, open-ended expression of a certain type of political thinking, we can better appreciate how this continuum might be understood as extending from the heights of heaven down to the variegated earthly world below; as encompassing a complex but differentiated social terrain that can involve people and divine beings in multiform arrangements; and as enmeshing the inner regions of the self or personality within a vast political kingdom that is conceived of as coextensive with the cosmos as a whole.[3] Indeed, one of the main contributions of this chapter is to show how Paul's letters adapt certain Greek traditions to imagine inner selves and communities as potentially unstable sites of threat, conflict, and victory.[4] Another will be to show how Paul weaves together these discourses about victimization and threat with notions of righteous persecution and election familiar from Enochic literature, Daniel 7–12, and certain Qumran texts, among others.

Self-Mastery and Platonic Victimization

Paul's letters articulate a highly influential discourse about the person, self, or personality, one in which passions, flesh, and body become sources of conflict and ongoing threat.[5] Such concerns prove especially marked in Romans 6–8 and 2 Corinthians 4–5, but they are also prominent in texts such as Rom 1:18–32, 13:14; 1 Cor 7:5, 9:27; and Gal 5:24. Though Paul develops and reappropriates these traditions in interesting ways, his thinking about passions and desires draws on a rich body of intellectual traditions. In particular, he frequently draws on Platonic analogies about victimizing passions that threaten from their "command base" in the body.[6]

Philosophical schools associated with Plato, Aristotle, Epicurus, and the Stoics make passions and emotions into central preoccupations of ethics. For all their differences, these schools share a common set of interests and goals. Not only do they agree that a central goal is to achieve human thriving or *eudaimonia*, but with the notable exception of Aristotle, they also agree that most human beings suffer and fail to thrive because of misguided beliefs and values taught to them from the cradle. They also share a kind of tempered optimism about the possibility of therapeutic remedy and ethical healing. Thus, rather than being merely speculative concerns, their ethical theories aim to provide practical remedies for the ethical afflictions that the philosophers construe as pandemic.

In the Hellenistic and Roman periods, the Stoics come to dominate specialized philosophical inquiry, but the evidence of Philo of Alexandria and Plutarch shows the enduring relevance of Platonism.[7] Plato's thought on the soul is varied and complex, but the Platonists who come after him effectively make his tripartite soul into "the Platonic position." This influential model becomes the basis for a therapeutic ethical discourse about how the best part of the soul (ideally) ought to take charge and discipline the lesser or lower parts. Because it is intrinsically hierarchical, the tripartite soul also lends itself to analogies involving political order, dominance, and submission.

The Platonic soul is a composite of three different types of motivating desire.[8] Each of these parts serves as a local command base for desires that hunger for different sorts of objects. The reasoning part inclines after wisdom (the highest good, according to this theory), and this desire for knowledge comes to motivate activities such as reasoning, thinking, and speaking. The spirited part goes after more traditional social goods such as honor, wealth, and social esteem. As a result, this part tends to produce emotions like anger, fear, and shame in response to perceived losses or hoped-for gains. A host of moral ills follows on the heels of these emotions, such as taking excessive revenge for perceived slights or acquiring wealth by unjust means. Nevertheless, the spirited part is at least amenable to discipline and can, with considerable effort, be trained to submit to the dictates of reason. In sharp contrast, the lowest, appetitive part of the soul relentlessly goes after the most base and multiform sorts of bodily pleasures.

In the ideal situation, reason subdues and rules over the lower faculties so that a person achieves full self-mastery or self-control. Even in the best possible scenario, however, the lower parts tend to chafe at their rightful master (reason), and so conflict remains the norm. The appetites are particularly dangerous because they seek transient pleasures and so tend inevitably toward excess. Left unchecked, they would storm the "citadel" of reason, and the person (as a whole body-soul complex) would become a glutton, drunkard, or some other extreme degenerate. When the appetites go undisciplined, they can effectively disable reason and motivate the person to go after unstable, misleading pleasures associated with the body. Though most cases fall in between, extreme cases of moral degeneracy are particularly important for moralizing writers like Philo, who makes frequent appeals to these types in the context of moral exhortation.

Platonic theory treats the body or flesh as dangerous precisely because of the way that the bodily senses interact with the appetites, in effect becoming their co-conspirators. In brief, appetites desire unstable pleasures, but they also rely on the bodily senses to rouse them to action by identifying external pleasures like beautiful bodies or sumptuous foods.[9] The appetites are thus doubly problematic: they desire unstable pleasures, and they also rely on the bodily senses, which can funnel to them only imperfect knowledge about the material world. For these reasons, Plato's celebrated charioteer analogy in the *Phaedrus* (253c–254e) pictures the appetitive horse as the more wild and uncontrolled of the pair. Here it is only by constant and hard reining-in that reason (the charioteer) can make the appetitive horse weak and pliable enough to do its bidding.[10] By contrast, the mind has other options; it can (uniquely, in this respect) turn inward and alienate itself from the lower faculties, from the bodily senses, and from the material world available to sight, smell, or touch. Platonists famously relate this superior intellectual kind of reasoning to an immaterial, immortal, noetic realm of being that contrasts sharply with its ontological other: the lower realm of matter, becoming, and change.

The precise relationships between the three parts of the soul and between the soul and the body are fairly complex, but Platonic writers sometimes develop simplifying binaries that pit body against soul, reason against passion, and virtue against vice. Furthermore, in thunderous exhortations about the dangers of the passions, moralists tend to construe passions and desires as stand-ins for the appetites, to imagine the appetites as a fierce opponent of the soul (rather than one of its parts), and to push the spirited faculty to the sidelines. (This last point is still basically consistent with Platonic theory, which treats the spirited part as a kind of moderate that can join forces with either reason or appetite, for good or ill.) Rather than renouncing the body as evil, however, Platonists tend to imagine the lowest of the faculties as a resilient insurrectionist, one that always threatens to conspire with the body-senses-flesh to plot overthrow and coups. However negatively writers may construe the body, flesh, pleasures, senses, and appetites in some contexts, the goal is not to destroy or be rid of the body but to discipline the lower parts with its menacing allies: bodily senses and pleasures. As Philo of Alexandria writes, "the business of wisdom is to be estranged from the body with its appetites" (*Leg.* 1.103; cf. 3.41, 81, 168). Harmony between the soul's parts thus constitutes the best-case scenario, but some level of inner conflict is normative as long as the soul remains embodied.

The Platonic divided soul blames immorality and vice on the successful rebellion of the nonrational faculties, especially the appetites. So in the *Republic,* Plato envisions the worst-case scenario as the perverse, lawless rule of appetites that rise to govern in place of reason. Here Plato introduces a range of possible types but builds a picture in book 9 of the most extreme case as the "tyrannical man" (*Rep.* 9.571a–592b). Making heavy use of military and political analogies, he imagines an evil appetitive army that storms the "citadel of the soul," enslaves and imprisons reason, and then perversely rules in reason's rightful place (esp. *Rep.* 9.572d–e). Later Platonists show relatively little interest in these sorts of extreme, limiting cases, but the specter of the ultimate degenerate becomes more prominent in the treatises of Philo of Alexandria and the Platonist medical writer Galen, especially where their interests center on ethical admonition and exhortation.

Philo warns of the perils of degeneracy in many of his writings and often evokes sharp, moralizing oppositions between virtue and vice. In this light, consider his allegorical rereading of God's warning that Adam will die if he eats from the tree of life (Gen 2:17):

> That death is of two kinds, one that of the man in general, the other that of the soul in particular. The death of the man is the separation of the soul from the body, but the death of the soul is the decay of virtue and the bringing in of wickedness (ὁ δὲ ψυχῆς θάνατος ἀρητῆς μὲν φθορά ἐστι, κακίας δὲ ἀνάληψις). It is for this reason that God says not only "die" but "die the death," indicating not the death common to us all, but that special death properly so called, which is that of the soul becoming entombed in passions and wickedness of all kinds (ὅς ἐστι ψυχῆς ἐντυμβευομένης πάθεσι καὶ κακίαις ἁπάσαις). And this death is practically the antithesis of the death which awaits us all. The latter is a separation of combatants that had been pitted against one another, body and soul, to wit (ἐκεῖνος μὲν γὰρ διάκρισίς ἐστι τῶν συγκριθέντων σώματός τε καὶ ψυχῆς). The former, on the other hand, is a meeting of the two in conflict. And in this conflict the worse, the body, overcomes, and the better, the soul, is overcome (οὗτος δὲ τοὐναντίον σύνοδος ἀμφοῖν κρατοῦντος μὲν τοῦ χείρονος σώματος κρατουμένου δὲ τοῦ κρείττονος ψυχῆς). (*Leg.* 1.105–107)[11]

At least four Platonic premises drive this allegory: that the soul is a composite of rational and irrational sources of motivation (with good and bad behavior resulting from whichever source dominates); that the passions co-conspire with the body and flesh; that in the worst case scenario, this conflict leaves mind as a tiny inner person imprisoned by passions-body-senses; and that the conflict between reason and the passions-body-senses complex, however it happens to be going at any one time, persists in the embodied soul. Philo's use of death as a metaphor for domination proves quite unusual, but it functions just like the more common political analogies that appear alongside it. The figure of the utter moral degenerate is well-represented elsewhere in Philo's treatises, whether or not it comes with language of death and dying. So death metaphors run through an excoriating attack on pleasures in *Leg.* 2.78, along with appetites pictured as a "turbulent mob" and a "vulgar herd" (see also *Post.* 73). Here and in other cases, the death language seems to derive from plays on language drawn from biblical texts.[12] Elsewhere Philo prefers more common analogies relating to warfare, exile, enslavement, and imprisonment (e.g., *Leg.* 3.116–117 and *Deus* 111–115).

The legacies of both popular and more technical or systematic forms of Platonism are also evident in the works of the second-century CE medical writer Galen. In Galen's more systematic treatises, for instance, he develops some of the finer points of Platonic tripartition (e.g., *Hippocr. et Plat.* 4.2.39–44). Here he shows some interest in the extreme case of *akolasia* (total loss of self-control), where a person is led by desire alone—"his reason following his desire like a servant (ἀκολουθοῦντος αὐτῇ τοῦ λόγου καθάπερ τινὸς οἰκέτου)."This case is noted, but it does not become a central concern. Galen's more technical interests here are also shaped by strong interschool polemics between Stoics and Platonists (e.g., *Hippocr. et Plat.* 4.2.43–4.3.14). For Galen, Stoic theories are particularly at issue because they envision a single mind or command center without the threatening, rebellious, and nonrational parts that are so basic to Platonic theory. In this connection, the Stoics also develop a very distinctive theory about the rational content of passions and emotions. In one of Galen's more popular works, *On the Passions and Errors of the Soul*, he lavishes attention on the kind of extreme case that he mentions only in passing in *On the Doctrines of Hippocrates and Plato*. Here Galen warns: "Strive to hold this most excessive (or violent) power in check before it grows and acquires unconquerable strength (ἰσχὺν δυσνίκητον). For then, even if you should want to, you will not be able to hold it in check; then you will say what I heard a certain lover say—that you wish to stop but you cannot (ἐθέλειν μὲν παύσασθαι, μὴ δύνασθαι δὲ)."[13] As with many of Philo's works, the finer points of Plato's theory fall away as Galen pursues a rather straightforward moralizing agenda: to warn of the looming threats of acute vice and abject degeneracy, here construed as the complete loss of self-control.

The Life and Death of the Soul in Romans 7–8

In the famous monologue of Rom 7:7–25, Paul creates a first-person speaker who goes on at length about an inner torment caused by sin, flesh, and the body. This speaker laments that sin "came to life" because of the law and deceived and killed "me"; associates sin with the body and flesh; and in vv. 14–25 insists some eleven times that though "I" truly understand the good and want to put this into action, "I" cannot do so because sin enslaves, makes war, imprisons, and kills "me." Taking certain originally Platonic premises seriously here explains the alienation between the speaker and sin, the speaker and the body, and the alienation of the whole person from the good generally as well as from the goodness of God's law as a particular case.[14] Understood in Platonic terms, the monologue also elaborates on the thesis spelled out in 7:5: "When we were in the flesh, the sinful passions were aroused by the law and worked in our bodily members (ὅτε γὰρ ἦμεν ἐν τῇ σαρκί, τὰ παθήματα τῶν ἁμαρτιῶν τὰ διὰ τοῦ νόμου ἐνηργεῖτο ἐν τοῖς μέλεσιν ἡμῶν) to bear fruit to death."[15] Fittingly, the speaker who emerges in v. 7 at first lingers over the claim that the law aroused sinful passions (vv. 7–13) and then shifts inward to explain this as the ingrained plight of self-contradiction (vv. 14–25). The case of mind imprisoned by the passions and the flesh also sets up for the partial remedy announced in Romans 8. For all the freedom and transformation won for those now "in Christ" in 8:1–17, the flesh still ominously threatens (esp. vv. 5–17), as it does also in Rom 6:12–23, 13:14, and Gal 5:24.

Platonic discourse about extreme moral failure illuminates Paul's claims about the passions, the body, sin, flesh, the mind, and the inner person as well as the self-contradiction that he renders normative in vv. 14–25. Traditions that portray the appetites as a rebellious horde with an evil commander make especially good sense of the role of sin throughout the monologue.[16] So the speaker identifies the passions as sinful (7:5); distinguishes sharply between sin and the law (7:7–13); imagines sin as seizing an opportunity (7:8, 7:11), inciting desires (7:8), coming to life (7:9), deceiving (7:11), killing (7:11), working death "in me" (7:13), enslaving (7:14), and dwelling "in me" (7:17, 7:20); and at the dramatic climax of the monologue explains that the "I" is made a captive by, at war with, and enslaved to the "law of sin" (7:23, 25). As noted already, Platonic writers use similar language to explain the rise of the appetitive part of the soul to rule in place of reason or mind. So Plato's appetitive king rules and enslaves (*Rep.* 8.553d–e), and this lawless ruler gets away from reason; commits all sorts of vice and immorality (*Rep.* 9.571d); leads other desires (*Rep.* 9.573a); and slays, deceives, and incites other appetites to open rebellion in a successful campaign to enslave mind (*Rep.* 9.577d–e). Similarly, Philo gives a warning, "lest the mind should, without noticing it, be made captive and enslaved (λαθὼν ὁ νοῦς αἰχμάλωτος ἀνδραποδισθεὶς)" by the wiles of pleasure (*Sacr.* 26); Plutarch personifies "vice" as stirring up the appetites so that it "awakens" (ἐπανεγείρει) depravity and wickedness (*Mor.* 101A); and Galen advises that the "the appetitive power often waxes so strong that it hurls us into love beyond all cure (ἐπιθυμητικὴν δύναμιν εἰς ἀνίατον ἔρωτα πολλάκις ἐμβαλεῖν)."[17] As with the monologue of Romans 7, these analogies, images, and personifications creatively elaborate on Platonic assumptions to imagine a true inner person alienated from the body with its evil passions and pleasures. Taking sin as a personified representation of the passions makes good sense of sin's attributes and functions in the monologue as well as the role of passions, sin, and flesh in texts such as Rom 1:18–32 and 6:12.

Platonic traditions also explain the first-person speaker as the voice of reason or mind coming to understand its own radical disempowerment.[18] So in vv. 7–13 the speaker laments that the law aroused sinful passions ("sin, finding an opportunity in the commandment, worked in me all kinds of desires" [v. 8]) and that as sin "comes to life," the speaker "dies." These statements makes good sense once the language of life and death is understood as metaphor for domination and the narrator as reason or mind, displaying its characteristic attributes: reason, reflection, judgment, and voice. From yet another angle, Platonic traditions explain why Paul develops a picture of spatial alienation between the speaker and sin, uses this alienation to explain that sin and the "I" have antithetical desires for evil and good, and then explains that mind cannot do what it really wants (whether the good generally or the law specifically) because it is actually a prisoner of sin. Consistent with this interpretation, the narrator explains its plight anew in 7:21–23: "I find it to be a law that when I want to do what is good, evil lies in wait for me; for though I delight in the law of God in my inner person (κατὰ τὸν ἔσω ἄνθρωπον), I see another law in the members of my body making war on the law of my mind (τοῦ νοός) and making me a captive to the law of sin in my bodily members." These statements describe the plight of mind overwhelmed by passions. The "law" in v. 21 conveys the "principle" that reason cannot put its good judgments into action (once again because of sin), a restatement of the dilemma described repeatedly in vv. 14–20. Likewise, in v. 23 the speaker claims that body/sin has its own "law," a play on words that evokes sin's incorrigible desires for evil.[19] In sharp contrast, the mind grasps God's good and just and holy law in v. 22 and reflects throughout the monologue on its desire to do the good.

Understood in this way, Paul uses this monologue to depict a mind that is unable to obey God's law because it is in dire moral-psychological straits. So his speaker suffers from a terrible condition that prevents the good part, the mind, from doing anything that it recognizes as good, up to and including God's law. Identifying the narrator as reason or mind also explains why the speaker identifies itself in the third person as "my mind" and "my inner person." Both mind and the inner person are good Platonic stand-ins for the reasoning faculty (e.g., Rep. 9.589a), and the speaker's alternation between first- and third-person self-identifications is also consistent with similar uses of the interior monologue.[20] Reason at once recognizes the good, God's law, and the evils of sin and also comes to understand that it is utterly powerless to put this into action because it is held as a prisoner within the sin-passions-body complex.

Certain philosophical discourses help to make sense of the imagery and argument of 7:7–25, but it is important to emphasize that Paul adapts these Platonic images and assumptions to fit with relatively traditional notions of divinity. This is especially clear in his celebrations of divine wrath in Rom 1:18, looming judgment in 2:1–11, and talk of enslavement and obedience to God in 6:12–23. So in Rom 6:16, Paul poses the rhetorical question: "Do you not understand that if you offer yourselves to anyone as obedient slaves, you are slaves to the one you obey, whether to sin with a view to death, or to obedience, with a view to righteousness?" These analogies build on conceptions of political hierarchy within and without, a point that is reinforced in vv. 22–23, which again connect slavery and submission. So Paul writes in v. 22, "But now you have been freed from sin and enslaved (δουλωθέντες) to God" and insists that this newfound submission will yield immortality (v. 23). The marriage analogies of Rom 7:1–3 work in similar ways. Here Paul evokes relationships of dominance and exclusive commitment to explore the relative status of the law and then arrives at the conclusion that the Christ-followers now "belong to another." As he explains: "Now you are free from the law, dead to that which held you down, so that you serve as slaves (δουλεύειν) in the new *pneuma* and not the old letter" (7:6; cf. 6:13–14).[21] The ideal remains submission in the form of slavery, even while the status of the Christ-followers changes in dramatic ways. Fittingly, the subsequent monologue first casts the Christ-elect as stricken with an inveterate, inner lawlessness and disobedience (7:7–25) and then announces a newfound freedom from their richly deserved death sentence (8:1–5), a solution that finally allows them to submit to the true king of heaven.

In Rom 8:1–17, Paul claims to liberate Christ-followers from the terrible plight he has just described at length in chapter 7. This solution involves a changed inner landscape, some sort of ethical rehabilitation, and new terms on which the Christ-elect are to be judged. As Rom 8:1–4 announces:

> There is therefore now no condemnation for those who are in Christ Jesus. For the law [or principle] of the *pneuma* of life in Christ Jesus has set you free from the law [or principle] of sin and of death. For God has done what the law, weakened through the flesh, could not do: by sending his own son in the likeness (ἐν ὁμοιώματι) of sinful flesh, and to deal with sin, he judged

sin in the flesh, so that the just requirement of the law (τὸ δικαίωμα τοῦ νόμου) might be fulfilled in us, who walk not according to the flesh but according to the *pneuma*.

Those "in Christ" obey a new kind of law or principle, one that is linked to the *pneuma* of Christ. Paul's claims about Christ condemning "sin in the flesh" probably allude to the idea that Christ played a central role as a "*pneuma*-bearer," as suggested by the function of *pneuma* in vv. 5–17 and elsewhere in the letters.[22] Though short on specifics, these lines emphasize God's controlling providence in sending Christ, Christ's assumption of the "form/likeness of sinful flesh," and the pivotal role of *pneuma* in rehabilitating the wayward elect.

Read as an answer to 7:7–25, Rom 8:1–4 would suggest that the *pneuma*-elect are now free from the prison of the passions, but these intimations are carefully qualified by the admonitions that follow (vv. 6–17). Though Paul envisions the *pneuma* as dramatically reorienting the person, he continues to portray the flesh as the victimizing, incorrigible seat of sin.[23] So he warns of inner struggle and ongoing conflict: "For those of the flesh reason (φρονεῦσιν) according to the flesh, but those of the *pneuma* reason according to *pneuma*. The thought of the flesh is death (τὸ γὰρ φρόνημα τῆς σαρκὸς θάνατος), but the thought of the *pneuma* (τὸ δὲ φρόνημα τοῦ πνεύματος) is life and peace. For this reason, the thought that is set on the flesh is hostile to God (τὸ φρόνημα τῆς σαρκὸς ἔχθρα εἰς θεόν); it does not submit to God's law—indeed it cannot, and those who are in the flesh cannot please God" (8:5–8). Consistent with the Platonic premise of lower versus higher parts, flesh and *pneuma* operate with distinct and antithetical motivations. A similar formulation appears in Gal 5:17–25, though here Paul describes an opposition between antithetical desires (*epithumiai*) rather than thoughts/minds (*phronēma*) as in Romans 8. Though it is not clear exactly how Paul imagines the *pneuma* as operating, he seems to conceive of a divine substance that empowers, intermingles with, and cooperates with mind so that it has a chance at winning the war within. His statements elsewhere also suggest an intimate link between human and divine reasoning, as in 1 Cor 2:10–16, where *pneuma* seems to be a mindlike substance that intermingles with human and divine minds. So Paul concludes that the authentic, mature Christ-elect in 1 Corinthians 2 "have the mind of Christ" (2:16), and in Romans 12 he urges them to be "transformed by the renewal of your minds" so as to do the will of God, here construed in ethical terms as "the good, the pleasing, and the perfect" (12:2).

The idea of an ongoing threat from the flesh proves key to Paul's construction of authentic versus inauthentic Christ-followers. In important ways, this threat also serves to qualify his claims about imminent perfection and reward in vv. 11–17. As he admonishes them: "For if the *pneuma* of the one who raised Jesus from the dead dwells inside you, then he who raised Jesus from the dead will give life to your mortal bodies also through the *pneuma* that dwells in you" (8:11). Though hopeful, such exhortations incite considerable anxiety about just how all of this will go, especially with equivocations such as "if you live in accord with the flesh, you will die; but if with the *pneuma* you put to death the deeds of the body, you will live" (8:13). The ongoing, intimate threats from the passions of the flesh thus serve to qualify (and to some extent, to destabilize) Paul's bold articulation of heavenly goals and aspirations: to submit to God and to become sons of God, even co-heirs with Christ (8:17).

Platonic Victimization in 2 Corinthians and Galatians

The image of the inner person familiar from Rom 7:22 also appears in 2 Cor 4:16, this time in a series of oppositions between the inner and the outer, the heavenly and the earthly, and perfect and imperfect bodies. The overall effect is to describe true understanding, strength, and resilience as located in an inner self, one that must struggle heroically against the body with which it is stuck. So Paul counsels:

> So we do not lose heart. Even though our outer person (ὁ ἔξω ἡμῶν ἄνθρω-πος) is wasting away, our inner person (ὁ ἔσω ἡμῶν [ἄνθρωπος]) is being renewed day by day. For this slight moment of affliction is working in us for the eternal weight of glory beyond all measure, since we look not to what is seen, but to what cannot be seen. For what is seen is temporary, but what cannot be seen is eternal. For we know that if the earthly tent we live in is destroyed, we have a building made by God, a house not made by human hands, eternal, in the heavens. (2 Cor 4:16–5:1)

The figure of the inner person derives from an influential analogy in Plato's *Republic*. In book 9, Plato represents the reasoning faculty as an inner man, the spirited part as a lion, and the appetites as a multifarious, grotesque, many-headed monster down below.[24] The figure of the inner human being—the true person within the person—captures the constraints and possibilities of the tripartite model; for all its special powers, this tiny person must rule a fractious mob of unwieldy desires while encased in a body whose senses mislead and goad the brutish, monstrous crowds on toward insurrection. Here in 2 Cor 4:16, Paul shows little interest in portraying reason's struggle for mastery over the passions, but his claims about inner versus outer persons resonate with the Platonic goal of alienating the true self from the body. Similarly, his dismissive characterizations of the visible world strongly resemble Platonic thought about the limited, imperfect world available to the bodily senses. Paul's use of these images sets up for a picture of Christ-followers as weighed down in an agonizing struggle with the body while also training their focus on the perfect, unseen, immortal realms above.[25]

As Paul continues in chapter 5, he develops these motifs but also begins to equivocate about just how the heavenly judgment may go. After evoking the earthly house that is subject to decay, he adds: "And so we groan because of this, longing to put on our heavenly home, if also having taken off [our earthly body] we are not found naked" (5:2–3). Here a perfect, immortal form awaits in heaven, one that will replace the earthly mortal "house" of the body that is subject to change and decay. Analogies relating to houses and clothing are common, but the language about nakedness and judgment seems to reflect a Platonic myth about postmortem judgments.[26] This story appears first in the *Gorgias* (523a–527a), which tells of a hoary time in the distant past when people were judged on the day of their death (and so as a complete body-soul complex) and then sent off to Tartarus or the Isles of the Blessed. After other gods intercede, Zeus agrees that too many souls are misleading their judges, whether because their handsome bodies obscure diseased souls or because they crowd the court with friendly witnesses who attest to their virtuous lives. The solution arrived at puts an end to this dissemblance. First of all, the gods make the time of death unknowable, so there can be no time to prepare a defense that might sway the judges. Second, they opt to judge the soul naked after death, once it has removed the deceptive clothing of the body and can be judged impartially (cf. Rom 2:28–29).[27]

Plutarch reproduces Plato's myth at length (*Mor.* 121A–C), but Philo riffs in interesting ways on the idea of beholding the soul's ugly, naked truth. In this light, consider the following warnings about sophistic trickery and pretensions to virtue:

> The vindicators will come strong and bold, inspired with zeal for virtue. They will strip off all this complication of wraps and bandages which the perverted art of the talkers has put together, and beholding the soul naked in her very self (γυμνὴν αὐτὴν ἐφ' αὐτῆς τὴν ψυχὴν) they will know the secrets hidden from sight in the recesses of her nature; and then exposing

to every eye in clear sunlight her shame and all her disgraces they will point the contrast between her real character, so hideous, so despicable, and the spurious comeliness which disguised in her wrappings she counterfeited. (*Mut.* 199)

Like Philo's naked truth, Paul's comments "if also having taken off [our earthly body] we are not found naked" (v. 3) and "not that we may be unclothed, but further clothed" (v. 5) seem to assume that naked souls will spell disaster in the heavenly tribunal. Thus, whereas 4:16–18 convey optimism about the heavenly future that awaits, in 5:1–5 the specter of naked souls incites some doubt about the coming judgment. Appropriately, then, Paul presents the rewards of elevation and perfection as accruing to those with the right disposition, especially with warnings such as "we all must show ourselves before the tribunal of Christ so that each person may receive back corresponding to what they have done in the body, whether good or bad" (5:10).

In 2 Cor 4:16–18, Paul treats the body as a burdensome weight that is associated not only with decay but also with imperfectly "seeing" the temporary earthly world. In significant contrast, the inner person longs to be rid of its bodily shell and can truly "see" the heavenly and eternal worlds, however dimly. Here again Paul also gives a central role to the all-important *pneuma:* "For while we are still in this tent we groan, weighed down, because of which we wish not to be unclothed but further clothed, so that the mortal may be swallowed up by life. The one who has made us for this very thing is God, the one who has given us the down-payment of the *pneuma*" (2 Cor 5:4–5). Though Paul does not explain the precise relationship between the *pneuma* and the inner person, the context suggests that the *pneuma* helps to strengthen and revive the inner, immortal part of the person that strains against the body and will survive its death. In this sense, the formulation of 2 Corinthians 4–5 may be profitably compared to other of Paul's discourses about transformation and renewal, whether or not the *pneuma* comes to the fore. So Rom 12:2 exhorts: "Do not be conformed to this age, but be transformed by the renewal of your mind (μεταμορφοῦσθε τῇ ἀνακαινώσει τοῦ νοὸς) so that you approve the will of God, what is good and acceptable and perfect (τὸ ἀγαθὸν καὶ εὐάρεστον καὶ τέλειον)."[28] Here the mind becomes the site of renewal, transformation, and alienation from "this age," perhaps like the scenario developed in Rom 8:1–17, where the *pneuma* allows true followers to win the war within and to serve God just as they ought to have done all along.

In a number of other contexts, Paul imagines Christ-followers as victimized by the incorrigible desires of their passions and flesh. So in 1 Corinthians 7, he advises married couples to have sex regularly so that *satanas* may not tempt them because of their lack of self-control (lit., "because of your *akrasia*" [7:5]).[29] As used here, the common moral-psychological term *akrasia* or habitual lack of self-mastery conveys a vulnerability to weakness and temptation.[30] Couples thus emerge as under threat from both sexual passions within and testing or tempting figures from without. In a different turn, in 1 Cor 9:24–27 Paul uses common athletic metaphors to characterize his own struggle for discipline and self-control (e.g., "an athlete exercises self-control in all things [ὁ ἀγωνιζόμενος πάντα ἐγκρατεύεται]," 9:25). Here at the climax of a long, embattled defense of his authority, Paul arrives at the analogy of athletic triumphs in which he receives an "imperishable crown" (9:25), insisting, "I pummel my body and make it a slave, lest after preaching to others I do not myself meet the test" (9:27). Once again, the body and flesh emerge as menacing threats, but here Paul claims to heroically discipline, subdue, and enslave them. Though there is little hint that Paul is a high-level intellectual, and certainly not a full-blown Platonist, he rather freely adapts and appropriates from Platonic discourses about self-mastery. In so doing, he exploits the idea of an inner political hierarchy, one that meshes rather easily with more traditional notions of a cosmic hierarchy or *scala naturae*.

Galatians 5 contains a quite elaborate discussion of victimizing passions. Though passions and desires are little discussed in the earlier chapters, here Paul introduces language about them in ways that reinforce his invectives about rival teachers and teachings that run throughout the letter.[31] First evoking a cohesive, harmonious community characterized by freedom and mutuality, Paul encourages the Christ-followers to "be servants of one another through love" (5:13). Then he goes on the attack:

> If, however, you bite and devour one another, take care that you are not consumed by one another. But I say, walk by the *pneuma*, and do not gratify the desires of the flesh (ἐπιθυμίαν σαρκὸς οὐ μὴ τελέσητε). For the desire of the flesh is opposed to the *pneuma* (ἡ γὰρ σὰρξ ἐπιθυμεῖ κατὰ τοῦ πνεύματος), and the desire of the *pneuma* is opposed to the flesh (τὸ δὲ πνεῦμα κατὰ τῆς σαρκός); for these are opposed to each other, so that you cannot do the things that you want (ταῦτα γὰρ ἀλλήλοις ἀντίκειται ἵνα μὴ ἃ ἐὰν θέλητε ταῦτα ποιῆτε). (5:15–17)

After blaming his competitors for rivalry and discord in vv. 7–12, here Paul suggestively relates this rivalry to the conflicted, potentially unstable world within. The stark oppositions drawn between the *pneuma* and flesh, each with its own desires (*epithumiai*), again play on Platonic images and assumptions. Fittingly, the subsequent verses catalogue a host of vices that run from *porneia* (harlotry) to *eidôlatria* (idolatry), with rivalry and social discord prominent among them (5:19–20). So Paul inveighs, "those who do such things will not inherit the kingdom of God" (5:21) and "those who belong to Christ have crucified the flesh with its passions and desires (τὴν σάρκα ἐσταύρωσαν σὺν τοῖς παθήμασιν καὶ ταῖς ἐπιθυμίαις)" (5:24). The analogy between Christ's heroic death and the goal of "killing" the passions of one's own flesh serves as a rhetorical climax to Paul's discourse about anxiety and threat. According to this presentation, the legitimate Christ-followers are those who successfully negotiate a panoply of threats, from passions and desires, factionalism and strife, to the malevolent influence of evil teachers who would enslave them to "old gods" (4:3–10) and to the earthly cares of their own mortal bodies (4:31). Likewise, Paul rages against rival teachers in Romans 16, charging that they serve "their own bellies" and cause dissension and discord (16:17–18), as do the alleged dogs and evil workers in Philippians 3, whose "god is the belly" (3:19). Taken together, these texts suggest significant points of continuity in Paul's thought about the "selves" of his Christ-elite, namely, that the ideal is to have an inner self that resists, subdues, and heroically alienates itself from its own passions, flesh, and body. This complex of ideas also aligns quite easily with calls for alienation from "this world" and "this age," as well as from more proximate threats posed by outsiders, competitors, and opponents of many stripes.

Heroic Obedience and Noncompetition Among the Christ-Elect

Though highly tendentious as representations of social reality, Christ-followers are rather consistently portrayed by Paul as members of a righteously alienated, victimized elect.[32] Indeed, one of Paul's organizing conceits is that his audiences are (or ought to be) highly integrated gatherings of like-minded "saints." To this end, he works to set off these alleged communities from varied classes of outsiders, whether it is the "crooked and perverse generation" (Phil 2:15), the wily tempter *satanas*, self-serving and insincere teachers, or the Christ-followers' own fleshly passions. In

1 Thessalonians 1–2, he imagines interrelated groups of believers who, though separated by geography, nevertheless share the same commitments, gifts of *pneuma*, and experiences of persecution (1:6–9, 2:14–20). In much more elaborate ways, he also idealizes the unity and harmony of the Christ-elect in 1 Corinthians by building images of a single corporate community united in its worship of a single God and sharing a single spirit, mind, and body (e.g., 1 Cor 2:16, 10:17, 12:22–27). This unified ideal provides the basis for an extended critique in 1 Corinthians 1–4 of factionalism, selfishness, and division, the principle source of which is immature "fleshly" knowledge. The claim that some possess a true heavenly *pneuma* also becomes prominent here, as it comes to distinguish those with legitimate knowledge (here conceived of as having a superior, divine, and secret wisdom, e.g., 2:6–7) from the "fleshly persons," that is, those creatures of this world that are given to selfishness (ζῆλος), strife (ἔρις), and "human conduct" (3:1–3).[33] As a seemingly necessary consequence, Paul goes on to insist that the heavenly *pneuma* enables a new kind of morality organized around the good of the social whole.

These issues loom large elsewhere in the letters, but in Philippians 1–3 Paul presents numerous exhortations about obedience, unity, and mutual concern. Chapter 3 of this book treats the much-discussed "Christ hymn" of Phil 2:6–11, but here I turn to somewhat broader issues with unity, concord, and mutual up-building that run throughout the letter. In Philippians 1, Paul urges Christ-followers to understand themselves as a single, united group: "Stand fast with one *pneuma*, struggling together as one soul (μιᾷ ψυχῇ συναθλοῦντες) with the faithfulness of the gospel and not being disturbed by anything from your opponents (μὴ πτυρόμενοι ἐν μηδενὶ ὑπὸ τῶν ἀντικειμένων). For them this is evidence of their destruction, for you, salvation" (1:27–28). These claims about a single *pneuma*, soul, and gospel build a picture of a unified social body with a single, self-consistent purpose. Further, the contrast with opponents destined for destruction works to portray this privileged elect as hemmed in by malevolent threats from outside. In this case, Paul even goes so far as to construe persecution as a divine gift: "For it has been given to you as a gift that you not only faithfully obey but also suffer on behalf of Christ (τὸ εἰς αὐτὸν πιστεύειν ἀλλὰ καὶ τὸ ὑπὲρ αὐτοῦ πάσχειν), since you have the same struggle (τὸν αὐτὸν ἀγῶνα) that you saw and now hear to be mine" (1:29–30; cf. 3:10).[34] Here Paul conjures an image of suffering obediently "on behalf of Christ" and then strategically relates this to the hardships he claims as his own. The rather abstract, nonspecific language about suffering proves key here precisely because it allows him to create a picture of a single shared experience of victimization, heroic endurance, and obedience.

This picture of a vulnerable but tightly bound community proves foundational for the warnings about discord and dissent that follow in Philippians 2 and 3. So Paul admonishes: "Do nothing from selfishness or conceit (μηδὲν κατ᾽ ἐριθείαν μηδὲ κατὰ κενοδοξίαν), but with humility consider one another as better than yourselves (ἀλλὰ τῇ ταπεινοφροσύνῃ ἀλλήλους ἡγούμενοι[35] ὑπερέχοντας ἑαυτῶν); let each of you concern yourselves not with your own interests but with those of others (μὴ τὰ ἑαυτῶν ἕκαστος σκοποῦντες ἀλλὰ καὶ τὰ ἑτέρων ἕκαστοι). Let there be this same frame of mind among you that there was also for Christ Jesus" (2:3–5). Here negatively charged traits such as conceit (*kenodoxia;* cf. Gal 5:26) and selfish ambition (*eritheia*) contrast sharply with humble self-regard, solidarity, and mutuality. As becomes clear in v. 4, Paul conceives of social virtues and vices as pivoting around self and other-directed interests. In v. 5, he again calls for unity but now in terms of thinking or sharing a common understanding, a motif that sets up nicely for the infamous Christ hymn that follows. The precise translation of 2:6 remains controversial, but vv. 6–11 as a whole tell of how Christ obediently accepted his station, dutifully lowered himself to the human realm, remained there obedient to the point of death, and then ascended upward to become the one before whom "every knee should bow in the heavens and on the earth and under the earth" (2:10). It is perhaps telling that Paul does not draw connections here between Christ's upward ascent and the elect's aspirations of heavenly reward, as he does, for instance, in Philippians 3 (3:20–21) and at a number of points in 1 Corinthians (e.g., 4:8; 6:3; 15:23, 51). Instead, he prefers to use this as an occasion for enjoining submission and obedience, which comes out clearly in the admonitions that follow: "Therefore, my beloved, just as you have always been obedient so also now, not only in my presence but even more in my absence, with fearfulness and trembling, work toward your salvation (μετὰ φόβου καὶ τρόμου τὴν ἑαυτῶν σωτηρίαν κατεργάζεσθε)" (2:12). In this context, Paul's Christ myth serves to reinforce a particular set of identifications and obligations: the Philippians must at once submit to one another, God and Christ, and their servant Paul.

To give only one further example, consider Paul's attacks on rival teachers, who also appear in Philippians 2 and 3. After celebrating his own leadership in 2:12–18, Paul returns to an anxious imaginary by raising the specter of illegitimate apostles. Beginning in 2:19, he praises Timothy and Epaphroditus but then warns of pernicious, insincere teachers who disguise themselves as Christ-workers but in reality are "looking out for their own interests (οἱ πάντες γὰρ τὰ ἑαυτῶν ζητοῦσιν), not those of Christ" (2:21; cf. Phil 3:2 and Rom 16:17–18). Self-seeking and rivalry thus come to characterize rival teachers. By contrast, Paul constructs a singular focus on the divine will, self-sacrifice, and struggle on behalf of others as the hallmarks of sincerity and authenticity. As with other menaces, these evil teachers are key to Paul's construction of an embattled but divinely empowered Christ-elect bound by an ethics of mutuality and love.

In the extended ethical discourses of Romans 12–15, the ideal of solidarity often appears as a pole star that orients ethical choices, a guiding principle from which many and varied practical lessons are to be derived. These chapters do not present a formal or systematic presentation of ethics, but they consistently return to the issues of mutual up-building and care for others. As Troels Engberg-Pedersen and Runar M. Thorsteinsson have shown, Stoic traditions provide an illuminating context for understanding many aspects of these teachings, particularly Paul's focus on the good of others, adaptability and love, and issues of mind and rationality.[36] Understood in this way, Paul adapts distinctive myths about God, Christ, and the Christ-elect to fit with well-known ethical traditions that are of an identifiably Stoic provenance.[37] Though the victimizing Platonic passions help with other areas of Paul's thought, comparisons with Stoic sources show that he draws quite freely on multiple traditions and discourses.[38] These patterns suggest that Paul adapts fairly high-level intellectual traditions without regard for systems of thought, boundaries, or interschool polemics.

In contrast to Plato's embattled, tripartite soul, the Stoics argue that the soul is singular, unified, and rational through and through. They also develop a very distinctive account of passions and emotions. Rather than all bad emotions being innate, incorrigible appetites, they argue that such emotions are simply failures, mistakes, or improper applications of the soul's reasoning capacities. On this basis, they argue that moral education can and should bring about the complete extirpation of bad emotions like anger, fear, and shame. Though often misrepresented by rivals and detractors, the goal of extirpation is to allow for the consistent, stable experience of good emotions, which is achieved when the mind perfects its innate rationality. The Stoic ideal of extirpating all bad emotions also comes as part of a larger program that aims to achieve a transformative ethical reorientation. According to this theory, the life of reason and virtue arrives together with a moral-intellectual realization that one's own self-interest harmonizes with that of humankind as a whole (e.g., Seneca, *Ep.* 95.51–53; Epictetus, *Disc.* 2.10.4–5). The basic theory of moral development (*oikeiôsis*) runs as follows: set in perfect sociopolitical environments, all human beings would naturally realize their innate rational potential, outgrow their self-directed goals—the natural but immature habits learned from infancy to early adulthood—and mature into fully wise sages (Cicero, *Fin.* 3.62–64; Seneca, *Ep.* 76, 121.14–24, 124.8–24; Diogenes Laertius, *Lives* 7.85–87). As ethical superhumans, they would be free from the destructive influence of bad emotions and would fully appreciate that the highest good is the good of the whole human race, a singular commitment that should organize all ethical choices. In practice, however, most fail to realize their inborn potential. Among other problems, they are stunted by social environments that teach them mistaken beliefs and values. To compound matters, during infancy they also develop self-directed attachments to goods such as protection and nourishment. Though natural for a tiny infant, these moral habits tend to become very ingrained and so fuel the fires of ethical delusion.[39] As a result, human beings generally fail to thrive as nature intended, but with great effort, and the appropriate Stoic teachings, they can hope to undo the damage.

The Stoic theory of moral development remains fairly consistent through the early, middle, and late Stoa, though later writers emphasize practical teachings and moral progress as ways of avoiding charges of ethical idealism.[40] In general, writers agree that the goal of moral education is to bring about an ethical transformation—a kind of rational revelation—in which a person rejects his or her old way of organizing ethical choices. In one sense, this also reflects the maxim that virtue is the only true good, though by "virtue" Stoics mean a life lived in accord with right reason—the rationality that structures all human beings, the universe, and everything in it. Ideally, this singular good will come to organize all motivations so that the person will become flawlessly rational and consistently moral, adapting to whatever the precise situation demands. This goal can also be described as acting in accord with the rational design of the universe, nature, Zeus, *logos,* and God. In another sense, because right reason leads inevitably to a revelation about the harmony between one's own needs and the needs of others, Stoic writers develop rich discourses about mutuality, friendship, adaptability, and love for all humankind. As Arius Didymus summarizes:

"A man who benefits someone also benefits himself, and one who does harm also harms himself" (*SVF* 3.626 = LS 60P).[41] Indeed, since true self-interest turns out to be other-directed, the mature person will choose the course of action that will best serve others in their midst, and ultimately, all humankind.[42] So Seneca writes, "You must live for your neighbor, if you would live for oneself" (*Ep.* 48.3) and "a sage considers nothing more truly his own than that which he shares in partnership with mankind" (*Ep.* 73.7; cf. 85.36).[43] This idea, that what is good for "me" is actually what is good for all humanity, thus becomes axiomatic within Stoic ethics, and writers frequently emphasize the obligation to care for and love others, up to and including one's enemies and abusers.[44]

Moral exhortations about the interests of others, mutual up-building, and adaptability run through many of Paul's letters, but in Romans 12–15 they are linked together with strong claims about moral maturity, rational worship, and transformations of mind. So at the beginning of chapter 12, Paul urges, "Offer your bodies as a living sacrifice, holy and pleasing to God, which is your rational worship (λογικὴν λατρείαν)" (12:1). Instead of sacrifice involving dead bodies on an altar, here he seems to recast sacrifice as a new way of life, one that comes to entail certain commitments to the deity, a new sort of community, and a distinctive set of moral obligations. These obligations have strong parallels with Stoic thought, and as Thorsteinsson shows, Paul's specific language about sacrifice and "rational worship (λογικὴν λατρείαν)" echoes Stoic reinterpretations of traditional religious practices.[45] A number of Stoic writers use similar language to depict the ideal of life according to nature/right reason as in itself an act of worship, sacrifice, and/or imitation of the deity (e.g., Epictetus, *Disc.* 1.16.20–21, 3.26.29–30; Seneca, *Ep.* 115.5). Paul does not seem to share this broader cosmology, but he seems to adapt distinctively Stoic language to articulate an intellectual kind of religious practice, one that is focused on habits of mind, inner commitments and loyalties, and knowledge or rationality in some form.

Issues of transformed minds and rational capacities also become prominent in the verses that follow. So Paul urges, "therefore do not be conformed to this world but be transformed by the renewal of your minds (τῇ ἀνακαινώσει τοῦ νοὸς) so that you may understand the will of God, what is good and acceptable and perfect" (12:2).[46] Paul's language about "this world" could conceivably carry some darkly apocalyptic sense, but read in context, this mainly serves to circumscribe the elect by portraying them as alienated but empowered, set apart, changed, and transformed by a "renewal" of their minds. Thus changed, they are now capable both of grasping and of putting into practice that otherwise elusive divine intent (cf. Rom 7:7–25). The subsequent verses continue to play on notions of knowledge and understanding, and they also expand the sphere of obligation: "Everyone among you should not consider yourself more highly than you ought to consider yourself but to think with proper moderation, each according to the measure of faith that God has assigned (ἐν ὑμῖν μὴ ὑπερφρονεῖν παρ᾽ ὃ δεῖ φρονεῖν ἀλλὰ φρονεῖν εἰς τὸ σωφρονεῖν, ἑκάστῳ ὡς ὁ θεὸς ἐμέρισεν μέτρον πίστεως)" (12:3–4).[47] Like the language about rational worship and transformed minds, Paul's claims about "rational judgment (εἰς τὸ σωφρονεῖν)" in 12:3 make reason into a central pivot of ethical action, and his use of multiple φρονη- roots in v. 3 (ὑπερφρονεῖν, φρονεῖν, and σωφρονεῖν) plays on issues of right-mindedness, prudence, and self-mastery.[48] Though issues of mind and rationality are central here, Paul connects this complex of ideas with faithfullness/loyalty—something that he seems to conceive of as doled out to each person by God.

Stoic preoccupations with love and adaptability also shed light on a number of Paul's arguments in Romans 12 and 14. For instance, Epictetus (*Disc.* 2.22) argues that right reason allows us to fully love others because it leads us to understand our solidarity with all humankind, and Seneca defends Stoic ethics against accusations of harshness by claiming, "no school is more kindly and gentle, none more full of love of man (*amantior hominum*) and more concerned for the common good (*communis boni*), so that it is its avowed object to be of service and assistance, and to regard not merely self interest, but the interests of each and all" (*Clem.* 2.5.3–4). The links drawn here between love, adaptability, and service to others fit well with Paul's moral advice in a number of contexts. For instance, in Romans 12 Paul urges nonretaliation as an ethical principle (12:14, 17–21) and encourages adaptability to the needs of others with exhortations such as "rejoice with those who rejoice, weep with those who weep" (12:2) and "think of one another as the same, do not think of yourselves as better but associate with the lowly; do not claim to be wiser than you are" (12:16).[49] Most of his moral advice is directed at insiders, but he also urges, "if possible, insofar as it depends on you, live peaceably with all mankind" (12:18). In Romans 14, Paul counsels the mature to tolerate the diverse views of others, whether about eating certain foods or treating some days as having special significance. These arguments pivot around two main points: first, that a person's particular beliefs and practices relating to food and "days" are matters of in-difference; and second, that the good of others must always be kept in view. Furthermore, these arguments about "the strong" and "the weak" require that the weak can and should be helped along toward greater strength and understanding, principally by the strong.[50] Ultimately, then, his ideal Christ community is to be a distinct, harmonious social arrangement in which all moral actions aim at mutual up-building and care for others.

At a number of points in Romans 12–15, Paul adapts Stoic moral teach-ings, but he also weaves them together with distinctively non-Stoic ideas about divine judgment and election. So Paul warns against criticism and judgment in chapter 14, in part by noting that it is God who will be the ultimate arbiter and judge (14:4, 10–12) and in part by elevating the sta-tus of the Christ-elect, those whom "God has welcomed" (14:4). Though clearly special and elevated above others, from another angle they are also enslaved to God. This comes out clearly as Paul imagines them as servants of a single master and urges, "Do not pass judgment on the servant of another" (14:4; cf. Rom 6:15–22). In other contexts, Paul alludes to Christ's role in establishing this new and special kind of elect as he warns, "Do not let what you eat cause the ruin of one for whom Christ died" (14:10). Thus dignified and elevated, however, the Christ-elect often become the objects of distinctively Stoic teachings. So in Romans 14 he insists, "Let us then pursue what makes for peace and for the up-building of one another (τὰ τῆς οἰκοδομῆς τῆς εἰς ἀλλήλους)" (14:19), and in Romans 15, "We who are strong ought to put up with the failings of the weak, and not to please ourselves" (15:1). Remarkably, in Romans 15 Paul goes on to draw a parallel with Christ, who "did not please himself" (15:3). Understood in this way, Paul uses the indifferent status of eating or keeping certain "days" to argue for an ethics of love and solidarity that aims at up-building, moral progress, and the improvement of others, particularly "the weak." Fittingly, this long ethical discourse then concludes by identifying these core principles with the supreme deity: "May the God of endurance and up-building (ὁ δὲ θεὸς τῆς ὑπομονῆς καὶ τῆς παρακλήσεως) grant you to think in the same way among yourselves (τὸ αὐτὸ φρονεῖν ἐν ἀλλήλοις), in accord with Christ, that together with one soul (ὁμοθυμαδὸν) and one mouth glorify the God and father of our lord Jesus Christ" (15:5–6).[51] Paul's imagined community is to engage in a single, organizing practice, one with moral ideals that are embodied by God and enabled by Christ.

Paul's basic teachings about mutual love, respect, and concern for others are not radically different from those found among writers such as Seneca and Epictetus (e.g., Seneca, *Clem.* 1.11.2, *Ira* 1.5.2–3, *Ep.* 5.4; Epictetus, *Disc.* 4.10.12–13), but there are also clear points of divergence and difference, particularly in the scope of their moral concern. Consider, for instance, Paul's use of body analogies in Rom 12:4–5, where he creates an idealized picture of Christ-followers as knit together into a harmonious community, like diverse members of a single Christ body. As is well-known, a wide range of Greek and Roman writers use such analogies to explore social and political relationships, typically to encourage a picture of a natural, necessary, but complementary hierarchy.[52] Many Stoics use body motifs, however, to quite different ends. For instance, Epictetus argues that if the hand and the foot were endowed with reason (*logismos*), they would never choose anything but the good of the whole (*Disc.* 2.10.4). In this case, the body analogy does not serve to exemplify a hierarchy of types and functions. Instead, Epictetus insists that were the parts endowed with the reasoning capacities that the mind has, the hand or foot would be fundamentally transformed in its ethical orientation and so arrive at a new appreciation of the good. To similar ends, Seneca appeals to body and architecture analogies to explore the natural accord of all humankind:

> I can lay down for mankind a rule, in short compass, for our duties in human relationships: all that you behold, that which comprises both god and man, is one—we are the parts of one great body. Nature produced us related to one another, since she created us from the same source and to the same end. She engendered in us mutual affection, and made us prone to friendships. She established fairness and justice; according to her ruling, it is more wretched to commit than suffer injury. Through her orders, let our hands be ready for all that needs to be helped. Let this verse be in you heart and on your lips: "I am a man; and nothing in man's lot do I deem foreign to me" [Terence, *Haut.* 77]. Let us possess things in common; for birth is ours in common. Our relations with one another are like a stone arch, which would collapse if the stones did not mutually support each other, and which is upheld in this very way. (*Ep.* 95.51–53)[53]

The models of the body and the arch serve to exemplify Stoic theory, particularly about the human dispositions toward friendliness and mutual aid. Seneca's strongly cosmopolitan arguments here also reflect a particular theory about the interplay between cosmology and ethics, one that is notably absent from Romans 12 and from the more extended body analogy found in 1 Cor 12:12–31. Unlike the examples drawn from Epictetus and Seneca, the body analogy in Romans 12 creates a picture of different parts or components that each have different functions, though they share one body and an organizing purpose. Despite these differences, the analogy fits relatively easily with Paul's broader arguments about mutuality and care for others, at least for the privileged few who make up his imagined elect.

Whereas Seneca enjoins "nature begot me loving all people" (*Ep.* 102.8) and "no one can live happily who has regard for himself alone and transforms everything into questions of his own utility" (*Ep.* 28.2), Paul typically limits the sphere of ethical concern to other Christ-followers.[54] In some cases he conceives of this elect as set off against the wayward, evil, outside world, but in others, outsiders appear on the scene in less bleak, negatively charged ways. For instance, in Philippians Paul often returns to images of a community under siege, but in Romans 12–15 he is more characteristically indifferent. So in Romans 12 we find rather passing comments about not being conformed to "this world" (12:2), general ethical maxims that seem cosmopolitan in scope (e.g., 12:13, 20; cf. 13:10), and in at least one case, some explicit advice about dealings with the outside world: "If possible, insofar as it depends on you, live peaceably with all mankind" (12:18). Romans 13 also contains a remarkable argument to the effect that all the world's political institutions serve the will of heaven. On this basis, Paul urges submission to all rulers and authorities (13:1–7) but then telescopes to focus on his Christ-elite, who are living on the cusp of a new age (13:11–14). Though clearly set apart, in this case the elect are portrayed as having a largely indifferent relationship to the outside world.

Suffering, Victimization, and Conflict on the Apocalyptic Horizon

Philosophical traditions are important for understanding many aspects of Paul's language and argument. Understood in context, these philosophical discourses often serve to reinforce and amplify relatively well-worn ideological claims, particularly surrounding issues of authority and election. To give only a few salient examples for comparison, consider how the writer of the Book of the Watchers develops images of a favored, elect people that are aligned with the will of heaven. In the prologue, the writer/editor predicts a time of cataclysm when the supreme God will descend from on high: "The earth will be wholly rent asunder, and everything on the earth shall perish, and there will be judgment on all. With the righteous he will make peace, and over the chosen there will be protection, and upon them there will be mercy" (1 En. 1:7–8). This myth of divine descent plays on the model of a *scala naturae,* a closed, finite cosmos of different realms, substances, and types of being. In this case, the hierarchy extends from the heavens down into the earthly domains to justify the very different ranks, values, and destinies of people below. In ideological terms, the writer/editor represents an all-encompassing world taxonomy as if it is just natural, universal, and inevitable. As the Book of the Watchers continues, this taxonomy comes to underwrite a tale of victimization and violence, one that carefully circumscribes an elect and imbues them with exceptional value, relationships, and identifications. Similar patterns inform the Animal Apocalypse, which tells a tale of degeneracy in which the "sheep" of Israel become blind. Eventually, however, a small, ignored, and persecuted elect emerge as "lambs" born with eyes open (1 En. 90:6). This elect plays a starring role when the supreme powers of heaven intervene to vindicate and elevate them; among other rewards, they win immortality and are worshipped by the gentile nations (cf. Dan 7:14). Playing on this same basic strategy, the writer/editor of the Epistle of Enoch labors over images of the righteous suffering at the hands of the wicked but also promises them vindication and protection. So they predict:

> And the Most High will be aroused on that day
>> to execute great judgment on all.
> He will set a guard of the holy angels over all the righteous and holy;
>> and they will be kept as the apple of the eye
>> until evil and sin come to an end. (100:4–5)

The writer here plays on a hierarchical model of the cosmic political order, like the theophany that opens the Book of the Watchers, to imagine an elect with unique access to the supreme powers above. In important ways, these tales of cosmic woe and restoration set up for the construction of a victimized, alienated people that are already (or are soon to be) transformed into a righteous superhuman elite. Implicitly and explicitly, they are also portrayed as having access to the providential plan for world history and, above all, as having unique ties to the upper ranks of divine power.

Similar conceptions of a victimized but righteous remnant are also central to 1QS, 1QM, and Daniel 11–12, among other literature. In 1QM, for instance, the writer/editor draws sharp distinctions between the righteous and the wicked, the princes of light versus darkness, and the spirits of truth versus wickedness. Though seemingly absolute, categorical opposites, these binaries inexorably resolve into more complex, hierarchical schemas that distinguish the favored righteous as an alienated but highly privileged elite, allied with the true powers above. To this end, the writer portrays the righteous as tested in a great battle. Because the outcome of this struggle is preordained, however, the elect fight a battle for a victory already won. In a different way, the wise *maśkîlîm* play a pivotal role in Daniel 11, where they serve as an elite force of teachers who stand firm during a period of crisis. So the writer predicts: "The wise among the people will instruct the common people, but they will fall by sword and flame . . . some of the wise will fall, to refine and purify and make them white until the time of the end for it is still at the appointed time" (11:33–35).[55] While "some of the wise" are killed, their deaths seem to serve a purifying or testing function. Similar images of violence appear in Daniel 12: "Many will be purified and made white and refined and the wicked will act wickedly. All the wicked will not understand, but the wise will understand" (12:10–12). The writer offers assurance that this religious-intellectual elite, set apart from the wicked and from the nonwise, will "shine like the stars forever" (12:3). This singles out a rather circumscribed group of teachers or scribes from the broader category of elect Israel. Nevertheless, the writer works with premises about victimization, vindication, and proximity to the divine (and knowledge about the divine plan) that are consistent with those found in other literature.

Visions of a victimized, alienated elect abound in apocalyptic literature, but Paul develops these ideas in interesting ways. In Paul's hands, the elect are described as being under threat from explicit acts of violence as well as from various social pressures, tensions, and conflicts that menace from inside and outside their bodies. For instance, Paul describes his own heroic endurance in 1 Thessalonians 2 in ways that play on moralizing tropes about self-control and frank speech: "Though we had already suffered and been shamefully treated (προπαθόντες καὶ ὑβρισθέντες) at Philippi, as you know, we dared to speak frankly (ἐπαρρησιασάμεθα) in our God to convey to you the gospel of God amidst a great struggle (ἐν πολλῷ ἀγῶνι)" (2:2). These statements play on common discourses about enduring hardships and daring to "speak frankly," and as it does also for the moralists, these images of heroic endurance help to create and reproduce Paul's authoritative position.[56] In the subsequent verses, he amplifies concerns about struggle and threat: "For you suffered the same things (τὰ αὐτὰ ἐπάθετε) from your own compatriots as they did from the Judeans, who killed both the lord Jesus and the prophets, and drove us out; they displease God and oppose all mankind (πᾶσιν ἀνθρώποις ἐναντίων) by hindering us from speaking to the gentiles so that they may be saved, in order to fill up the measure of their sins, as always" (2:14–16). Here the elect are portrayed as a single, transcontinental body that shares a common plight. Though hemmed in by the complex, threatening, and wayward world around them, a singular elect heroically struggles against persecution, social pressure, and opposition to form an elite of like-minded, highly agreeable superhumans (cf. 2 Cor 4:9–11, Phil 2:29–30).[57] The conceit of a single community, a serenely unified, integrated, and tightly bounded social whole, proves central to Paul's rhetorical strategy; indeed, it operates as something of an ideological "river" toward which many of his arguments flow.

Elsewhere in his letters, Paul alludes to concrete acts of persecution (as Phil 2:17, 3:10; 1 Thess 3:3; cf. Rom 8:36), but in a number of other cases he prefers to make much more abstract and nonspecific comments about suffering. So Philippians 3 contains an infamous description of Paul's own self-transformation that includes a powerful analogy with the suffering of Christ. Here he explains that though he was formerly accustomed to place a high value on his Hebrew lineage and on keeping the law, he came to understand these as "rubbish" compared with the ultimate good of "knowing Christ" (3:7–11). This new orientation comes to include suffering of some kind, for he now aims "to know him and the power of his resurrection and the sharing of his sufferings (κοινωνίαν παθημάτων) by becoming like him in his death (συμμορφιζόμενος τῷ θανάτῳ αὐτοῦ), so that I might also attain resurrection from the dead" (3:10–11).[58] It is difficult to say precisely what is meant by "sharing his sufferings" and "becoming like him in his death." It seems likely that Paul means to cast his work as a form of agonizing but righteous suffering that has some analogy with Christ's obedience, rejection, and persecution (cf. Gal 6:17), a view that may help to explain his adaptation of so-called hardship catalogues in other contexts. Nevertheless, these comments appear briefly and with little explanation. Elsewhere in the letters, Paul also suggests that enduring hardships is a more general condition for election and reward. In Romans 5, he draws on common moral metaphors about enduring distress as proof of character. Though he offers few specifics about precisely what is to be endured, he insists: "We boast in our hope of sharing the glory of God. And not only that, but we also boast in our distress (θλίψεσιν), knowing that distress produces endurance (ὑπομονὴν), and endurance character (δοκιμήν), and character produces hope (ἐλπίδα), and hope does not put us to shame, because God's love has been poured into our hearts through the divine *pneuma*" (5:2–5).[59] Similarly, Rom 8:17–18 evokes a larger scheme of heavenly power in which the *pneuma*-elect become children of God: "And if children, then heirs, heirs of God and fellow heirs with Christ, if in fact we suffer with him (συμπάσχομεν) so that we may also be glorified with him (ἵνα καὶ συνδοξασθῶμεν). I consider that the sufferings of this present time (τὰ παθήματα τοῦ νῦν καιροῦ) are not worth comparing with the glory about to be revealed to us." Though nonspecific and allusive, the "if in fact we suffer with him" clause could include a struggle to defeat the passions, especially because these concerns predominate in Romans 6–8. This suffering could also encompass a host of other social conflicts and pressures, but if so, they are not specified here. Instead, Paul passes over suffering or struggle very quickly and soon arrives at a highly simplified scheme that links together righteous alienation, empowerment, submission, and reward.

Paul's basic notions of election and victimization prove relatively traditional, but he incites very distinctive anxieties about passions that still threaten from within. His adaptation of Greek traditions thus serves to introduce a quite important sphere of interest and anxiety that centers on the hidden inner regions of the person. In this light, consider the way that Romans 13 weaves together the promise of imminent rescue with ongoing anxieties about the passions.[60] Arguing that love should serve as a unifying ethical principle, Paul urges:

> Besides this, you know what time it is, how it is now the time for you to wake from sleep. For salvation is nearer to us now than when we became believers; the night is far gone, the day is near. Let us then cast off the works of darkness and clothe ourselves with the armor of light; let us live honorably as in the day, not in reveling and drunkenness, not in debauchery and licentiousness, not in quarreling and jealousy. Instead, clothe yourselves with the lord Jesus Christ, and make no provision for the flesh, to gratify its desires (ἐνδύσασθε τὸν κύριον Ἰησοῦν Χριστὸν καὶ τῆς σαρκὸς πρόνοιαν μὴ ποιεῖσθε εἰς ἐπιθυμίας). (13:11–14; cf. 1 Thess 5:8–15)

The oppositions between day/night, sober/drunk, and awake/asleep work to solidify group identifications with states and dispositions that Paul construes as positive. These exhortations also organize a range of anxieties and aspirations along a singular ideological axis: empowered, heroic submission to God and to God's servants, Christ and Paul. His warnings about fractious rivalry and infighting are familiar (and distinctively Stoic), but here they blend seamlessly into a discourse about self-control. So the Christ-followers should "put on" Christ as a kind of moral-intellectual armor that will empower them to resist the passions and the social discord that follows from them, among countless other vices.⁶¹ In this way, Paul gives pride of place to an intimate, inner conflict with the passions. The result is a distinctive sphere of interest, anxiety, and instability, a new sort of territory for articulating issues of morality, conviction, struggle, and threat. As in many other cases, Paul uses these hidden, inner reaches of the person in ways that at once incite and resolve anxieties about the passions. Little about these discussions is entirely novel, but these anxious selves and communities will prove to be one of the most enduring legacies of Pauline thought.

In Romans 14, Paul again ties together his vision of the grand cosmopolitical drama with a more intimate, local discourse about ethics. Here he again raises the issue of self-interest and urges the imagined audience to defer judgments to the supreme deity:

> We do not live to ourselves (ἑαυτῷ), and we do not die to ourselves (ἑαυτῷ). If we live, we live to the Lord, and if we die, we die to the Lord; so then, whether we live or whether we die, we are the Lord's. For this Christ died and lived, so that he might rule over (κυριεύσῃ) both the dead and the living. Why do you judge your brother? Or why do you hate your brother? For we will all stand before the judgment seat of God. For it is written, "As I live, says the Lord, every knee shall bow to me, and every tongue shall give praise to God." ⁶² So then, each of us shall give an account of his own (περὶ ἑαυτοῦ λόγον δώσει) to God. (14:7–12)

Here Paul imagines Christ as lord over both the living and dead, evokes an impending divine judgment, and construes this judgment as a time of absolute submission, when all will be brought to their knees before God. In this context, however, a fundamentally hierarchical taxonomy of power and privilege works to reinforce claims about ethical solidarity, love, and concern for others. The result is an otherworldly justification for a distinctively this-worldly morality, one that centers on mutuality, solidarity, and shared interests.

Finally, it is important to stress that Paul's simplistic idealizations of community and his ethics of love and mutuality quite consistently work to legitimize his right to teach, speak, write, advise, contest, rebuke, and accept money or refuse it.⁶³ In this light, notice how his claims about the Christ-elect vacillate between calls to realize his vision of an ideal community and exhortations that incite anxiety about just what will happen when the new age finally dawns. In Galatians 5, for instance, Paul builds a catalogue of virtues and vices, only to conclude, "I am warning you, as I warned you before: those who do such things will not inherit the kingdom of God" (5:21; similarly, 1 Cor 6:9–11). Likewise, in 1 Thessalonians Paul reflects on his own toil among the "saints," which he describes as "encouraging and imploring that you walk in ways that are worthy of God, who calls you to his own kingdom and glory" (2:12). In these contexts, the imminent horizon of reward offers a kind of integrated, panoramic vision of reality that furthers his characterizations of the elect and that implicitly reproduces his authoritative status as an interpreter of divine secrets. An especially powerful image appears in Philippians 1 where Paul adapts priestly imagery to imagine presenting the Philippians as a spotless, pure, and blameless offering on the "day of Jesus Christ" (1:6, 10; 2:14–15; cf. Rom 15:16 and 2 Cor 1:13).[64] The Christ-followers are thus portrayed as communities of elite, perfectly unified, moral superhumans who have unique access to the intentions, power, and protection of the supreme (but largely unrecognized) world ruler. At the same time, Paul now becomes the priest who delivers them, whole, pristine, and perfect to the high God looming over all.

Conclusion

I have argued that Paul's letters adapt Greek traditions about inner conflict and ethical solidarity to construct a Christ-elect with distinctive plights and privileges. Though Greek moral traditions prove illuminating for certain features of the letters, Paul consistently organizes these interests and anxieties around rather traditional notions of divine rule, election, and righteous victimization. In fact, one of the most remarkable aspects of Paul's letters is that they greatly expand the discourse of victimization that is also featured in much other literature. His Christ-followers thus frequently appear as embattled and beset by threat, whether from the passions and the flesh, the wiles of *satanas,* inauthentic teachers, or their own penchants for conflict, factionalism, and indulgence of the dissolute. Likewise, he portrays the chosen as an alienated, victimized elite who have been empowered by *pneuma* but must still struggle mightily to master their own passions, maintain unity, and submit to the supreme deity through Christ. Their alienation from the temporary, earthly, and evil ways of others emerges as a seemingly necessary corollary to their elite status in the broader cosmo-political drama, as does their implicit acceptance of Paul as a masterful interpreter of divine intent.

Conclusion:
Apocalypse as Holy War

In popular usage, the term "apocalypse" often evokes profoundly visual cues, be it blood-soaked battles, violent upheavals, or catastrophes on a grand scale. Inflected with a specifically Christian sense, the term usually carries notions of a worldwide reckoning or judgment long delayed. Whether taken as intriguing, exciting, or revolting, such notions rely on the claims of particular myths and mythmakers. At a minimum, such senses of "apocalypse" accept that these myths are indeed about looming threats of world catastrophe and judgment, if not also claims about the alleged coherence of the world historical order. Singular evocations of "the apocalypse" or "the end" also mislead, as they stretch the sense of an ending in curious ways. Even a cursory reading of Revelation should give the reader pause about just what "end" is envisioned here, since the world emerges anew after having been violently cleansed of disagreement. Such a free-form bricolage of associations is to be expected in popular discourse but not in critical scholarship. Somewhat like these popular characterizations, however, interpreters of Christian apocalypticism have tended to rely on uncritical, hodge-podge conceptions, albeit ones more clearly shaped to suit certain theological agendas. In fact, much of the scholarly literature selectively appropriates images and rhetoric drawn from a diverse array of sources and then weaves these rather disparate pieces together into a single normative tapestry, one that has plausible ties to the hoary past and thus some presumed claim to authenticity. For instance, in place of popular notions of "the apocalypse," scholarly interpreters more commonly hold that apocalyptic literature, though notable for its plurality and diversity rather than singularity and consistency, is most fundamentally concerned with a great battle between good and evil.[1] Thus construed, evidence that is quite varied, complex, and historically contingent turns out to have a singular agenda and an overriding theological intent.

Though I do not claim some objective point of view, I have tried to reframe the discussion of apocalypticism in ways that are consistent with the norms of historical inquiry in the humanities and social sciences of the secular academy, while also keeping in view certain parochial approaches that have tended to dominate the field. In keeping with the norms of critical inquiry, I have sought in this study to drive a wedge between first- and second-order analysis, between folk definitions and critical historical ones. To this end, I have found it helpful to understand the relevant literature as myths concerned with politics in the divine world. This critical reframing allows for a great deal more literature to become relevant for understanding apocalyptic myths and for the work of comparison and contextualization to become more richly illuminating. Different patterns of continuity and discontinuity also come into relief. As I have argued, the bulk of the texts and traditions I treat in this study work to suppress the possibility of conflict and competition in the divine world, in large part by extolling the supreme, incomparable powers of the true deity conceived of as ruling from on high. So the unknown writers and editors of works such as 1 Enoch, Daniel 7–12, 1QM, and 1QS labor to avoid the possibility of rivalry and rebellion, whether by deriding other gods as dead and lifeless statues; extolling the harmonious subservience of all the lesser ranks; or developing myths about senseless fools who stray from their divine decree, overzealous middle managers who deviate, ever so slightly, from the will of heaven, or an amorphous class of minor gods who haunt and harass in the distant earthly regions far below.

Comparisons with Mesopotamian, Syrian, and Greek myths about divine war bring out these patterns especially well. Though many others could be added, texts such as the Baal Cycle, the Enuma Elish, the Epic of Anzu, and the *Theogony* do not agree on the names, roles, and relationships of the gods or the precise ways that they influence the cosmos they engender, shape, and rule. To the extent that they do show patterns of agreement, these tend to involve rather basic sensibilities about the anthropomorphic nature of the gods, especially their humanlike political arrangements. Traditions like the Enuma Elish and the *Theogony* also celebrate the emergence of a settled hierarchy among the gods after cycles of rivalry, battle, and attempted coups. They thus lend legitimacy to particular visions of settled political order, in large part through tales about heroic military campaigns fought to establish, solidify, and renegotiate relationships of power, and in ways construed as mutually beneficial for all. Though biblical and Hellenistic Jewish traditions play on similar patterns of assumptions, they also show a distinctive tendency to centralize power in the supreme deity while stripping lesser gods of powers and independence. One result is a tendency to hymn the supposedly unique, incomparable standing of the supreme deity while continuing to conceive of this deity as presiding over ranks of divine subordinates. Another is a tendency to suppress competition and rivalry between this supreme God and lower-ranking divinities. On the whole, writers continue to assume that the world functions as a single political hierarchy, but this world undergoes what Mark Smith terms a process of "collapse and telescoping."[2] As part of this reorganization, other gods often appear in quite limited roles, such as the anonymous but adoring host, obedient warriors, heavenly bodies, and minions of heavenly worshippers, the submissive posture of which serves to illustrate the towering, incomparable might of the supreme sovereign over them. These patterns have important implications for depictions of warfare and conflict, which tend to become highly asymmetrical affairs. For instance, in biblical texts such as Exodus 15 and Deuteronomy 32–33, and prophetic texts like Habakkuk 3, Isaiah 13, Joel 2–3, and Zechariah 14, writers and editors work to reclassify enemies and would-be opponents as relatively powerless non-gods, mere statues, instrumental enemies, and human beings foolishly arrayed against the powers of heaven. Conveniently, such formulations suppress intimations that the gods of others—especially those of the conquering Assyrian, Babylonian, and Persian Empires—could possibly defeat Israel's deity.

These findings have important implications for understanding discussions about conflict, battle, and relationships of power in Hellenistic sources such as 1 Enoch, Jubilees, Daniel 7–12, the War Scroll, and the Community Rule. Eschewing categories such as "angels" and "demons" in favor of lesser or lower-ranking deities, I understand these figures as idiosyncratic, context-specific elaborations of the lower tiers of the divine order. So we find myths about occasional insubordinates like the watchers, overzealous divine managers like the Enochic shepherds, and even arrogant human rulers like Antiochus IV Epiphanes. In many cases, these figures come to exemplify something about the perils of insubordination, and in at least some of them, they are also identified with the gods of the gentiles. The identification with gentile gods is explicit in texts where harmful spirits lead gentiles into idolatry (as in the Book of the Watchers and Jubilees) and in the Animal Apocalypse, where they are a class of lesser, managerial deities charged with punishing Israel. This association also seems clear in cases where outsiders are charged with worshipping the heavenly bodies (as in the Astronomical Book of Enoch) and perhaps in Daniel 10, which tells of a conflict between lesser divine subordinates (cf. Rev 12). Though gentile gods often play relatively minor, supporting roles, their assimilation suggests a kind of tacit admission that—however perverse, foolish, and/or intentionally planned by the supreme deity—other peoples persist in non-Yahweh–centered beliefs and practices. Relatedly, I have argued that notions of a future reckoning or punishment of gentile gods is often implicit in myths about the eschatological punishment of the watchers, evil spirits, and overzealous shepherd-managers and the eschatological destruction of "idols" that appear in a range of biblical and Hellenistic literature.

Along with the supposed battle between good and evil, a resilient scholarly consensus holds that apocalypticists envision the world as in rebellion against God. As argued here, however, the evidence rather suggests that writers and editors work hard to push conflict and opposition to the periphery, not the center, of the world political stage. Of course, the scribes seem to agree that deities preside over the cosmos and govern the world's political order, including but by no means limited to its military affairs. Yet the idea of an eternal, stable, unchallenged, and ultimately just divine order proves foundational for Paul and other mythmakers, even if this comes to require (as it often does) that political defeats come at the hands of Israel's patron deity or that the vast majority of the world's inhabitants are blind to this true divine ruler and master puppeteer. Claims about a temporary time of evil or punishment, blinded outsiders, and instrumental enemies all serve this agenda, as does the premise of a time right on the horizon of the expected future when God will fully display the true political order that has been there all along. These patterns shed light on Paul's brief discussion of divine war in 1 Corinthians 15, and they explain the much-discussed "principalities and powers" as lesser deities and mistaken objects of gentile worship. Like a range of other Jewish writers, Paul in 1 Corinthians 15 imagines Christ defeating enemies and opponents even though (somewhat paradoxically) he more consistently maintains that God and Christ, rightly conceived, have no enemies and opponents of comparable power. Understood in this way, Paul's letters evoke an imminent transformation that will complete, restore, and perfect the system of divine rule already inherent in the existing cosmic and historical orders. Comparisons with Jewish traditions also make good sense of why Paul stresses Christ's submission and noncompetition in 1 Corinthians 15 and Philippians 2, as well as his protean arguments about gentile gods in Galatians 4 and 1 Corinthians 8–10.

I have also focused attention on Paul's formulations of a victimized but righteous elect. Indeed, many of his discussions of ideal Christ communities work to organize and incite anxieties in ways that greatly expand the discourse about victimization and alienation that appears in much apocalyptic literature. To this end, Paul reappropriates Platonic traditions to imagine the Christ-elect as engaged in an ongoing, anxious struggle against their own passions and flesh, the goal of which seems to be submission and subservience to God, often conceived of as heroic. To somewhat similar ends, he also adapts Stoic traditions to articulate a distinctive ethics that centers on adaptability, mutuality, and submission to one another (as well as to God, Christ, and Paul). Like the ongoing menace of the passions, however, these imagined communities are hemmed in by looming threats, whether from inauthentic teachers, persecuting outsiders, or their own penchants for immature, fractious rivalry and self-directed ways. Paul's Christ-followers thus routinely emerge as engaged in conflict and struggle, whether with their own bodies, passions, and flesh; with persecutors and oppressors; with insincere teachers and teachings; or with bad moral habits that threaten to erode these ideal communities from within.

In advancing these arguments, I have consciously resisted the temptation to conceptualize authors, texts, traditions, genres, or religions as having relatively stable, common worldviews or distinctive (and mutually exclusive) systems of thought. My aim has been to treat particular texts as fragments of the worlds inhabited by particular writers, editors, and mythmakers, not as representing stable systems of thought that stretch across time and space. Though Judaism, Jewish apocalypticism, Hellenism, and Christianity are sometimes understood in this way, little in the evidence encourages us to reify them as thought worlds, theologies, or religious traditions that arrive in the minds of their ethno-religious heirs as inevitable "package deals." As an alternative, this study finds continuity—at least for the texts and traditions considered here—mainly at the level of rather modest, taken-for-granted premises and assumptions. Chief among them are that the cosmos is a singular, closed, hierarchically organized continuum; that this continuum or *scala naturae* functions more or less like a human political arrangement; and that divine beings create, organize, and preside over all of its affairs. These minimal shared assumptions allow us to better understand a number of difficult features of the literature in question. Understood in this way, for instance, we can account for the lesser deities who come onstage in some Jewish literature without imagining that some new class of beings has been added to an otherwise coherent and stable Jewish theological system (and with special names like "angels" and "demons"). Instead, we can conceive of mythmakers working to adapt the lower ranks of the *scala naturae* as suits their particular interests and aims.

In addition, this approach has the effect of normalizing the premise that a single supreme deity stands over all, whether envisioned as Yahweh, Marduk, or Zeus. Attention to this rather basic point allows us to understand claims about the exceptional status of Israel's deity as rhetorical overstatements rather than straightforward depictions of Israel's political imaginary.[3] By resisting the allures of alleged monotheism, more illuminating patterns of continuity and discontinuity can emerge in the literature, whether in the longer mythic narratives that survive from Babylon, Ugarit, and Greece or in Exodus 15, Daniel 7–12, the Apocalypse of Weeks, or the letters of Paul. Conversely, this minimalistic account of continuity allows considerably more space for imagining the particularities of any one literary creation. As argued here, for instance, taking Paul's thought as rather modestly structured in this way can provide enough conceptual flexibility to explain his creative adaptations of multiple traditions and discourses, whether about an impending "day of Christ," gentile gods, or the victimizing Platonic passions that threaten from within.

Throughout this study, I have stressed dissimilarity and difference in an effort both to deconstruct theories about overarching, transhistorical dualisms and to develop a more constructive alternative. In this light, consider a few brief examples drawn from Colossians and Ephesians, which have often been implicated in theories about evil apocalyptic forces and powers. In the approach taken here, these texts are best construed not as receiving, transmitting, or commenting on a distinctively Pauline system of thought (or replaying a dualistic theology), but as the products of unknown writers who sometimes play with certain images and ideas in selective and indeterminate ways. So the unknown author of Colossians plays with the temporal, spatial, and material dimensions of Paul's thought to evoke bodily resurrection as a present rather than future reality (Col 2:12; cf. Rom 6:4–5).

Thus, Paul's tense expectations of imminent transformation are changed quite dramatically, even though the cosmos itself allegedly stays the same. In a similar play with ideas of time and location, Ephesians imagines the Christ-elect as having already assumed their true heavenly station: "[God] raised us together and seated us with him in the heavenly places in Christ Jesus" (2:6). What for Paul was to take place on the horizon of the near future is here projected onto the recent past, suggesting that past and future are equally productive as imaginative locales, perhaps precisely because they are not "right here." Similarly, Colossians imagines a battle "to disarm the principalities and powers" (2:15), not as a kind of future war of Christ on par with 1 Cor 15:23–28 but rather as a victory that has already been won. Though one can discern some clear resonance with Paul's thought, little else about these claims is quite the same.

I have stressed the significant differences between Paul's thought about conflict and transformation and that found in Colossians and Ephesians, but they do share some basic premises about the divine political order as well as certain argumentative strategies. So the writer of Colossians warns about being duped into the "worship of *aggeloi*" (2:18) and insists that the implied audience has in fact died to "the *stoicheia kosmou*" (2:20). Many scholars have labored to reconstruct the beliefs and opponent figures that might be the target of such claims. Yet more basically, and less speculatively, these verses suggest that the writer of Colossians finds reclassification polemics congenial for attacking rival teachings and teachers. Whether or not gentile gods are specifically in view, these *aggeloi* and *stoicheia* are clearly made out as deities of lesser power, and they are clearly illegitimate. In a similar vein, the writer of Ephesians 6 pictures an anxious faithful beset by the wiles of the devil and struggling against "principalities and powers, against the cosmic rulers of this darkness, against the spirits of wickedness" (6:12). Elided with 1 Cor 15:23–28, this could plausibly seem to be the crucible for the much discussed battle against "powers of darkness." The preceding analysis suggests a different approach, one that draws attention to clear differences between the ways that these writers imagine participants, opponents, and sources of threat, to say nothing of the quite different temporal schemes operative in Ephesians 6 and 1 Corinthians 15. Nevertheless, the writer of Ephesians builds a familiar image of an anxious faithful and, like a range of other writers, incites anxiety about threats from lesser divine beings. Against these threats, however, one is to put on the "armor of God" so that the struggle is inexorably to be resolved by the help of greater heavenly powers against lesser ones (6:10–12, 13–17).[4] Understanding these claims as the work of local, historically contingent mythmakers helps us to resist the allure of transtemporal coherence. At the same time, appreciating how writers play on relatively common strategies of argument helps us to understand just how much has changed in such formulations, and yet, how much has also stayed the same.

Notes

Introduction

1. See also the "day of Jesus Christ" in 1 Cor 1:8, Phil 1:6, 2:16; cf. Rom 14:7–12, 17–18; Phil 3:12–21; 1 Thess 4:13–18; 1 Cor 15:20–28, 50–58.
2. On myths and mythmaking, I draw especially on Lincoln, *Theorizing Myth*, e.g., 141–147, and Ballentine, *Conflict Myth*, 1–13.
3. This has important implications for notions of alleged "monotheism," as well as for classes of beings often termed "angels" or "demons." On monotheism, see especially Fredriksen, "Mandatory Retirement"; M. Smith, *Origins*, 41–53; Olyan, "Is Isaiah 40–55 Really Monotheistic?"; and Porter, "Anxiety of Multiplicity." The essays collected in Athanassiadi and Frede, eds., *Pagan Monotheism in Antiquity*, and Mitchell and Van Nuffelen, eds., *One God*, are also valuable, but some of the contributors adapt language about monotheism in unhelpful ways.
4. For instance, see the diverse essays collected in Horsley, ed., *Paul and Politics*, and Stanley, ed., *Colonized Apostle*; Elliott, *Arrogance of the Nations*; Portier-Young, *Apocalypse Against Empire*. For criticisms, see Collins, *Apocalyptic Imagination*, 10, 37–38; Adler, "Introduction," 6, 19–20; J. Z. Smith, "Wisdom and Apocalypticism"; Johnson-DeBaufre and Nasrallah, "Beyond the Heroic Paul." For attempts to appropriate apocalyptic rhetoric in contemporary philosophy, see Milbank, Žižek, and Davis, *Paul's New Moment*.
5. Translated and edited by Hiers and Holland; the German original was published in 1892.
6. See the concerns voiced by Koch, *Rediscovery of Apocalyptic;* cf. Schnackenburg, *God's Rule and Kingdom*, e.g., 69; Dodd, *New Testament Studies*, 67–128.
7. Weiss, *Jesus' Proclamation*, 74–70; here Weiss relies heavily on Matt 12:28, Luke 17:21, and Rev 12:10.
8. Weiss, *Jesus' Proclamation;* see also 80, 93, 101. Weiss's conclusion seems to equivocate on the precise status of Satan's kingdom (e.g., ibid., 129–130), but his earlier claims are much stronger.

211

9. *State in the New Testament* and *Christ and Time*. More recently, see N. T. Wright, *Jesus and the Victory of God*, 193–197, 226–229.

10. Schweitzer (*Mysticism*, 54) maintained a strong link between "late Judaism" and Paul's thought but rendered Hellenism a later, second-century contribution; on "late Judaism" as a product of nineteenth-century scholarship, see Collins, *Apocalyptic Imagination*, 1–2.

11. *Mysticism*, 55.

12. See *Theology of the New Testament* and "Romans 7 and the Anthropology of Paul." See also Bultmann and Bartsch, *Kerygma and Myth*, 5.

13. The former claim appears in "Beginnings of Christian Theology," 102, and the latter in *Commentary on Romans*, 150. See also Käsemann, "On the Subject of Primitive Christian Apocalyptic." Bultmann responded in "Ist Apokalyptik die Mutter der christlichen Theologie?"

14. See e.g., *Commentary on Romans*, 92, 159.

15. *Commentary on Romans*, 150.

16. So Daniel J. Harrington ("Review of Ernst Käsemann") finds the work commendable as a theological project but not as an historical one; so also Scroggs, "Ernst Käsemann," 260, and Dunn, "Review of Ernst Käsemann." For stronger critiques, see also E. P. Sanders, *Paul, the Law, and the Jewish People*, 155–156; and Donaldson, *Paul and the Gentiles*, 93–100. See also Stanley Stowers's sharp critique of powers theories in "Paul's Four Discourses" and *A Rereading of Romans*, 179–189.

17. Loren Stuckenbruck makes this problem especially clear for the interpretation of Paul in "Overlapping Ages." He writes, for instance: "God's definitive activity is not only a matter for the future; rather, it is God's invasive presence to defeat evil *in the past* (e.g. at the time of the Great Flood) that guarantees its annihilation in the future (1 En. 10, 15–16; 91:5–10; 106:13–107:1; Jub. 5–10; Book of Giants at 4Q530 2 ii + 6–7 + 8–12, lines 4–20). Thus in essence, evil, however rampant and overwhelming in the present age, *is but a defeated power whose time is marked*" (ibid., 323; emphasis in the original). See also Adler's critique of Philip Vielhauer's strict two-age scheme ("Introduction," 2–7); cf. Vielhauer and Strecker, "Apocalyptic and Early Christianity."

18. So Morrison, *Powers That Be*; Schlier, *Principalities and Powers*; Caird, *Principalities and Powers*; and Beker, *Triumph of God*. For focused studies of particular texts, see MacGregor, "Principalities and Powers"; Lee, "Interpreting the Demonic Powers"; M. Black, "'Πᾶσαι ἐξουσίαι αὐτῷ ὑποταγήσονται'"; de Boer, *Defeat of Death*; Martyn, *Galatians*, 393–406; Martyn, "Apocalyptic Antinomies"; Arnold, "Returning to the Domain;" Moses, *Practices of Power*. For some helpful criticisms, see Forbes, "Paul's Principalities and Powers"; Forbes, "Pauline Demonology"; Carr, *Angels and Principalities*, 30–35; and Matlock, *Unveiling the Apocalyptic Paul*.

19. Wink's *Naming the Powers* is the first of a series that addresses the powers from the perspective of liberation theology; see Arnold's appeal to the Satanic

influences of "popular witchcraft and sorcery, channeling, the heavy metal culture, parapsychology (including ESP, clairvoyance, telepathy, etc.)," in Arnold, *Powers of Darkness*, 211.

20. See Beker, *Triumph of God;* Martyn, "Apocalyptic Antinomies" and "Deapocalypticizing Paul," and the contributions to his Festschrift, Marcus and Soards, eds., *Apocalyptic and the New Testament;* Gaventa, *Our Mother Saint Paul;* and Eastman, *Recovering Paul's Mother Tongue.*

21. For instance, David Aune ("Apocalypticism") qualifies this as "limited dualism" but still imagines "this age" as dominated by hostile, ungodly powers; similar problems characterize John G. Riley's treatment of Paul in "Demons," 240.

22. *Triumph of God,* 135–152, esp. 145.

23. Stuckenbruck, "Overlapping Ages"; see also Collins, "Genre, Ideology, and Social Movements," 26–27.

24. *Triumph of God,* 145.

25. "Paul and Apocalyptic Eschatology"; see also his "Paul and Jewish Apocalyptic Eschatology" and *Defeat of Death.*

26. "Paul and Apocalyptic Eschatology," 348. Though de Boer appeals to Schweitzer for this view of the two ages (e.g., "Paul and Apocalyptic Eschatology," 354–355), he misconstrues Schweitzer's more subtle formulation (e.g., Schweitzer, *Mysticism of the Apostle Paul,* 98–99).

27. "Paul and Apocalyptic Eschatology," 367–368.

28. "Introduction," 9; see von Rad, *Old Testament Theology,* 2:330, for the idea of a mixed genre.

29. Contrast Koch, *Rediscovery of Apocalyptic,* which distinguished six specific features, and Russell's longer list in *Method and Message,* 104–139.

30. "The Jewish Apocalypses," 28; see also his "Genre, Ideology, and Social Movements," 27–28. Christopher Rowland (*Open Heaven,* 70–72) and Jean Carmignac ("Qu'est-ce que l'Apocalyptique") prefer to stress the revelation of divine mysteries as the most distinctive feature; similarly, Stegemann, "Die Bedeutung der Qumranfunde."

31. So Michael Stone complains, "there are some of the books which are conventionally regarded as apocalypses which are for all practical purposes devoid of apocalypticism," and "truly apocalyptic apocalypses are the exception rather than the rule" ("Lists of Revealed Things," 440, 443); see also E. P. Sanders's critique in "Genre of Palestinian Jewish Apocalypses." For an attempted emendation to the definition offered by *Semeia* 14, see Hellholm, "Problem of Apocalyptic Genre," 27; cf. Collins's responses: *Apocalyptic Imagination,* 41–42, and "Genre, Ideology, and Social Movements," 25–38.

32. Some of the most fruitful areas of research have focused on prophetic, mantic, and wisdom literature. See, e.g., Hanson, *Dawn of Apocalyptic;* Cook, *Prophecy and Apocalypticism,* 123–165; Collins, "From Prophecy to Apocalypticism"; Collins, "Cosmos and Salvation"; Kvanvig, *Roots of Apocalyptic;* Attridge, "Greek and Latin Apocalypses"; J. Z. Smith, "A Pearl of Great Price"; J. Z. Smith,

"Wisdom and Apocalypticism"; Müller, "Mantische Weisheit und Apokalyptik"; and Neujahr, *Predicting the Past.*

33. So "Genre, Ideology, and Social Movements," 25–38. More recently, see Sacchi, *Jewish Apocalyptic,* for an evolutionary theory that construes apocalypticism as responding to the problem of evil (cf. Collins's critique, *Apocalyptic Imagination,* 10–11), and the unifying social-scientific approach of Schmithals, *Apocalyptic Movement.*

34. *Apocalyptic Imagination,* 9. A similar focus on angels and demons characterizes a much-quoted definition in the *Encyclopedia of Apocalypticism,* 1:x.

35. Cf. Zech 8:20–23; Isa 2:2–4, 14:5–7; 3 Sib. Or. 703–720; 1 En. 10:21–22; and 11QMelch.

36. See, e.g., Gager, *Curse Tablets.*

Chapter 1. Creation, Battle, and Cosmic Intrigue

1. Gunkel, *Creation and Chaos;* von Rad, *Holy War in Ancient Israel;* von Rad, "Origin of the Concept"; Cross, "Divine Warrior"; Miller, *Divine Warrior;* Hanson, *Dawn of Apocalyptic.* For more recent treatments, see Clifford, *Creation Accounts;* Forsyth, *Old Enemy;* Day, *God's Conflict;* Fishbane, *Biblical Myth;* Angel, *Chaos and the Son of Man;* Scurlock and Beal, eds. *Creation and Chaos;* and Ballentine, *Conflict Myth.* For an unconvincing critique, see Tsumura, *Creation and Destruction.*

2. Hanson's *Dawn of Apocalyptic* chronicled precise developments, but his proposals have been sharply criticized by scholars such as Cook, *Prophecy and Apocalypticism;* cf. Gunkel, *Creation and Chaos,* 110–111.

3. So Cross, "Divine Warrior"; von Rad, "Origin of the Concept"; Miller, *Divine Warrior;* Clifford, "Roots of Apocalypticism"; and Collins, "From Prophecy to Apocalypticism." Somewhat differently, J. Z. Smith argues that the loss of native kingship informs wisdom, apocalyptic, and gnostic literature ("Pearl of Great Price" and "Wisdom and Apocalypticism"); cf. von Rad, *Old Testament Theology,* 2:301–308, and *Wisdom in Israel,* 263–283.

4. Furthermore, as J. Z. Smith argues, the Enuma Elish "is not simply, or even primarily, a cosmogony. It is pre-eminently a myth of the establishment of Marduk's kingship, the creation of his city (Babylon) and his central capital, Esagila" ("Pearl of Great Price," 7). On the Babylonian New Year festival, see van der Toorn, "Babylonian New Year Festival"; and Sommer, "Babylonian Akitu Festival."

5. I draw on Lincoln, *Theorizing Myth,* esp. 141–147; Ballentine, *Conflict Myth,* 1–21; and J. Z. Smith, *Map Is Not Territory.* See also Oden, "Interpreting Biblical Myths."

6. See, e.g., Eliade, *Myth and Reality,* 5–6, 13; cf. Lincoln, *Theorizing Myth,* 141–147.

7. Cross, for instance, finds that Baal's battles with Yamm, Leviathan, and Mot are alloforms portraying the victory of life over death (*Canaanite Myth,* 120, 149);

elsewhere he relies on problematic notions of the "mythopoetic mind" (*Canaanite Myth*, 135; and *From Epic to Canon*, 81). For criticisms and refinements, see Peter Machinist's foreword to Gunkel's *Creation and Chaos*, xvi. Clifford ("Roots of Apocalypticism," 4–5, 19) and Collins ("From Prophecy to Apocalypticism," 129) appeal to similar "battles with chaos" categories but also accept the political dimensions of these myths.

8. *Conflict Myth*, esp. 186–189. As she notes, for instance, interpreters use categories like "chaos" in varied and imprecise ways, sometimes suggesting "a state of disorder," in other contexts something like "primordial matter," and in others, a deity of some kind.

9. Ballentine, *Conflict Myth*, 2–8; Lincoln, *Theorizing Myth*, 147–150. For similar approaches to Greek traditions, see also Laks ("Between Religion and Philosophy," 137–139) on the Darveni Papyrus and creation narratives generally; cf. Guthrie, "Pre-Socratic World-Picture"; and Finkelberg, "On the Unity of Orphic and Milesian Thought."

10. For a broader treatment that begins with Gilgamesh, see Forsyth, *Old Enemy;* relevant literature that I do not treat here includes Egyptian traditions about Horus's battle with Seth and the Sumerian Lugale epic.

11. Similarly, Miller, *Divine Warrior*, 59–63.

12. *Conflict Myth*, esp. 1–2, 14–15, 20–21. See also Tugendhaft, "Babel-Bible-Baal."

13. For a comparative analysis of Greek and Near Eastern traditions, see López-Ruiz, *When the Gods Were Born.*

14. Similarly Ballentine, *Conflict Myth*, e.g., 21–22, though with more emphasis on the appropriation of certain mythic taxonomies and ideological forms by actors in different sociopolitical contexts.

15. For overviews of much of the literature, see Clifford, *Creation Accounts;* and Lambert, "Mesopotamian Creation Stories," with a translation of the Enuma Elish, 37–59.

16. The most recent critical edition is Talon, *Enuma Elish;* Talon's edition updates Lambert and Parker, *Enuma Elish*, and supplements it with relevant fragments.

17. Lambert, "Mesopotamian Creation Stories," 17; Lambert, "Studies in Marduk"; Vanstiphout, "Enuma Elish as a Systematic Creed," esp. 48; Sommerfeld, *Der Aufstieg Marduks;* for a date ca. 1250, see Jacobsen, *Treasures of Darkness*, 167; cf. Dalley, *Myths from Mesopotamia*, 228–231.

18. For instance, Marduk takes on the roles played by Enlil in other myths and renegotiates the status of Nabû as his son while also expropriating attributes of Enlil's son (Ninurta); so Livingstone, *Mystical and Mythological Explanatory Works*, 155–156; and Porter, "What the Assyrians Thought." On the relation to Ninurta traditions, see Lambert, "Ninurta Mythology," 56; and Vanstiphout, "Enuma Elish as a Systematic Creed," 44–45. Lambert ("Mesopotamian Creation Stories," 35–37) notes that earlier traditions make Nippur the central

meeting place and envision the whole assembly as ruled by Enlil rather than Marduk; he finds similar claims in Sumerian and Akkadian incantations where Marduk becomes the primary god who creates all things, even the Anunnaki. In contrast, the law code of Hammurabi casts Anu as "king of the Anunnaki," while Enlil remains "lord of heaven and earth," and Marduk gains power over human beings as well as an elevated status among the Igigi; so Roth, *Law Collections,* 76; and Ballentine, *Conflict Myth,* 34–35.

19. Lambert, "Mesopotamian Creation Stories," 17–18. For evidence that the Marduk myths were explicitly used to legitimate local kings, see Ballentine, *Conflict Myth,* 36–39; and Weissert, "Creating a Political Climate."

20. In other Babylonian myths, Ea appears as god of the subterranean waters pooled beneath the earth (Lambert, "Mesopotamian Creation Stories," 19).

21. See also Ballentine, *Conflict Myth,* 30–39; Lambert, "Mesopotamian Creation Stories," 17–28; and Tugendhaft, "Unsettling Sovereignty."

22. Marduk requests this status at II, 155–162, and the gods grant it beginning in IV, 1. So, for instance, the assembly cries:

> Marduk, you are the most honored among the great gods,
>> Your destiny is unequalled, your command is like Anu's.
> Henceforth your order will not be annulled,
>> It is in your power to exalt and abase.
> Your utterance is sure, your command cannot be rebelled against,
>> None of the gods will transgress the line you draw.
> Shrines for all the gods need provisioning,
>> That you may be established where their sanctuaries are.
> You are Marduk, our avenger,
>> We have given you kingship over the sum of the whole universe.
>> (IV, 5–14; trans. Lambert)

See also the acclamation of Marduk at V, 109.

23. At other points, the Enuma Elish claims that Marduk has merely subdued Tiamat (as VII, 130–134), which suggests her ongoing presence in the domesticated but still threatening waters. On other domestication motifs, see Forsyth, *Old Enemy,* 49; and Ballentine, *Conflict Myth,* 150–166.

24. On the three-tiered heavens with Anu, Enlil, and Ea, see Lambert, "Mesopotamian Creation Stories," 22–23.

25. Lambert, "Mesopotamian Creation Stories," 24.

26. On democracy and agreement in the assembly, see Jacobsen, "Primitive Democracy" and "Battle Between Marduk and Tiamat."

27. The critical text is Annus, *Standard Babylonian Epic of Anzu;* Vogelzang, *Bin šar dadmē.* The dating of these tablets varies widely; see Dalley, *Myths from Mesopotamia,* 203. Ballentine, *Conflict Myth,* 23, opts for a range between 1500 and 600 BCE.

28. Annus, *Standard Babylonian Epic of Anzu*, ix–xi; Lambert, "Ninurta Mythology," 55–60; Wazana, "Anzu and Ziz."

29. Various other traditions about Anzu and Ninurta also survive, some of which name a different god as the heroic slayer of Anzu. So Ninurta appears in older Sumerian myths about Lugale and Angim that dramatize Marduk's elevation. Another Old Babylonian version has Ningirsu taking Anzu's place; see Ballentine, *Conflict Myth*, 27; Annus, *Standard Babylonian Epic of Anzu*, ix–xi; and Black and Green, *Gods, Demons, and Symbols*, 138, 142–143.

30. Ballentine, *Conflict Myth*, 23, 190–191; George, *House Most High*, 116–117.

31. Translation by Dalley, *Myths from Mesopotamia*. On the inconsistencies in Ninurta's genealogy, see Livingstone, *Mystical and Mythological Explanatory Works*, 153.

32. Lambert ("New Look," 296) connects this to the damming of water during an intermediate phase of creation, parallel to the third day in Genesis 1. Annus (*Standard Babylonian Epic of Anzu*, x–xi) suggests that Enlil establishes decrees of missions/destinies (*têrêtu*) for the other gods and that his appointing Anzu as his doorkeeper is an exemplary case (I, 62–64). Other doorkeeper gods are familiar from Gilgamesh and Ligalbanda (Annus, *Standard Babylonian Epic of Anzu*, xi–xii), which may help to explain the image of "blocking" or controlling the flood.

33. On the Tablets of Destiny motifs in other traditions (including Jubilees and 1 Enoch), see Annus, *Standard Babylonian Epic of Anzu*, xxviii–xxix; and Dalley et al., "Sassanian Period," 166; cf. Paul, "Heavenly Tablets."

34. Annus, *Standard Babylonian Epic of Anzu*, x–xi; cf. Vogelzang, *Bin šar dadmē*, 76–77 n. 61.

35. See Annus, *Standard Babylonian Epic of Anzu*, xxiii, on the role of secret lore/wisdom.

36. See Annus, *Standard Babylonian Epic of Anzu*, xiv; Hallo and Moran, "First Tablet of the SB Recension," 68 n. 11; and Lambert, "Ninurta Mythology," 58.

37. For the association of Anzu with water, see Annus, *Standard Babylonian Epic of Anzu*, x–xi; with seasonal patterns, ibid., xxxii–xxxiii; Jacobson, *Treasures of Darkness*, 132–133.

38. The critical edition and translation is M. S. Smith, *Ugaritic Baal Cycle Volume I*; and Smith and Pitard, *Ugaritic Baal Cycle Volume II*; see also Smith's translation in Parker, ed., *Ugaritic Narrative Poetry*. Smith (*Ugaritic Baal Cycle*, 1:1) dates the work to 1400–1350 BCE on the basis of archaeological evidence and a reference in the text to *ngmd*, most likely Niqmaddu II, who ruled ca. 1380–1346.

39. See Clifford, "Cosmogonies in the Ugaritic Texts"; Margalit, *Matter of "Life" and "Death"*; and M. S. Smith, *Ugaritic Baal Cycle*, 1:1–28. Tablets 2–6 clearly focus on Baal, but the narrative continuity of the whole text is doubtful (M. S. Smith, *Ugaritic Baal Cycle*, 1:4–19); relatedly, see M. S. Smith (*Ugaritic Baal*

Cycle, 1:20–25; and in Parker, ed., *Ugaritic Narrative Poetry*, 81–82) on the order of the columns. A fragmentary tradition about the binding of Yamm also survives; see Pitard, "Binding of Yamm."

40. The text also twice mentions Athtar (an astral deity) as a possible rival to Baal, which suggests that Baal's dominion may have included the heavens alongside the sea and the underworld, at least at some point; see Caquot, "Le dieu 'Athtar"; M. S. Smith, *Ugaritic Baal Cycle*, 1:240–250; Parker, ed., *Ugaritic Narrative Poetry*, 82; and Miller, *Divine Warrior*, 18–20. On the structure of the pantheon, see the discussions in Handy, "Dissenting Deities"; and M. S. Smith, *Origins*, esp. 41–66.

41. On the divine family and "the seventy sons of Athirat," see M. S. Smith, *Ugaritic Baal Cycle*, 1:92–93.

42. On the help given by other deities and the political situation at Ugarit, see Parker, ed., *Ugaritic Narrative Poetry*, 84–85; M. S. Smith, *Ugaritic Baal Cycle*, 1:96–110; and Ballentine, *Conflict Myth*, 57–59.

43. This victory is recalled as a mighty deed of Baal at *KTU* 1.3 III, 38–40; cf. *KTU* 1.3 III, 41–47, which also refers to other enemies that Baal has defeated.

44. On this translation, see Parker, ed., *Ugaritic Narrative Poetry*, 169 n. 94.

45. It is clear from the context that El remains king over all; on the relative use of status titles and designations, see M. S. Smith and Pitard, *Ugaritic Baal Cycle*, 2:354–355.

46. Translations of tablets 5 and 6 are from Parker, ed., *Ugaritic Narrative Poetry*.

47. On the servant language used here, see M. S. Smith, *Ugaritic Baal Cycle* 1:59–60.

48. M. Smith, "Structure of Divinity," 45; for connections with biblical traditions, see Parker, ed., *Ugaritic Narrative Poetry*, 85–86.

49. See Cross, *Canaanite Myth*, ix; Grabbe, "Seasonal Pattern"; and Wyatt, "Arms and the King," esp. 833–844.

50. On the tripartite domains, see M. Smith, *Early History of God*, 94–96; and Handy, "Dissenting Deities," 21–22.

51. Tugendhaft ("Unsettling Sovereignty") suggests some important qualifications on the notions of political hierarchy envisioned here. Others emphasize the continued threats posed by "chaos"; so Parker, ed., *Ugaritic Narrative Poetry*, 85; M. S. Smith, *Ugaritic Baal Cycle*, 1:59; Gibson, "Theology of the Ugaritic Baal Cycle"; and Kapelrud, "Ba'al, Schöpfung und Chaos."

52. See the critical text and commentary by West, *Hesiod: Theogony;* and Solmsen, Merkelbach, and West, *Hesiodi: Theogonia*. The text survives in fragments of Greek papyri dating between the first century BCE and the sixth century CE and in some sixty-nine manuscripts that date from the medieval and Renaissance periods.

53. Herodotus, *Hist.* 2.53, distinguishes four traditions of early poetry: those of Homer, Hesiod, Orpheus, and Mousaius. Some texts briefly mention a theogony, as in Apollonius of Rhodes, *Argonautika*, 496–511; *Hymn to Hermes*,

54–61; cf. *Il.* 9.189; *Od.* 1.325–359, 4.17–18, 8.487–520. The later Darveni Papyrus preserves a form of the succession myth (col. 10–11, 13) but reinterprets it as philosophical allegory; see Laks, "Between Religion and Philosophy"; and West, *Orphic Poems*. In a similar vein, Diogenes Laertius (*Lives* 1.119) credits the Pre-Socratic Pherecydes of Syros with first writing on nature and the gods and claims that he construes Zeus, Time, and Earth as first principles.

54. The *terminus post quem* is the late ninth century BCE, since the Greek alphabet is unknown before then (Lamberton, *Hesiod*, 13–14). West (*Hesiod: Theogony*, 40–48) dates the *Theogony* to the last quarter of the eighth century BCE; Kirk, *Songs of Homer*, prefers a somewhat later date, but López-Ruiz (*When the Gods Were Born*, 48–49) argues for the decades around 700 BCE. On Hesiod in relation to other traditions of myth, see Lambert and Walcot, "New Babylonian Theogony"; West, *Theogony*, 18–31; and López Ruiz, *When the Gods Were Born*, 48–83; cf. Lambert, *Background of Jewish Apocalyptic*, on possible connections with Dan 11.

55. Lamberton, *Hesiod*, 27–37; Griffith, "Personality in Hesiod."

56. On the oral tradition, see Lamberton, *Hesiod*, 11–27; Kirk, *Songs of Homer;* and Lord, *Singer of Tales.*

57. Translations are from Lombardo, trans., *Hesiod*, unless noted. On the prologue, see Lamberton, *Hesiod*, 44–69.

58. See especially Mondi, "Tradition and Innovation." As Mondi argues, for instance, the writers/editors transform the Prometheus myth from an etiological tale into a cautionary one about the dangers of disobeying Zeus. Jeffrey M. Duban ("Poets and Kings") also treats Zeus's relationship to favored human kings, with their similar scepters, laws, and claims of divine descent (cf. *Homeric Hymn* 25, where Zeus is also the patron of kings). Duban focuses attention on the king's place of honor among the Muses (*Th.* 81), his powers to enunciate law (*Th.* 85), his ability to settle conflicts (*Th.* 87, cf. 72–75, which recalls Zeus's Titanomachy), and as revered in the assembly like a god (*Th.* 90–91). The effect is to represent the king's unerring pronouncements as "the moral safeguards to the universe's physical stability" ("Poets and Kings," 19). For connections with the fertility of the earth, see *Od.* 9.109–114; *Hymn. Dem.*, 470–474; *Il.* 16.384–393; and *Op.* 225–237, 238–247.

59. Lamberton (*Hesiod*, 69) suggests translations such as "gaping," "division," or "separation."

60. On the place of Night here and in other Greek cosmologies, see West, *Hesiod: Theogony*, 197.

61. On the pejorative language about Gaia and her offspring, especially the Titans, see Lamberton, *Hesiod*, 72–81, though his argument about male lust versus female rage is overstated. He also flattens the complexity and nuance of the created order by construing *Th.* 211–232 as an account of the origins of evil (ibid., 81).

62. On the castration and eating of genitals in other contexts, see Lamberton, *Hesiod*, 41–42; cf. West, *Hesiod: Theogony*, 20–21.

63. On Hesiod's misogyny, see Lamberton, *Hesiod*, 101–103; Loraux, "Sur la race des femmes"; Arthur, "Cultural Strategies"; and Arthur, "Dream of a World Without Women."

64. As Robert Mondi ("Titanomachy," 27–29) shows, many scholars seek to excise this *aristeia* as an artless addition, but it fits quite well with "Hesiod's" political agenda.

65. For a somewhat different account of Typhon's genealogy and a more extended account of the battle, see *Il.* 2.781–783; cf. Pindar, *Pythian Ode* 1.19–20; Aeschylus, *Prometheus Bound* 370; and Fontenrose, "Typhon Among the Arimoi," esp. 64–65. On some possible connections with Near Eastern myths, see Cross, *Canaanite Myth*, 113.

66. West, *Hesiod: Theogony*, 337–338. In the *Theogony*, the battle with Typhon puts an end to the cycles of violence between different generations of gods, but some sources tell of other rebellions against Zeus, especially the so-called Gigantomachy, which is a standard "noble theme" in rhetorical theory; so Cicero, *Part. Or.* 56; Demetrius, *On Style* 75; Hermogenes, *On Ideas* 2.287–290; cf. Aristophanes, *Frogs* 1021; Quintilian, *Inst.* 10.1.46. D. C. Innes ("Gigantomachy and Natural Philosophy") shows that Augustan-age poets exploit it to celebrate emperors and kings, as Horace, *Odes* 3.4.5–8 and Ovid, *Am.* 2.1.11–18, *Tristia* 2.61–72, 331–334. In general, however, such references prove relatively brief and allusive (so Manilius *Astr.* 3.5; *Aetna* 41–73). On theomachy as a feature of imperial poetry, see Chaudhuri, *War with God.*

67. Similarly, Mondi, "Tradition and Innovation," 25–48; Mondi, "Ascension of Zeus"; and Philips, "Narrative Compression."

68. On the influence of Hesiod's Titanomachy on Latin tradition, see Ripoll, "Adaptations latines."

69. Lamberton, *Hesiod*, 105–133; the text gives no explanation for the progressive deterioration, but others traditions do; see Lovejoy and Boas, *Primitivism and Related Ideas*, 31.

70. Some early manuscripts lack this addition about Chronos in 195–200 (see Lombardo, trans., *Hesiod*, 54). Cf. Proteus's fate in *Od.* 4.561–570. In Plato's *Gorgias* (523a–b), the good go to the Isles of the Blessed and the bad to Tartarus, but in 523c–524a Zeus reorganizes so that all the dead will be judged naked (as also their judges) by a group of three.

71. I prefer Richmond Lattimore's translation here. This tradition proves popular, and its influence is especially clear in the later works of Ovid and the Augustan poets. On just kingship in the *Works and Days*, see Mordine, "'Speaking to Kings.'"

72. In *Il.* 15.187–193 they have separate domains but rule as equals in Olympus; cf. *Hymn to Demeter*, 85–86; Pindar, *Olympian* 7.54–55; Plato, *Gorg.* 523a; Virgil, *Aen.* 1.139; Innes, "Gigantomachy," 165–171.

73. Innes, "Gigantomachy," 166.

74. Much of the Near Eastern data have been collected in van der Deijl, *Protest or Propaganda*, 303–659. See also Rowlett, *Joshua and the Rhetoric of Violence*, 71–120; Kang, *Divine War*, 11–110; Weinfeld, "Divine Intervention"; and Younger, *Ancient Conquest Accounts*.

75. For overviews of the extensive scholarship, see J. Wright, "War, Ideas of"; and Trimm, "Recent Research." See especially Niditch, *War in the Hebrew Bible;* Niditch, "War and Reconciliation"; Kelle and Ames, eds., *Writing and Reading War;* and Crouch, *War and Ethics;* cf. the wide-ranging critique of Schmitt, *Der "Heilige Krieg."*

76. Grayson and Novotny, *Royal Inscriptions of Sennacherib.*

77. Leichty, *Royal Inscriptions of Esarhaddon.*

78. On Ninurta-centered traditions, see Ballentine, *Conflict Myth*, 23–30; Annus, *Standard Babylonian Epic of Anzu*, xiv–xxii, esp. xiv–xvi; and Otto, "Human Rights." For the sources from Mari, see Parker, ed., *Ugaritic Narrative Poetry*, 84; Wyatt, "Arms and the King," 833–882; and Ballentine, *Conflict Myth*, 111–123. Rowlett (*Joshua and the Rhetoric of Violence*, 73) notes the relative absence of war oracles and battle reports from the surviving literature of Ugarit.

79. Wellhausen, *Prolegomena to the History of Israel*, 434–435. Various terms for war appear in biblical traditions, but language about the "wars of Yahweh" (1 Sam 18:17, 25:28; Num 21:14) appears in abundance; cf. Thucydides, *Peloponnesian Wars* 1.112; Aristophanes, *Birds* 5.556; Miller (*Divine Warrior*, 2–3) justifies the use of the term "holy war" for the traditions about Yahweh; for an alternative, see Jones, "'Holy War.'"

80. Ben C. Ollenburger ("Gerhard von Rad's Theory of Holy War") treats the scholarship between Wellhausen and von Rad; Trimm ("Recent Research") surveys more recent literature. For new approaches, see the essays collected in Kelle, Ames, and Wright, eds., *Warfare, Ritual, and Symbol.*

81. Von Rad, *Holy War;* summarized as authoritative by Toombs, "War, Ideas of"; treated more critically in Gottwald, "War, Holy"; see also de Vaux, *Ancient Israel*, 1:213–266.

82. Similarly, Peter Weimar ("Die Jahwekriegserzählungen") finds an opposition between (northern) prophecy and the monarchy; cf. Rowlett, *Joshua and the Rhetoric of Violence*, 53–54.

83. See Weippert, "Heiliger Krieg in Israel und Assyrien"; and Smend, *Yahweh War and Tribal Confederation*, 26–27. Fritz Stolz (*Jahwes und Israels Kriege*) also attacks the distinction between holy and nonholy war and the theory of a unified institutional structure (the tribal league) that was later reimagined in the literature of Deuteronomy, Joshua, and Judges.

84. Both are reprinted in Cross, *Canaanite Myth and Hebrew Epic*, 91–144. This work shows a keen interest in precise historical reconstructions, though it is sharply critical of von Rad's distinctions between supposed royal traditions and pure holy war ones.

85. The Ugaritic Baal Cycle and the *Phoenician History* of Philo of Byblos are Miller's main comparative materials. On the antiquity of the latter, see the more skeptical approach of Attridge and Oden, eds., *Philo of Byblos*, 1–10.

86. See also Cross, "Council of Yahweh"; Mullen, *Assembly of the Gods;* and M. Smith, *Origins*, 41–66.

87. Miller argues that the epic of Israel's origins "took its shape at least in part out of the hymnic accounts of God's leading his armies in the primal march of holy war and conquest" (*Divine Warrior*, 7), and Cross (*Canaanite Myth and Hebrew Epic*, 138) notes that the Reed Sea becomes fused with the crossing of the Jordan in Josh 3–5, Ps 114, and Hab 3:7–9; see also Cross, "Divine Warrior." For passing references to the exodus as exemplifying Yahweh's power, see, e.g., Num 23:22, 24:8; Deut 1:29–30; and Josh 2:10–11.

88. Verses 1b–18 are ascribed to the Yahwist (J); v. 21 may be an incipit of the same hymn, preserved by the Elohist (E); Cross (*Canaanite Myth and Hebrew Epic*, 123–124) draws helpful contrasts between the prose account in Exod 14 (P), where Moses divides the sea and the people pass through it (Exod 14:16, 21c–22, 26, 29), while in 15:1b–18, Yahweh's breath casts Pharaoh into the sea. The account in Exod 14 combines J, E, and P (see Cross, *Canaanite Myth and Hebrew Epic*, 318); cf. Noth, *Exodus*, 105–120. On the early poetry, see Freedman, "Archaic Forms in Early Hebrew Poetry"; and Robertson, *Linguistic Evidence;* for attempts at dating, see Cross, *Canaanite Myth and Hebrew Epic*, 121–144; Cross and Freedman, "Song of Miriam"; Coats, "Song of the Sea"; and Freedman, "Moses and Miriam." Martin L. Brenner (*Song of the Sea*) argues for a postexilic date, but his arguments have not been well-received.

89. The LXX has ἐμπλήσω ψυχήν μου.

90. Unless otherwise noted, quotations from the Bible are from New Revised Standard Version Bible, copyright © 1989 National Council of the Churches of Christ in the United States of America. Used by permission. All rights reserved.

91. For instance, Anzu I 72–76 depicts Anzu as motivated by a desire to usurp Enlil's power.

92. Cross (*Canaanite Myth and Hebrew Epic*, 129) prefers "underworld" for 'ereṣ on the basis of similar uses (e.g., Gen 2:6; Isa 14:9, 21:9, 29:4; Jonah 2:7; Obed 1:3; Pss 147:6, 148:7; see Cross and Freedman, "Song of Miriam," 247 n. 39).

93. Similarly, Cross, *Canaanite Myth and Hebrew Epic*, 131–132; and Cross and Freedman, "Song of Miriam," 239, though misleadingly construed as "naturalistic." Cf. Miller, *Divine Warrior*, 115–117.

94. Following von Rad and others, Miller (*Divine Warrior*, 116) takes this as evidence that biblical representations of holy war emphasize terror and dread rather than numbers and weapons, as in Exod 23:27–29; Josh 2:9, 24; and Deut 2:25, 11:25. On similar patterns in non-Yahweh traditions, see Rowlett, *Joshua and the Rhetoric of Violence*, 71–120; and Albrektson, *History and the Gods*.

95. So Cross ("Divine Warrior," 19, and *Canaanite Myth and Hebrew Epic*, 142–143) notes that the sanctuary is most likely Gilgal; cf. Josh 3–5 and Ps 24; see also Cross and Freedman, "Song of Miriam," 240; and Clifford, *Cosmic Mountain.*

96. With Cross and Freedman ("Song of Miriam," 247 n. 35), I read *qĕdōš(îm)* as "who is like thee, feared among the holy ones," in accord with the LXX and the Syro-hexaplar version.

97. Cross (*Canaanite Myth and Hebrew Epic*, 138) reconstructs *kl* for *ḥl* so 7a reads "Before the lord of all the earth."

98. See M. Smith, *Ugaritic Baal Cycle*, 1:101, on similar uses of cosmogonic imagery in the Baal Cycle, as in *CTA* 5 I 1–5, where Baal kills a dragon and the heavens wilt and droop.

99. The Ugaritic text reads "Lift up, O Gods, Your Heads!" (*CTA* 2 I 27); Cross, *Canaanite Myth*, 97–99.

100. Cross distinguishes direct references to Yahweh as battling the sea or sea dragon (Pss 89, 93; Isa 27:1; Job 7:12, 9:8, 26:12, 38:7–11; Nah 1:4) from texts that also make reference to the Reed Sea myth (Ps 77; Isa 43:16–17, 50:2, 51:9–11; Pss 106:9, 114:1–5), though Josh 2:9 proves ambiguous, and in 24:6–7 the story involves a cloud (Cross, *Canaanite Myth and Hebrew Epic*, 135). Cross regards some of the later texts as instances of recrudescence, esp. Isa 24–27 and Isa 34–35. Ballentine (*Conflict Myth*, 81–82) also includes Pss 29:3, 65:7–8, 74:12–17, 78:13; and Nahum 1:3b–5 on the grounds that they share a marked concern with Yahweh's power, whether this involves kingly, creative, or military attributes. See also Miller, "El the Warrior"; and M. Smith, *Early History of God*, 32–42. Smith understands the twin roles of Yahweh as creator and warrior as originally separate on analogy with El and Baal; though see Cross, *Canaanite Myth and Hebrew Epic*, 44–75, for a different view.

101. See, e.g., Hanson, *Dawn of Apocalyptic;* and Clifford, "Roots of Apocalypticism." Clifford identifies four stages in the use of the conflict myth: early poetry like Exod 15, liturgical poems that date from the monarchy (especially hymns and laments like Pss 74, 77, 89, 93, 96, 114), second temple literature like Isa 40–66 and Zech 9–14, and finally apocalyptic texts like Dan 7 and Rev 12. By contrast, Ballentine prefers a taxonomy organized by types of interventions and enemies (e.g., *Conflict Myth*, 123–126).

102. See Freedman, "'Who Is Like Thee?,'" which focuses on biblical poetry in Gen 49, Exod 15, Num 23–24, Deut 33, and Judg 5.

103. On the appropriation of Exod 15 in Ps 77, see Clifford, *Psalms 73–150*, 39–40. Clifford (ibid., 38–39) argues for the unity of Ps 77, while Erhard S. Gerstenberger (*Psalms, Part 2, and Lamentations*) argues that the *Chaoskampf* motif suggests that the hymn was an originally separate composition. See also Jefferson, "Psalm 77."

104. See Clifford, *Psalms 73–150*, 41.

105. Cross (*Canaanite Myth and Hebrew Epic*, 136) notes the allusion to the writhing dragon Yamm; cf. Ps 29:8.

106. The translation of *galgal* ("whirlwind" in the NRSV) is difficult; Dahood (*Psalms II*, 232 n. 19) prefers "in the dome of the heavens."

107. Psalm 106 depicts the Israelites as consistently disloyal, and Yahweh saves them only for "the sake of his name" (106:8). For similar laments, see Pss 1, 19, 78, 106, 119; Neh 9; Ezra 9; and Dan 9; on bearing ancestral punishments, see LXX Isa 64:4; Dan 9:16; 2 Kgs 17:7–13, 23:26–27, 24:3–4. For punishments that are to last for only a set time, see Ps 106:3–4; cf. Pss 103:9, 39:4, 90:11–12; Jer 25:11–12, 29:10. An omen text about the capture of a statue of Bel also states, "It is said that after 30 years vengeance will be exercised, and the gods will return to their place," in Roberts, "Of Signs, Prophets, and Time Limits," 478.

108. Cf. v. 34; extermination is commanded in Exod 34:11–16; Deut 7:1–5, 12:1–3; cf. the disobedience in Josh 9; Judg 1:17–35, 2:23–3:6; cf. Exod 23:23–24, 34:10–16; Judg 2:6–3:6. On the rather free reediting of the sequence when compared with the canonical narratives, see Gerstenberger, *Psalms, Part 2*, 240–241.

109. Reading 74:12b in accord with Ballentine, *Conflict Myth*, 84.

110. On the difficulties with the translation of *lĕ ʿ ām lĕṣiyim*, see Ballentine, *Conflict Myth*, 84 n. 17; the LXX has βρῶμα λαοῖς τοῖς Αἰθίοψιν.

111. Gerstenberger (*Psalms, Part 2*, 78) argues that 74:13–15 refers to a *Chaoskampf* rather than the Reed Sea myth from Exodus, finding parallels in Isa 27:1, 51:1–11, 63:7–19; Jer 10:6–24; and Ps 77:17–21.

112. Note that the text does not summon the powers of earth alongside heaven, as in Pss 29 and 148. On the ethnic superiority implied here, see Gerstenberger, who justifies this as a fight for survival in a "multi-religious, autocratic imperium" (*Psalms, Part 2*, 188); more critically, see Clifford (*Psalms 73–150*, 122–123), who also draws connections with polemics about gentile deities in texts such as Pss 58, 82; and Isa 40–55.

113. Cf. Pss 97:1; 99:1, 10b; 93:1, 10c; 7:9; 1 Sam 2:10; 1 Chr 16:23–33.

114. On the language of festal celebrations in other psalms, see Pss 97:1, 8, 12; 67:5–6; 68:4; 69:33; 70:5.

115. Similarly, Gerstenberger, *Psalms, Part 2*, 190; Gunkel (*Creation and Chaos*, 421) characterizes Ps 96 as an eschatological psalm. On the coming of the king motif, see Ringgren, "Behold Your King Comes."

116. On the translation of *bĕnê ʾēlim*, see Ballentine, *Conflict Myth*, 83 n. 20; Cross, *Canaanite Myth and Hebrew Epic*, 45–46; for other examples of assemblies (and heavens) that acclaim Yahweh, see 1 Kgs 22:19–22; Job 1–2; Pss 82; 29:1–2; 50:6; 97:6; 148:1, 4, 13; 50:4; and Cross, "Council of Yahweh."

117. Dahood translates more literally as "Strong Yah, your faithfulness surrounds you;" cf. "Your strength and your fidelity surround you" (Cross, *Canaanite Myth and Hebrew Epic*, 160 n. 66); cf. 2 Sam 7:22.

118. The enemies are nonspecific here, but see Ballentine (*Conflict Myth*, 83 n. 25) for suggestions; Rahab is also named in Isa 51:9 and Job 9:13.

119. For more literal translations see Dahood (*Psalms II*, 308–315) and Ballentine

(*Conflict Myth*, 83). See also Sarna, "Psalm 89"; on the question of unity, see Gerstenberger, *Psalms, Part 2*, 153–154.

120. In this context, the acclamation of Yahweh also serves to legitimize David as a king who is enthroned on the waters in v. 25; cf. Mari Letter A. 1968 (where Adad endorses the king) and the one "like a son of man" in Dan 7. On kingship motifs, see Clifford, *Creation Accounts*, 59–61, 66–71; Malamat, *Mari and the Bible*, 157–164, and Heim, "(God-)Forsaken King."

121. On whole narrative articulations of the myth versus more compressed motifs such as this, see Ballentine, *Conflict Myth*, 14–15.

122. By contrast, Clifford (*Psalms 73–150*) treats the "raising up" of the sea in Ps 93:1–4 as a form of attack rather than of celebration, as does Gerstenberger (*Psalms, Part 2*, 175).

123. See Miller, *Divine Warrior*, 36–37, on resonances with the characterization of Baal.

124. On some difficulties with the language and subject matter, see Clifford, *Psalms 73–150*, 314–315. W. F. Albright theorized that Ps 68 collects incipits taken from a number of other poems (*Yahweh and the Gods*, 23–24). Its unity was subsequently defended by S. Mowickel, but some scholars regard the text as corrupt, as Tate, *Psalms 51–100*, 170; Klingbeil, *Yahweh Fighting from Heaven*, 122; and Miller, *Divine Warrior*, 103. Cf. Fokkelman, "Structure of Psalm 68."

125. The translation of the hapax *šin'ān* is disputed. Tate (*Psalms 51–100*, 161–166) follows Albright in glossing this as "thousands of warriors," but this requires taking the aleph as dittography. Klingbeil (*Yahweh Fighting from Heaven*, 124) instead suggests translating the MT as "bright ones," on the theory that it alludes to the astral association of the host in other texts; cf. Deut 33:2; Cross, "Divine Warrior," 102.

126. On language about the heights as "heaven," see Job 16:19; Pss 71:19, 93:4, 102:20.

127. On the display of captives in a victory march, see Isserlin, "Psalm 68:14"; cf. Keel, *Die Welt der altorientalischen Bildsymbolik*, 76–78.

128. Miller and others (e.g., Albright, *Yahweh and the Gods*, 24; Dahood, "Mišmār 'muzzle'") amend 68:23b so that it appeals to Yahweh's battle with a sea dragon; cf. *CTA* 3 III 37–38. So Miller, "Two Critical Notes on Psalm 68," 240, follows Dahood and S. Loewenstamm in revocalizing the text to yield "I muzzled the deep sea" (v. 23b), with the full text as: "The lord said: I muzzled the serpent, I muzzled the deep sea that you may wash your feet in blood, the tongues of your dogs from the enemies their portion (?)" (Miller, *Divine Warrior*, 110).

129. According to the MT of Deut 32:8, El apportions the nations among the "sons of Israel," but the LXX has υἱῶν θεοῦ (and ἀγγέλων θεοῦ in some manuscripts) and 4QDeutʲ supports this reading with *běnê 'ĕlōhîm*. See Ulrich et al., eds., *Qumran Cave 4. IX*, 90; Tov, *Textual Criticism*, 269; and Schenker, "Le monothéisme israélite," 438. So S. B. Parker ("Sons of [the] Gods") argues for the consensus view that the MT of 32:8 redacts the earlier text so as to render

Yahweh supreme, in ways similar to Ps 82; cf. 1 Kgs 22:19–22. See further, Mullen, *Assembly of the Gods,* 202–203; Niehr, "Host of Heaven"; Skehan, *Studies in Israelite Poetry and Wisdom,* 69 (on Sir 17:17); and Glasson, *Greek Influence,* 69–73.

130. *Early History of God,* 32.

131. Alternatively, Elyon could be taken as an alias for Yahweh, so Cross, *Canaanite Myth and Hebrew Epic,* 44–95. See M. Smith, *Early History of God,* 32–48, on the similarities between the iconographies and attributes of El, Baal, and Yahweh; on Yahweh's origins in Edom, see van der Toorn, *Family Religion,* 266–315, esp. 281–286; and van der Toorn, "Yahweh"; cf. Day, *Yahweh and the Gods and Goddesses of Canaan,* 91–116. M. Dijkstra argues that El is merely a title of Yahweh ("El, YHWH and Their Asherah"), but M. Smith's critique (*Early History of God,* 33 n. 45) is persuasive.

132. So Cross, *Canaanite Myth and Hebrew Epic,* 44–95.

133. See Miller's discussion, *Divine Warrior,* 75–80; Cross and Freedman ("Blessing of Moses") date the poem to the eleventh century BCE; cf. Gaster, "An Ancient Eulogy on Israel"; Gordis, "Text and Meaning"; and Gordis, "Critical Notes."

134. See Miller, "Two Critical Notes," 242–243, and *Divine Warrior,* 78–80, for the suggestion that the original might be *ʾšd* ("warriors") in v. 2 instead of the MT *ʾēšědāt,* in keeping with the parallelism and the LXX ἄγγελοι, yielding "warriors of the gods"; cf. 1QM 15.14; and Cross and Freedman, "Blessing of Moses," 191–210.

135. This term appears also in Ps 106:37 and Lev 17:7; as a Near Eastern deity, see Kuemmerlin-McLean, "Demons," 139; Riley, "Demons," 237; and D. Martin, "When Did Angels Become Demons?," 658–659; see also Brenk, "'In the Light of the Moon.'"

136. On sacrifice to "demons," see 2 Bar. 4:7; 1 En. 19:1; Jub. 1:11; T. Job 3:3; Philo, *Mos.* 1.276; Acts 17:18; Rev 9:20 (cf. Isa 13); *Ep. Barn.* 16.7; Justin, *Dialogue with Trypho* 30.3, 55.2, 73.2; cf. Plutarch, *Mor.* 316B, 417C; D. Martin, "When Did Angels Become Demons?," 663–664.

137. The NRSV of 32:43 is here emended to accord with 4QDeut[q] and the LXX, omitted in the MT and missing from 4QDeut[j]. Similarly, see Karrer, "Epistle to the Hebrews," 350–352; cf. Ps 96:7.

138. See von Rad, "Origin of the Concept"; von Rad, *Old Testament Theology,* 2:119–225; and Cross, "Divine Warrior." Von Rad's and Cross's main comparative material consists of combat myths, but others have appealed to traditions of theophany, as M. Weiss ("Origin of the 'Day of the Lord'"), or combined both traditions, as Wolff, Janzen, and McBride, *Joel and Amos,* 33–34. See also Cross, *Canaanite Myth and Hebrew Epic,* 144, for proposals about the synthesis and reinvention of earlier epic and royal themes.

139. Similar images and ideas appear in other literature, but von Rad ("Origin of

the Concept," 97–108) suggests the following basic texts: Isa 2:12; 13:6, 9; 22:5; 34:8; Jer 46:10; Ezek 7:19; 13:5; 30:3; Joel 1:15; 2:1, 11; 3:4; 4:14; Amos 5:18–20; Obad 15; Zeph 1:7–8, 14–18; for past battles construed as "days of Yahweh," see also Ezek 13:5, 34:12; Lam 1:12, 2:22. Subsequent studies have treated individual texts, sometimes adding to this basic constellation, as Beck, "Das Tag JHWHs-Verständnis von Zephanja iii"; see also Beck, *Der "Tag JHWHs"*; Everson, "Days of Yahweh." Von Rad (*Old Testament Theology*, 2:119–225) also notes connections between the imagery used in "day of Yahweh" texts and other literature about the wars of Yahweh (e.g., Isa 9:4 [5]; 28:21 = 2 Sam 5:20, 25), including images of thunder (1 Sam 7:10), darkness (Exod 14:20, Josh 24:7), clouds dripping water (Judg 5:4–5), and panic and confusion in the enemy (Exod 15:14–16, 23:27–28; Josh 2:9, 24; 5:1; 7:5).

140. Many scholars view Hab 1–3 as a composite that has been more or less unified by its editor (as Sweeney, "Habakkuk"), though some attempt to identify unified underlying compositions. Complicating factors are that the MT appears disjointed and other versions attest many variants; 1QpHab, for instance, preserves only Hab 1–2. J. A. Sanders ("Text and Canon") argues for greater confidence in the MT, but scholars such as Albright ("Psalm of Habakkuk") and Hiebert (*God of My Victory*, 4–57) treat it as corrupt and opt to heavily amend it. Hiebert argues, for instance, that chapter 3 was an originally distinct hymn from the premonarchic era that was incorporated into Hab 1–2 by postexilic editors "caught in the apocalyptic fervor of their era" (*God of My Victory*, 1).

141. Verses 3–7 and 8–15 may date significantly earlier, as suggested by Miller, *Divine Warrior*, 118–20; see also Albright, "Psalm of Habakkuk"; Eaton, "Origin and Meaning"; and Cross, *Canaanite Myth and Hebrew Epic*, 102–103.

142. With Hiebert (*God of My Victory*, 19, 91–94) and others (e.g., Miller, *Divine Warrior*, 119), I take Deber and Reshep as names, against the NRSV's translation as "plague and pestilence."

143. Contrast Hiebert (*God of My Victory*, 20–21), who suggests "Ancient mountains were shattered, Eternal hills collapsed, Eternal orbits were destroyed" (3:7), following Albright's suggestion ("Psalm of Habakkuk," 14 n. 6) that *hălîkôt* refers to celestial orbits.

144. For similar patterns in Ugaritic texts, see Cross, *Canaanite Myth and Hebrew Epic*, 147–163, and Hiebert, *God of My Victory*, 94–102. The participation of the sun and moon could allude to favorable astrological omens, as suggested by Hiebert, *God of My Victory*, 94–102; Holladay, "Day(s) the Moon Stood Still"; Miller, *Divine Warrior*, 123–128.

145. For comparisons between v. 9 and Akkadian and Ugaritic myths that specify the weapons of the divine warrior, see Hiebert, *God of My Victory*, 26–27.

146. Hiebert (*God of My Victory*, 30) prefers "clouds poured down water," by revocalizing *zrm* as a Poel perfect (*zōrĕmû*), "to storm," and reading "clouds" (*'ābôt*) from an alternate manuscript.

147. Somewhat speculatively, Hiebert (*God of My Victory*, 34–36) reconstructs 13a as "You advanced for the victory of your militia," with Albright ("Psalm of Habakkuk," 16–17).

148. Miller (*Divine Warrior*, 136) takes 13a as a call for celestial deities to participate in battle, reminiscent of Judg 5:20, Hab 3:11, and Josh 10. The heavenly bodies are assimilated into Yahweh's assembly in texts like Ps 148:3 but commonly appear as gods in Near Eastern traditions (*Divine Warrior*, 240 n. 180); cf. Job 31:26.

149. See further, Wildberger, *Isaiah 13–27*, 1–39; Eidevall, *Prophecy and Propaganda*, esp. 107–113; and Blenkinsopp, *Isaiah 1–39*, 270–280.

150. For arguments that 13:2–16 constitutes a retrospect of the imminent events in vv. 17–22 (an attack on Babylon), see Wildberger (*Isaiah 13–27*, 11–15) and Eidevall (*Prophecy and Propaganda*, 110); for possible connections with Jer 50–51, see Blenkinsopp, *Isaiah 1–39*, 277–280.

151. Wildberger (*Isaiah 13–27*, 7) identifies the weapons (*kēlîm*) as the host itself.

152. Wildberger (*Isaiah 13–27*, 416) prefers *za'mô* as "execution," cf. Isa 10:5, Prov 22:14.

153. Wildberger (*Isaiah 13–27*, 4) prefers "whole land," which would qualify the seeming universalism evoked in the NRSV translation.

154. Some of the language suggests a call to war amidst an assembly of deities (but see the important qualifications of Miller, *Divine Warrior*, 136). Others argue for more specific enemies, as Erlandson, *Burden of Babylon*; cf. Wildberger, *Isaiah 13–27*, 13–14; Blenkinsopp, *Isaiah 1–39*, 411; and Eidevall, *Prophecy and Propaganda*, 98–101.

155. See Eidevall, *Prophecy and Propaganda*, 110; and Vanderhooft, *Neo-Babylonian Empire*, 126.

156. Wildberger (*Isaiah 13–27*, 8) suggests that the term *ûkĕsîlêhem* (here "constellations") may be a gloss.

157. For allusions to an assembly (as evident in the use of first-person language in 13:3, e.g.), see Miller, *Divine Warrior*, 136.

158. On oracles in relation to treaty curses, see Hillers, *Treaty Curses*, 44–54; and Vanderhooft, *Neo-Babylonian Empire*, 127.

159. The role of the Medes here is curious, and many scholars take them as a stand-in for the Persians; see Wildberger, *Isaiah 13–27*, 12.

160. Similarly, Eidevall, *Prophecy and Propaganda*, 177–186.

161. Miller (*Divine Warrior*, 140), for instance, views Zech 14 as emblematic of holy war's "full eschatological bloom in late prophecy." Meyers and Meyers (*Zechariah 9–14*, 409–410) argue that the preexilic prophets view this "day" as imminent, while the postexilic ones take the exile as the beginning of "the day" that is still to be completed in the future. Thus construed, postexilic writings imagine an eschatological drama that has already begun (as in Joel and Malachi).

162. For debates about the unity of the text, see Wolff, Janzen, and McBride, *Joel and Amos*, 6–8; and Crenshaw, *Joel*, 29–34.

163. Motifs familiar from divine war traditions include the call to war (as also in, e.g., Judg 5:12 and Isa 51:9) and the sanctification of the armies (e.g., Josh 3:5, 2 Sam 11:11, 1 Sam 21:5); Miller, *Divine Warrior*, 37–38; cf. the "consecrated ones" (*limquddāšāy*) in Isa 13:3.

164. See Wolff, Janzen, and McBride, *Joel and Amos*, 46, on the idea of "fixed marching routes" (cf. Joel 1:6 and Prov 30:27).

165. Some manuscripts attest to the singular, so Wolff, Janzen, and McBride (*Joel and Amos*, 38–39) read "mighty is he [Yahweh] who carries out his word."

166. Wolff, Janzen, and McBride (*Joel and Amos*, 73) arrive at "That Yahweh may [shatter] your heroes," by preferring the text of Targum Jonathan and the Vulgate and on the basis of similar formulations in other literature. Cf. Crenshaw (*Joel*, 189–190) for arguments for and against taking this as a gloss.

167. Other images of Yahweh sitting in judgment appear in 1 Sam 3:13; Pss 9:8–9 [7–8], 122:5; cf. Jer 26:10b, Ruth 4:2.

168. *Divine Warrior*, 138; for *gibbōrîm*, see also Ps 103:20 and Judg 5:23; this term is often used for lesser divine beings in Qumran literature.

169. Wolff (*Isaiah 13–27*, 72) prefers the Greek reading, "Tumult! Tumult"; by contrast, Crenshaw (*Joel*, 192) takes *hāmônîm* as the noise of a great crowd, as in Isa 13:4 and 17:12.

170. Crenshaw (*Joel*, 192–193) notes the seeming contradiction between images of Yahweh sitting in judgment in a valley and marching forth from Zion; he explains this as reflecting dual judicial and military roles. For other images of Yahweh dwelling on Zion, see, e.g., Isa 8:18 and Zech 2:14.

171. Cf. the assault of the nations in Zech 12:3.

172. Meyers and Meyers (*Zechariah 9–14*, 410–411) suggest that this future defeat is modeled on the fall of Jerusalem to the Babylonians (cf. the partial success of Gog in Ezek 38). Cf. also the fifty-fifty split of Jerusalem here to that envisioned in Zech 13:8–9.

173. For other images of Yahweh "going forth" (*yāṣā'*) to battle, see Isa 26:21, 42:13.

174. Translations of Zechariah are from Meyers and Meyers, *Zechariah 9–14*. On the use of the rare term *qěrāb*, see ibid., 418.

175. Meyers and Meyers, *Zechariah 9–14*, 412–413.

176. On the divine council language here and in Zech 1–8, see Meyers and Meyers *Zechariah 9–14*, 429–430; Hanson, *Dawn of Apocalyptic*, 375.

177. Language about "all the earth" appears also in Zech 1:11 and 6:5.

178. Meyers and Meyers (*Zechariah 9–14*, 440) argue that the language reimagines Deut 6:4 in terms of the global sovereignty of Yahweh; cf. Zech 13:2 where the names of other gods will be removed.

179. On deities positioning themselves on a mountain at the center of the cosmos, see Meyers and Meyers, *Zechariah 9–14*, 419; and M. Smith, *Early History of God*, 73 n. 86; cf. Hag 1:8; Mic 1:2–4; Amos 4:13, 9:5–6.

180. The phrase "on that day" (14:4) occurs seven times in Zech 14 alone; cf. Zech 12:3 and 13:1.

181. See Miller, *Divine Warrior*, 66–74, 132–133; and Handy, "Dissenting Deities." In some cases, Israel's armies are envisioned as fighting alongside the heavenly armies, as in 2 Kgs 6:15–19 (cf. 2 Kgs 7:6, 2:11–12), but Israel's human armies often play relatively passive roles. The host also functions as part of the assembly in some cases (2 Kgs 22:19) and includes the sun, the moon, and the stars in others (Deut 4:19, 17:3; Pss 103:20–21, 148:2–3); cf. Job 38:7, where the morning stars appear in a parallelism with *běnê 'ĕlōhîm*, and Ps 82, where Yahweh executes a death sentence against other gods.

182. Similarly, Miller, *Divine Warrior*, 162.

183. See M. S. Smith, *Origins*, 41–53; Miller, "Cosmology and World Order"; Mullen, *Assembly of the Gods*, 114–120; and Olyan, "Is Isaiah 40–55 Really Monotheistic?"

184. In many cases, mythmakers also expropriate the powers and iconography of other gods. The biblical anthology, for instance, attests to the fusing of El and Yahweh, the latter of which also assimilates attributes of Baal and Asherah, as argued by M. Smith, *Early History of God*, esp. 32–64; and Cross, *Canaanite Myth and Hebrew Epic*, 44–75; cf. M. S. Smith, *Ugaritic Baal Cycle*, 1:89–96, on the relationship between El and Baal.

Chapter 2. Assemblies, Councils, and Ranks of Divinity

1. So Morrison, *Powers that Be*; Schlier, *Principalities and Powers*; Caird, *Principalities and Powers*; Beker, *Triumph of God*; and Moses, *Practices of Power*. For focused studies of particular texts, see MacGregor, "Principalities and Powers"; Lee, "Interpreting the Demonic Powers"; Black, "Πᾶσαι ἐξουσίαι αὐτῷ ὑποταγήσονται"; de Boer, *Defeat of Death*; Martyn, *Galatians*; Martyn, "Apocalyptic Antinomies"; and Arnold, "Returning to the Domain."

2. Many scholars claim that a developing angelology or demonology is characteristic of testamentary and apocalyptic literature, as Newsom, "Angels"; and Koch, "Monotheismus und Angelologie." Lower-level beings also populate the landscape in 4 Ezra, the Testaments of the Twelve Patriarchs, and 2 Enoch, but other texts show little or no such interests (e.g., Sirach, Wisdom, 2 Baruch, Epistle of Jeremiah, Susanna 1–4, Maccabees, and the Psalms of Solomon). The contrasts are especially striking when one compares 1–2 Chr with the parallel account in Sam–Kgs (e.g., 2 Sam 24:16–17 versus 2 Chr 21:15–30). Some explain these interests by positing Babylonian influence, as Bousset and Gressman, *Religion des Judentums*, 499–505; and Russell, *Method and Message of Jewish Apocalypticism*, 257–262, or an increasingly remote deity that requires intermediaries (so Bousset and Gressman, *Religion des Judentums*, 319–321, 329–331), though this has been sharply criticized (Olyan, *A Thousand Thousands Served Him*, 6). John Collins (*Apocalyptic Vision*, 101–104, and *Apocalypticism*, 133) suggests that angel speculation more basically reflects popular views; see also Gruenwald, *From Apocalypticism to Gnosticism*, 125–144; Meier, *Messenger in the Ancient Semitic World*; Greene, *Role of the Messenger and Message*; Kasher, "Angelology"; and Garrett, *No Ordinary Angel*.

3. M. Smith, *Origins*, 41–53; M. Smith, *Early History of God;* Nissinen, "Prophets and the Divine Council"; Seitz, "Divine Council"; Cross, "Council of Yahweh"; Mullen, *Assembly of the Gods;* Miller, "Cosmology and World Order"; Freedman, "Who Is Like Thee?" Of course, such work has also proved controversial. For instance, Robert Wilson objects to Cross's argument that Isa 40:1–8 addresses divine heralds within the council, in part, by insisting that these other deities are not true deities because they cannot "do anything in the cosmos" ("Community of the Second Isaiah," 54), but Seitz's critique ("Divine Council," 10–11) is persuasive.

4. Smith (*Origins*, 48) suggests that Ps 82 preserves a tradition in which Yahweh is not the high god but a son who takes over the patrimonies of the others; see also Dietrich and Loretz, *Jahwe und seine Aschera;* Seybold, *Die Psalmen;* Parker, "Beginning of the Reign of God"; and Sawyer, "Biblical Alternatives."

5. The MT of Deut 32:8 has El apportioning the nations among the "sons of Israel," but the LXX has υἱῶν θεοῦ (and ἀγγέλων θεοῦ in some manuscripts) and 4QDeut^j supports this reading with *běnê 'ělōhîm;* see Tov, *Textual Criticism,* 269; and Ulrich et al., eds., *Qumran Cave 4. IX,* 900.

6. Smith (*Origins*, 167–178) suggests that the rise of the Neo-Assyrian Empire may have informed a shift away from the framework of shared governance developed in Deut 32 and toward the kind of violent usurpation found in Ps 82; cf. the reduction of Baal's retinue in *CTA* 1.5, V 6–9.

7. *Origins*, 47; M. Smith, *Early History of God,* 145 n. 143; Mullen, *Assembly of the Gods,* 114–120.

8. On the host, see Olyan, "Is Isaiah 40–55 Really Monotheistic?"; Mettinger, "YHWH SABAOTH"; and Miller, *Divine Warrior,* 152. Earlier studies sought to avoid identifying the host with divine beings. For instance, scholars argued that this language referred to the human armies of Israel (as Maier, *Das altisraelitische Ladeheiligtum,* 50–51), the totality of all creatures, like *ṣābā'* in Gen 2:1 and Isa 34:2 (as Wambacq, *L'épithète divine,* 276), as well as an abstraction or epithet of God (as Tsevat, "Studies"); cf. Miller, *Divine Warrior,* 256.

9. On Reshep and Deber as plague gods, see van der Toorn, "Theology of Demons," 64; Hiebert, *God of My Victory,* 19, 91–94; and Miller, *Divine Warrior,* 119.

10. See Pope, *Job,* 9–11; and Schoors, "Isaiah." On other accuser figures, see, e.g., Meyers and Meyers, *Haggai, Zechariah 1–8,* 183–184; and Oppenheim, "Eyes of the Lord."

11. M. Smith, *Origins,* 51–52. Similarly, Miller, "Cosmology and World Order," 73–74; Levenson, *Creation and the Persistence of Evil,* 131; and J. Z. Smith, "Wisdom and Apocalypticism."

12. On Ezekiel's language about "angels," see Newsom, "Angels," 1:251; cf. 2 Bar. 6–8. Cherubim also appear in Ezek 1 and 10, which Newsom takes as watchdog figures or guardians (cf. Gen 3:24; Ezek 28:14; 2 Sam 22:1; Pss 18:11 [18:10], 80:1, 99:1; Isa 37:16), noting that they often appear in throne decorations (Exod

25:18–20, 26:31; 1 Sam 4:4; 1 Kgs 6:23–36); see also the Seraphim of Isa 14:29 and 30:6; cf. Num 21:6–9 and 2 Kgs 18:4. Isaiah seems to assimilate them to the divine council, but later writers make them a special class of *aggeloi*.

13. In chapter 36 the writer also envisions cleansing the people of their idols and remaking their hearts with the deity's spirit (*rûaḥ*) (36:25–32); cf. 11:18–21.

14. See Meyers and Meyers, *Haggai, Zechariah 1–8*. Meyers and Meyers suggest that 1:11 alludes to the peace and political reorganization under Darius (ibid., 116–117); cf. 2 Chr 36:21 and Dan 9:2.

15. The term *ša'ănān* (translated as "securely") may be meant ironically (Meyers and Meyers, *Haggai, Zechariah 1–8*, 121–122); that is, it could connote the nations' false assumptions about their continued peace and prosperity (as 2 Kgs 19:28–31 and Amos 6:1).

16. Translation by Meyers and Meyers. See Meyers and Meyers (*Haggai, Zechariah 1–8*, 122) on the unusual use of ʿzr with *lĕrā'â*, "they helped to/for evil." P. R. Ackroyd (*Exile and Restoration*, 176) proposes an alternate root for ʿzr, yielding "to be copious" and hence "they multiply calamity"; in a different way, P. R. Driver ("Hebrew Notes," 173) emends the text with *zārĕ'û* (from zrʿ, "to plow"), yielding "they sow/plot (evil)."

17. The nation alluded to here is most likely Persia (Meyers and Meyers, *Haggai, Zechariah 1–8*, 121).

18. Cf. Zech 3:1–7, where lower-level deities deliver Yahweh's promises. On the *mal'ak* of Yahweh (in Zech 3:1 and other literature), see Meyers and Meyers, *Haggai, Zechariah 1–8*, 183; as the head of the divine council, see Cooke, "Sons of (the) God(s)"; Kingsbury, "Prophets and the Council"; and Newsom, "Angels," 250.

19. The accuser is rebuked, and Joshua is re-dressed in purified clothing and promised rule. On clothing as marks of status, see Oppenheim, "Golden Garments"; and Meyers and Meyers, *Haggai, Zechariah 1–8*, 119.

20. Translations of 1 Enoch are from Nickelsburg and VanderKam (*1 Enoch*), which works with an eclectic text based on multiple Ethiopic, Greek, and Aramaic manuscripts; the commentaries by Nickelsburg (*1 Enoch: A Commentary*) and Nickelsburg and VanderKam (*1 Enoch 2: A Commentary*) provide extensive notes on the textual reconstructions used in this translation. Where I provide transliterations of the Ethiopic and/or the Greek texts, I use Charles's critical edition (*Ethiopic Version*) and note other editions and possible reconstructions in the notes where relevant. I have also consulted Knibb's edition and translation (*Ethiopic Book of Enoch*), which is based on a single complete Ethiopic manuscript; Milik's edition of the Aramaic fragments (*Books of Enoch*); and the commentaries of Black (*Book of Enoch or 1 Enoch*) and Charles (*Book of Enoch or 1 Enoch*).

21. This analysis could be extended to the Similitudes, but I have avoided this text because of constraints of space and difficulties with dating. See Knibb, "Date of the Parables of Enoch."

22. As VanderKam notes (*Enoch and the Growth*, 103 n. 84), Uriel has a revealing role elsewhere (72:1; 74:2; 75:3–4; 78:10; 79:2, 6; 82:7), acts as the guide of all celestial bodies (72:1), and gives light to humankind (82:8). Other stars are called leaders (*marāḥi*) (e.g., 72:3, 75:1; cf. 80:1, 82:18) or heads (*'ar'est*) over the thousands (75:1; 82:4, 12–14), and the sun, moon, and stars ride chariots across the sky (sun, 72:5, 75:3, 82:8; moon, 73:2, 75:3, 82:8; stars, 75:3, 82:8). In 82:10 leaders watch over the celestial bodies to ensure they appear at the correct times and in the right places; see also Schäfer, *Revalität zwischen Engeln und Menschen*, 23–26. On the language of leaders (*marāḥi, xabây,* or *'ar'est*) for the luminaries, see Davidson, *Angels at Qumran*, 93, 327–331.

23. On seasonal weather patterns and agriculture, see Melkeyal's ninety-one-day rule, which involves three leaders beneath him and brings "sweat, heat, and sadness; all the trees bear fruit and leaves come out on all the trees; (there is) a harvest of wheat, roses, and all the flowers that bloom in the field, but the winter trees are dried up" (82:16). Similarly, the ninety-one days of Helememelek bring "heat, drought, trees bearing their fruit ripe" (82:19).

24. See Nickelsburg and VanderKam (*1 Enoch 2*, 359–365) on the literary unity (or lack thereof). VanderKam (*Enoch and the Growth*, 79) argues that 82:9–20 belongs before chapter 79, whereas 82:1–8 forms a "credible conclusion" to the work as a whole; 4Q211 may preserve an originally longer ending. Jonathan Ben-Dov (*Head of All Years*, 69–118) argues that the Astronomical Book contains at least two originally independent treatises (1 En. 72–74 and 78–79), a position originally taken by Neugebauer ("'Astronomical' Chapters"). For other proposals, see VanderKam, *Enoch and the Growth*, 106–107.

25. Some manuscripts read "stars of the command." On this translation, see Nickelsburg and VanderKam (*1 Enoch 2*, 521, 528). Against Knibb, who translates as "heads of stars in command" (*'ar'estihomu la-kawākebt te'ezāz*), Black argues for the reading "stray from the commandments (of God)," insisting (with Charles, *Book of Enoch or 1 Enoch*, 172, and others) that the noun *te'ezāz* (Greek ἐντολή) is part of the predicate even though the grammatical structure is unusual (Black, *Book of Enoch or 1 Enoch*, 253). Black (ibid., 253) takes the Greek original as τῆς ἐντολῆς (to be taken with the verb, as in 3 Macc 4:16), mistakenly connected with the stars by the Ethiopic translator.

26. Though they differ from this Enochic myth in a number of important ways, certain Greek, Roman, and Babylonian texts discuss ideas of the cyclical consummation of civilizations as well as that of the cosmos itself, often involving astrological realignments. See, e.g., Virgil, *Ecl.* 4; Seneca, *Nat.* 3.29; *Epistle of Barnabas* 6.13; *Life of Adam and Eve* 49.3; Josephus, *Ant.* 1.2.3; and 2 Pet 3:10–12. David E. Hahm (*Origins of Stoic Cosmology*, 185–187) relates such patterns to Stoic theories of a conflagration (ἐκπύρωσις) and focuses especially on the myths of Phaethon and Deucalion (Plato, *Tim.* 22b–23c), Aristotle on the great or (greatest) year (frag. 19 of the *Protrepticus*), the Pythagorean Philolaus (DK 44A 18), and certain Epicurean texts (e.g., Lucretius, *De Rer.* 5.338–347).

See also Lucan, *Bellum* 1.649–665. On the appropriation of specifically Stoic imagery in 2 Pet, see, e.g., Harrill, "Stoic Physics."

27. The Psalms of Solomon 18 offers a clarifying addendum to the order and obedience of the luminaries: "[the luminaries] have not wandered (οὐκ ἐπλανήθησαν) from the day he created them, from ancient generations. They have not veered off their course (οὐκ ἀπέστησαν ὁδῶν αὐτῶν) except when God directed them by the command of his servants" (18:12).

28. The Greek of the Book of Watchers 1–16 uses ἐγρήγοροι for the watchers but uses ἄγγελοι (the Ethiopic has *malā'ekt*) for heavenly beings generally (like 1 En. 1–36 and 83–108) and watchers on occasion (1 En. 20:1, 39:12–13, 71:7; cf. the Aramaic of 22:6 and 93:2, in place of the ἄγγελοι/*malā'ekt* of the other versions); cf. 1QapGen ii 1, 16; 4 QEnGiants; and 4QAmram. It is notable also that the fragments from Qumran rarely use the term *mal'ak* for the watchers. Nickelsburg (*1 Enoch*, 140–141) and others (e.g., Collins, "Watchers") suggest that the Aramaic original may have been *'yr* (see Dan 4:10, 14, 20; CD 2.18; cf. 2 Pet 2:4), perhaps reflecting a derivation from the root *'wr*, "to be awake/watchful," which was then translated into the Greek as ἐγρήγοροι. Though this argument has not been well-received, Glasson (*Greek Influence*, 69–73) connects this language with Hesiod's guardians ("For upon the bounteous earth Zeus has thrice ten thousand spirits, watchers [φύλακες] of mortal men, and these keep watch on judgments and deeds of wrong as they roam, clothed in mist, all over the earth" [*Works and Days*, 292–295]) and the regional gods and spirits of Plato's *Politicus, Laws,* and *Critias;* cf. Philo of Byblios, *Phoenician History*, 1.10.2.

29. Nickelsburg (*1 Enoch*, 142) supplies "quake," in keeping with the Ethiopic text and the sense of 1 En. 13:3, but then takes the watchers as the subject of both verbs against both the Greek and the Ethiopic, a move that defies logic. The Greek Akhmim papyrus has "and all will fear and the watchers will believe (καὶ φοβηθήσονται πάντες καὶ πιστεύσουσιν οἱ ἐγρήγοροι)," whereas the Ethiopic has "and all will fear and the watchers will quake (*wa-yefarrehu kwellu wa-yādlaqallequ teguhān*)."

30. See VanderKam, "Theophany of Enoch." Here the watchers are confined at the outer edges of the earth, but in other cases there is ambiguity about their precise location, both before and after their judgment (e.g., 10:13, 18:10–19:1, 21:7–10). See Glasson (*Greek Influence*, 64–65) for speculation about the influence of Greek traditions about the Titans; alternatively, A. Lods (*Livre d'Henoch*) takes this as a later (perhaps Christian) interpolation.

31. For other texts that use the order and obedience of the natural world and the heavenly bodies in similar ways, see Sir 16:24–30, 1QS 3.15–4.26, 1Q34bis 3 ii, 1–4, Ps. Sol. 18:10–12, 1 Clement 19–20, and T. Naph. 3:2–4:1; Nickelsburg, *1 Enoch*, 152–155.

32. This translation follows Syncellus's Greek manuscript, which has πνεύματα

πονηρά, in agreement with the Ethiopic *manfasāta 'ekuyāna*, against the Akhmim's ἰσχυρά.

33. Syncellus has πνεύματα πονηρὰ [ἔσονται, τὰ πνεύματα] ἐξεληλυθότα ἀπὸ τοῦ σώματος [τῆς σαρκὸς] αὐτῶν. Where the Ethiopic and Greek Akhmim read more simply, πνεύμα[τα] τὰ πονηρὰ ἐξῆλθον ἀπὸ τοῦ σώματος αὐτῶν. Nickelsburg (*1 Enoch*, 268) takes "body of the flesh" as a kind of semiticism familiar from Sir 23:16, 1 En. 102:5, and 1QpHab 9.2. On the language of πνεύματα πονηρά, see 1 Sam 16:14–23, 18:10; 1 En. 99:7; Tob 6:7; Jub. 10:3, 13; 12:20; Luke 7:21, 8:2, 11:26; Matt 12:43; Acts 19:12–16; T. Sim. 3:5, 4:9, 6:6; T. Levi 5:6, 18:12; T. Jud. 16:1; and T. Ash. 1:8, 6:5.

34. This reading of 15:9 follows the Ethiopic. Syncellus omits most of 9b; Nickelsburg (*1 Enoch*, 268) reconstructs the Greek original as πνεύματα πονηρά ἐπὶ τῆς γῆς ἔσονται καὶ πνεύματα πονηρὰ κληθήσεται.

35. Charles's edition has *wa-manfasa ra 'ayt* [*damanāta*]; τὰ πνεύματα τῶν γιγάντων [νεφέλας]/τὰ πνεύματα τῶν γιγάντων νεμόμενα. Charles (*Book of Enoch*, 36–37) takes Syncellus's νεμόμενα as "afflict" while Nickelsburg (*1 Enoch*, 268) takes νεμόμενα as "pasturing" and therefore as a translation of the Aramaic *r'yn*, which he takes as corrupt for *t'yn* ("lead astray") or *r''yn* ("shatter"). As F. Crawford Burkitt (*Jewish and Christian Apocalypses*, 22) notes, the wrestling language fits with demonic seizures as found in Mark 9:20.

36. The text here is very difficult. Both Greek manuscripts agree on δρόμους ποιοῦντα, "making flights/races." Charles (*Book of Enoch*, 37) suggests that δρόμους may be corrupt for τρόμους, yielding "but nevertheless hunger"; Nickelsburg (*1 Enoch*, 268) suggests that δρόμους may translate *mrwṣh*, which can be translated as "running/oppression" or may be corrupt for *mrw'*, "illness." See also Black's reconstruction for the translation "causing injuries" and of 15:11 generally (*Book of Enoch*, 153–154).

37. Cf. Jub. 10:5–11; Matt 8:29.

38. See Nickelsburg (*1 Enoch*, 273–274) on the textual problems here. Knibb (*Ethiopic Book*, 2:102) prefers the Greek, while Black (*Book of Enoch*, 35) takes the Ethiopic as the better reading; cf. Knibb, "1 Enoch," 205 n. 2. See Glasson, *Greek Influence*, 57–61, on the possible influence of Hesiod's *Works and Days*.

39. See also Deut 32:17; Ps 106:36–39; Jub. 15; Justin Martyr, *2 Apol.* 5; and Tertullian, *De Idol.* 4.

40. See also Stuckenbruck, *1 Enoch 91–108*, 401–403.

41. VanderKam (*Enoch and the Growth*, 361–363) dates the Book of Dreams (which includes the Animal Apocalypse in 85–90) to sometime before 161 BCE when Judas Maccabeus died. Most others agree on a date sometime in the 160s (e.g., Tiller, *Commentary*, 61–82). The Book of Dreams is extant in complete form only in Ethiopic, but Greek fragments of 89:42–49 survive (Charles, *Book of Enoch*, 195–198; Black, ed., *Apocalypsis Henochi graece*, 36–37), as do parts of the Animal Apocalypse in Aramaic fragments (Milik, ed., *Books of Enoch*, 6).

42. For the argument that the first vision is originally independent of the Animal Apocalypse, see Tiller, *Commentary*, 98–100.

43. The Ethiopic manuscripts add "for you see all things," but the editors take this as a doublet of the previous line.

44. Cf. similar language in Wis 9 (esp. 2, 4, 9, 10) and Book of the Watchers 9.

45. Tiller, *Commentary*, 15–20.

46. See also Isa 2:2, 8:3; Zech 14; 5Q 15; Tiller, *Commentary*, 46. As Tiller explains (ibid., 47–51), the Animal Apocalypse also idealizes the desert camp rather than the temple.

47. The leader himself is later transformed, but because the text is corrupt, it is not clear into what he is transformed (Tiller, *Commentary*, 17).

48. Tiller, *Commentary*, 38–40.

49. So VanderKam, *Enoch and the Growth*, 164–167. Cf. also the scheme of Dan 9. In some contrast, Nickelsburg (*1 Enoch*, 391) also emphasizes connections with Ezek 34 and Zech 11. Tiller (*Commentary*, 54–60, modifying Milik's argument) shows that other schemes of periodization may influence the writer here, such as the seventy generations of 1 En. 10:12; cf. Nickelsburg, *1 Enoch*, 391–392, for the argument that the first period begins with the rule of Manasseh. On similar analogies in Greek tradition, especially Plato's *Critias*, see Glasson, *Greek Influence*, 70.

50. I avoid language about angels here, but such concepts abound in the scholarly literature, beginning with Charles (*Book of Enoch*, 200). Though in other cases Tiller seems to represent the shepherds as human kings, here (*Commentary*, 53) he goes a step farther and introduces language about harmful deities (or demons) even though they are not construed in this way in the text. A similar problem emerges in Tiller's reading of 90:13 as a battle where "the forces of heaven and hell are arrayed against one another" (ibid., 73).

51. See Tiller (*Commentary*, 327–328) on the textual problem here.

52. The figure of the "ram with a horn" is most likely Judas Maccabeus, but some have attempted to identify this figure as John Hyrcanus (Tiller, *Commentary*, 7–8).

53. VanderKam (*Enoch and the Growth*, 167) suggests connections with Jer 25:12, but the shepherds in the Animal Apocalypse are clearly construed as divine beings.

54. The Ethiopic text of 1 En. 90 proves difficult; see VanderKam, *Enoch and the Growth*, 162–163, who resists a number of proposals for emending or reordering vv. 13–19; cf. Nickelsburg, *1 Enoch*, 396–397.

55. This translation reflects the emendation of "every word" to "every thing" (Tiller, *Commentary*, 377; Nickelsburg, *1 Enoch*, 402–403).

56. Some scholars discern originally separate compositions in the Epistle. So Stuckenbruck (*1 Enoch 91–108*, 2–4) distinguishes between an exhortation (91:1–10, 18–19), the Apocalypse of Weeks (93:1–10, 91:11–17), the Epistle proper (92:1–5, 93:11–105:2), the Birth of Noah (106:1–107:3), and a concluding Eschatologi-

cal Admonition (108:1–15). Nickelsburg (*1 Enoch*, 416–421) follows a similar schema, but VanderKam (*Enoch and the Growth*, 145) argues that the thematic unity of the Epistle suggests a unifying editorial hand. Knibb ("Apocalypse of Weeks") also argues that 91:1–9, 18–19 form the introduction to the work, a view supported by Aramaic fragments that place chapter 91 at the beginning of the work.

57. VanderKam (*Enoch and the Growth*, 142–149) argues that only the Apocalypse of Weeks offers sufficient evidence for dating and that it may not be as independent of the Epistle as sometimes thought. He dates the work to between 175 (the first year of the reign of Antiochus IV) and 167 BCE by identifying the apostate generation in 93:9 as a Hellenizing movement within Palestine that worked together with Antiochus, and the "sword" in 91:12 as alluding to an eschatological battle. In contrast, Nickelsburg (*1 Enoch*, 427) dates the Epistle to ca. 200–160 BCE on the grounds that the author knows the Book of the Watchers, that the text was composed to fit an Enochic testament that either predated or included the animal visions, and that Jubilees knows the testamentary form of 1 Enoch but shows no knowledge of the Epistle, so the terminus post quem becomes the date of Jubilees. Nickelsburg admits that a terminus ante quem proves difficult to establish but suggests the time of Ben Sira (198–175) or Alexander Jannaeus (103–76). Stuckenbruck (*1 Enoch 91–108*, 8–14) suggests that some parts of the Epistle may be pre-Maccabean, especially the Apocalypse of Weeks.

58. For similarities with 2 Bar. 56–77, see Nickelsburg, *1 Enoch*, 439; and Henze, "Apocalypse of Weeks," 209. On the paired structure of the Apocalypse of Weeks, see VanderKam, *Enoch: A Man for All Generations*, 65–70; Henze, "Apocalypse of Weeks," 208–209; and Tiller, *Commentary*, 96–98.

59. The scheme becomes difficult in the seventh age, which may allude to the period leading up to the Maccabean revolt (e.g., 91:11).

60. The precise identification of "they" here is difficult. The context suggests that the referent is to the people, but it could also include the powers of heaven, since the sins of the watchers are recalled in v. 15, and the heavens and heavenly powers are re-created in v. 16. On these verses, see also Nickelsburg (*1 Enoch*), 450.

61. The text of vv. 7–8 is difficult. Nickelsburg (*1 Enoch*, 482–483) reconstructs "Those who worship stones—and who carve images of silver and gold and wood and stone and clay and worship phantoms (φαν]τάσμασιν) and demons (δαιμονίοι[ς) and abominations (βδελύγ]μασι) and evil spirits (πνεύμασιν πονη[ροῖς) and all errors, not according to knowledge" (v. 7) by drawing on the Greek of Chester Beatty and Tertullian's Latin. See the further discussion of this text below.

62. Nickelsburg and VanderKam translate as "learn to do the commandments of the Most High." They rely on the Greek of Chester Beatty (τὰς ἐντολάς) against the Ethiopic *lafenāwāta* ("the ways of") (*1 Enoch*, 483).

63. On heavenly record-keeping, see also 1 En. 89:70, 90:20; Ps 56:9; Isa 65:6; and Mal 3:16.

64. Nickelsburg's translation follows the Greek manuscript (γραφήν [τὴν] ἀναγκαίαν) here against the Ethiopic witnesses, which have "holy writings (ṣeḥfata qeddusāta)" or "writings of the holy ones (ṣeḥfata qeddusān)."

65. Manuscripts do not agree on the precise word order of 4a, but the sense of the text seems basically consistent; see Nickelsburg, *1 Enoch*, 496; cf. Milik, ed., *Books of Enoch*, 52.

66. Nickelsburg (*1 Enoch*, 483) follows the Greek text of Chester Beatty here: καὶ λατρεύ[οντες φαν]τάσμασιν καὶ δαιμονίοι[ς καὶ βδελύγ]μασι καὶ πνεύμασιν πονη[ροῖς, which gains support from the witness of Tertullian. The Ethiopic witnesses have "and who worship evil spirits and demons (wa-ʾella yesaggedu la-nafsāt ʾekuyāt/ān [or rekusāt/ān] wa-ʾagānent)," which may suggest attempted revisions.

67. Nickelsburg (*1 Enoch*, 483) follows the Greek of Chester Beatty: καὶ τὰ ὁρ[ά]ματα τῶν ἐνυπνίων [ὑμῶν] καταπλανήσουσιν ὑμᾶς; the Ethiopic manuscript has "and in the visions of their dreams they will err and they will fear (wa-bareʾya ḥelmomu bomu yerasseʿu wa-yefarrehu)."

68. Dan 7–12 may be the work of multiple hands and redactors, but most source critical and redaction theories remain highly speculative. For an overview of the relevant scholarship, see, Collins, *Daniel*, 26–38. As with other texts, I use designations such as "writer(s)" and "editor(s)" as a way of drawing attention to these literary possibilities.

69. Modern commentators take the empires as Babylonian, Median, Persian, and Greek; on the history of scholarship, see Collins, *Daniel*, 312. Cf. also the "trees" of Babel and Persia in 4Q552 and 4Q553.

70. Translations are from Collins, *Daniel*.

71. On the alleged *Chaoskampf* backgrounds of the larger conflict, see Collins, *Daniel*, 280–294; Ps 82; and 11QMelch ii, 9–10. "Holy ones" here most likely alludes to lower-level beings such as the stars and the host in 8:9–12; on the extended scholarly discussion about whether these beings should be construed as divine or human, see Collins, ibid., 312–318.

72. Many commentators take the ten horns as Seleucid kings, though the identities of some of the rulers are disputed: Collins, *Daniel*, 320–321; Rowley, *Darius the Mede*, 108–115. Andreas Blasius ("Antiochus IV Epiphanes") argues (following Elias Bickermann) that the last three are the Ptolemaic co-regents of Egypt (Ptolemy VI, VIII, and Cleopatra).

73. On dominion granted to secondary divine beings (e.g., Baal in *KTU* 1.1–6 and 1.2), see Collins, *Daniel*, 286–294; and Ballentine, *Conflict Myth*, 194–197.

74. The language here is difficult; some manuscripts suggest that the word for host (ḥaṣṣābāʾ) is a gloss; Collins, *Daniel*, 334–335.

75. For language about trampling underfoot, see also 7:24, 8:7, 8:10, and 11:36; cf. Isa 14:12–15 and Rev 12:4.

76. E.g., Isa 10:5–34, 14:3–21, 37:16–35; Ezek 27, 28, 31; 2 Kgs 19. See Collins, *Daniel,* 386–388, and Clifford, "History and Myth in Daniel."

77. The prayer in 9:3–19 has Deuteronomistic overtones and could be the work of a different hand, though see Collins's cautious assessment (*Daniel,* 347–348); similar prayers appear in Ezra 9:6–15; Neh 1:5–11, 9:5–37; Ps 79; and the Words of the Heavenly Luminaries (4Q504), among others.

78. On the alleged offense/pollution of the temple, see 1 Macc 1:54, 4:43; 2 Macc 5:6; Josephus, *Ant.* 12.5.4. Some suggest that chapter 9 was composed shortly after these events (Collins, *Daniel* 359).

79. On the convoluted sequence of 10:20–24, see Charles, *Critical and Exegetical Commentary,* 265–267, and J. Collins, *Daniel,* 376.

80. 4QDanᶜ has *sarim;* on this term used for divinities, see Dan 8:11; Josh 5:14; the "prince of lights" in 1QS 3.20; CD 5.14; 1QM 13.10; "prince of holiness " in 4Q 401; the "prince of the dominion of wickedness" in 1QM 17.5–6; J. Collins, *Daniel,* 375; and Newsom, *Songs of the Sabbath Sacrifice,* 26–27.

81. See Collins, "Mythology of Holy War," 602–603; Collins, *Daniel,* 313–317; and Miller, *Divine Warrior,* 158–159. Collins argues for a two-story interpretation of the combat, but he also allows that the two intermingle in texts like Judg 5 and 1QM 12.7–8.

82. See Collins, *Daniel,* 375–376; 1 En. 20:5 (cf. 9:1 and 10:11) gives a similar role to Michael, but compare Isa 63:9 and Jub. 15:31–32 and the strong role of the angel of the presence and the prince of light in the War Scroll (1QM 13.10, cf. 13.14 and 17.7). Michael plays a military role in 1QM 17.7–8 but elsewhere more diverse ones; Melchizedek plays military, priestly, and judicial roles in 11QMelchizedek (Collins, "Son of Man," 64–65), and 4QAmram seems to identify him with Melchizedek and with the prince of light; cf. Steudel, "Eternal Reign," on Dan 7:18; 4Q246; and 1QM. Cf. also *Animal Apocalypse,* 89–90; Matt 16:27; Mark 8:38; 1 Thess 4:16; 2 Thess 1:7; 4 Ezra 13; and T. Moses 10. The Shepherd of Hermas equates Christ and Michael. In other literature, human enemies take the place of would-be divine opponents, as in Pss 2, 47, and 48. In Ps 2, for instance, Yahweh (like Baal) ridicules the kings massing against his impregnable mountain (Clifford, *Cosmic Mountain,* 144–155).

83. Similarly, Collins, "Son of Man," 55–56, and "Mythology of Holy War," 596–612. See the further debate between Collins and Philip R. Davies: Davies, "Dualism and Eschatology in the War Scroll," esp. 28–29; Davies, "Dualism and Eschatology in 1 QM"; and Collins "Dualism and Eschatology in 1 QM."

84. So Clifford ("History and Myth in Daniel," 24) takes Antiochus's outrage as directed at the council and the supreme deity. Texts such as Deut 32:8–9, 4:19; Sir 17:17; Jub. 15:31; and Acts 7:42–43 are frequently brought to bear on the princes of Dan 10, but Collins (*Daniel,* 374–375) also adds Greek texts such as Plato's *Critias* and *Laws.* For the view that the princes are human rulers, see Shea, "Wrestling with the Prince of Persia"; and Meadowcroft, "Who Are the Princes?"

85. See, e.g., M. Smith, *Origins*, 47, and *Early History*, 145 n. 143; Mullen, *Assembly of the Gods*, 114–120.

86. Jubilees was originally composed in Hebrew and then translated into Greek. Though not extant, the Greek version was the basis for translations into Ethiopic and Latin. Hebrew fragments have been uncovered at Qumran and Masada, but the only complete manuscripts that survive are in Ethiopic. A partial version also survives in Latin, and some later Greek and Syriac texts allude to the work; VanderKam, *Book of Jubilees*, 2:v–xxxiv. Though the work is not typically regarded as a full-blown apocalypse, chapter 23 contains a discourse about an end-time horizon that may be implicit elsewhere (as 1:23–29). See Collins, *Apocalyptic Imagination*, 79–84; Davenport (*Eschatology of the Book of Jubilees*), argues that the eschatological sections are the work of multiple redactors.

87. See VanderKam, "Demons."

88. Trans. VanderKam, *Book of Jubilees*.

89. That the "spirits and angels" in 1.25 do not currently recognize Israel suggests that the lesser ranks may not have been fully briefed on the divine plan. This seems implicit also for the shepherd-managers in the Animal Apocalypse and perhaps also the "rulers of this age" in 1 Cor 2:8.

90. In 2:8 the sun, moon, and stars are created "to rule over day and night."

91. Cf. also 11Q5 XIX (11QPs^a): "Let not a satan rule over me, nor an unclean spirit; neither let pain nor evil inclination have power over my bones;" see Flusser, "Qumrân and Jewish 'Apotropaic' Prayers."

92. Similarly, VanderKam, "Demons," 340.

93. The Ethiopic terms translated as "angels" and "spirits" here are consistently *malā'ekt* and *manfas*, respectively. The seemingly odd phrase "angels of the spirits" is thus simply *malā'ekta manfasa*. On the text, see VanderKam, *Book of Jubilees*, 7–8.

94. The language about spirits and "angels" does not reappear in the subsequent discussion of waters, plants, and luminaries though they do have anthropomorphic attributes (e.g., the waters obey commands in 2:6).

95. On this verse, see VanderKam, "Demons," 357–358; and Charles, *Book of Jubilees*, 45; cf. Josephus, *Ant.* 1.3.70–75; and Philo, *Mos.* 2.65, on the flood as *paliggenesia*. Cf. Jub. 6:32–37 on the calendar.

96. The writer also emphasizes human responsibility with statements such as, "All the thoughts and wishes of mankind were (devoted to) thinking up what was useless and wicked all the time" (7:24); cf. 7:25 where the supreme deity destroys them all "because of their actions."

97. See VanderKam, "Demons," 342–343, on the tendency to equate eating meat with blood and shedding blood (6:18, 6:38, 7:29); cf. VanderKam, "Viewed from Another Angle"; and VanderKam, "Angel Story," esp. 160–163.

98. For the idea of "hymnic exorcisms," see Lange, "Essene Position"; Charles, *Jubilees*, 141; and VanderKam, "Demons," 347.

99. See VanderKam, "Demons," 344 n. 12; some of the manuscripts prefer simple adjectives rather than the construct ("spirits of wickedness"), thus rendering them more simply as "savage spirits" and "evil/wicked spirits."

100. Similarly, in Jub. 15:33 "all the people of Belial will leave their sons uncircumcised."

101. See VanderKam, "Demons," 346–347; and Charles, *Jubilees*, xliv, 78–81, 111–112. Cf. Tg. Ps-J. on Deut 32:8; Pss 106:35–37, 96:4–5.

102. Mastema carries out the slaughter of the Egyptian firstborn (49:2) and appears in the Aqedah scene in 17:15–18:19 (though without a host of evil spirits); cf. 1Q225; VanderKam and Milik, "225.4Qpseudo-Jubilees^a"; and VanderKam, "*Aqedah, Jubilees*, and Pseudojubilees," esp. 258–259.

103. For instance, Collins understands Jubilees as dualistic in the sense that "humanity is torn between two ways, each controlled by supernatural powers, in a manner similar to what we will find at Qumran" (*Apocalyptic Imagination*, 83); similarly, VanderKam, *Textual and Historical Studies*, 265–267. Cf. Testuz, *Les idées religieuses*, 75–92.

104. For instance, see Metso, *Serekh Texts*, 26–27; Stuckenbruck, "Interiorization of Dualism," 162; Tigchelaar, "Evil Inclination," 353; and Charlesworth, "Critical Comparison," 76 n. 1. Others have pushed farther on the issue of dualism, as Frey ("Different Patterns," 281–285), who discerns some eleven distinct forms of dualism; in some contrast, Dimant ("Demonic Realm," 104–105) objects that such diverse formulations have the effect of distracting from or diluting the strong, coherent core of dualism that characterizes the literature.

105. For a lucid assessment of the evidence for Zoroastrianism, see De Jong, "Iranian Connections"; on arguments for and against Iranian influence, see Levison, "Two Spirits," 2:172–177. In many cases, scholars also explain these dualisms by appealing to exhortations about two paths or types, such as those found in Prov 29:27 and Sir 42:24 and 33:9, as Stuckenbruck, "Interiorization of Dualism," 159–184, esp. 161; Frey, "Different Patterns," 295–300; and Metso, *Serekh Texts*, 26.

106. This perspective is well-represented in the work of Duhaime, "Dualism"; Frey, "Different Patterns," 275–335; Dimant, "Composite Character," esp. 602; Dimant, "Between Qumran Sectarian and Non-Sectarian"; and Koch, "History as a Battlefield," esp. 196. Cf. Lange, *Weisheit und Prädestination*, 126; and Collins, "Sectarian Consciousness," esp. 185–192.

107. Dimant is a champion of this view (e.g., "Demonic Realm," 103–117, among other of her essays), but she builds on the earlier work of scholars such as von der Osten-Sacken, *Gott und Belial*.

108. Recently, see Popović, "Anthropology," 58–98, and the essays collected in Xeravits, ed., *Dualism at Qumran*, especially Davies, "Dualism in the Qumran War Texts," 8, and Hempel, "*Treatise on the Two Spirits*," 119. Earlier studies also challenge the coherence of some of these theories and the priority of the Treatise in Qumran thought, as Levison, "Two Spirits," 2:169–193; and

Stegemann, "Zu Textbestand." For instance, Stegemann (ibid., 125–130) suggests that the Treatise expresses the idiosyncratic views of the scribe who composed or edited the work.

109. Popović ("Anthropology") is especially critical of so-called psychological dualisms, as is Rosen-Zvi ("Two Rabbinic Inclinations?") and Tigchelaar ("Evil Inclination").

110. For the latter view, see Hempel, "*Treatise on the Two Spirits*," 102–104. Here she suggests that 1QS 3–4 may supply the final redacted form of the text but also argues that dualism is not a consistent characteristic of 1QS as a whole, and certainly not of many other sectarian works, with the possible exceptions of CD 13.12 and 4QZodiacal Physiognomy (4Q186); on 4Q186, see Popović, *Reading the Human Body*, 206–208.

111. A number of scholars consider the treatise to be a later addition, in part because some manuscripts of 1QS lack this section (4QS^d, 4QS^e, and the fragments of 4QS^b). Of the twelve fragments preserved from Cave 4, only two preserve some portion of the Treatise (4Q255 and 4Q257). For speculation about whether the original form was shorter or longer, see Alexander, "Redaction-History," and Metso, *Textual Development*, 135–140; for its possible fit within the literary development of 1QS, see Hempel, "*Treatise on the Two Spirits*," who notes some similarities with 1QS 5–9, though these chapters lack the language about the sons of light/darkness. See further, Metso, "In Search of the Sitz im Leben"; Metso, *Serekh Texts;* Alexander and Vermes, eds., *Qumran Cave 4. XIX;* Knibb, "Rule of the Community"; Tigchelaar, *To Increase Learning,* 201–203; and Tigchelaar, "'These Are the Names."

112. Views differ as to whether the *maskil* headings and the introduction are original to 1QS 3–4; see Hempel, "*Treatise on the Two Spirits*," 112–114; Metso, *Textual Development,* 135–140; and Lange, *Weisheit und Prädestination,* 141–143.

113. I agree with Popović ("Anthropology") that it is impossible to discern whether the term *rûḥôt* in 3.14 here alludes to a deity of some kind or to internal dispositions of human beings. He also suggests that the *mînê rûḥôtām* of 3.14 conveys something like "all [i.e., many] types of spirits," not just two (cf. CD 4.15–16), consistent with the multiple ranks or types of spirits evoked a few lines later; in 1QS 2.20 the same term seems to refer to ranks or varieties of "spiritual" attainment; cf. Ps. 51.

114. On the sense of *tôlēdôt* here as "generations" or "origins," see Popović, *Reading the Human Body,* 180 n. 29.

115. Trans. modified from García Martínez and Tigchelaar, *Dead Sea Scrolls Study Edition.*

116. On the universalism characteristic of these lines (and of 1QS 9.12–26), see Hempel, "*Treatise on the Two Spirits*," 115.

117. Collins ("In the Likeness of the Holy Ones," 612) suggests that the use of *'ĕnôš* here alludes to Adam.

118. I follow Popović, against García Martínez and Tigchelaar, in translating "placed before him two spirits" (3.18) instead of "placed within him two spirits." This makes better sense of the context (Gen 43:32, 2 Sam 12:20, 1 Sam 9:20, Deut 32:46; cf. Isa 63:11) and the meaning of *śîm* with the preposition; similarly, Levison, "Two Spirits," 2:170; and Charlesworth, "Critical Comparison," 83–86.

119. For an overview of the diverse proposals, see Sekki, *Meaning of Ruaḥ*, 193–219. Though rarely found in other literature from Qumran, the term *rûaḥ* occurs sixteen times in the Treatise, frequently in expressions such as "in all the generations of the spirits," "two spirits" (3.18), "spirits of truth and deceit" (3.18, 19; cf. 4.23), and "spirits of light and darkness" (3.25).

120. Other literature (such as CD 12.2–4, 4Q271 5 i 18–19) tells of multiple spirits within, not only two.

121. A number of scholars have challenged the coherence and consistency of *yeṣer* traditions even in later rabbinic literature, as Popović, "Anthropology;" Rosen-Zvi, "Two Rabbinic Inclinations?," 513–539; and Tigchelaar, "Evil Inclination," 347–357. For a more traditional view, see van der Horst, "Evil Inclination."

122. Similarly, Collins, *Apocalypticism*, 47.

123. Some scholars speculate about the relationship between 1QS 3 and 4. On the basis of shared vocabulary, for instance, Tigchelaar (*To Increase Learning*, 201–203) distinguishes 3.18–4.1 as the most original layer and treats 4.2–14 as an addition, one that has some affinities to the vocabulary of 4QInstruction. According to this theory, at the final stage, the whole treatise was reframed with the addition of the introductory material in 3.13–18 and 4.15–26. For a different view, see Hempel, "*Treatise on the Two Spirits,*" 102–120.

124. Among others, see J. Z. Smith, "Differential Equations."

125. Other Qumran texts are frequently compared with the Treatise, such as CD 2.2–13, 1QHᵃ 5.12–6.18, 4QInstruction (on which, see Tigchelaar, *To Increase Learning*, 194–207), and portions of the War Scroll and Testaments of the Twelve Patriarchs. The work known as 4QAmram also reports a vision of two angelic beings who "rule over all humanity"; see esp. 4Q544 frags. 1.10–3.2, 4Q543 2–6, 4Q548 1–2 (Collins, *Apocalypticism*, 45–46; Popović, "Anthropology," 35–38); 4Q177 2.7 contains language about the "lot of light" and the "dominion of Belial," and 4Q286 curses Belial and the spirits of his lot and points to their destiny in "the pit." See also the language about Belial in 11Q11 5.5–8, which Alexander ("Demonology of the Dead Sea Scrolls," esp. 346) interprets in psychological terms; cf. Tob 6:6–7.

126. Lange (*Weisheit und Prädestination*, 241–242) insists on a literary relationship between CD and 1QS 3, but Davies (*Damascus Covenant*, 72–73) argues that they are independent; Collins (*Apocalypticism*, 50) prefers to take 1QS as influenced by CD as well as certain Zoroastrian concepts.

127. Duhaime ("Dualistic Reworking," esp. 51–55) argues that this is part of a longer secondary addition running from CD 5.14b–6.2a, but Dimant ("Qumran

Sectarian Literature," 493) understands Belial as "at the heart of the sectarian thought."

128. Trans. García Martínez and Tigchelaar.

129. The original edition is Baillet, *Qumran Grotte 4*. Most agree that columns 1 and 15–19 were originally distinct from 2–9; on further problems associated with the fragments from Cave 4, see Duhaime, "War Scroll" and *War Texts;* cf. Abegg, "Messianic Hope"; on the dating, see Cross, *Ancient Library of Qumran*, 110–111.

130. See Collins, *Apocalypticism,* 91–92.

131. Divine beings seem to intermingle with human armies also in columns 7 and 12; cf. 1QSa 2; Florilegium on Ps 2 (4Q174); Pesher on Isaiah (4Q161); CD 7.20–21; and 1QH^a 11.35.

132. For a different interpretation of 1QM 2, 6–15, see Alexander, "Evil Empire," esp. 27–29. Alexander argues that the first seven years consist of a war for Israel's independence, but the remaining thirty-three involve an all-encompassing war against the nations of the world. In contrast, Schultz (*Conquering the World*) argues that columns 1–9 and 15–19 allude to different kinds of eschatological wars against the Kittim, the former developing the thought of Dan 11, the latter of Ezek 38–39; Davies (*1QM, the War Scroll,* 113–120) prefers to understand column 1 as the work of an editor seeking to reconcile columns 2–10 and 15–19.

133. As Collins (*Apocalypticism,* 91) argues, 1QM vacillates between drawing traditional oppositions between Israel/gentile nations (often evoked as the Kittim, King of Assur, and so on) and imagining opponents in more conceptually expansive terms, such as the armies of Belial or the lot of the sons of darkness. For examples of the former, see 1QM 1.1–2, which at times defines these enemies as the combined forces of Edom, Moab, the sons of Ammon, Philistia, and the Kittim of Ashur, the last of which it envisions as in league with the covenant violators. By contrast, the sons of light are imagined as the exiles of the desert and the sons of Levi, Judah, and Benjamin who will (seemingly) rule together as a "nation of God" (*lĕʿam ʾēl*) with the "men of his lot."

134. The Songs of the Sabbath Sacrifice frequently depict a supreme deity exalted among the holy ones, gods, and *ʾēlîm* (so 4Q401) or as "king of the heavenly beings" (4Q402 12); Newsom, *Songs of the Sabbath Sacrifice,* 23–38; and Collins, *Apocalypticism,* 138–139. In some cases, however, Melchizedek is named as the leader of the general or of the whole heavenly host, as in 4Q401 11; cf. 11QMelchizedek and 4QAmram.

135. See Alexander, "Demonology"; Angel, "Maskil"; Kosmala, "Maskil"; and Newsom, "Sage in the Literature."

136. The original manuscript has *sd ʾym,* read together by Baillet, *Qumran Grotte 4* 216.

137. Against García Martínez and Tigchelaar, Alexander ("Demonology," 346) reads "howlers and yelpers" instead of "owls and [jackals]."

138. See also the more fragmentary texts of the Song, especially 4Q511 frag. 1, 10, 35, 48, 49, and 51.

139. See, e.g., Collins, "Mythology of Holy War," 607–608. Paul Heger's arguments against Persian influence are unconvincing, in "Another Look at Dualism."

140. Collins, "Mythology of Holy War," 604–612.

141. See, e.g., Duhaime, "Dualism."

142. For similar motifs in Greek literature, especially surrounding the Titans, see Glasson (*Greek Influence*, 61–68); Jude 6; 2 Pet 2:4; 2 Sib. Or. 228–235.

143. Among many others, see Beker, *Triumph of God;* MacGregor, "Principalities and Powers," 17–28; Lee, "Demonic Powers in Paul's Thought," 54–69; Black, "Πᾶσαι ἐξουσίαι αὐτῷ ὑποταγήσονται," 74–82; de Boer, *Defeat of Death;* Martyn, "Apocalyptic Antinomies"; "De-apocalypticizing Paul"; Arnold, "Returning to the Domain"; Gaventa, *Our Mother Saint Paul;* and Eastman, *Recovering Paul's Mother Tongue.* The theory is represented as a settled scholarly consensus in much of the scholarship on Paul. On 1 Cor, for instance, see Conzelmann, *1 Corinthians,* 271–272; Fee, *First Epistle,* 471–475; Fitzmyer, *First Corinthians,* 330–352, 393–394; Horsley, *1 Corinthians,* 141; and D. Martin, *Corinthian Body,* 132–133. To similar ends, see Riley, "Demons."

Chapter 3. Conflict, Competition, and Paul's "Principalities and Powers" Reconsidered

1. By "satirical identification" I mean that these polemics misrepresent the beliefs and practices of other peoples, particularly in claims that identify (or elide) their gods with cult statues. As Nathaniel B. Levtow (*Images of Others,* esp. 86–129) and others have shown, these satires and polemics deliberately misrepresent the ways that other peoples understand their deities, especially in relation to their iconodules or cult statues.

2. The texts are helpfully collected in Donaldson, *Judaism and the Gentiles.* See also Donaldson, *Paul and the Gentiles,* 70–78; Donaldson, "Proselytes or Righteous Gentiles?"; Sanders, *Jesus and Judaism;* McKelvey, *New Temple,* 12–17; and Jeremias, *Jesus' Promise.* As Donaldson ("Proselytes or Righteous Gentiles?") notes, in some cases the gentiles are utterly destroyed (as in Jub. 15:26; 4 Ezra 12:33, 13:38; 2 Bar. 40:1; Apoc. Abr. 31:2; 1QM; Test. Mos. 10:10), but they are more frequently brought in to serve Israel and Israel's patron deity (as in Isa 18:7, 60:1–22, 66:18–21; Hag 2:21–22; Ps. Sol. 17:30–31; Jub. 32:19; Tg. Isa. 25:6–10), sometimes as full participants: so Isa 2:2–4; Mic 4:1–3; Isa. 25:6–10a, 56:6–8; Zech 8:20–23; Tob 13:11, 14:5–7; 1 En. 10:21, 90:27–33; 3 Sib. Or. 657–808; Philo, *Mos.* 2.43–44; *Praem.* 164–172; 2 Bar. 72–73 (but only those who have not "trodden Israel" will survive in 72:4); T. Levi 18; T. Naph. 8:3–4; T. Jud. 24:6, 25:5; T. Zeb. 9:8; T. Benj. 10:9.

3. On the category of nations/gentiles, see Johnson Hodge, *If Sons, Then Heirs,*

52–58; and Buell, *Why This New Race,* esp. 138–165; cf. Rosen-Svi and Ophir, "Paul and the Invention of the Gentiles."

4. Collins, *Apocalypticism,* 91–93; Nickelsburg, *Jewish Literature,* 9–18.

5. LXX: ἐν τῷ ἁγιασθῆναί με ἐν σοὶ ἐνώπιον αὐτῶν.

6. Cf. Wolff, Janzen, and McBride (*Joel and Amos,* 73), who have, "That Yahweh may [shatter] your heroes," by preferring Targum Jonathan and the Vulgate to the MT; they find similar formulations in Isa 13:3b, Zech 14:5b, and 2 Chr 20:22; cf. 1 En. 56:5 and 1QM 1.10–11.

7. LXX: βασιλείας τῆς οἰκουμένης.

8. LXX: τὴν οἰκουμένην ὅλην.

9. LXX: ἔδωλα.

10. LXX: ὁ Θεὸς μόνος.

11. See Levtow, *Images of Others;* W. Roth, "For Life"; von Rad, *Wisdom in Israel,* 177–185; and Preuss, *Verspottung.*

12. See Gordon, "Gods Must Die."

13. Translations of Zechariah are from Meyers and Meyers. This language adapts Deut 6:4 to fit with the global sovereignty of Yahweh (LXX Θεος); Meyers and Meyers, *Zechariah 9–14,* 440.

14. LXX: τὰ ὀνόματα τῶν εἰδώλων.

15. See Levtow, *Images of Others;* and Roth, "For Life," 21–47.

16. See Collins, *Between Athens and Jerusalem,* 62–72. The charge of worshipping dead kings adapts euhemeristic traditions to polemical ends; similarly, see Wis 13 and Rom 1:23.

17. The LXX avoids language about the gods of others: "All the peoples walk each in their own way (πορεύσονται ἕκαστος τὴν ὁδὸν αὐτοῦ) but we walk in the name of the Lord our God (πορευσόμεθα ἐν ὀνόματι κυρίου θεοῦ ἡμῶν)" (Mic 4:5).

18. See also Ps. Sol. 17 where Jerusalem is purified of gentiles (17:25) and the nations come to "see his glory," bringing Israel's own sons as gifts (17:34); cf. Jdt 8:20; Philo, *Virt.* 102, 179, 214; *Spec.* 1.52; 2 Bar. 4–5; Rev 21:4; Jos. Asen. 8:5–7; Donaldson, *Paul and the Gentiles,* 82–88. On the absence of ingathering motifs in some literature, see Wise, "Eschatological Vision," though the Temple Scroll does envision foreigners serving in the eschatological temple. Likewise, Jub. 1–2 has a reconciliation of Israel (and even a world renewal) but does not include the gentiles; cf. Wis 3:5–8.

19. The NRSV (reflecting the MT) has "the nations shall inquire of him."

20. See also Isa 49:6–26; 56:1–8; 60:3–7, 10–14; 66:18–24; Israel's participation in these affairs is clear in, e.g., Isa 54:3, 60:16, 61:6; Jer 3:17.

21. LXX: βουλεύσασθε ἅμα.

22. LXX: πρὸς θεούς οἳ οὐ σῴζουσιν.

23. The LXX translation has "the order/*kosmos* of heaven" in place of the "host" of the MT: ἐπάξει ὁ θεὸς ἐπὶ τὸν κόσμον τοῦ οὐρανοῦ τὴν χεῖρα; note that some versions of LXX 34:5 describe the destruction of the "powers of heaven

(αἱ δυνάμεις τῶν οὐρανῶν)," but Zeigler's edition prefers ἐμεθύσθη ἡ μάκαιρά μου ἐν τῷ οὐρανῷ, which is close to the MT.

24. Cf. 4QAgesCreat B, where God "delivered the sons of the he[avens] and the earth to a wicked community until its end" 4Q181 B 1 ii, 3.

25. For instance, see the renewal of the luminaries in Jub. 1:29 and Zech 14:6–7; their destruction in 3 Sib. Or. 88–90; and the new heaven in Isa 65:17 and 66:22; cf. Isa 60:19–20; Rev. 22:5.

26. On the "savage spirits" (or alternately, "evil/wicked spirits"), see VanderKam's discussion of the manuscripts in "Demons," 344 n. 12.

27. See Collins (*Apocalypticism*, 91), on how 1QM vacillates between the traditional opposition between Israel/the nations and more expansive categories of opponents such as the armies of Belial or sons of darkness.

28. Schultz (*Conquering the World*) argues that columns 1–9 and 15–19 allude to different kinds of eschatological wars; Davies (*1QM*, 113–120) prefers to see 1QM 1 as the work of an editor seeking to reconcile columns 2–10 and 15–19.

29. On the recensions of 1QM and the reappropriation of Gog in 4Q285 as king of the Kittim, see Alexander, "Evil Empire."

30. But see, e.g., 1QM 4.12 and 14.5; on these and other Qumran texts, see Donaldson, *Judaism and the Gentiles*, 195–215.

31. Cf. 2 Thess 1–2, which could be authentic.

32. The "smiths," *ḥārāšîm*, of v. 20 (perhaps drawing on Ezek 21:36 [NRSV 21:31]) destroy the nations that have overrun Judah, Israel, and Jerusalem; see Meyers and Meyers, *Haggai, Zechariah 1–8*, 139–143.

33. On the use of Ps 110 here, see Hay, *Glory at the Right Hand*, 60–62; on the symbolic humiliation of the enemy by portraying them as under the foot of the conquering warrior, see also 1QM 12.11 and related texts.

34. The contrast with Greek traditions was not lost on Didymus of Alexandria, who understands Paul's text as countering impious Greek myths in which gods commit parricide; Staab, *Pauluskommentare*, 8.

35. Black, "Πᾶσαι ἐξουσίαι αὐτῷ ὑποταγήσονται"; de Boer, "Meaning of the Phrase"; Martyn, *Galatians*, 393–406; Arnold, "Returning to the Domain"; Forbes, "Paul's Principalities and Powers"; cf. Glasson, *Greek Influence*, 69–73.

36. For instance, Black ("Πᾶσαι ἐξουσίαι αὐτῷ ὑποταγήσονται," 78) explains the enemies in 1 Cor 15:24 by appealing to texts that do not envision them as rebellious (1 En. 61:10, T. Levi 3:8, and 4Q209 28 [4QEnastrᵇ]).

37. The LXX translation is similar (using the language of εἰδώλοις τῶν ἐθνῶν), but the second stanza is somewhat awkward: "And whether the sky will give its abundance (καὶ εἰ ὁ οὐρανὸς δώσει πλησμονὴν αὐτοῦ)" (NETS).

38. The LXX adds "βουλεύσασθε ἅμα" (take counsel together).

39. The LXX has "gods" in the plural: πρὸς θεούς οἳ οὐ σῴζουσιν.

40. The LXX version prefers "kosmos" of heaven (πάντα τὸν κόσμον τοῦ οὐρανοῦ), usually translated along the lines of the NETS "any ornament of the sky."

41. So also Deut 17:3; 2 Kgs 21:5, 23:5; Job 31:26; Cross, "Council of Yahweh in Second Isaiah," 274, n. 1; Miller, *Divine Warrior in Early Israel,* 240 n. 180. The heavenly bodies and divine messengers are assimilated to Yahweh's assembly in texts like Ps 148:3 but commonly appear as gods in Near Eastern traditions. In more celebratory contexts, the host also functions as part of the assembly (as in 1 Kgs 22:19), as do the sun, the moon, and the stars in other contexts (Pss 103:20–21, 148:2–3; Job 38:7; cf. Ps 29:1–2).

42. Among many examples, see *Opif.* 45–46; *Conf.* 173–174; and *Dec.* 52–80; cf. *Vit. Cont.* 3–12; Winston, *Wisdom of Solomon,* 248–249; Dillon, *Middle Platonists,* 46–47. For the idea that religion originates with the worship of heavenly bodies, see Plato, *Crat.* 397d; Diodorus Siculus, *Bibl.* 2.30.

43. Though his language is shot through with normative rhetoric, Black makes a similar suggestion: "They are cosmic or celestial potentates whose empires are among the 'hosts of heaven' κοσμοκράτορες τοῦ σκότους τούτου, Eph 6:12, and most probably the astral deities of Hellenistic religions accommodated within a Jewish-Hellenistic angelology" ("Πᾶσαι ἐξουσίαι αὐτῷ ὑποταγήσονται," 76).

44. See Schweitzer, *Mysticism of the Apostle Paul,* 67, for views about an interregnum (as Rev 20:4–6; 4 Ezra 7:26–31; 2 Bar. 29:1–30:5, 40:3); de Boer, "Paul and Apocalyptic Eschatology," 1:377–378, and Davies, *Paul and Rabbinic Judaism,* 285–298, modify this view.

45. Others treat the role of gentiles in Paul's eschatological scenario in similar ways, as Donaldson, *Paul and the Gentiles,* 69–74, 224–230; Fredriksen, "Judaism"; E. P. Sanders, *Paul, the Law,* 171–179, and *Jesus and Judaism,* 79–90, 96–98; Gager, *Reinventing Paul,* 119–126; Stowers, *A Rereading of Romans,* esp. 95–97; Schweitzer, *Mysticism of the Apostle Paul,* 181–187. Unpublished portions of Nongbri, "Paul Without Religion," also help to contextualize Paul's thought about the timing of gentile inclusion by appealing to Isaiah (esp. 10:20–22 and 11:11–12).

46. See Engberg-Pedersen, *Cosmology and Self,* 21–38.

47. Some passages in Heraclitus's *Homeric Problems* offer intriguing hints of such possibilities. For instance: "Some think that Homer in this episode has revealed the conjunction of the seven planets in a single zodiacal sign. Now whenever this happens, total disaster ensues. He is therefore hinting at the destruction of the universe, bringing together Apollo (the sun), Artemis (the moon), and the stars of Aphrodite, Ares, Hermes, and Zeus" (*Hom. Prob.* 53; cf. 25). See Dillon, *Alcinous,* 130, on the great year; Seneca, *Nat.* 3.29, Apuleius, *de Plat.* 1.10.203.

48. Black ("Πᾶσαι ἐξουσίαι αὐτῷ ὑποταγήσονται," 74–82, and "Two Unusual Nomina Dei") argues that the lord of spirits in the Similitudes and 2 Macc 3:24 derives from the biblical title "Lord of Hosts."

49. Inspired by such material, Forbes ("Paul's Principalities and Powers") attempts

to show that Paul's language appropriates from Middle Platonic traditions, but his arguments are not convincing.

50. For polemics about philosophers who allegorize the heavenly bodies and elements as gods, see Plutarch, *Mor.* 377B–378A; cf. *Mor.* 20A; Winston, *Wisdom of Solomon*, 248–251.

51. For instance, the Astronomical Book refers to heavenly bodies as having dominion (*šelṭānāt*) (e.g., 72:1 and 82:10; see also 4QEnastr^b (4Q209) 7 iii, 4, 1QM 17.6–7, Dan 7:27), which probably refers to their having certain positions on certain days (Black, "Πᾶσαι ἐξουσίαι αὐτῷ ὑποταγήσονται," 79–81), and in Jub. 2:7–10 the heavenly bodies are said to "rule over day and night." See the diverse terminology explored in Newsom, "Angels (OT)."

52. Similarly, Aune, "Archon."

53. The term usually translated as "eager longing" or "eager expectation" (ἀποκαραδοκία) in 8:19 (cf. Phil 1:20) is ambiguous and could be taken in a negative way; see Fitzmyer, *Romans*, 508; and Denton, "Apokaradokia." Some interpreters have found allusions to Adam or Satan in v. 20, but most take the "one who subjected the creation to futility and hope (τῇ γὰρ ματαιότητι ἡ κτίσις ὑπετάγη, οὐχ ἑκοῦσα ἀλλὰ διὰ τὸν ὑποτάξαντα ἐφ᾽ ἐλπίδι)" as the supreme creator God. It should be noted, however, that expressions of agency using δία plus the accusative are not well-attested; see Fitzmyer, *Romans*, 508; and Hill, "Construction of Three Passages," 296–297.

54. Engberg-Pedersen (*Cosmology and Self,* 34–37) finds hints of a Stoic-like conflagration here and elsewhere in the text; see also van der Horst, "'Elements Will Be Dissolved.'"

55. Similarly, see Cranfield, *Critical and Exegetical Commentary,* 1:441–444. Fitzmyer (*Romans,* 535) takes these as "cosmic powers" of some kind but does not take a position on whether they are conceived of as good or bad; see also Weiss, "ἀρχή."

56. On the textual problem with the placement of *dunameis,* see Sanday and Headlam, *Critical and Exegetical Commentary,* 223. The heights and depths are sometimes used in astrological contexts; see Black ("Πᾶσαι ἐξουσίαι αὐτῷ ὑποταγήσονται," 76–77); cf. Ps. Sol. 18:10.

57. Cf. 2 Bar. 51:10–12, "For they will live in the heights of that world and they will be like the angels and be equal to the stars." For an interpretation of this transformation as purely spiritual, see Yarbro Collins, "Otherworld and the New Age."

58. See Asher, *Polarity and Change;* Stowers, "What Is 'Pauline Participation'?"; D. Martin, *Corinthian Body,* esp. 117–136.

59. Asher ("ΣΠΕΙΡΕΤΑΙ") makes a plausible case that the sowing metaphors reflect philosophical adaptations of anthropogenic myths. He elsewhere argues (*Polarity and Change,* esp. 156 n. 20), against Martin (*Corinthian Body,* 126), that Paul does not envision body and soul as left behind but rather as fully

transformed into a fine, material substance; so also Engberg-Pedersen, *Cosmology and Self,* 34 n. 85.

60. See Stowers, "What Is 'Pauline Participation'?"; D. Martin, *Corinthian Body,* esp. 117–136; Koyre, *From the Closed World.*

61. On this language in relation to kinship and the idea of bearing the image of the father, see Johnson Hodge, *If Sons, Then Heirs,* esp. 111–115.

62. See Steudel, "Eternal Reign," esp. 517.

63. See the overview of scholarship in R. Martin, *Carmen Christi,* 134–164; and Reumann, *Philippians,* 333–365. Scholars often compare the text with other traditions about divine beings, but they differ considerably on how to characterize them. For instance, Martin Dibelius appeals to supposed myths of a descending/ascending deity, drawing mainly on the Ascension of Isaiah (*Die Briefe des Apostels Paulus,* 53–55, and *Die Geisterwelt im Glauben des Paulus,* 203–205), while Ernst Lohmeyer appeals to various Satan figures (*Kurios Jesus,* esp. 27–29) and Ernst Käsemann ("Critical Analysis") appeals to the Corpus Hermeticum 1.12–26, where an *anthrôpos* figure "demonstrated to nature below the beautiful *morphê* of God." More recently, J. Sanders ("Dissenting Deities") works with Jewish literature about the divine council, with particular attention to watchers traditions familiar from 1 Enoch and Jubilees. Scholars have also debated whether or not the text is pre-Pauline and whether this fits the form of a hymn. For arguments that construe it as Pauline and not a formal hymn at all, see Fee, "Philippians 2:5–11"; similarly, Brucker, "*Christushymnen*"; as a Greek translation of an Aramaic original, Fitzmyer, "Aramaic Background," esp. 481–482; as a prose hymn that involves "wisdom speculation," Tobin "World of Thought," 92.

64. R. Martin, *Carmen Christi,* 99–133, 138–139. Scholars conventionally distinguish these positions by using the Latin phrases *res rapta* (something already seized) and *res rapienda* (something to be seized).

65. R. Martin, *Carmen Christi,* 137–143; more recently, see Vollenweider, "'Raub' der Gottgleichheit"; Yarbro Collins, "Psalms, Phil 2:6–11"; M. Martin, "ἁρπαγμός Revisited"; and Reumann, *Philippians,* 335–383.

66. R. Martin (*Carmen Christi,* 100–133) treats much of the relevant scholarship but goes on to argue that Christ is best understood as the second Adam who is "the image [or perhaps the 'glory'] of God," even though such ideas are meagerly attested in the extant literature.

67. So J. Sanders, "Dissenting Deities;" Yarbro Collins ("Worship of Jesus") prefers a number of other possibilities such as a hypostatis of God, divine logos, or principal angel.

68. In agreement with Yarbro Collins ("Psalms, Phil 2:6–11," 367) and Vollenweider ("'Raub' der Gottgleichheit," 417–419), among others. Cf. M. Martin, "ἁρπαγμός Revisited;" and Reumann, *Philippians,* esp. 365–366.

69. Vollenweider also draws on scholarship that compares traditions about the Godlike status of Alexander the Great, Heracles, and Caligula with Phil 2

("'Raub' der Gottgleichheit," 423–425; see also R. Martin, *Carmen Christi*, 155–157; Fee, *Paul's Letter to the Philippians*, 97. One problem with Vollenweider's approach is that it almost entirely excludes political discourse about the heavenly world (though see the brief comments in "'Raub' der Gottgleichheit," 423). Another is that emperors and rulers are not typically portrayed as having come from the divine world, though see Hengel, *Son of God*, 35–41. Others appeal to the emperor cult, as Erik M. Heen ("Phil 2:6–11"), but Yarbro Collins ("Worship of Jesus") shows that such practices can more successfully be compared to the elevation of Christ in vv. 9–11 and to the Christian worship of Jesus generally.

70. "Dissenting Deities," 279–290.

71. Charlesworth, ed., *Old Testament Pseudepigrapha*.

72. This translation of Deut 32:43 emends the NRSV, in keeping with the text of 4QDeut[j] and the LXX. This language is omitted from the MT and 4QDeut[j]; cf. Ps 96:7.

73. Collins, "Throne in the Heavens."

74. Similarly Yarbro Collins, "Psalms, Phil 2:6–11," 366–367; and Vollenweider, "'Raub' der Gottgleichheit," 424–425.

75. "Dissenting Deities," 290; cf. Enoch in 1 En. 71.

76. See Tobin ("World of Thought," 93–94) on Christ as an instrument of creation in 1 Pet 1:20–21, 2 Cor 8:6, 1 Tim 3:16; cf. Prov 8:22–31, Sir 24, Wis 7:21–8:1.

77. Forbes, "Paul's Principalities and Powers," 64–65. Engberg-Pedersen (*Cosmology and Self*, 92–98) notes that *aggeloi* play ambivalent roles in Paul's letters whereas "demons" prove less so. With many others, he insists that Paul's world is in the grip of evil demonic forces (drawing especially on Martin Dibelius, among others). Helpfully, Dale B. Martin ("When Did Angels Become Demons?") offers a programmatic challenge to the theory that demons are "fallen angels," arguing that in Jewish and early Christian texts, "angels" and "demons" play relatively ambiguous and inconsistent roles, as is the case with Paul's letters (ibid., 673). The scholarly literature on angels in Jewish and Christian tradition is quite robust but rarely engages with Paul's texts. See Davidson, *Angels at Qumran*; Olyan, *A Thousand Thousands Served Him*; Fossum, *Name of God*; Schäfer, *Rivalität zwischen Engeln und Menschen*; Halperin, *Faces of the Chariot*; Halperin, "Ascension or Invasion"; and Stuckenbruck, *Angel Veneration*.

78. D. Martin (*Corinthian Body*, 168–174) offers a helpful interpretation of *pneuma* and the purity logic at work in this text; less satisfying is his appropriation of traditional notions of apocalyptic dualism. Engberg-Pedersen (*Cosmology and Self*, 34–36) explores the possibility that the "fire" here may reflect a Stoic-like conception of conflagration.

79. Some argue that this could be an interpolation, as Fitzmyer, "Qumrân and the Interpolated Paragraph"; others take Beliar as a stand-in for the anti-Christ or the forces of Satan, often in connection with Qumran literature. For an overview of the scholarship, see Tucker, "Reconsidering Βελιάρ," esp. 169–170.

80. So also Engberg-Pedersen, *Cosmology and Self,* esp. 92–98.

81. Though the Hebrew Bible makes no mention of other divine beings, the LXX adds an accompanying entourage to Deut 33:2 (ἄγγελοι μετ᾽αὐτοῦ). Some interpreters find similar implications in the LXX of Pss 102:20 and 103:4 as well as Jub. 2:2, 1 En. 60, and (perhaps) Josephus, *Ant.* 15.136; others question whether *aggelôn* in Gal 3:19 refers to human or divine beings; on the scholarship, see Betz, *Galatians,* 168–172; cf. Davies, "Note on Josephus"; Walton, "Messenger of God."

82. Some early manuscripts read πράξεων here rather than παραβάσεων (as P⁴⁶) and one has παραδόσεων; for discussion see Metzger, *Textual Commentary,* 594.

83. See Betz (*Galatians,* 170) for the view that the mediator is Moses, as Exod 19–20; 24:3, 4, 12; 31:18; 32:16, 19, 30; 34:1–28; Deut 4:14; 5:4–5; and others. See Bruce, *Epistle of Paul,* 176–178, and *Acts of the Apostles,* 209. See also Susan A. Meier, "Mediator I," and Feldmeier, "Mediator II," on the use of *mesitês* in Greek and Hellenistic Jewish contexts, esp. Plato, *Symp.* 203a; Plutarch, *Mor.* 369E; Ps-Lucian, *Amor.* 47; Josephus, *Ant.* 4.133; Philo, *Spec.* 4.31. The term is never applied to Moses in the LXX (cf. Philo, *Mos.* 2.166, *Her.* 206, *Somn.* 1.142–143), but a Greek fragment of the Testament of Moses claims that Moses was preordained before creation to be the mediator of the covenant; cf. T. Dan 6:2–6; 1 Tim 2:5–6; Heb 8:6, 9:15, 12:24; Irenaeus, *Adv. Haer.* 3.18.7; Clement of Alexandria, *Paed.* 3.1.

84. See Gropp and Bernstein et al., eds., *Wadi Daliyeh II.* See also Deut 34:10–12; 1 En. 89:36; T. Moses 11:16–17; and Ezekiel the Tragedian, *Exag.* 68–89; Collins, "Throne in the Heavens," 43–57.

85. See Najman, "Angels at Sinai"; on the rabbinic literature, see Segal, *Two Powers,* 64, 189, 211; Urbach, "Homiletical Interpretations," esp. 253–57; and Urbach, *Sages,* 152–53.

Chapter 4. Idols and Other Gods in 1 Corinthians, Galatians, and Romans

1. For instance, see Exod 32–33; Deut 9:10–29; 1 Kgs 12:25–30; Judg 8:22–28; Dan 3; Hab 2; Pss 115, 135; Epistle of Jeremiah; Bel and the Dragon; *Aristeas* 135–137; and the writings of Philo and Josephus. See Levtow, *Images of Others;* Roth, "For Life"; von Rad, *Wisdom in Israel,* 177–185; Preuss, *Verspottung fremder Religionen;* Bergmann, "Idol Worship"; Murphy, "Retelling the Bible." Much of the relevant Jewish literature is treated by Richard Liong-Seng Phua (*Idolatry and Authority*) but his study offers very little critical analysis of the sources.

2. See Levtow, *Images of Other,* 86–129, on iconic practices in Mesopotamian traditions. As Levtow and others have shown, such polemics deliberately misrepresent the way other traditions distinguish between divinities and their iconodules or cult statues. Some Greek and Roman philosophers also criticize

the use of statuary, as Heraclitus of Ephesus, Frag. 117; similarly, Epictetus (*Disc.* 2.8.12–13) attacks reverence for gods "made of gold and silver" instead of the true god within, and Plutarch's "superstitious" person (*Mor.* 167E) worships the works of stone, metal, and wax; see also Juvenal, *Sat.* 13.114–115; Horace, *Sat.* 1.8.1–3; Cicero, *De nat.* 1.27.77; M. R. Wright, *Cosmology in Antiquity,* 163–184. See also Boys-Stones, "Ancient Philosophy of Religion," esp. 7–9.

3. Verse 12 is an Aramaic addition to the MT; among others, see the discussion of Levtow, *Images of Others,* 46 n. 12.

4. As with other citations of the LXX, the Greek text of Jeremiah is from Zeigler's edition. In contrast to the MT (which reproduces 10:12–17 as a doublet at 51:15–19, almost exactly), the LXX repeats much of 10:12–17 at 28:15–19 but with significant alterations. Translations of the Greek are from the NETS, unless noted.

5. On sacrifice to "demons," see 2 Bar. 4:7; 1 En. 19:1; Jub. 1.11; T. Job 3:3; Philo, *Mos.* 1.276; Acts 17:18; Rev 9:20 (cf. Isa 13); *Ep. Barn.* 16:7; Justin, *Dialogue with Trypho* 30.3, 55.2, 73.2; cf. Plutarch, *Mor.* 316B, 417C; and D. Martin, "When Did Angels Become Demons?," 663–664.

6. The NRSV translation of Deut 32:43a reflects the sense of 4QDeut^q and the LXX; the line is omitted in the MT. Cf. Ps 96:7.

7. See Olyan, "Is Isaiah 40–55 Really Monotheistic?" esp. 193–194.

8. Trans. modified; the NETS translates τὸν κόσμον as "ornamentation," but "host" better fits the context.

9. See Levtow, *Images of Others,* 68, on the wordplays.

10. "For Life," 45–47; see also Tatum, "LXX Version"; cf. van der Horst, "'Thou Shalt Not Revile'"; Borgen, "'Yes,' 'No,' 'How Far?'"

11. This figure is probably envisioned as a *paidogôgos,* a household slave charged with overseeing children, consistent with the earlier analogy in Gal 3:24; see Young, "Paidagogos."

12. Unless otherwise noted, translations of Paul's letters are my own.

13. *Pneuma* is often misleadingly translated as "spirit" but is best understood as an airy breathlike substance. Much recent scholarship agrees on this but not on how to contextualize Paul's conception of it. See Johnson Hodge, *If Sons, Then Heirs;* Stowers, "What Is 'Pauline Participation'?"; D. Martin, *Corinthian Body,* 108–132; and Engberg-Pedersen, *Cosmology and Self,* esp. 1–105.

14. De Boer, "Meaning of the Phrase"; Martyn, *Galatians,* 393–406; Rusam, "Neue Belege"; Betz, *Galatians,* 213–217; Arnold, "Returning to the Domain." Though otherwise helpful, these studies frequently appeal to language about demonic forces, evil powers, and angels that bear the stamp of Christian ideology. For different approaches, see Glasson, *Greek Influence,* 69–73; and DeMaris, "Element, Elemental Spirit."

15. For an overview, see de Boer, "Meaning of the Phrase," 205–208.

16. Cf. Philo, *Gig.* 7, where the "elements" seem to be different domains or regions, each of which contains beings proper to it.

17. Against, e.g., Schweizer, "Slaves of the Elements"; and Rusam, "Neue Belege."
18. Other scholars prefer to understand the law here as an evil enslaving power that holds the world in its grip. For instance, de Boer notes that Josephus uses similar language about the law as father and master (*Contr. Ap.* 2.174) but insists that for Josephus the idea of being "'under the Law' implies accountability, not enslavement and oppression as it does for Paul" ("Meaning of the Phrase," 212 n. 39); see also Marcus, "'Under the Law'"; and Betz, *Galatians,* 204–205.
19. Debates have also centered on the unity of the text, the place of chapter 9, and the existence or nonexistence of discreet factions at Corinth, especially in light of Paul's language about "the strong" and "the weak." For an overview, see Willis, "1 Corinthians 8–10." Arnold, "Returning to the Domain," 70, helpfully discusses 1 Cor 8 and 10 in light of polemics in Isaiah, Jeremiah, and the Epistle of Jeremiah.
20. On the preference for δαιμόνιον rather than δαίμων, see D. Martin, "When Did Angels Become Demons?," 658 n. 4. There is a good deal of other literature on "demonology" in Paul, but it tends to involve theories of warring powers and kingdoms that are untenable; see, e.g., Dibelius, *Die Geisterwelt im Glauben des Paulus;* Lee, "Interpreting the Demonic Powers"; and Arnold, "Returning to the Domain"; cf. Riley, "Demons," which provides a valuable overview of other literature but finds a distinctive view of "warring kingdoms" in the letters of Paul. On demonology generally, see Brenk, "'In the Light of the Moon'"; Gager, *Curse Tablets;* and the essays collected in Graf et al., eds., *Archiv für Religionsgeschichte* 14 (2013).
21. This view is especially associated with Fee, *First Epistle;* Fee, "εἰδωλόθυτα Once Again"; and Witherington, *Conflict and Community.* More recently, see Newton, *Deity and Diet,* 331–71; Horrell, "Theological Principle"; and Horrell, "Idol-Food," 121. Dale Martin (*Corinthian Body*) takes exception on the grounds that there are no clear textual signals of different practical contexts and that the theory works with untenable public/private distinctions. By contrast, Horrell ("Idol Food," 104; "Theological Principle," 101, 103) follows others in drawing attention to the prohibition of εἰδωλολατρία in 10:14, in contrast to the more flexible concerns with εἰδωλόθυτα (8:1, 4, 7, 10; 10:19) and ἱερόθυτος (10:28); see also Horrell, "Domestic Space"; and Stambaugh, "Functions of Roman Temples." Other positions are too numerous and disparate to summarize, but see Fotopoulos, "Arguments Concerning Food"; Fotopoulos, *Food Offered to Idols;* Cheung, *Idol Food;* Smit, *About the Idol Offerings;* and Meeks, "Polyphonic Ethics."
22. Interpreters dispute some of the finer points of the translation, though not the overall sense. Fitzmyer takes the εἴπερ as concessive, indicating a simple, real condition with ὥσπερ: "For even if there are so-called gods either in heaven or on earth—indeed there are many 'gods' and many 'lords'" (*First Corinthians,* 340–341); Smit (*About the Idol Offerings,* 75) takes the εἴπερ as indicating the hypothetical nature of the ὥσπερ clause: "If indeed there are so-called gods

either in heaven or on earth, then in that sense there are many gods and many lords;" Fee (*First Epistle*, 372) takes the second clause as parenthetical: "Even if there are so-called gods, whether heavenly or earthly (just as there are indeed gods many and lords many)."

23. Though awkward, the whole second clause is attested in P⁴⁶; cf. Col 1:15–20.

24. For recent discussions, see the essays collected in Knust and Várhelyi, eds., *Ancient Mediterranean Sacrifice.*

25. See Malherbe, "Determinism and Free Will"; Glad, *Paul and Philodemus;* and Thorsteinsson, *Roman Christianity.*

26. Newton (*Deity and Diet*) follows Fee (among others) in eliding the concerns of 8:1–13 with 10:14–22. This helps with Paul's caveat about being observed reclining in an εἰδωλείῳ in 8:10 but does not fit easily with his statements about the indifferent status of idol meat in 8:8 and 10:25.

27. Meeks, "'And Rose Up,'" esp. 66.

28. On table fellowship and sacrifice here, see Hollander, "Idea of Fellowship," who helpfully discusses similar language in Philo, *Spec.* 1.221 and the bread of the presence in Hebrew Bible/LXX traditions. See, e.g., Exod 25:23–30; Lev 24:5–9; 1 Kgs 7:48; 1 Macc 1:22; 4:49, 51; 1 Clement 43:2; T. Jud. 21:5.

29. E.g., Jub. 1:8, 7:27, 10:1–13, 11:4–5, 22:16–18; cf. 1:19–21; Deut 4:28; Ps 115:4–8; Isa 44:9–20; Wis 15:15–19; Arnold "Returning to the Domain," 66; Betz, *Galatians*, 216 n. 32.

30. Trans. VanderKam, *Book of Jubilees.*

31. This translation relies generally on the Greek text, but the manuscripts pose some difficulties. See the discussion of Nickelsburg (*1 Enoch*, 483), who prefers the Greek text of Chester Beatty (καὶ λατρεύ[οντες φαν]τάσμασιν καὶ δαιμονίοι[ς καὶ βδελύγ]μασι καὶ πνεύμασιν πονη[ροῖς), which is quite close to the Latin witness of Tertullian. The Ethiopic witnesses have simply "evil spirits and demons" (*la-nafsāt 'ekuyāt/ān* [or *rekusāt/ān*] *wa-'agānent*), which may suggest attempted revisions.

32. This translation follows the Greek of Chester Beatty (καὶ τὰ ὁρ[ά]ματα τῶν ἐνυπνίων [ὑμῶν] καταπλανήσουσιν ὑμᾶς); the Ethiopic manuscript has "and in the visions of their dreams they will err and they will fear (*wa-bare'ya ḥelmomu bomu yerasse'u wa-yefarrehu*)."

33. Horrell ("Theological Principle," 47) similarly notes a "hedging strategy" in 1 Cor 8.

34. Sterling, "Prepositional Metaphysics," esp. 232–238; Wasserman, "Metaphysical Contradictions," 201–227; Runia, *Philo of Alexandria*, 171–174; this phrase originates with Theiler, *Die Vorbereitung des Neuplatonismus.* See Horsley (*1 Corinthians*, 133) for an argument that identifies 1 Cor 8:6 with Middle-Platonic tendencies to construe the *logos* as Sophia, similar to Wis 7:20–29 and 9:1–2; cf. Philo, *Leg.* 3.96; *Opif.* 24–25; *Spec.* 1.81; and *Det.* 54; cf. *Fug.* 190; *Deus* 57; *Her.* 199; *Ebr.* 30–31; *Sacr.* 8; and *Leg.* 2.49.

35. Aristotle does not use prepositions in the way later philosophers do but in some contexts he does use prepositions in relation to efficient causes. On his material, formal, efficient, and final causes, see e.g., *Phys.* 194b–200b, *Metaph.* 1013a–b.; Sterling, "Prepositional Metaphysics," 220–221; Sprague, "The Four Causes." For Peripatetic developments of the four causes and Platonic and Neo-Platonic additions, see Sterling, "Prepositional Metaphysics," 224–225.

36. Trans. Dillon, *Alcinous*, 115. As Dillon notes, it remains unclear whether the paradigm or the model is inside or outside the mind of the demiurge or even whether the demiurge is the supreme God.

37. Varro (apud Augustine, *Civ.* 7.28) and Aëtius (*Plac.* 1.11.2) prefer three, while Alcinous (*Did.* 12.1–2) and Seneca (*Ep.* 65.7–10) add more. See also *Tim.* 29d7–e2 (quoted in Seneca, *Ep.* 65.10); and Philo, *Opif.* 16–25, 173, where the goodness of the demiurge becomes final cause.

38. See Attridge, "Philo and John," and "Philosophical Critique."

39. Sterling ("Prepositional Metaphysics," 219–220) shows that interpreters at least from the time of Basil of Caesarea noted problems with taking this language as strictly Platonic; on the mixed Platonic and Stoic tendencies of 1 Cor 8:6, see Sterling, "Prepositional Metaphysics," 235–237.

40. Sterling, "Prepositional Metaphysics," 220–223; e.g., Pseudo-Aristotle: "all things are from God (ἐκ θεοῦ) and through God (διὰ θεοῦ) hold together for us" (*De Mundo* 397b); Aelius Aristides, "for all things everywhere are through you (διὰ σοῦ) and have become for us on account of you (διὰ σε)" (*Or.* 45.14; in 43.9, 23 the writer also replaces "you" with "Zeus" and "Διος"); cf. Pseudo-Apuleius, *Asclepius* 34; *Corp. Herm.* 5.10 and the alternative Stoic positions discussed in Sterling, "Prepositional Metaphysics," 223. Such formulations inspired Eduard Norden (*Agnostos Theos*, 240–250) and resonate with early Christian texts such as Rom 11:36 and Heb 2:10 (cf. Eph 4:5; Heb 1:2; John 1:3, 10); see also Dörrie, "Präpositionen und Metaphysik"; and Runia, *Philo of Alexandria*, 171–172.

41. The idea that Christ might be the instrument in 8:6 is not lost on the later writer of Col 1:15, who develops even more elaborate uses of Platonic imagery (cf. Heb 1:2 and John 1:1–8). On Heb 2:10, see Attridge, *Epistle to the Hebrews*, 79–82; Attridge, "Philo and John"; and Tobin, "Prologue of John."

42. Scholars have often discussed the "strong" and "weak" here and in Romans as if they were discreet factions rather than part of Paul's strategic imaginary (e.g., Willis, "1 Corinthians 8–10"); for a strong critique, see Stowers, "Concept of 'Community.'" The most convincing analyses construe this as Paul's strategic reuse of philosophical discourses about ethical maturity, but that does not mean that this can be easily identified with any one "faction"; so Thorsteinsson, *Roman Christianity*, 152–155; Glad, *Paul and Philodemus*, esp. 277–336; and Malherbe, "Gentle as a Nurse," 43–48.

43. Interpreters often take this as a condemnation of all humanity based on conjectured allusions to an Adamic fall. As a number of scholars have argued,

however, the text fits with common Jewish stereotypes of gentiles as sex-crazed sinners, e.g., Stowers, *Rereading of Romans*, 86–89; Thorsteinsson, *Paul's Interlocutor*, 165–176; and Thiessen, *Paul and the Gentile Problem*, 47–52. On the language about "nature" in vv. 26–27, see Brooten, *Love Between Women*, 267–302; and D. Martin, "Heterosexism."

44. As Roth notes ("For Life," 30), the focus on issues of knowledge and understanding led some commentators to typify idol parodies as "rationalist;" see also von Rad, *Wisdom in Israel*, 177–185; and Crüsemann, *Studien zur Formgeschichte*, 113–114.

45. In *Phaedo* 97c, Plato attributes this view to the Pre-Socratic Anaxagoras. As David Sedley shows (*Creationism and Its Critics*, 87–89), Socrates and Plato often misconstrue the Pre-Socratics as atheists and use them as stand-ins for their antiteleological rivals, the atomists.

46. Xenophon (*Mem.* 1.1.11–16) also pillories the early scientists for their antisocial and religiously aberrant behaviors such as worshipping "stocks and stones and beasts" (1.1.14).

47. Plato, *Laws* 886a; Epictetus, *Disc.* 1.6.7, 1.19.11; Cicero, *De nat.* 1.20.53; 2.37.95, on Aristotle; Diodorus Siculus, *Bibl.* 1.11.1; Pseudo-Aristotle, *De Mundo* 399b12–399b22; Philo, *Opif.* 7–12 (adapting *Tim.* 28a–28c); *Spec.* 1.3; *Mos.* 2.12; *Aet.* 10–19; Josephus, *Ant.* 1.7.1; *Bellum* 7.8.7; *Aristeas* 132; Wis 13:5; cf. Jub. 12, where Abraham infers knowledge of God by observing the heavens (12:17).

48. It should be noted that Philo's claims about deifying the elements could reflect a critique of Stoic theology specifically. The Stoics tended to construe many of the traditional Olympian gods as allegories for the elements, qualities of the elements, and principles (including their theory of an all-pervading, rational divine *pneuma*). The charge of deifying the world could also (in theory, at least) fit with statements made by a wide array of Platonist, Peripatetic, and Stoic philosophers. See, e.g., *Tim.* 29b–c, where Plato describes the created world as "a blessed god." The association with Stoicism is, however, quite common. According to Cicero (*De nat.* 1.15.38–41), Chrysippus described the world as a god and identified the elements as gods (so Jupiter becomes aether, Neptune the air in the sea, and Ceres the earth); see further *De nat.* 2.25–28; Diogenes Laertius, *Lives* 7.147; Plutarch, *Mor.* 363D, 367C–E; cf. *Mor.* 364A–E, 365C–E. See the important qualification of Long, "Allegory in Philo."

49. In less polemical settings, Philo treats the elements as a self-evident feature of the cosmos (*Her.* 281–282; cf. *Dec.* 31); see also *Plant.* 281–283; *Somn.* 1.21; *Deus* 46; *Opif.* 27, 144; *Gig.* 7–9; *Conf.* 173; *Dec.* 52–63; *Spec.* 1.207; and *Vit. Cont.* 3–12. Of course, the attack on the sun, moon, planets, and fixed stars could allude to Greek and Roman myths that associate the gods with heavenly bodies, but this is more easily understood as an ungenerous repurposing of the cosmological argument.

50. Cf. Philo's critique in *Opif.*, which impugns those who hold "the world in admiration rather than the maker of the world (κοσμοποιὸν)" (*Opif.* 7) and insists

that the true God is the "perfectly pure and unsullied mind of the universe, transcending virtue, transcending knowledge, transcending the good itself and the beautiful itself" (*Opif.* 8).

51. Winston (*Wisdom of Solomon*, 249–251) shows that the language of the artificer in 13:1 derives from Stoic traditions (adapted by Philo in similar ways), but the "primal author of beauty" in 13:3 seems more Platonic.

52. See Winston (*Wisdom of Solomon*, 248) for speculations about Jewish Hellenistic traditions that might have been common to Philo and Pseudo-Solomon.

53. James D. G. Dunn (*Romans*, 1:57–58) notes the unusual language here and connects it to Stoicism, with the Wisdom of Solomon as a possible conduit (so, e.g., ἀΐδιος appears in Wis 7:26); likewise, Joseph A. Fitzmyer (*Romans*, 279–281). Dunn (*Romans*, 1:58) also notes connections with Philo's language about ἀΐδιος and ἀόρατα but evokes Christian categories, noting, for instance, that Paul uses the term κτίζω in ways that are consistent with "a qualitative distinction between Creator and creature" that proves so central to "Judeo-Christian theology."

54. See Stowers, "Paul's Four Discourses," 108–113.

55. See Stowers, *Rereading of Romans*, 8–94; Stowers, "Paul and Self-Mastery"; and Wasserman, *Death of the Soul*, 118–128.

Chapter 5. Victimization, Alienation, and Privilege Among the Christ-Elect

1. It should be emphasized, however, that such language should not be taken as expressing objective or reified social realities. On the problems with conceiving of groups in these ways, see Brubaker, *Ethnicity Without Groups;* and Stowers, "Concept of 'Community.'"

2. Many versions of the "powers" theories do just this; see, e.g., Käsemann, *Commentary on Romans;* Beker, *Triumph of God;* and the contributions in Gaventa, ed., *Apocalyptic Paul.*

3. As will become clear, I use the term "self" to designate diverse and interrelated attributions of mind, soul, emotion, personality, ethical disposition, and moral responsibility that are central concerns of much ancient literature, not some modern Kantian or other notion of fully self-conscious, autonomous individualism. For an excellent discussion of these distinctions, see Gill, *Personality in Greek Epic,* 1–28.

4. I use "victimization" as an umbrella term for Paul's varied claims about the dangers and threats that afflict his imagined Christ communities. I am sympathetic with the approaches advocated by James A. Kelhoffer (*Persecution, Persuasion and Power,* esp. 1–25) and Elizabeth A. Castelli (*Imitating Paul*), which treat language about persecution, strength, and suffering as part of an authorizing discourse about Paul's own power and legitimate standing. In this respect, connections could also be drawn with so-called hardship catalogues

(e.g., Kelhoffer, ibid.; and Fitzgerald, *Cracks in an Earthen Vessel*). Here, however, I focus on the ways that these discourses work rhetorically to create imagined outsiders, insiders, and threats and less on Paul's heroic self-presentation (cf. Castelli, *Martyrdom and Memory*, esp. 35–38).

5. This section draws on some of my previously published work: "Paul Beyond the Judaism/Hellenism Divide?" and *Death of the Soul*.

6. Scholars have tended to deny that Paul's letters meaningfully appropriate from Greek or Hellenistic traditions. For instance, see the apologetics about Hellenic-gnostic dualism in the work of Bultmann, *Theology of the New Testament*, e.g., 109, 164–183; Jewett, *Paul's Anthropological Terms*, esp. 396–401 (though see now his *Commentary on Romans*, 440–473); Betz, "Concept of the 'Inner Human Being'"; and Heckel, "Body and Soul in Paul," 122, and *Der Innere Mensch*. In some contrast, David E. Aune ("Human Nature and Ethics") treats Hellenistic traditions more seriously but arrives at a formulation of a diffuse and vaguely defined culture of Hellenism that contributes little to Paul's thought.

7. Aune ("Human Nature and Ethics," 292–293) develops a fairly subtle portrayal of Platonism but overemphasizes the inconsistencies in Plato's writings and ignores the way later Platonists develop these views. See Wasserman, "Paul Among the Philosophers," esp. 387–401, on the resilience of Platonic moral psychology.

8. This draws on Plato's theory as described in the *Phaedrus*, *Republic*, and *Timaeus* rather than the earlier *Phaedo*. See Price, *Mental Conflict*, 30–103, and Cooper, "Plato's Theory of Human Motivation."

9. Though they cannot reason in a developed sense, the appetites do have some kind of low-level rational capacities; see Gill, "Did Galen Understand?"

10. See, e.g., *Tim.* 86b–90a and Galen, *On the Passions and Errors of the Soul* (Kühn, ed., *Claudii Galeni opera Omnia*, 5:28), on cultivating the strength and weakness of the soul's parts.

11. See Zeller, "Life and Death of the Soul." Though otherwise excellent, this study explores the origins of these metaphors rather than the underlying moral-psychological phenomenon they capture.

12. Philo can also speak positively of dying to bodily life as in *Mos.* 1.279; *Gig.* 14; cf. *Ebr.* 70; *Fug.* 90; being truly alive in *Leg.* 1.32, 35; 2.93; 3.52; *Post.* 12, 45; *Migr.* 21; *Her.* 201; *Congr.* 87; *Mut.* 213; *Somn.* 2.64; *Virt.* 17; *QG* 1.16, 70; 2.45; 4.46, 149, 238; truly dead in *Her.* 53, 201; *Leg.* 3.35, 72; *Spec.* 1.345; cf. Plato, *Gorg.* 492e.

13. Kühn, ed., *Claudii Galeni opera Omnia*, 5:29; Harkins, trans., *Galen*, 48. I have modified the translation from Harkins. The Greek text is from Kühn, page references are for both Kühn and Harkins.

14. Stowers also notes connections with Platonism in *Rereading of Romans*, 269–272; see also his "Paul and Self-Mastery."

15. Translations of Paul's letters are my own.

16. Other theories about sin have proved to be popular. So Käsemann (*Commentary on Romans*, 150, and "On Paul's Anthropology") argues that sin is an invading apocalyptic power. Among others, these views are adapted by many contributors to Gaventa, ed., *Apocalyptic Paul*. Others have understood sin in terms of an evil impulse, as Keck, "Absent Good"; Murphy, "*Yeser* in the Qumran Literature"; and Marcus, "Evil Inclination in the Epistle of James" and "Evil Inclination in the Letters of Paul." Still others appeal to supposed confessional texts from Qumran, as Seifrid, "Subject of Rom 7:14–25," 322; Fitzmyer, *Romans*, 465–466; and Stuhlmacher, *Paul's Letter to the Romans*, 109–110. Though plausible at first blush, these theories do not specify very precise points of continuity among the texts in question, and they do little to illuminate the specifics of Paul's language and argument. For an alternative to such readings of Qumran literature, see Wills, "Ascetic Theology?," esp. 906–907.

17. Kühn, ed., *Claudii Galeni opera Omnia*, 5:29; Harkins, trans., *Galen*, 48.

18. The identity of the speaker has been widely disputed, with no consensus emerging. For the autobiographical reading, see Dodd, *Epistle of Paul to the Romans*, 104–105; Jewett, *Commentary on Romans*, 442–444; and Engberg-Pederson, "Reception of Greco-Roman Culture," 37; that of a Jewish boy before a mature interaction with the law, Gundry, "Moral Frustration of Paul"; the plight of humankind generally in 7:7–13 and the Christian in 7:14–25, Cranfield, *Critical and Exegetical Commentary*, 341; Dunn, *Romans*, 1:382–383; the unregenerate human being generally, Fitzmyer, *Romans*, 462–477; Adam, Israel, and Paul himself, Byrne, *Romans*, 218; and Lichtenberger, *Ich Adams*, 160–166; as a kind of Adamic gentile, Holland, "Self Against the Self"; and as Eve, Busch, "Figure of Eve in Romans 7:5–25." As Stowers argues, however, the monologue reflects the conventions of speech-in-character (προσωποποιία), a rhetorical technique in which the writer creates a fictitious persona and/or interlocutor to advance his or her argument; see Stowers, "Apostrophe"; Stowers, *Rereading of Romans*, 16–21, 264–284; and Stowers, "Romans 7:7–25"; see also Harrill, *Slaves in the New Testament*, 18–33; Wasserman, *Death of the Soul*, 77–81; and Jewett, *Commentary on Romans*, 27–28, 441–445, 455–456. For some recent but unpersuasive challenges, see Anderson, *Ancient Rhetorical Theory*, 181, and Timmins, "Romans 7 and Speech-in-Character."

19. Many commentators have been eager to deny that Paul could adapt Platonism or Greek philosophy of any kind (e.g., Betz, "Concept of the 'Inner Human Being'"; and Heckel, "Body and Soul in Paul," 122), but Troels Engberg-Pedersen (most recently in "A Stoic Concept?") has argued that the monologue envisions a Stoic form of *akrasia* (typically translated as "weakness of will"). As I argue below, Stoicism does prove illuminating for many other aspects of Paul's language and argument, but the metaphors, analogies, and normative character of self-contradiction in Rom 7 reflect well-established Platonic traditions about extreme types (and not, per se, *akrasia*; see Wasserman, *Death*

of the Soul, 98–103). Stoic moral psychology, by contrast, posits the vacillation of a single mind that turns first one way and then another; see, e.g., Gill, "Did Galen Understand?"; Brennan, "Stoic Moral Psychology"; and Brennan, *Stoic Life.* Engberg-Pedersen's Stoic reading of Rom 7 seems to derive from a concern to find a relatively consistent (and Stoic) picture of Paul's thought, not a careful consideration of the case for the adaptation of Platonism.

20. Stowers, *Rereading of Romans,* 269–272; Stowers, *Diatribe and Paul's Letter;* Gill, "Did Chrysippus Understand Medea?"; Gill, "Two Monologues."

21. *Pneuma* is some sort of airy breathlike substance; see Johnson Hodge, *If Sons, Then Heirs;* Stowers, "What Is 'Pauline Participation'?"; D. Martin, *Corinthian Body,* 108–132; and Engberg-Pedersen, *Cosmology and Self,* esp. 1–105.

22. On Christ as the *pneuma*-bearer, see Stowers, "What Is 'Pauline Participation'?," 352–71.

23. This conception of *pneuma* has certain resonances with Stoic thought, but Stoic traditions do not typically imagine *pneuma* as an instrument of anthropomorphic deities or as dolled out to a favored elect. See Stowers, "Paul and Self-Mastery," on the synthesis of Platonism and Stoicism in Rom 7–8; Engberg-Pedersen, *Paul and the Stoics,* 239–246; Engberg-Pedersen, *Cosmology and Self,* 106–138; Long, *Epictetus,* esp. 142–179.

24. *Rep.* 9.588c–591b. For a persuasive argument that 1 Cor 15:32 alludes to the lion and the many-headed beast, see Malherbe, "Beasts at Ephesus."

25. C. K. Barrett (*Commentary,* 146) dismisses any psychological dualism in 4:16 on the grounds that the tension is eschatological and not psychological; likewise, Victor Paul Furnish (*II Corinthians,* 261–301) entertains the relevance of so-called Hellenistic ideas but insists that their meaning is uniquely Pauline; similarly, Aune, "Human Nature and Ethics," 301–302; and Heckel, "Body and Soul," 129–130. Such approaches obfuscate more than they clarify.

26. Among many other examples, consider Philo's use of housing analogies in *Opif.* 137, where God fashions Adam out of the best earth to serve as a house or a sacred shrine (οἶκος γάρ τις ἢ νεὼς ἱερὸς) for the reasoning faculty, "which man was to carry like a holy image, of all images the most Godlike."

27. Cf. Plato, *Crat.* 403b. Aune ("Human Nature and Ethics," 302) suggests these connections but does not develop them.

28. See Thorsteinsson, *Roman Christianity,* 141–146.

29. See Stowers "Paul and Self-Mastery," esp. 290–300.

30. Stowers, "Paul and Self-Mastery."

31. Stowers, "Paul and Self-Mastery."

32. See Brubaker, *Ethnicity Without Groups;* Stowers, "Concept of 'Community.'"

33. On *pneuma,* see Stowers, "What Is 'Pauline Participation'?" and Johnson Hodge, *If Sons, Then Heirs.*

34. On imitation, see Castelli, *Imitating Paul;* Thorsteinsson, *Roman Christianity,* 149–156.

35. P⁴⁶ and other witnesses have προηγούμενοι.

36. Thorsteinsson, *Roman Christianity*, esp. 92–104, 137–189; Thorsteinsson, "Stoicism as a Key"; Engberg-Pedersen, *Paul and the Stoics*. Engberg-Pedersen generally relies on Cicero's account, but Thorsteinsson helpfully shifts the focus to Roman Stoics.

37. Abraham Malherbe and Clarence Glad have also shown that Paul's arguments about adaptability are strikingly similar to those found in a range of Greco-Roman moral traditions, including but not limited to Stoic ones. See especially Malherbe, "Determinism and Free Will"; and Glad, *Paul and Philodemus*, esp. 38–45, 236–326.

38. Engberg-Pedersen makes very significant contributions to our understanding of Paul's thought, but his arguments to the effect that Paul's moral psychology is Stoic (*Paul and the Stoics*, 239–246, and "Reception of Greco-Roman Culture") are not convincing. He maintains this view largely by insisting that there is a coherent, basically Stoic core to Paul's thought and by ignoring the Platonic evidence.

39. See Gill, "Did Galen Understand?"

40. Colish, *Stoic Tradition*, 38–41; Annas, *Morality of Happiness*, 262–276; more recently, Reydams-Schils, *Roman Stoics*, 53–82. As Reydams-Schils shows (ibid., 68–70), Roman Stoics treat social relationships as goods in themselves, even if they are inevitably subordinate to the overarching good of life in harmony with nature; see, e.g., Cicero *Fin.* 3.55; Arius Didymus *SVF* 3.106–112; Epictetus, *Disc.* 3.3.5–10. See also Engberg-Pedersen, "Marcus Aurelius on Emotions"; and Thorsteinsson, *Roman Christianity*, 175–189.

41. Long and Sedley, trans., *Hellenistic Philosophers*. Some writers also distinguish spheres of social concern, as Hierocles apud Stobeus, *Flor.* 84.23.

42. The focus on the rationality of the sage may seem at odds with other-directed values, but as Reydams-Schils shows (*Roman Stoics*, 58–59), the Stoics view these as different aspects of *oikeiôsos*.

43. Similarly, Cicero, *Off.* 1. 153, 3.52; *Fin.* 3.67–68; Marcus Aurelius, *Med.* 6.39; 7.13, 55; 8.12, 26; 11.1.

44. See, e.g., Seneca, *Ben.* 7.30–32; *Ira.* 2.34; Epictetus, *Disc.* 3.22.54; Musonius Rufus, *Frag.* 41; Marcus Aurelius, *Med.* 7.22; Rom 12:17, 13:8–10; Thorsteinsson, *Roman Christianity*, 166–175, and "Stoicism as a Key," 29–32.

45. "Stoicism as a Key," 23–25.

46. On mind and moral praxis, see Thorsteinsson, *Roman Christianity*, 143–144.

47. Concerns about pretension and arrogance are a regular feature of Greco-Roman moral discourses. See, e.g., Philodemus, *On Frank Criticism*, 15b–21a; Glad, *Paul and Philodemus*, 150–152; Stowers, *Diatribe and Paul's Letter*, 93–96; Stowers, *Rereading of Romans*, 144–149; see also Meeks, "Judgment and the Brother."

48. See Thorsteinsson, "Stoicism as a Key," 25–28, and *Roman Christianity*, 148–149.

49. Thorsteinsson, *Roman Christianity*, 166–175, and "Stoicism as a Key," 29–32. On nonretaliation, see, e.g., Seneca, *Ira.* 1.16.1; *Ben.* 7.31.1; Musonius Rufus, *Frag.* 10.78.26–33.

50. Scholars have often identified the language of strong and weak here and in 1 Corinthians with parties or groups that have distinct habits, attributes, and conflicts (see Willis's overview in "1 Corinthians 8–10"). Such approaches tend to engage in a problematic mirror reading of Paul's identifications and to work with naïve constructions of social reality; for a robust critique, see Brubaker, *Ethnicity Without Groups;* and Stowers, "Concept of 'Community.'" The most convincing analyses construe this as Paul's strategic reuse of philosophical discourses about ethical maturity. See Thorsteinsson, *Roman Christianity*, 152–155; Glad, *Paul and Philodemus*, esp. 277–336; and Malherbe, "Gentle as a Nurse."

51. On imitation and "clothing oneself" with Christ, see Thorsteinsson, *Roman Christianity*, 149–156, who compares Paul's model of Christ with the ideal of the sage, particularly as embodied by Socrates.

52. See, e.g., Livy, *Hist.* 2.32.9–12; Seneca, *Clem.* 1.3.5–1.4.1, 1.5.1; Thorsteinsson, *Roman Christianity*, 164–165; Lee, *Paul, the Stoics*, esp. 29–102; and McVay, "Human Body."

53. See also *Ira* 2.31.7; Marcus Aurelius, *Med.* 7.13; cf. 2.1. Elsewhere Seneca uses body analogies in more traditional ways, as *Clem.* 1.4.1–3, 2.2.1.

54. Similarly, Thorsteinsson, *Roman Christianity*, 28–29, and "Stoicism as a Key."

55. See Collins, *Daniel*, 403–404; language about suffering as refinement also appears in Isa 53:11; Wis 2–3; 2 Macc 7; Sir 2:5; cf. Test. Mos. 9; and Rev 6:10–11.

56. See Malherbe, "Gentle as a Nurse," esp. 43–48; Fredrickson, "Parrêsia"; on hardship catalogues, see 1 Cor 15:30–31, 4:9–13; 2 Cor 4:8–10, 6:4–10, 11:23–28, 12:10; Fitzgerald, *Cracks in an Earthen Vessel*, e.g., 37; Kelhoffer, *Persecution, Persuasion and Power*, 30–64.

57. See also Paul's more oblique language about "this age" in Gal 1:4; 1 Cor 1:20, 2:6, and "the end of the ages" in 1 Cor 11:10; cf. 2 Cor 5:17.

58. On orientation around a single good as distinctive to Hellenistic philosophical ethics, see Stowers, "Does Pauline Christianity Resemble?"

59. Some scholars have drawn connections with "eschatological suffering" but not victimization generally, as Jewett, *Romans*, 353; Dunn, *Romans*, 1:468–469. For a helpful and programmatic reassessment, see Kelhoffer, *Persecution, Persuasion and Power.*

60. On martial imagery in discussions of self-mastery, see Malherbe, "Antisthenes and Odysseus"; see, e.g., Diogenes Laertius, *Lives* 6.13; Seneca, *Ep.* 96.5; Epictetus, *Disc.* 4.8.33; 2 Cor 10:3–6; on the use of clothing imagery to similar ends, see Malherbe's discussion of the "harsh cynics" (e.g., Ps-Crates, *Ep.* 19, 23; Ps-Diogenes, *Ep.* 15), ibid.

61. For comparisons with discussions of imitating or "putting on" Socrates and other wise men, see Thorsteinsson, *Roman Christianity*, 33–34, 150–156.

62. This seems to draw on the LXX of Isa 45:23 (with slight modifications to the word order) and adds the common prophetic motif, "as I live, says the Lord."

63. See also Kelhoffer, *Persecution, Persuasion and Power,* 1–64.

64. On Paul's priestly language in Rom 12:1–2 and 15:16, see Thorsteinsson, *Roman Christianity,* 138.

Conclusion

1. Such theories became especially popular in post–World War II biblical theology because of figures like Oscar Cullman (*State in the New Testament*) and Ernst Käsemann (*Commentary on Romans* and "On the Subject of Primitive Christian Apocalyptic"). For Cullmann and Käsemann, for instance, the evil apocalyptic overlords provide a corollary to the evils of the modern world where Christians find themselves under the dominion of evil political and military regimes. More recently, see the contributions to Gaventa, ed., *Apocalyptic Paul;* and Moses, *Practices of Power.*

2. *Origins of Biblical Monotheism,* 47; see also Mullen, *Assembly of the Gods,* 114–120; and Miller, "Cosmology and World Order."

3. A number of critics take issue with the category of alleged "monotheism." Among others, see Fredriksen, "Mandatory Retirement" and "Review of Larry Hurtado"; also M. Smith, *Origins,* 41–53; and Olyan, "Is Isaiah 40–55 Really Monotheistic?"

4. Some manuscripts add "wicked spirits in the heavens (ἐν τοῖς ἐπουρανίοις)" to 6:12, but this is absent from P⁴⁶.

Bibliography

Critical Editions and Translations

Alexander, Philip S., and Geza Vermes, eds. *Qumran Cave 4. XIX: Serekh ha-Yaḥad and Two Related Texts.* Discoveries in the Judaean Desert 26. Oxford: Clarendon, 1998.

Annus, Amar. *The Standard Babylonian Epic of Anzu.* Helsinki: Neo-Assyrian Text Corpus Project, 2001.

Attridge, Harold W., and Robert A. Oden Jr., eds. *Philo of Byblos: The Phoenician History.* Catholic Biblical Quarterly Monograph Series 9. Washington, DC: Catholic Biblical Association of America, 1981.

Baillet, Maurice. *Qumran Grotte 4, III (4Q482–520).* Discoveries in the Judaean Desert 7. Oxford: Clarendon, 1982.

Black, Matthew, ed. *Apocalypsis Henochi Graece: Fragmenta pseudepigraphorum quae supersunt Graeca, collegit et ordinavit Albert-Marie Denis.* Leiden: Brill, 1970.

Black, Matthew. *The Book of Enoch or 1 Enoch: A New English Edition with Commentary and Textual Notes.* Studia in Veteris Testamenti Pseudepigrapha 7. Leiden: Brill, 1985.

Charles, R. H. *The Book of Enoch or 1 Enoch.* 2nd ed. Oxford: Clarendon, 1912.

Charles, R. H. *The Book of Jubilees or the Little Genesis: From the Editor's Ethiopic Text.* London: Adam and Charles Black, 1902.

Charles, R. H. *The Ethiopic Version of the Book of Enoch.* Oxford: Clarendon, 1906.

Charlesworth, James H., ed. *The Old Testament Pseudepigrapha.* 2 vols. New York: Doubleday, 1983–1985.

Dalley, Stephanie. *Myths from Mesopotamia: Creation, the Flood, Gilgamesh, and Others.* Edited and translated with an introduction and notes by Stephanie Dalley. Oxford: Oxford University Press, 2000.

Duhaime, Jean. "War Scroll." Pages 180–203 in vol. 2 of *The Dead Sea Scrolls: Hebrew, Aramaic, and Greek Texts with English Translations.* Edited by J. H. Charlesworth. Louisville, KY: Westminster John Knox, 1995.

Duhaime, Jean. *The War Texts: 1QM and Related Manuscripts.* Companion to the Dead Sea Scrolls 6. London: T & T Clark, 2004.

García Martínez, Florentino, and Eibert J. C. Tigchelaar. *The Dead Sea Scrolls Study Edition.* 2 vols. Grand Rapids, MI: Eerdmans, 1997, 1998.

Grayson, A. Kirk, and Jamie Novotny, *The Royal Inscriptions of Sennacherib, King of Assyria (704–681 BC), Part 2.* Royal Inscriptions of the Neo-Assyrian Period 3/2. Winona Lake, IN: Eisenbrauns, 2014.

Gropp, Douglas M., and Moshe Bernstein et al., eds. *Wadi Daliyeh II: The Samaria Papyri from Wadi Daliyeh and Qumran Cave 4. XXVIII, Miscellanea, Part 2.* Discoveries in the Judaean Desert 28. Oxford: Clarendon, 2000.

Harkins, Paul W., trans. *Galen: On the Passions and Errors of the Soul.* Columbus: Ohio State University Press, 1963.

Knibb, Michael A. *The Ethiopic Book of Enoch: A New Edition in the Light of the Aramaic Dead Sea Fragments.* 2 vols. Oxford: Clarendon, 1978.

Kühn, C. G., ed. *Claudii Galeni opera omnia. V, 4, 1, 2.* Edited and translated by Philip De Lacy. Berlin: Akademie-Verlag, 1978.

Lambert, W. G. "Mesopotamian Creation Stories." Pages 15–59 in *Imagining Creation.* Edited by Markham J. Geller and Mineke Schipper. Studies in Judaica 5. Leiden: Brill, 2008.

Lambert, W. G., and S. B. Parker. *Enuma Elish: The Babylonian Epic of Creation, the Cuneiform Text.* London: Oxford, 1966.

Lattimore, Richmond. *Hesiod: Works and Days, Theogony, and the Shield of Achilles.* Ann Arbor: University of Michigan Press, 1959.

Leichty, Erle. *The Royal Inscriptions of Esarhaddon, King of Assyria (680–669 BC).* Royal Inscriptions of the Neo-Assyrian Period 3/4. Winona Lake, IN: Eisenbrauns, 2011.

Lods, A. *Le Livre d'Hénoch: Fragments grecs découverts à Akhmim (Haute-Égypte), publiés avec les variantes du texte éthiopien, traduits et annotés.* Paris: Leroux, 1892.

Lombardo, Stanley, trans. *Hesiod: Works and Days and Theogony.* Indianapolis, IN: Hackett, 1993.

Long, A. A., and David Sedley, eds. *The Hellenistic Philosophers.* 2 vols. Cambridge: Cambridge University Press, 1987.

Milik, J. T., ed., with Matthew Black. *Books of Enoch: Aramaic Fragments of Qumran Cave 4.* Oxford: Clarendon, 1976.

Newsom, Carol. *Songs of the Sabbath Sacrifice: A Critical Edition.* Harvard Semitic Studies 27. Atlanta: Scholars, 1985.

Nickelsburg, George W. E., and James C. VanderKam. *1 Enoch: The Hermeneia Translation.* Minneapolis: Fortress, 2004.

Parker, Simon B., ed. *Ugaritic Narrative Poetry.* Society of Biblical Literature Writings from the Ancient World Series 9. Atlanta: Scholars, 1997.

Smith, Mark S. *The Ugaritic Baal Cycle Volume I: Introduction with Text, Translation, and Commentary of KTU/CAT 1.1–1.2.* Leiden: Brill, 1994.

Smith, Mark S., and Wayne T. Pitard. *The Ugaritic Baal Cycle Volume II: Introduction with Text, Translation, and Commentary of KTU/CAT 1.3–1.4.* Leiden: Brill, 2009.

Solmsen, F., R. Merkelbach, and M. L. West. *Hesiodi: Theogonia, Opera et Dies, Scutum, Fragmenta Selecta.* Oxford: Oxford University Press, 1983.

Talon, Philippe. *Enuma Elish: The Standard Babylonian Creation Myth.* State Archives of Assyria Cuneiform Texts 4. Helsinki: Neo-Assyrian Text Corpus Project, 2005.

Ulrich, E., F. M. Cross, S. W. Crawford, J. A. Duncan, P. W. Skehan, E. Tov, J. C. Trebolle Barrera. *Qumran Cave 4. IX: Deuteronomy, Joshua, Judges, Kings.* Discoveries in the Judaean Desert 14. Oxford: Clarendon, 1995.

VanderKam, James C. *The Book of Jubilees.* 2 vols. Corpus Scriptorum Christianorum Orientalium 510–511. Leuven: Peeters, 1989.

Vogelzang, M. E. *Bin šar dadmē: Edition and Analysis of the Akkadian Anzu Poem.* Groningen: Styx, 1988.

West, M. L. *Hesiod: Theogony.* Oxford: Oxford University Press, 1966.

Zeigler, J., ed. *Septuaginta. Vetus Testamentum Graecum Auctoritate Academiae Scientiarum Gottingensis editum.* 20 vols. Göttingen: Vandenhoeck & Ruprecht, 1931–.

Secondary Sources

Abegg, Martin G., Jr. "Messianic Hope and 4Q285: A Reassessment." *Journal of Biblical Literature* 113.1 (1994): 81–91.

Ackroyd, P. R. *Exile and Restoration: A Study of Hebrew Thought of the Sixth Century BC.* London: SCM, 1968.

Adler, William. "Introduction." Pages 1–31 in *The Jewish Apocalyptic Heritage in Early Christianity.* Edited by James C. VanderKam and William Adler. Minneapolis: Fortress, 1996.

Albrektson, Bertil. *History and the Gods: An Essay on the Idea of Historical Events as Divine Manifestations in the Ancient Near East and in Israel.* Coniectanea Biblica Old Testament Series 1. Winona Lake, IN: Eisenbrauns, 2011. Reprint of 1st edition, 1967.

Albright, W. F. "Psalm of Habakkuk." Pages 1–18 in *Studies in Old Testament Prophecy Dedicated to T. H. Robinson.* Edited by H. H. Rowley. Edinburgh: Clark, 1950.

Albright, W. F. *Yahweh and the Gods of Canaan: A Historical Analysis of Two Contrasting Faiths.* London: Athlone, 1968.

Alexander, Philip S. "The Evil Empire: The Qumran Eschatological War Cycle and the Origins of Jewish Opposition to Rome." Pages 17–31 in vol. 1 of *Emanuel: Studies in Hebrew Bible, Septuagint, and Dead Sea Scrolls in Honor of Emanuel Tov.* 2 vols. Edited by Shalom Paul, Robert A. Kraft, Lawrence H. Schiffman, and Weston W. Fields, Leiden: Brill, 2003.

Alexander, Philip S. "The Demonology of the Dead Sea Scrolls." Pages 331–353 in vol. 2 of *The Dead Sea Scrolls After Fifty Years: A Comprehensive Assessment*. 2 vols. Edited by Peter W. Flint and James C. VanderKam. Leiden: Brill, 1998.

Alexander, Philip S. "The Redaction-History of Serekh ha-Yaḥad: A Proposal." *Revue Qumran* 17 (1996): 437–453.

Anderson, R. Dean, Jr. *Ancient Rhetorical Theory and Paul*. Contributions to Biblical Exegesis and Theology 18. Leuven: Peeters, 1999.

Angel, Andrew. *Chaos and the Son of Man: The Hebrew Chaoskampf Tradition in the Period 515 BCE to 200 CE*. New York: T & T Clark, 2006.

Angel, Joseph A. "Maskil, Community, and Religious Experience in the *Songs of the Sage* (4Q510–511)." *Dead Sea Discoveries* 19.1 (2012): 1–27.

Annas, Julia. *The Morality of Happiness*. New York: Oxford, 1993.

Arnold, Clinton E. *Powers of Darkness: Principalities and Powers in Paul's Letters*. Downers Grove, IL: InterVarsity, 1992.

Arnold, Clinton E. "Returning to the Domain of the Powers: 'Stoicheia' as Evil Spirits in Galatians 4:3, 9." *Novum Testamentum* 38.1 (1996): 55–76.

Arthur, Marilyn B. "Cultural Strategies in Hesiod's *Theogony:* Law, Family, and Society." *Arethusa* 15 (1982): 63–82.

Arthur, Marilyn B. "The Dream of a World Without Women: Poetics and Circles of Order in the *Theogony* Prooemium." *Arethusa* 16 (1983): 97–116.

Asher, Jeffrey R. "ΣΠΕΙΡΕΤΑΙ: Paul's Anthropogenic Metaphor in 1 Corinthians 15:42–44." *Journal of Biblical Literature* 120.1 (2001): 101–122.

Asher, Jeffrey R. *Polarity and Change in 1 Corinthians 15: A Study of Metaphysics, Rhetoric, and Resurrection*. Tübingen: Mohr Siebeck, 2000.

Athanassiadi, Polymnia, and Michael Frede, eds. *Pagan Monotheism in Antiquity*. Oxford: Oxford University Press, 1999.

Attridge, Harold W. *The Epistle to the Hebrews: A Commentary on the Epistle to the Hebrews*. Philadelphia: Fortress, 1989.

Attridge, Harold W. "Greek and Latin Apocalypses." Pages 159–186 in *Apocalypse: The Morphology of a Genre*. Edited by J. J. Collins. Semeia 14. Missoula, MT: Scholars, 1979.

Attridge, Harold W. "Philo and John: Two Riffs on One Logos." *Studia Philonica Annual* 17 (2005): 103–117.

Attridge, Harold W. "The Philosophical Critique of Religion Under the Early Empire." Pages 45–78 in *Aufstieg und Niedergang der römischen Welt: Geschichte aud Kultur Roms im Spiegel der neueren Forschung (ANRW)* 2.16.1. Edited by W. Haase. Berlin: de Gruyter, 1978.

Aune, David E. "Apocalypticism." Pages 25–35 in *The Dictionary of Paul and His Letters*. Edited by Gerald F. Hawthorne, Ralph P. Martin, and Daniel G. Reid. Downers Grove, IL: InterVarsity, 1993.

Aune, David E. "Archon." Pages 82–85 in *The Dictionary of Deities and Demons in the Bible*. Edited by Karel van der Toorn, Bob Becking, and Pieter W. van der Horst. 2nd ed. Leiden: Brill, 1999.

Aune, David E. "Human Nature and Ethics in Hellenistic Philosophical Traditions and Paul: Some Issues and Problems." Pages 291–312 in *Paul in His Hellenistic Context*. Edited by Troels Engberg-Pedersen. Minneapolis: Fortress, 1995.

Ballentine, Debra Scoggins. *The Conflict Myth and the Biblical Tradition*. New York: Oxford University Press, 2015.

Barrett, C. K. *A Commentary on the Second Epistle to the Corinthians*. London: Adam and Charles Black, 1973.

Beck, Martin. "Das Tag YHWHs-Verständnis von Zephanja iii." *Vetus Testamentum* 58 (2008): 159–177.

Beck, Martin. *Der "Tag YHWHs" im Dodekapropheton. Studien im Spannungsfeld von Traditions- und Redaktionsgeschichte*. Beihefte zur Zeitschrift für die alttestamentliche Wissenschaft 356. Berlin: de Gruyter, 2005.

Beker, Johan Christiaan. *The Triumph of God: The Essence of Paul's Thought*. Translated by Loren T. Stuckenbruck. Minneapolis: Fortress, 1990.

Ben-Dov, Jonathan. *Head of All Years: Astronomy and Calendars at Qumran in Their Ancient Context*. Studies on the Texts of the Desert of Judah 78. Leiden: Brill, 2008.

Bergmann, Claudia D. "Idol Worship in *Bel and the Dragon* and Other Jewish Literature from the Second Temple Period." Pages 207–223 in *Septuagint Research: Issues and Challenges in the Study of the Greek Jewish Scriptures*. Edited by W. Kraus and R. G. Wooden. Society of Biblical Literature Septuagint and Cognate Studies 53. Atlanta: Society of Biblical Literature, 2006.

Betz, Hans Dieter. "The Concept of the 'Inner Human Being' (ὁ ἔσω ἄνθρωπος) in the Anthropology of Paul." *New Testament Studies* 46.3 (2000): 315–341.

Betz, Hans Dieter. *Galatians: A Commentary on Paul's Letter to the Churches in Galatia*. Philadelphia: Fortress, 1979.

Black, Matthew. "'Πᾶσαι ἐξουσίαι αὐτῷ ὑποταγήσονται (All Powers Will Be Subject to Him).'" Pages 74–82 in *Paul and Paulinism: Essays in Honour of C. K. Barrett*. Edited by Morna D. Hooker and Stephen G. Wilson. London: SPCK, 1982.

Black, Matthew. "Two Unusual Nomina Dei in the Second Vision of Enoch." Pages 53–59 in vol. 1 of *The New Testament Age: Essays in Honor of Bo Reicke*. 2 vols. Edited by William Weinrich. Macon, GA: Mercer University Press, 1984.

Black, Jeremy, and Anthony Green, eds. *Gods, Demons, and Symbols of Ancient Mesopotamia: An Illustrated Dictionary*. Austin: University of Texas Press, 1992.

Blasius, Andreas. "Antiochus IV Epiphanes and the Ptolemaic Triad: The Three Uprooted Horns in Dan 7:8, 20, and 24 Reconsidered." *Journal for the Study of Judaism in the Persian, Hellenistic and Roman Period* 37.4 (2006): 521–547.

Blenkinsopp, Joseph. *Isaiah 1–39: A New Translation with Introduction and Commentary*. New York: Doubleday, 2000.

Borgen, Peder. "'Yes,' 'No,' 'How Far?' The Participation of Jews and Christians in Pagan Cults." Pages 30–59 in *Paul in His Hellenistic Context*. Edited by Troels Engberg-Pedersen. Minneapolis: Fortress, 1995.

Bousset, Wilhelm, and H. Gressman. *Die Religion des Judentums im späthellenistichen Zeitalter.* 3rd ed. Tübingen: Mohr Siebeck, 1966.

Boys-Stones, George. "Ancient Philosophy of Religion: An Introduction." Pages 1–22 in vol. 1 of *Ancient Philosophy of Religion: The History of Western Philosophy of Religion.* Edited by Graham Oppy and N. N. Trakakis. Durham: Acumen, 2009.

Brenk, Frederick E. "'In the Light of the Moon': Demonology in the Early Imperial Period." Pages 2068–2145 in *Aufstieg und Niedergang der römischen Welt: Geschichte und Kultur Roms im Spiegel der neueren Forschung (ANRW)* 2.16.3. Edited by W. Haase. Berlin: de Gruyter, 1986.

Brennan, Tad. *The Stoic Life: Emotions, Duties, and Fate.* Oxford: Clarendon, 2005.

Brennan, Tad. "Stoic Moral Psychology." Pages 257–294 in *The Cambridge Companion to the Stoics.* Edited by Brad Inwood. Cambridge: Cambridge University Press, 2003.

Brenner, Martin L. *The Song of the Sea: Ex. 15:1–21.* Beihefte zur Zeitschrift für die alttestamentliche Wissenschaft 195. Berlin: de Gruyter, 1991.

Brooten, Bernadette. *Love Between Women: Early Christian Responses to Female Homoeroticism.* Chicago: University of Chicago Press, 1996.

Brubaker, Rogers. *Ethnicity Without Groups.* Cambridge, MA: Harvard University Press, 2004.

Bruce, F. F. *The Acts of the Apostles: The Greek Text with Introduction and Commentary.* 3rd ed. Grand Rapids, MI: Eerdmans, 1990.

Bruce, F. F. *The Epistle of Paul to the Galatians: A Commentary on the Greek Text.* Exeter: Paternoster, 1982.

Brucker, Ralph. *"Christushymnen" oder "epideiktische Passagen"? Studien zum Stilwechsel im Neuen Testament und seiner Umwelt.* Forschungen zur Religion und Literatur des Alten und Neuen Testaments 176. Göttingen: Vandenhoeck & Ruprecht, 1997.

Buell, Denise Kimber. *Why This New Race: Ethnic Reasoning in Early Christianity.* New York: Columbia University Press, 2008.

Bultmann, Rudolf. "Ist Apokalyptik die Mutter der christlichen Theologie? Eine Auseinandersetzung mit Ernst Käsemann." Pages 64–69 in *Apophoreta: Festschrift für E. Haenchen.* Edited by W. Eltester and F. H. Kettler. Beihefte zur Zeitschrift für die neutestamentliche Wissenschaft 30. Berlin: Töpelmann, 1964.

Bultmann, Rudolf. "Romans 7 and the Anthropology of Paul." Pages 147–157 in *Existence and Faith: Shorter Writings of Rudolf Bultmann.* Translated by Schubert Ogden. Cleveland, OH: Meridian, 1960.

Bultmann, Rudolf. *The Theology of the New Testament.* Translated by Kendrick Grobel. 2 vols. New York: Scribner, 1951.

Bultmann, Rudolf, and Hans-Werner Bartsch. *Kerygma and Myth: A Theological Debate.* Translated by Reginald H. Fuller. New York: Harper and Row, 1961.

Burkitt, F. Crawford. *Jewish and Christian Apocalypses.* London: Oxford University Press, 1914.

Busch, Austin. "The Figure of Eve in Romans 7:5–25." *Biblical Interpretation* 12.1 (2004): 1–36.

Buttrick, G. A. *The Interpreter's Dictionary of the Bible.* New York: Abingdon, 1962.

Byrne, Brendan. *Romans.* Collegeville, MN: Liturgical, 1996.

Caird, G. B. *Principalities and Powers: A Study in Pauline Theology.* Oxford: Clarendon, 1956.

Caquot, André. "Le dieu 'Athtar et les textes de Ras Shamra." *Syria* 35 (1958): 45–60.

Carmignac, Jean. "Qu'est-ce que l'Apocalyptique: Son emploi à Qumran." *Revue de Qumran* 10 (1979): 3–33.

Carr, Wesley. *Angels and Principalities: The Background, Meaning, and Development of the Pauline Phrase hai archai kai hai exousiai.* Society for New Testament Studies Monograph Series 42. Cambridge: Cambridge University Press, 1981.

Castelli, Elizabeth A. *Imitating Paul: A Discourse on Power.* Louisville, KY: Westminster John Knox, 1991.

Castelli, Elizabeth A. *Martyrdom and Memory: Early Christian Culture Making.* New York: Columbia University Press, 2004.

Charles, R. H. *A Critical and Exegetical Commentary on the Book of Daniel.* Oxford: Clarendon, 1929.

Charlesworth, James H. "A Critical Comparison of the Dualism in 1 QS 3:13–4:26 and the 'Dualism' Contained in the Gospel of John." Pages 76–102 in *John and Qumran.* Edited by James H. Charlesworth. London: Geoffrey Chapman Publisher, 1972.

Chaudhuri, Pramit. *The War with God: Theomachy in Roman Imperial Poetry.* New York: Oxford University Press, 2014.

Cheung, Alex T. *Idol Food in Corinth: Jewish Background and Pauline Legacy.* Journal for the Study of the New Testament Supplement Series 176. Sheffield: Sheffield Academic, 1999.

Clifford, Richard J. *The Cosmic Mountain in Canaan and the Old Testament.* Harvard Semitic Monographs 4. Cambridge, MA: Harvard University Press, 1972.

Clifford, Richard J. "Cosmogonies in the Ugaritic Texts and in the Bible." *Orientalia* 53 (1984): 183–201.

Clifford, Richard J. *Creation Accounts in the Ancient Near East and the Bible.* Catholic Biblical Studies Monograph Series 26. Washington, DC: Catholic Biblical Association of America, 1994.

Clifford, Richard J. "History and Myth in Daniel 10–12." *Bulletin of the American Schools of Oriental Research* 220 (1975): 23–26.

Clifford, Richard J. *Psalms 73–150.* Nashville: Abingdon, 2003.

Clifford, Richard J. "The Roots of Apocalypticism in Near Eastern Myth." Pages 3–38 in vol. 1 of *The Encyclopedia of Apocalypticism: The Origins of Apocalypticism in Judaism and Christianity.* 3 vols. Edited by J. J. Collins, B. McGinn, and S. Stein. New York: Continuum, 2000.

Coats, George W. "The Song of the Sea." *Catholic Biblical Quarterly* 31 (1969): 1–17.

Colish, Marcia L. *The Stoic Tradition from Antiquity to the Early Middle Ages*, 2 vols. I: *Stoicism in Classical Latin Literature*. Leiden: Brill, 1985.

Collins, John J. *The Apocalyptic Imagination: An Introduction to Jewish Apocalyptic Literature*. 2nd ed. Grand Rapids, MI: Eerdmans, 1998.

Collins, John J. *Apocalypticism in the Dead Sea Scrolls*. London: Routledge, 1997.

Collins, John J. *The Apocalyptic Vision of the Book of Daniel*. Harvard Semitic Monographs 16. Missoula, MT: Scholars, 1977.

Collins, John J. *Between Athens and Jerusalem: Jewish Identity in the Hellenistic Diaspora*. New York: Crossroad, 1983.

Collins, John J. "Cosmos and Salvation: Jewish Wisdom and Apocalyptic in the Hellenistic Age." Pages 317–338 in *Seers, Sibyls, and Sages in Hellenistic-Roman Judaism*. Leiden: Brill, 2001.

Collins, John J. *Daniel: A Commentary on the Book of Daniel*. Minneapolis: Fortress, 1993.

Collins, John J. "Dualism and Eschatology in 1 QM: A Reply to P. R. Davies." *Vetus Testamentum* 29.2 (1979): 212–216.

Collins, John J. "From Prophecy to Apocalypticism: The Expectation of the End." Pages 129–161 in vol. 1 of *The Encyclopedia of Apocalypticism: The Origins of Apocalypticism in Judaism and Christianity*. 3 vols. Edited by J. J. Collins, B. McGinn, and S. Stein. New York: Continuum, 2000.

Collins, John J. "Genre, Ideology, and Social Movements in Jewish Apocalypticism." Pages 25–38 in *Seers, Sibyls, and Sages in Hellenistic-Roman Judaism*. Leiden: Brill, 2001.

Collins, John J. "In the Likeness of the Holy Ones: The Creation of Humankind in a Wisdom Text from Qumran." Pages 609–618 in *The Provo International Conference on the Dead Sea Scrolls: Technological Innovations, New Texts, and Reformulated Issues*. Edited by D. W. Parry and E. Ulrich. Studies on the Texts of the Desert of Judah 30. Leiden: Brill, 1999.

Collins, John J. "Introduction: Towards the Morphology of the Genre." Pages 1–20 in *Apocalypse: The Morphology of a Genre*. Semeia 14. Missoula, MT: Scholars, 1979.

Collins, John J. "The Jewish Apocalypses." Pages 21–59 in *Apocalypse: The Morphology of a Genre*. Edited by J. J. Collins. Semeia 14. Missoula, MT: Scholars, 1979.

Collins, John J. "The Mythology of Holy War in Daniel and the Qumran War Scroll: A Point of Transition in Jewish Apocalyptic." *Vetus Testamentum* 25.3 (1975): 596–612.

Collins, John J. "Sectarian Consciousness in the Dead Sea Scrolls." Pages 177–192 in *Heavenly Tablets: Interpretation, Identity and Tradition in Ancient Judaism*. Edited by L. LiDonnici and A. Lieber. Leiden: Brill, 2007.

Collins, John J. "The Son of Man and the Saints of the Most High in the Book of Daniel." *Journal of Biblical Literature* 93.1 (1974): 50–66.

Collins, John J. "A Throne in the Heavens: Apotheosis in Pre-Christian Judaism." Pages 41–56 in *Death, Ecstasy, and Otherworldly Journeys*. Edited by John J. Collins and Michael Fishbane. Albany: State University of New York, 1995.

Collins, John J. "Watchers." Pages 893–895 in *The Dictionary of Deities and Demons in the Bible*. Edited by Karel van der Toorn, Bob Becking, and Pieter W. van der Horst. 2nd ed. Leiden: Brill, 1999.

Conzelmann, Hans. *1 Corinthians: A Commentary on the First Epistle to the Corinthians*. Translated by James W. Leitch. Philadelphia: Fortress, 1975.

Cook, Stephen L. *Prophecy and Apocalypticism: The Postexilic Social Setting*. Minneapolis: Fortress, 1995.

Cooke, G. "The Sons of (the) God(s)." *Zeitschrift für die alttestamentliche Wissenschaft* 76.1 (1964): 22–47.

Cooper, John M. "Plato's Theory of Human Motivation." Pages 118–137 in *Reason and Emotion: Essays on Ancient Moral Psychology and Ethical Theory*. Princeton: Princeton University Press, 1999.

Cranfield, C. E. B. *A Critical and Exegetical Commentary on the Epistle to the Romans*. 2 vols. Edinburgh: T & T Clark, 1975, 1979.

Crenshaw, James L. *Joel: A New Translation with Introduction and Commentary*. New York: Doubleday, 1995.

Crim, Keith, ed. *The Interpreter's Dictionary of the Bible: Supplementary Volume*. Nashville: Abingdon, 1976.

Cross, Frank Moore. *The Ancient Library of Qumran*. 3rd ed. New York: Doubleday, 1995.

Cross, Frank Moore. *Canaanite Myth and Hebrew Epic: Essays on the History of Israel*. Cambridge, MA: Harvard University Press, 1973.

Cross, Frank Moore. "The Council of Yahweh in Second Isaiah." *Journal of Near Eastern Studies* 12.4 (1953): 274–277.

Cross, Frank Moore. "The Divine Warrior in Israel's Early Cult." Pages 91–111 in *Canaanite Myth and Hebrew Epic: Essays on the History of Israel*. Cambridge, MA: Harvard University Press, 1973.

Cross, Frank Moore. *From Epic to Canon: History and Literature in Ancient Israel*. Baltimore: Johns Hopkins University Press, 1998.

Cross, Frank Moore, and David Noel Freedman. "The Blessing of Moses." *Journal of Biblical Literature* 67.3 (1948): 191–210.

Cross, Frank Moore, and David Noel Freedman. "The Song of Miriam." *Journal of Near Eastern Studies* 14 (1955): 237–250.

Crouch, Carly L. *War and Ethics in the Ancient Near East: Military Violence in Light of Cosmology and History*. Beihefte zur Zeitschrift für die alttestamentliche Wissenschaft 407. Berlin: de Gruyter, 2009.

Crüsemann, Frank. *Studien zur Formgeschichte von Hymnus und Danklied in Israel*. Wissenschaftliche Monographien zum Alten und Neuen Testament 32. Neukirchen-Vluyn: Neukirchener Verlag, 1969.

Cullmann, Oscar. *Christ and Time: The Primitive Christian Conception of Time and History.* Translated from the revised edition by Floyd V. Filson. Philadelphia: Westminster, 1964.

Cullmann, Oscar. *The State in the New Testament.* New York: Scribner, 1956.

Dahood, Mitchell. "Mišmār 'Muzzle' in Job 7:12." *Journal of Biblical Literature* 80.3 (1961): 270–271.

Dahood, Mitchell. *Psalms II: Psalms 51–100.* Anchor Yale Bible 17. New Haven: Yale University Press, 1995.

Dalley, Stephanie, A. T. Reyes, David Pingree, Alison Salvesen, and Henrietta McCall. "The Sassanian Period and Early Islam, c. AD 224–651." Pages 163–181 in *The Legacy of Mesopotamia.* Edited by Stephanie Dalley. Oxford: Oxford University Press, 1998.

Davenport, G. L. *The Eschatology of the Book of Jubilees.* Studia Post-Biblica 20. Leiden: Brill, 1971.

Davidson, Maxwell J. *Angels at Qumran: A Comparative Study of 1 Enoch 1–36, 72–108 and Sectarian Writings from Qumran.* Journal for the Study of the Pseudepigrapha Supplement Series 11. Sheffield: Sheffield Academic, 1992.

Davies, Philip R. *The Damascus Covenant: An Interpretation of the "Damascus Document."* Journal for the Study of the Old Testament Supplement Series 25. Sheffield: Journal for the Study of the Old Testament, 1983.

Davies, Philip R. "Dualism and Eschatology in 1 QM: A Rejoinder." *Vetus Testamentum* 30.1 (1980): 93–97.

Davies, Philip R. "Dualism and Eschatology in the War Scroll." *Vetus Testamentum* 28.1 (1978): 28–36.

Davies, Philip R. "Dualism in the Qumran War Texts." Pages 8–19 in *Dualism in Qumran.* Edited by Géza G. Xeravits. New York: T & T Clark, 2010.

Davies, Philip. R. *1QM, the War Scroll from Qumran: Its Structure and History.* Biblica et Orientalia 32. Rome: Pontifical Biblical Institute, 1977.

Davies, W. D. "A Note on Josephus, *Antiquities* 15:136." *Harvard Theological Review* 47.3 (1954): 135–140.

Davies, W. D. *Paul and Rabbinic Judaism: Some Rabbinic Elements in Pauline Theology.* New York: Harper Torchbooks, 1967.

Day, John. *God's Conflict with the Dragon and the Sea: Echoes of a Canaanite Myth in the Old Testament.* Cambridge: University of Cambridge Press, 1985.

Day, John. *Yahweh and the Gods and Goddesses of Canaan.* Sheffield: Sheffield Academic, 2000.

de Boer, Martinus C. *The Defeat of Death: Apocalyptic Eschatology in 1 Corinthians 15 and Romans 5.* Journal for the Study of the New Testament Supplement Series 22. Sheffield: JSOT, 1988.

de Boer, Martinus C. "The Meaning of the Phrase τὰ στοιχεῖα τοῦ κόσμου in Galatians." *New Testament Studies* 53.2 (2007): 204–224.

de Boer, Martinus C. "Paul and Apocalyptic Eschatology." Pages 345–383 in vol. 1 of *The Encyclopedia of Apocalypticism: The Origins of Apocalypticism in Judaism and*

Christianity. 3 vols. Edited by J. J. Collins, B. McGinn, and S. Stein. New York: Continuum, 2000.

de Boer, Martinus C. "Paul and Jewish Apocalyptic Eschatology." Pages 169–190 in *Apocalyptic and the New Testament: Essays in Honor of J. Louis Martyn.* Edited by Joel Marcus and Marion L. Soards. Journal for the Study of the New Testament Supplement Series 24. Sheffield: JSOT, 1989.

De Jong, Albert. "Iranian Connections in the Dead Sea Scrolls." Pages 479–500 in *The Oxford Handbook of the Dead Sea Scrolls.* Edited by Timothy H. Lim and John J. Collins. Oxford: Oxford University Press, 2010.

DeMaris, Richard E. "Element, Elemental Spirit." Pages 444–445 in vol. 2 of *The Anchor Bible Dictionary.* Edited by David Noel Freedman. 6 vols. New York: Doubleday, 1992.

Denton, D. R. "Apokaradokia." *Zeitschrift für die Neutestamentliche Wissenschaft* 73 (1982): 138–140.

de Vaux, Roland. *Ancient Israel: Social Institutions.* 2 vols. New York: McGraw-Hill, 1965.

Dibelius, Martin. *Die Briefe des Apostels Paulus an die Thessalonicher I, II; an die Philipper.* Tübingen: Mohr, 1911.

Dibelius, Martin. *Die Geisterwelt im Glauben des Paulus.* Göttingen: Vandenhoeck & Ruprecht, 1909.

Dietrich, Manfred, and Oswald Loretz. *Jahwe und seine Aschera: Anthropomorphes Kultbild in Mesopotamien, Ugarit und Israel: das biblische Bilderverbot.* Ugaritisch-Biblische Literatur 9. Münster: Ugarit-Verlag, 1992.

Dijkstra, M. "El, YHWH and Their Asherah: On Continuity and Discontinuity in Canaanite and Ancient Israelite Religion." Pages 43–73 in *Ugarit: Eine ostmediterranes Kulturzentrum in Alten Orient. Ergebnisse und Perspektiven der Forschung, Band I: Ugarit und seine altorientalische Umwelt.* Edited by M. Dietrich and O. Loretz. Abhandlungen zur Literatur Alt-Syriens-Palästinas 7. Münster: Ugarit-Verlag, 1995.

Dillon, John M. *Alcinous: The Handbook of Platonism.* Oxford: Clarendon, 1993.

Dillon, John M. *The Middle Platonists: 80 BC to AD 220.* Ithaca, NY: Cornell University Press, 1996.

Dimant, Devorah. "Between Qumran Sectarian and Non-Sectarian Texts: The Case of Belial and Mastema." Pages 235–256 in *The Dead Sea Scrolls and Contemporary Culture: Proceedings of the International Conference Held at the Israel Museum, Jerusalem (July 6–8, 2008).* Edited by Adolfo D. Reitman, L. H. Schiffman, and S. Tzarev. Studies on the Texts of the Desert of Judah 93. Leiden: Brill, 2011.

Dimant, Devorah. "The Composite Character of the Qumran Sectarian Literature as an Indication of Its Date and Provenance." *Revue de Qumran* 88 (2006): 615–630.

Dimant, Devorah. "The Demonic Realm in Qumran Sectarian Literature." Pages 103–117 in *Gut und Böse in Mensch und Welt: Philosophische und religiöse Konzeptionen vom Alten Orient bis zum frühen Islam.* Edited by Heinz-Günther Nesselrath and Florian Wilk. Tübingen: Mohr Siebeck, 2013.

Dimant, Divorah. "Qumran Sectarian Literature." Pages 483–550 in *Jewish Writings of the Second Temple Period: Apocrypha, Pseudepigrapha, Qumran, Sectarian Writings, Philo, Josephus*. Edited by M. E. Stone. Compendia Rerum Iudaicarum ad Novum Testamentum, Section 2. Philadelphia: Fortress, 1984.

Dodd, C. H. *The Epistle of Paul to the Romans*. London: Collins, 1959.

Dodd, C. H. *New Testament Studies*. Manchester: Manchester University Press, 1967.

Donaldson, Terrance L. *Judaism and the Gentiles: Jewish Patterns of Universalism (to 135 CE)*. Waco, TX: Baylor University Press, 2007.

Donaldson, Terrance L. *Paul and the Gentiles: Remapping the Apostle's Convictional World*. Minneapolis: Fortress, 1997.

Donaldson, Terrance L. "Proselytes or Righteous Gentiles? The Status of Gentiles in Eschatological Pilgrimage Patterns of Thought." *Journal for the Study of the Pseudepigrapha* 7 (1990): 3–27.

Dörrie, H. "Präpositionen und Metaphysik: Wechselwirkung zweier Prinzipienreihen." *Museum Helveticum* 26 (1969): 217–228.

Driver, P. R. "Hebrew Notes on Prophets and Proverbs." *Journal of Theological Studies* 41 (1940): 162–175.

Duban, Jeffrey M. "Poets and Kings in the *Theogony* Invocation." *Quaderni Urbinati di Cultura Classica* 4 (1980): 7–21.

Duhaime, Jean. "Dualism." Pages 215–220 in vol. 1 of *The Encyclopedia of the Dead Sea Scrolls*. 2 vols. Edited by Lawrence H. Schiffman and James C. VanderKam. Oxford: Oxford University Press, 2000.

Duhaime, Jean. "Dualistic Reworking of the Scrolls from Qumran." *Catholic Biblical Quarterly* 49 (1987): 32–56.

Dunn, James D. G. "Review of Ernst Käsemann, *Commentary on Romans*." *Journal for the Study of the New Testament* 17 (1983): 117–119.

Dunn, James D. G. *Romans*. 2 vols. Dallas: Word, 1988.

Eastman, Susan G. *Recovering Paul's Mother Tongue: Language and Theology in Galatians*. Grand Rapids, MI: Eerdmans, 2007.

Eaton, J. H. "The Origin and Meaning of Habakkuk 3." *Zeitschrift für die alttestamentliche Wissenschaft* 76.2 (1964): 144–171.

Eidevall, Göran. *Prophecy and Propaganda: Images of Enemies in the Book of Isaiah*. Coniectanea Biblica Old Testament Series 56. Winona Lake, IN: Eisenbrauns, 2009.

Eliade, Mircea. *Myth and Reality*. Translated by W. Trask. New York: Harper and Row, 1968.

Elliott, Neil. *The Arrogance of the Nations: Reading Romans in the Shadow of Empire*. Minneapolis: Fortress, 2008.

Engberg-Pedersen, Troels. *Cosmology and Self in the Apostle Paul: The Material Spirit*. Clarendon: Oxford, 2010.

Engberg-Pedersen, Troels. "Marcus Aurelius on Emotions." Pages 305–337 in *The Emotions in Hellenistic Philosophy*. Edited by Juha Sihvola and Troels Engberg-Pedersen. Dordrecht, Netherlands: Kluwer Academic, 1998.

Engberg-Pedersen, Troels. *Paul and the Stoics*. Louisville, KY: Westminster John Knox, 2000.

Engberg-Pedersen, Troels. "The Reception of Greco-Roman Culture in the New Testament: The Case of Romans 7.7–25." Pages 32–57 in *The New Testament as Reception*. Edited by Mogens Müller and Henrik Tronier. Journal for the Study of the New Testament Supplement Series 230. London: Sheffield, 2002.

Engberg-Pedersen, Troels. "A Stoic Concept of the Person in Paul? From Galatians 5:17 to Romans 7:14–25." Pages 85–112 in *Christian Body, Christian Self: Concepts of Early Christian Personhood*. Edited by Clare K. Rothschild and Trevor W. Thompson. Wissenschaftliche Untersuchungen zum Neuen Testament 284. Tübingen: Mohr Siebeck, 2011.

Erlandson, Seth. *The Burden of Babylon: A Study of Isaiah 13:2–14:23*. Coniectanea Biblica Old Testament Series 4. Lund: Gleerup, 1970.

Everson, Joseph A. "The Days of Yahweh." *Journal of Biblical Literature* 93.3 (1974): 329–337.

Fee, Gordon D. "εἰδωλόθυτα Once Again: An Interpretation of 1 Corinthians 8–10." *Biblica* 61.2 (1980): 172–197.

Fee, Gordon D. *The First Epistle to the Corinthians*. Rev. 2nd ed. Grand Rapids, MI: Eerdmans, 2014.

Fee, Gordon D. *Paul's Letter to the Philippians*. Grand Rapid, MI: Eerdmans, 1995.

Fee, Gordon D. "Philippians 2:5–11: Hymn or Exalted Pauline Prose?" *Bulletin for Biblical Research* 2 (1992): 29–46.

Feldmeier, R. "Mediator II." Pages 557–560 in *The Dictionary of Deities and Demons in the Bible*. Edited by Karel van der Toorn, Bob Becking, and Pieter W. van der Horst. 2nd ed. Leiden: Brill, 1999.

Finkelberg, Aryeh. "On the Unity of Orphic and Milesian Thought." *Harvard Theological Review* 79.4 (1986): 321–335.

Fishbane, Michael. *Biblical Myth and Rabbinic Mythmaking*. Oxford: Oxford University Press, 2003.

Fitzgerald, John T. *Cracks in an Earthen Vessel: An Examination of the Catalogues of Hardships in the Corinthian Correspondence*. Society of Biblical Literature Dissertation Series 99. Atlanta: Scholars, 1988.

Fitzmyer, Joseph A. "The Aramaic Background of Philippians 2:6–11." *Catholic Biblical Quarterly* 50.3 (1988): 470–483.

Fitzmyer, Joseph A. *First Corinthians: A New Translation with Introduction and Commentary*. New Haven, CT: Yale University Press, 2008.

Fitzmyer, Joseph A. "Qumrân and the Interpolated Paragraph in 2 Cor 6:14–7:1." *Catholic Biblical Quarterly* 23.3 (1961): 271–280.

Fitzmyer, Joseph A. *Romans: A New Translation with Introduction and Commentary*. New York: Doubleday, 1993.

Flusser, David. "Qumrân and Jewish 'Apotropaic' Prayers." *Israel Exploration Journal* 16 (1966): 194–205.

Fokkelman, J. P. "The Structure of Psalm 68." Pages 72–83 in *In Quest of the Past: Studies on Israelite Religion, Literature and Prophetism: Papers Read at the Joint British-Dutch Old Testament Conference, Held at Elspeet, 1988*. Edited by A. S. Van der Woude. Oudtestamentische Studiën 26. Leiden: Brill, 1990.

Fontenrose, Joseph. "Typhon Among the Arimoi." Pages 64–82 in *The Classical Tradition: Literary and Historical Studies in Honor of Harry Caplan*. Edited by Luitpold Wallach. Ithaca, NY: Cornell University Press, 1966.

Forbes, Christopher. "Pauline Demonology and/or Cosmology? Principalities, Powers and the Elements of the World in Their Hellenistic Context." *Journal for the Study of the New Testament* 85 (2002): 51–73.

Forbes, Christopher. "Paul's Principalities and Powers: Demythologizing Apocalyptic?" *Journal for the Study of the New Testament* 82 (2001): 61–88.

Forsyth, Neil. *The Old Enemy: Satan and the Combat Myth*. Princeton, NJ: Princeton University Press, 1987.

Fossum, Jarl E. *The Name of God and the Angel of the Lord: Samaritan and Jewish Concepts of Intermediation and the Origin of Gnosticism*. Wissenschaftliche Untersuchungen zum Neuen Testament 2.36. Tübingen: J. C. B. Mohr (Paul Siebeck), 1985.

Fotopoulos, John. "Arguments Concerning Food Offered to Idols: Corinthian Quotations and Pauline Refutations in a Rhetorical Partitio (1 Corinthians 8:1– 9)." *Catholic Biblical Quarterly* 67.4 (2005): 611–631.

Fotopoulos, John. *Food Offered to Idols in Roman Corinth: A Social-Rhetorical Reconsideration of 1 Corinthians 8:1–11:1*. Wissenschaftliche Untersuchungen zum Neuen Testament 2.151. Tübingen: Mohr Siebeck, 2003.

Fredrickson, David. "Parrêsia in the Pauline Epistles." Pages 163–183 in *Friendship, Flattery, and Frankness of Speech: Studies on Friendship in the New Testament World*. Edited by John T. Fitzgerald. Supplements to Novum Testamentum 82. Leiden: Brill, 1996.

Fredriksen, Paula F. "Judaism, the Circumcision of Gentiles, and Apocalyptic Hope: Another Look at Galatians 1 and 2." *Journal of Theological Studies* 42.2 (1991): 532–564.

Fredriksen, Paula F. "Mandatory Retirement: Ideas in the Study of Christian Origins Whose Time Has Come to Go." *Studies in Religion/Sciences religieuses* 35.2 (2006): 231–246.

Fredriksen, Paula F. "Review of Larry Hurtado, *Lord Jesus Christ.*" *Journal of Early Christian Studies* 12 (2004): 537–541.

Freedman, David Noel. "Archaic Forms in Early Hebrew Poetry." *Zeitschrift für die Alttestamentliche Wissenschaft* 72 (1960): 101–107.

Freedman, David Noel. "Moses and Miriam: The Song of the Sea (Exodus 15:1–18, 21)." Pages 67–83 in *Realia Dei: Essays in Archaeology and Biblical Interpretation in Honor of Edward F. Campbell, Jr. at His Retirement*. Edited by P. H. Williams and T. Hiebert. Atlanta: Scholars, 1999.

Freedman, David Noel. "'Who Is Like Thee Among the Gods?' The Religion of Early Israel." Pages 315–335 in *Ancient Israelite Religion: Essays in Honour of Frank Moore Cross.* Edited by P. D. Miller, P. D. Hanson, and S. D. McBride. Philadelphia: Fortress, 1987.

Frey, Jörg. "Different Patterns of Dualistic Thought in the Qumran Library: Reflections on Their Background and History." Pages 275–335 in *Legal Texts and Legal Issues: Proceedings of the Second Meeting of the International Organization for Qumran Studies, Cambridge, 1995, Published in Honour of Joseph M. Baumgarten.* Edited by Moshe Bernstein, Florentino García Martínez, and John Kampen. Studies on the Texts of the Desert of Judah 23. Leiden: Brill, 1997.

Furnish, Victor Paul. *II Corinthians: A New Translation with Introduction and Commentary.* New York: Doubleday, 1984.

Gager, John G. *Curse Tablets and Binding Spells from the Ancient World.* New York: Oxford University Press, 1992.

Gager, John G. *Reinventing Paul.* Oxford: Oxford University Press, 2002.

Garrett, Susan R. *No Ordinary Angel: Celestial Spirits and Christian Claims About Jesus.* New Haven, CT: Yale University Press, 2008.

Gaster, Theodore H. "An Ancient Eulogy on Israel: Deuteronomy 33:3–5, 26–29." *Journal of Biblical Literature* 66.1 (1947): 53–62.

Gaventa, Beverly Roberts, ed. *Apocalyptic Paul: Cosmos and Anthropos in Romans 5–8.* Waco, TX: Baylor University Press, 2013.

Gaventa, Beverly Roberts. *Our Mother Saint Paul.* Louisville, KY: Westminster John Knox, 2007.

George, Andrew R. *House Most High: The Temples of Ancient Mesopotamia.* Winona Lake, IN: Eisenbrauns, 1993.

Gerstenberger, Erhard S. *Psalms, Part 2, and Lamentations.* The Forms of Old Testament Literature 15. Grand Rapids, MI: 2001.

Gibson, J. C. L. "The Theology of the Ugaritic Baal Cycle." *Orientalia* 53 (1984): 202–219.

Gill, Christopher. "Did Chrysippus Understand Medea?" *Phronesis* 28 (1983): 136–149.

Gill, Christopher. "Did Galen Understand Platonic and Stoic Thinking on Emotions?" Pages 113–148 in *Emotions in Hellenistic Philosophy.* Edited by Juha Sihvola and Troels Engberg-Pedersen. Dordrecht, Netherlands: Kluwer Academic, 1998.

Gill, Christopher. *Personality in Greek Epic, Tragedy, and Philosophy: The Self in Dialogue.* Oxford: Clarendon, 1996.

Gill, Christopher. "Two Monologues of Self-Division: Euripides, *Medea* 1021–80 and Seneca, *Medea* 893–977." Pages 25–37 in *Homo Viator: Classical Essays for John Bramble.* Edited by Michael Whitby, Philip Hardie, and Mary Whitby. Bristol: Classical, 1987.

Glad, Clarence E. *Paul and Philodemus: Adaptability in Epicurean and Early Christian Psychagogy.* Supplements to Novum Testamentum 81. Leiden: Brill, 1995.

Glasson, T. F. *Greek Influence in Jewish Eschatology, with Special Reference to the Apocalypses and Pseudepigraphs.* Biblical Monographs 1. London: SPCK, 1961.

Gordis, Robert. "Critical Notes on the Blessing of Moses (Deut xxxiii)." *Journal of Theological Studies* 34 (1933): 390–392.

Gordis, Robert. "The Text and Meaning of Deuteronomy 33:27." *Journal of Biblical Literature* 67 (1948): 69–72.

Gordon, Robert P. "The Gods Must Die: A Theme in Isaiah and Beyond." Pages 45–61 in *Isaiah in Context: Studies in Honour of Arie van der Kooij on the Occasion of his Sixty-Fifth Birthday.* Edited by Michaël N. van der Meer, Percy van Keulen, Wido van Peursen, and Baster Haar Romeny. Supplements to Vetus Testamentum 138. Leiden: Brill, 2010.

Gottwald, N. "War, Holy." Pages 942–944 of *Interpreter's Dictionary of the Bible: Supplementary Volume.* Edited by Keith Crim. Nashville: Abingdon, 1976.

Grabbe, Lester L. "The Seasonal Pattern and the Baal Cycle." *Ugarit-Forschungen* 8 (1976): 57–63.

Graf, Fritz, Tonio Hölscher, Ludwig Koenen, John Scheid, Jan Assmann, eds. *Archiv für Religionsgeschichte* 14. Berlin: de Gruyter, 2013.

Greene, J. T. *The Role of the Messenger and Message in the Ancient Near East.* Brown Judaic Studies 169. Atlanta: Scholars, 1989.

Griffith, Mark. "Personality in Hesiod." *Classical Antiquity* 2 (1983): 37–65.

Gruenwald, Ithamar. *From Apocalypticism to Gnosticism: Studies in Apocalypticism, Merkavah Mysticism, and Gnosticism.* Beiträge der Erforschung des Alten Testaments und des antiken Judentums 14. Frankfurt: Lang, 1988.

Gundry, Robert H. "The Moral Frustration of Paul Before His Conversion: Sexual Lust in Romans 7:7–25." Pages 228–245 in *Pauline Studies: Essays Presented to Professor F. F. Bruce on His 70th Birthday.* Edited by Donald A. Hagner and Murray J. Harris. Grand Rapids, MI: Eerdmans, 1980.

Gunkel, Hermann. *Creation and Chaos in the Primeval Era and the Eschaton: A Religio-Historical Study of Genesis 1 and Revelation 12.* Translated by K. William Whitney Jr.. Grand Rapids, MI: Eerdmans, 2006. German original published in 1895.

Guthrie, W. K. C. "The Pre-Socratic World-Picture." *Harvard Theological Review* 45.2 (1952): 87–104.

Hahm, David E. *The Origins of Stoic Cosmology.* Columbus: Ohio State University Press, 1977.

Hallo, W. W., and W. L. Moran. "The First Tablet of the SB Recension of the Anzu-Myth." *Journal of Cuneiform Studies* 31 (1979): 65–115.

Halperin, David J. "Ascension or Invasion: Implications of the Heavenly Journey in Ancient Judaism." *Religion* 18 (1988): 47–67.

Halperin, David J. *The Faces of the Chariot: Early Jewish Responses to Ezekiel's Vision.* Texte und Studien zum antiken Judentum 16. Tübingen: J. C. B. Mohr (Paul Siebeck), 1988.

Handy, Lowell K. "Dissenting Deities or Obedient Angels: Divine Hierarchies in Ugarit and the Bible." *Biblical Research* 35 (1990): 18–35.

Hanson, Paul. *Dawn of Apocalyptic: The Historical and Sociological Roots of Jewish Apocalyptic Eschatology.* Philadelphia: Fortress, 1979.

Harrill, J. Albert. *Slaves in the New Testament: Literary, Social, and Moral Dimensions.* Minneapolis: Fortress, 2006.

Harrill, J. Albert. "Stoic Physics, the Universal Conflagration, and the Eschatological Destruction of 'the Ignorant and Unstable' in 2 Peter." Pages 115–140 in *Stoicism in Early Christianity.* Edited by Tuomas Rasimus, Troels Engberg-Pedersen, and Ismo Dunderberg. Grand Rapids, MI: Baker Academic, 2010.

Harrington, Daniel J. "Review of Ernst Käsemann, *An Die Römer.*" *Biblica* 55.4 (1974): 583–587.

Hay, David M. *Glory at the Right Hand: Psalm 110 in Early Christianity.* Society of Biblical Literature Monograph Series 18. Nashville: Abingdon, 1973.

Heckel, Theo K. "Body and Soul in Paul." Pages 117–132 in *Psyche and Soma: Physicians and Metaphysicians on the Mind-Body Problem from Antiquity to the Enlightenment.* Oxford: Clarendon, 2003.

Heckel, Theo K. *Der Innere Mensch: Der paulinische Verarbeitung eines platonischen Motivs.* Wissenschaftliche Untersuchungen zum Neuen Testament 2.53. Tübingen: Mohr Siebeck, 1993.

Heen, Erik M. "Phil 2:6–11 and Resistance to Local Timocratic Rule: *Isa theô* and the Cult of the Roman Emperor in the East." Pages 125–153 in *Paul and the Roman Imperial Order.* Edited by Richard A. Horsley. Harrisburg, PA: Trinity Press International, 2004.

Heger, Paul. "Another Look at Dualism in Qumran Writings." Pages 39–101 in *Dualism in Qumran.* Edited by Géza G. Xeravits. New York: T & T Clark, 2010.

Heim, Knut M. "The (God-)Forsaken King of Psalm 89: A Historical and Intertextual Enquiry." Pages 296–322 in *King and Messiah in Israel and the Ancient Near East.* Edited by John Day. Sheffield: Sheffield Academic, 1998.

Hellholm, David. "The Problem of Apocalyptic Genre and the Apocalypse of John." Pages 13–64 in *Early Christian Apocalypticism: Genre and Social Setting.* Edited by Adela Yarbro Collins. Semeia 36. Decatur, GA: Scholars, 1986.

Hempel, Charlotte. "The *Treatise on the Two Spirits* and the Literary History of the *Rule of the Community.*" Pages 102–120 in *Dualism in Qumran.* Edited by Géza G. Xeravits. New York: T & T Clark, 2010.

Hengel, Martin. *Son of God: The Origin of Christology and the History of Jewish Hellenistic Religion.* Translated by John Bowden. Eugene, OR: Wipf and Stock, 2007.

Henze, Matthias. "The Apocalypse of Weeks and the Architecture of the End Time." Pages 207–209 in *Enoch and Qumran Origins: New Light on a Forgotten Connection.* Edited by Gabriele Boccaccini. Grand Rapids, MI: Eerdmans, 2005.

Hiebert, Theodore. *God of My Victory: The Ancient Hymn in Habakkuk 3.* Harvard Semitic Monographs 38. Atlanta: Scholars, 1986.

Hill, Edmund. "The Construction of Three Passages from Saint Paul." *Catholic Biblical Quarterly* 23 (1961): 296–301.

Hillers, Delbert R. *Treaty Curses and the Old Testament Prophets.* Biblica et Orientalia 16. Rome: Pontifical Biblical Institute, 1964.

Holladay, J. S. "The Day(s) the Moon Stood Still." *Journal of Biblical Literature* 87.2 (1968): 166–178.

Holland, Glen. "The Self Against the Self in Romans 7:7–25." Pages 260–271 in *The Rhetorical Interpretation of Scripture: Essays from the 1996 Malibu Conference.* Edited by S. E. Porter and D. L. Stamps. Journal for the Study of the New Testament Supplement Series 180. Sheffield: Sheffield Academic, 1999.

Hollander, Harm W. "The Idea of Fellowship in 1 Corinthians 10:14–22." *New Testament Studies* 55.4 (2009): 456–470.

Horrell, David G. "Domestic Space and Christian Meetings at Corinth: Imagining New Contexts and the Buildings East of the Theatre." *New Testament Studies* 50.3 (2004): 349–369.

Horrell, David G. "Idol-Food, Idolatry, and Ethics in Paul." Pages 120–140 in *Idolatry: False Worship in the Bible, Early Judaism, and Christianity.* Edited by Stephen C. Barton. London: T & T Clark, 2007.

Horrell, David G. "Theological Principle or Christological Praxis? Pauline Ethics in 1 Corinthians 8:1–11:1." *Journal for the Study of the New Testament* 67 (1997): 83–114.

Horsley, Richard A. *1 Corinthians.* Nashville: Abingdon, 1998.

Horsley, Richard A., ed. *Paul and Politics: Ekklesia, Israel, Imperium, Interpretation: Essays in Honor of Krister Stendahl.* Harrisburg, PA: Trinity Press International, 2000.

Innes, D. C. "Gigantomachy and Natural Philosophy." *Classical Quarterly* 29.1 (1979): 165–171.

Isserlin, B. S. J. "Psalm 68:14: An Archaeological Gloss." *Palestine Exploration Quarterly* 103 (1971): 5–8.

Jacobsen, Thorkild. "The Battle Between Marduk and Tiamat." *Journal of the American Oriental Society* 88 (1968): 104–108.

Jacobsen, Thorkild. "Primitive Democracy in Ancient Mesopotamia." Pages 157–170 in *Toward the Image of Tammuz and Other Essays on Mesopotamian History and Culture.* Edited by William L. Moran. Cambridge, MA: Harvard University Press, 1970.

Jacobson, Thorkild. *The Treasures of Darkness: A History of Mesopotamian Religion.* New Haven, CT: Yale University Press, 1976.

Jefferson, Helen G. "Psalm 77." *Vetus Testamentum* 13 (1963): 87–91.

Jeremias, Joachim. *Jesus' Promise to the Nations.* Translated by S. H. Hooke. Studies in Biblical Theology 14. London: SCM, 1958.

Jewett, Robert. *Paul's Anthropological Terms: A Study of Their Use in Conflict Settings.* Arbeiten zur Geschichte des Antiken Judentums und des Urchristentums 10. Leiden: Brill, 1971.

Jewett, Robert. *Romans: A Commentary.* Minneapolis: Fortress, 2007.

Johnson-DeBaufre, Melanie, and Laura S. Nasrallah. "Beyond the Heroic Paul: Toward a Feminist and Decolonizing Approach to the Letters of Paul." Pages 161–174 in *The Colonized Apostle: Paul Through Postcolonial Eyes*. Edited by Christopher D. Stanley. Minneapolis: Fortress, 2011.

Johnson Hodge, Caroline. *If Sons, Then Heirs: A Study of Kinship and Ethnicity in Paul's Letters*. Oxford: Oxford University Press, 2007.

Jones, Gwilym H. "'Holy War' or 'Yahweh War'?" *Vetus Testamentum* 25.3 (1975): 642–658.

Kang, Sa-Moon. *Divine War in the Old Testament and in the Ancient Near East*. Beihefte zur Zeitschrift für die alttestamentliche Wissenschaft 177. Berlin: de Gruyter, 1989.

Kapelrud, Arvid S. "Ba 'al, Schöpfung und Chaos." *Ugarit-Forschungen* 11 (1979): 407–412.

Karrer, Martin. "The Epistle to the Hebrews and the Septuagint." Pages 335–353 in *Septuagint Research: Issues and Challenges in the Study of the Greek Jewish Scriptures*. Society of Biblical Literature Septuagint and Cognate Studies 53. Edited by Wolfgang Kraus and R. Glenn Wooden. Atlanta: Society of Biblical Literature, 2006.

Käsemann, Ernst. "The Beginnings of Christian Theology." Pages 82–107 in *New Testament Questions of Today*. Translated by W. J. Montague. Philadelphia: Fortress, 1969.

Käsemann, Ernst. *Commentary on Romans*. Translated and edited by Geoffrey W. Bromiley. 3rd ed. Grand Rapids, MI: Eerdmans, 1980.

Käsemann, Ernst. "Critical Analysis of Philippians 2:5–11." Pages 45–88 in *God and Christ: Existence and Providence*. Edited by Robert W. Funk, translated by Alice Carse. New York: Harper and Row, 1968.

Käsemann, Ernst. "On Paul's Anthropology." Pages 1–31 in *Perspectives on Paul*. Translated by Margaret Kohl. Philadelphia: Fortress, 1971.

Käsemann, Ernst. "On the Subject of Primitive Christian Apocalyptic." Pages 108–137 in *New Testament Questions of Today*. Translated by W. J. Montague. Philadelphia: Fortress, 1969.

Kasher, Rimon. "Angelology and the Supernal Worlds in the Aramaic Targums to the Prophets." *Journal for the Study of Judaism in the Persian, Hellenistic and Roman Period* 27.2 (1996): 168–191.

Keck, Leander. "The Absent Good: The Significance of Rom 7:18a." Pages 66–75 in *Text und Geschichte: Facetten theologischen Arbeitens aus dem Freundes- und Schülerkreis, Dieter Lührmann zum 60 Geburtstag*. Edited by Stefan Maser and Egbert Schlarb. Marburg: Elwert, 1999.

Keel, Othmar. *Die Welt der altorientalischen Bildsymbolik und das Alte Testament: Am Beispiel der Psalmen*. Göttingen: Vandenhoeck & Ruprecht, 1996.

Kelhoffer, James A. *Persecution, Persuasion and Power: Readiness to Withstand Hardship as a Corroboration of Legitimacy in the New Testament*. Wissenschaftliche Untersuchungen zum Neuen Testament 270. Tübingen: Mohr Siebeck, 2010.

Kelle, Brad E., and Frank Ritchel Ames, eds. *Writing and Reading War: Rhetoric, Gender, and Ethics in Biblical and Modern Contexts.* Society of Biblical Literature Symposium Series 42. Atlanta: Society of Biblical Literature, 2008.

Kelle, Brad E., Frank Ritchel Ames, and Jacob L. Wright, eds. *Warfare, Ritual, and Symbol in Biblical and Modern Contexts.* Society of Biblical Literature, Ancient Israel and Its Literature 18. Atlanta: Society of Biblical Literature, 2014.

Kingsbury, Edwin. C. "The Prophets and the Council of Yahweh." *Journal of Biblical Literature* 83 (1964): 279–286.

Kirk, G. S. *The Songs of Homer.* Cambridge: Cambridge University Press, 1962.

Klingbeil, M. *Yahweh Fighting from Heaven: God as Warrior and as God of Heaven in the Hebrew Psalter and Ancient Near Eastern Iconography.* Orbis Biblicus et Orientalis 169. Göttingen: Vandenhoeck & Ruprecht, 1999.

Knibb, Michael A. "The Apocalypse of Weeks and the Epistle of Enoch." Pages 213–219 in *Enoch and Qumran Origins: New Light on a Forgotten Connection.* Edited by Gabriele Boccaccini. Grand Rapids, MI: Eerdmans, 2005.

Knibb, Michael A. "The Date of the Parables of Enoch: A Critical Review." *New Testament Studies* 25.3 (1979): 345–359.

Knibb, Michael A. "1 Enoch." Pages 169–319 in *The Apocryphal Old Testament.* Edited by H. Sparks. Oxford: Clarendon, 1984.

Knibb, Michael A. "Rule of the Community." Pages 793–797 in vol. 2 of the *Encyclopedia of the Dead Sea Scrolls.* 2 vols. Edited by L. Schiffman and J. C. VanderKam. New York: Oxford University Press, 2000.

Knust, Jennifer Wright, and Zsuzsanna Várhelyi, eds. *Ancient Mediterranean Sacrifice.* New York: Oxford University Press, 2011.

Koch, Klaus. "History as a Battlefield of Two Antagonistic Powers in the Apocalypse of Weeks and in the Rule of the Community." Pages 185–199 in *Enoch and Qumran Origins: New Light on a Forgotten Connection.* Edited by Gabriele Boccaccini. Grand Rapids, MI: Eerdmans, 2005.

Koch, Klaus. "Monotheismus und Angelologie." Pages 565–581 in *Ein Gott allein? JHWH Verehrung und biblischer Monotheismus im Kontext der israelitischen und altorientalische Religionsgeschichte.* Edited by W. Dietrich and M. A. Klopfenstein. Orbis Biblicus et Orientalis 139. Göttingen: Vandenhoeck & Ruprecht, 1994.

Koch, Klaus. *The Rediscovery of Apocalyptic: A Polemical Work on a Neglected Area of Biblical Studies and Its Damaging Influence on Theology and Philosophy.* Translated by Margaret Kohl. Studies in Biblical Theology 2.22. Naperville, IL: Allentown, 1972. German original published in 1970.

Kosmala, Hans. "Maskil." Pages 235–241 in *The Gaster Festschrift.* Edited by D. Marcus. Journal for the Ancient Near Eastern Society of Columbia University. New York: Ancient Near Eastern Society, 1974.

Koyre, Alexander. *From the Closed World to the Infinite Universe.* Baltimore: Johns Hopkins University Press, 1957.

Kuemmerlin-McLean, Joanne K. "Demons: Old Testament." Pages 138–140 in vol. 2 of *The Anchor Bible Dictionary*. Edited by David Noel Freedman. 6 vols. New York: Doubleday, 1992.

Kvanvig, Helge. *The Roots of Apocalyptic: The Mesopotamian Background of the Enoch Figure and of the Son of Man*. Wissenschaftliche Monographien zum Alten und Neuen Testament 61. Neukirchen-Vluyn: Neukirchener Verlag, 1988.

Laks, André. "Between Religion and Philosophy: The Function of Allegory in the 'Derveni Papyrus.'" *Phronesis* 42.2 (1997): 121–142.

Lambert, W. G. *The Background of Jewish Apocalyptic*. London: Athlone, 1978.

Lambert, W. G. "Mesopotamian Creation Stories." Pages 15–59 in *Imagining Creation*. Edited by Markham J. Geller and Mineke Schipper. Institute of Jewish Studies, Studies in Judaica 5. Leiden: Brill, 2008.

Lambert, W. G. "A New Look at the Babylonian Background of Genesis." *Journal of Theological Studies* 16 (1965): 185–300.

Lambert, W. G. "Ninurta Mythology in the Babylonian Epic of Creation." Pages 55–60 in *Keilschriftliche Literaturen, Ausgewählte Vorträge der XXXII. Rencontre Assyriologique Internationale, Münster, 8–12 Juli, 1995*. Edited by K. Hecker and W. Sommerfeld. Berlin: Deitrich Reimer, 1986.

Lambert, W. G. "Studies in Marduk." *Bulletin of the School of Oriental and African Studies* 47 (1984): 1–9.

Lambert, W. G., and Peter Walcot. "A New Babylonian Theogony and Hesiod." *Kadmos* 4 (1965): 64–72.

Lamberton, Robert. *Hesiod*. New Haven, CT: Yale University Press, 1988.

Lange, Armin. "The Essene Position on Magic and Divination." Pages 377–423 in *Legal Texts and Legal Issues*. Edited by M. Bernstein, F. García Martínez, and J. Kampen. Studies on the Texts of the Desert of Judah 23. Leiden: Brill, 1997.

Lange, Armin. *Weisheit und Prädestination: Weisheitliche Urordnung und Prädestination in den Textfunden von Qumran*. Studies on the Texts of the Desert of Judah 18. Leiden: Brill, 1995.

Lee, Jung Young. "Interpreting the Demonic Powers in Paul's Thought." *Novum Testamentum* 12.1 (1970): 54–69.

Lee, Michelle V. *Paul, the Stoics, and the Body of Christ*. Society for New Testament Studies Monograph Series 137. Cambridge: Cambridge University Press, 2006.

Levenson, Jon D. *Creation and the Persistence of Evil: The Jewish Drama of Divine Omnipotence*. Princeton, NJ: Princeton University Press, 1988.

Levison, John R. "The Two Spirits in Qumran Theology." Pages 169–194 in vol. 2 of *The Bible and the Dead Sea Scrolls: The Princeton Symposium on the Dead Sea Scrolls*. 2 vols. Edited by James H. Charlesworth. Waco, TX: Baylor University Press, 2006.

Levtow, Nathaniel B. *Images of Others: Iconic Politics in Ancient Israel*. Biblical and Judaic Studies from the University of California, San Diego 11. Winona Lake, IN: Eisenbrauns, 2008.

Lichtenberger, Hermann. *Das Ich Adams und das Ich der Menschheit: Studien zum Menschenbild in Römer 7.* Wissenschaftliche Untersuchungen zum Neuen Testament 2.164. Tübingen: Mohr Siebeck, 2004.

Liddell, Henry George, Robert Scott, Henry Stuart Jones. *A Greek-English Lexicon.* 9th ed. Oxford: Clarendon, 1996.

Lincoln, Bruce. *Theorizing Myth: Narrative, Ideology, and Scholarship.* Chicago: University of Chicago Press, 1999.

Livingstone, Alasdair. *Mystical and Mythological Explanatory Works of Assyrian and Babylonian Scholars.* Winona Lake, IN: Eisenbrauns, 2007.

Lohmeyer, Ernst. *Kurios Jesus: Eine Untersuchung zu Phil. 2, 5–11.* Heidelberg: Karl Winter, 1928.

Long, A. A. "Allegory in Philo and Etymology in Stoicism: A Plea for Drawing Distinctions." *Studia Philonica Annual* 9 (1997): 198–210.

Long, A. A. *Epictetus: A Stoic and Socratic Guide to Life.* Oxford: Oxford University Press, 2002.

López-Ruiz, Carolina. *When the Gods Were Born: Greek Cosmogonies and the Near East.* Cambridge, MA: Harvard University Press, 2010.

Loraux, Nicole. "Sur la race des femmes et quelques-unes de ses tribus." *Arethusa* 11 (1978): 43–88.

Lord, Albert B. *The Singer of Tales.* Edited by David L. Elmer. Cambridge, MA: Harvard University Press, 2017.

Lovejoy, Arthur O., and George Boas. *Primitivism and Related Ideas in Antiquity.* Baltimore: Johns Hopkins University Press, 1935.

MacGregor, G. H. C. "Principalities and Powers: The Cosmic Background of Paul's Thought." *New Testament Studies* 1 (1954): 17–28.

Maier, J. *Das altisraelitische Ladeheiligtum.* Beihefte zur Zeitschrift für die alttestamentliche Wissenschaft 93. Berlin: Töpelmann, 1965.

Malamat, Abraham. *Mari and the Bible.* Studies in the History and Culture of the Ancient Near East 12. Leiden: Brill, 1998.

Malherbe, Abraham J. "Antisthenes and Odysseus, and Paul at War." *Harvard Theological Review* 76.2 (1983): 143–173.

Malherbe, Abraham J. "The Beasts at Ephesus." Pages 79–89 in *Paul and the Popular Philosophers.* Minneapolis: Fortress, 1989.

Malherbe, Abraham J. "Determinism and Free Will in Paul: The Argument of 1 Corinthians 8 and 9. " Pages 231–255 in *Paul and His Hellenistic Context.* Edited by Troels Engberg-Pedersen. Minneapolis: Fortress, 1995.

Malherbe, Abraham J. "Gentle as a Nurse: The Cynic Background to 1 Thessalonians 2." Pages 35–48 in *Paul and the Popular Philosophers.* Minneapolis: Fortress, 1989.

Marcus, Joel. "The Evil Inclination in the Epistle of James." *Catholic Biblical Quarterly* 44.4 (1982): 606–621.

Marcus, Joel. "The Evil Inclination in the Letters of Paul." *Irish Biblical Studies* 8 (1986): 8–21.

Marcus, Joel. "'Under the Law': The Background of a Pauline Expression." *Catholic Biblical Quarterly* 63.1 (2001): 72–83.

Marcus, Joel, and Marion L. Soards, eds. *Apocalyptic and the New Testament: Essays in Honor of J. Louis Martyn.* Journal for the Study of the New Testament Supplement Series 24. Sheffield: JSOT, 1989.

Margalit, Baruch. *A Matter of "Life" and "Death": A Study of the Baal-Mot Epic (CTA 4-5-6).* Alter Orient und Altes Testament 206. Kevelaer: Butzon and Bercker / Neukirchen-Vluyn: Neukirchener Verlag, 1980.

Martin, Dale B. *The Corinthian Body.* New Haven, CT: Yale University Press, 1995.

Martin, Dale B. "Heterosexism and the Interpretation of Rom 1:18–32." Pages 51–64 in *Sex and the Single Savior: Gender and Sexuality in Biblical Interpretation.* Louisville, KY: Westminster John Knox, 2006.

Martin, Dale B. "When Did Angels Become Demons?" *Journal of Biblical Literature* 129.4 (2010): 657–677.

Martin, Michael W. "ἁρπαγμός Revisited: A Philological Reexamination of the New Testament's 'Most Difficult Word.'" *Journal of Biblical Literature* 135.1 (2016): 175–194.

Martin, Ralph P. *Carmen Christi: Philippians 2:5–11 in Recent Interpretation and in the Setting of Early Christian Worship.* 2nd ed. Grand Rapids, MI: Eerdmans, 1983.

Martyn, J. Louis. "Apocalyptic Antinomies in Paul's Letter to the Galatians." Pages 111–123 in *Theological Issues in the Letters of Paul.* Nashville: Abingdon, 1997.

Martyn, J. Louis. "De-apocalypticizing Paul: An Essay Focused on *Paul and the Stoics* by Troels Engberg-Pedersen." *Journal for the Study of the New Testament* 86 (2002): 61–102.

Martyn, J. Louis. *Galatians: A New Translation with Introduction and Commentary.* New York: Doubleday, 1997.

Matlock, R. Barry. *Unveiling the Apocalyptic Paul: Paul's Interpreters and the Rhetoric of Criticism.* Journal for the Study of the New Testament Supplement Series 127. Sheffield: Sheffield Academic Press, 1996.

McKelvey, R. J. *The New Temple: The Church in the New Testament.* Oxford: Oxford University Press, 1969.

McVay, John K. "The Human Body as Social and Political Metaphor in Stoic Literature and Early Christian Writers." *Bulletin of the American Society of Papyrologists* 37 (2000): 135–147.

Meadowcroft, Tim. "Who Are the Princes of Persia and Greece (Daniel 10)? Pointers Towards the Danielic Vision of Earth and Heaven." *Journal for the Study of the Old Testament* 29.1 (2004): 99–113.

Meeks, Wayne A. "'And Rose Up to Play': Midrash and Paraenesis in 1 Corinthians 10:1–22." *Journal for the Study of the New Testament* (1982): 64–78.

Meeks, Wayne A. "Judgment and the Brother: Romans 14:1–15:13." Pages 153–166 in *In Search of the Early Christians: Selected Essays.* Edited by Allen R. Hilton and H. Gregory Snyder. New Haven, CT: Yale University Press, 2002.

Meeks, Wayne A. "The Polyphonic Ethics of the Apostle Paul." Pages 196–209 in *In Search of the Early Christians: Selected Essays*. Edited by Allen R. Hilton and H. Gregory Snyder. New Haven, CT: Yale University Press, 2002.

Meier, Samuel A. *The Messenger in the Ancient Semitic World*. Harvard Semitic Monographs 45. Atlanta: Scholars, 1989.

Meier, Susan A. "Mediator I." Pages 554–557 in *The Dictionary of Deities and Demons in the Bible*. Edited by Karel van der Toorn, Bob Becking, and Pieter W. van der Horst. 2nd ed. Leiden: Brill, 1999.

Metso, Sarianna. "In Search of the Sitz im Leben of the Community Rule." Pages 306–315 in *The Provo International Conference on the Dead Sea Scrolls: Technological Innovations, New Texts, and Reformulated Issues*. Edited by D. W. Parry and E. Ulrich. Studies on the Texts of the Desert of Judah 30. Leiden: Brill, 1999.

Metso, Sarianna. *The Serekh Texts*. Library of Second Temple Studies 62, Companion to the Qumran Scrolls 9. London: T & T Clark, 2006.

Metso, Sarianna. *The Textual Development of the Qumran Community Rule*. Studies on the Texts of the Desert of Judah 21. Leiden: Brill, 1997.

Mettinger, Tryggve N. D. "YHWH SABAOTH—The Heavenly King on the Cherubim Throne." Pages 109–138 in *Studies in the Period of David and Solomon and Other Essays: Papers Read at the International Symposium for Biblical Studies, Tokyo, 5–7 December, 1979*. Edited by T. Ishida. Winona Lake, IN: Eisenbrauns, 1982.

Metzger, Bruce. *A Textual Commentary on the Greek New Testament*. London: United Bible Societies, 1971.

Meyers, Carol L., and Eric M. Meyers. *Haggai, Zechariah 1–8: A New Translation with Introduction and Commentary*. New York: Doubleday, 1987.

Meyers, Carol L., and Eric M. Meyers. *Zechariah 9–14: A New Translation with Introduction and Commentary*. New York: Doubleday, 1993.

Milbank, John, Slavoj Žižek, and Creston Davis. *Paul's New Moment: Continental Philosophy and the Future of Christian Theology*. Grand Rapids, MI: Brazos, 2010.

Miller, Patrick D. "Cosmology and World Order in the Old Testament: The Divine Council as Cosmo-Political Symbol." *Horizons in Biblical Theology* 9.2 (1987): 53–78.

Miller, Patrick D. *The Divine Warrior in Early Israel*. Harvard Semitic Monographs 5. Cambridge, MA: Harvard University Press, 1973.

Miller, Patrick D. "El the Warrior." *Harvard Theological Review* 60 (1967): 411–431.

Miller, Patrick D. "Two Critical Notes on Psalm 68 and Deuteronomy 33." *Harvard Theological Review* 57 (1964): 240–243.

Mitchell, Stephen, and Peter Van Nuffelen, eds. *One God: Pagan Monotheism in the Roman Empire*. Cambridge: Cambridge University Press, 2010.

Mondi, Robert. "The Ascension of Zeus and the Composition of Hesiod's Theogony." *Greek, Roman, and Byzantine Studies* 25.4 (1984): 325–344.

Mondi, Robert. "Tradition and Innovation in the Hesiodic Titanomachy." *Transactions of the American Philological Association* 116 (1986): 25–48.

Mordine, Michael J. "'Speaking to Kings': Hesiod's ΑΙΝΟΣ and the Rhetoric of Allusion in the *Works and Days*." *Classical Quarterly* 56.2 (2006): 363–373.

Morrison, Clinton. *The Powers That Be*. Studies in Biblical Theology 29. Naperville, IL: Allenson, 1960.

Moses, Robert Ewusie. *Practices of Power: Revisiting the Principalities and Powers in the Pauline Letters*. Minneapolis: Fortress, 2014.

Mullen, Theodore. *The Assembly of the Gods: The Divine Council in Canaanite and Early Hebrew Literature*. Chico, CA: Scholars, 1980.

Müller, Hans-Peter. "Mantische Weisheit und Apokalyptik." Pages 268–293 in *Congress Volume: Uppsala 1971*. Vetus Testamentum Supplement Series 22. Leiden: Brill, 1972.

Murphy, Frederick J. "Retelling the Bible: Idolatry in Pseudo-Philo." *Journal of Biblical Literature* 107.2 (1988): 275–287.

Murphy, Roland. "*Yeser* in the Qumran Literature." *Biblica* 39 (1958): 334–344.

Najman, Hindy. "Angels at Sinai: Exegesis, Theology, and Interpretative Authority." *Dead Sea Discoveries* 7.2 (2000): 313–333.

Neugebauer, Otto. "The 'Astronomical' Chapters of the Ethiopic Book of Enoch (72–80.1 and 82.4–20)." Pages 386–419 in *The Book of Enoch or 1 Enoch: A New English Edition with Commentary and Textual Notes*. By Matthew Black, in consultation with James C. VanderKam, with an appendix on the "astronomical" chapters (72–82) by Otto Neugebauer. Leiden: Brill, 1985.

Neujahr, Matthew. *Predicting the Past in the Ancient Near East: Mantic Historiography in Ancient Mesopotamia, Judah, and the Mediterranean World*. Providence: Brown University, 2012.

Newsom, Carol. "Angels (OT)." Pages 248–253 in vol. 1 of *The Anchor Bible Dictionary*. Edited by David Noel Freedman. 6 vols. New York: Doubleday, 1992.

Newsom, Carol. "The Sage in the Literature of Qumran: The Functions of the Maskil." Pages 373–382 in *The Sage in Israel and the Ancient Near East*. Edited by J. G. Gammie and L. G. Perdue. Winona Lake, IN: Eisenbrauns, 1990.

Newton, Derek. *Deity and Diet: The Dilemma of Sacrificial Food at Corinth*. Journal for the New Testament Supplement Series 169. Sheffield: Sheffield Academic, 1998.

Nickelsburg, George W. E. *1 Enoch: A Commentary on the Book of 1 Enoch*. Minneapolis: Fortress, 2001.

Nickelsburg, George W. E. *Jewish Literature Between the Bible and the Mishnah: A Historical and Literary Introduction*. Philadelphia: Fortress, 1981.

Nickelsburg, George W. E., and James C. VanderKam. *1 Enoch 2: A Commentary on the Book of 1 Enoch, Chapters 37–82*. Minneapolis: Fortress, 2011.

Niditch, Susan. "War and Reconciliation in the Traditions of Ancient Israel: Historical, Literary, and Ideological Considerations." Pages 141–160 in *War and Peace in the Ancient World*. Edited by K. A. Raaflaub. Malden, MA: Blackwell, 2007.

Niditch, Susan. *War in the Hebrew Bible: A Study in the Ethics of Violence*. Oxford: Oxford University Press, 1993.

Niehr, Herbert. "Host of Heaven." Pages 428–430 in *The Dictionary of Deities and Demons in the Bible*. Edited by Karel van der Toorn, Bob Becking, and Pieter W. van der Horst. 2nd ed. Leiden: Brill, 1999.

Nissinen, Martti. "Prophets and the Divine Council." Pages 4–19 in *Kein Land für sich allein: Studien zum Kulturkontakt in Kanaan, Israel/Palästina und Ebirnâri für Manfred Weippert zum 65. Geburtstag*. Edited by U. Hübner and E. A. Knauf. Göttingen: Vandenhoeck & Ruprecht, 2002.

Nongbri, Brent. "Paul Without Religion: The Creation of a Category and the Search for an Apostle Beyond the New Perspective." PhD diss., Yale University, 2008.

Norden, Eduard. *Agnostos Theos: Untersuchungen zur Formengeschichte religiöser Rede*. Stuttgart: Teubner, 1913.

Noth, Martin. *Exodus: A Commentary*. Translated by J. S. Bowden. Philadelphia: Westminster, 1962.

Oden, Robert A., Jr. "Interpreting Biblical Myths." Pages 40–91 in *The Bible Without Theology: The Theological Tradition and Alternatives to It*. San Francisco: Harper and Row, 2000.

Ollenburger, Ben C. "Gerhard von Rad's Theory of Holy War." Pages 1–33 in Gerhard von Rad, *Holy War in Ancient Israel*. Translated and edited by Marva Dawn. Grand Rapids, MI: Eerdmans, 1991. Translation from the 3rd German edition published in 1958.

Olyan, Saul M. "Is Isaiah 40–55 Really Monotheistic?" *Journal of Ancient Near Eastern Religions* 12 (2012): 190–201.

Olyan, Saul M. *A Thousand Thousands Served Him: Exegesis and the Naming of Angels in Ancient Judaism*. Tübingen: J. C. B. Mohr/Paul Siebeck, 1993.

Oppenheim, A. L. "The Eyes of the Lord." *Journal of the American Oriental Society* 88 (1968): 173–180.

Oppenheim, A. L. "The Golden Garments of the Gods." *Journal of Near Eastern Studies* 8.3 (1949): 172–193.

Otto, E. "Human Rights: The Influence of the Hebrew Bible." *Journal of Northwest Semitic Languages* 25 (1999): 1–20.

Parker, S. B. "The Beginning of the Reign of God: Psalm 82 as Myth and Liturgy." *Revue Biblique* 102 (1995): 532–559.

Parker, S. B. "Sons of (the) Gods." Pages 794–800 in *The Dictionary of Deities and Demons in the Bible*. Edited by Karel van der Toorn, Bob Becking, and Pieter W. van der Horst. 2nd ed. Leiden: Brill, 1999.

Paul, Shalom M. "Heavenly Tablets and the Book of Life." *Journal of the Ancient Near Eastern Society* 5 (1974): 345–353.

Philips, F. C. "Narrative Compression and the Myths of Prometheus in Hesiod." *Classical Journal* 68 (1973): 289–305.

Phua, Richard Liong-Seng. *Idolatry and Authority: A Study of 1 Corinthians 8:1–11:1 in the Light of the Jewish Diaspora*. Library of New Testament Studies 299. London: T & T Clark, 2005.

Pitard, Wayne T. "The Binding of Yamm: A New Edition of KTU 1.83." *Journal of Near Eastern Studies* 57.4 (1998): 261–280.

Pope, Marvin. *Job*. Garden City, NY: Doubleday, 1965.

Popović, Mladen. "Anthropology, Pneumatology, and Demonology in Early Judaism: The *Two Spirits Treatise* (1QS 3:13–4:26) and Other Texts from the Dead Sea Scrolls." Pages 58–98 in *Dust of the Ground and Breath of Life (Gen 2.7): The Problem of a Dualistic Anthropology in Early Judaism and Christianity*. Edited by Jacques van Ruiten and George Van Kooten. Leiden: Brill, 2016.

Popović, Mladen. *Reading the Human Body: Physiognomics and Astrology in the Dead Sea Scrolls and Hellenistic-Early Roman Judaism*. Studies on the Texts of the Desert of Judah 67. Leiden: Brill, 2007.

Porter, Barbara N. "The Anxiety of Multiplicity: Concepts of Divinity as One and Many in Ancient Assyria." Pages 211–271 in *One God or Many? Concepts of Divinity in the Ancient World*. Edited by Barbara N. Porter. Transactions of the Casco Bay Assyriological Institute 1. Chebeague Island, ME: Casco Bay Assyriological Institute, 2000.

Porter, Barbara N. "What the Assyrians Thought the Babylonians Thought About the Relative Status of Nabû and Marduk in the Late Assyrian Period." Pages 253–260 in *Assyria 1995: Proceedings of the 10th Anniversary Symposium of the Neo-Assyrian Text Corpus Project*. Edited by Simo Parpola and Robert M. Whiting. Helsinki: Neo-Assyrian Text Corpus Project, 1997.

Portier-Young, Anathea E. *Apocalypse Against Empire: Theologies of Resistance in Early Judaism*. Grand Rapids, MI: Eerdmans, 2011.

Preuss, Horst Dietrich. *Verspottung fremder Religionen im Alten Testament*. Beiträge zur Wissenschaft vom Alten und Neuen Testament 5.12. Stuttgart: Kohlhammer, 1971.

Price, A. W. *Mental Conflict*. London: Routledge, 1995.

Reumann, John. *Philippians: A New Translation with Introduction and Commentary*. New Haven, CT: Yale University Press, 2008.

Reydams-Schils, Gretchen. *The Roman Stoics: Self, Responsibility, and Affection*. Chicago: University of Chicago Press, 2005.

Riley, John G. "Demons." Pages 235–240 in *The Dictionary of Deities and Demons in the Bible*. Edited by Karel van der Toorn, Bob Becking, and Pieter W. van der Horst. 2nd ed. Leiden: Brill, 1999.

Ringgren, Helmer. "Behold Your King Comes." *Vetus Testamentum* 24 (1974): 207–211.

Ripoll, François. "Adaptations Latines d'un Thème Homérique: La Théomachie." *Phoenix* 60 (2006): 236–258.

Roberts, J. J. M. "Of Signs, Prophets, and Time Limits: A Note on Psalm 74:9." *Catholic Biblical Quarterly* 39 (1977): 474–481.

Robertson, David A. *Linguistic Evidence in Dating Early Hebrew Poetry*. Society of Biblical Literature Dissertation Series 3. Missoula, MT: Society of Biblical Literature, 1972.

Rosen-Zvi, Ishay. "Two Rabbinic Inclinations? Rethinking a Scholarly Dogma." *Journal for the Study of Judaism* 39 (2008): 513–539.

Rosen-Zvi, Ishay, and Adi Ophir. "Paul and the Invention of the Gentiles: Towards a Genealogy of the Goy." *Jewish Quarterly Review* 105.1 (2015): 1–41.

Roth, Martha T. *Law Collections from Mesopotamia and Asia Minor.* Writings from the Ancient World 6. Atlanta: Scholars, 1995.

Roth, Wolfgang M. W. "For Life, He Appeals to Death (Wis 13:18): A Study of Old Testament Idol Parodies." *Catholic Biblical Quarterly* 37.1 (1975): 21–47.

Rowland, Christopher. *The Open Heaven: A Study of Apocalyptic in Judaism and Early Christianity.* New York: Crossroad, 1982.

Rowlett, Lori L. *Joshua and the Rhetoric of Violence: A New Historicist Analysis.* Journal for the Study of the Old Testament Supplement Series 223. Sheffield: Sheffield Academic, 1996.

Rowley, H. H. *Darius the Mede and the Four World Empires in the Book of Daniel: A Historical Study of Contemporary Theories.* Cardiff: University of Wales Press, 1959.

Runia, David T. *Philo of Alexandria and the Timaeus of Plato.* Leiden: Brill, 1986.

Rusam, Dietrich. "Neue Belege zu den στοιχεῖα τοῦ κόσμου (Gal 4,3.9; Kol 2,8.20)." *Zeitschrift für die Neutestamentliche Wissenschaft und die Kunde der Älteren Kirche* 83 (1992): 119–125.

Russell, D. S. *The Method and Message of Jewish Apocalyptic: 200 BC–AD 100.* London: SCM, 1964.

Sacchi, Paolo. *Jewish Apocalyptic and Its History.* Sheffield: Sheffield Academic, 1997.

Sakenfeld, Katharine Doob. *New Interpreter's Dictionary of the Bible.* 5 vols. Nashville: Abingdon, 2009.

Sanday, William, and Arthur C. Headlam. *Critical and Exegetical Commentary on the Epistle to the Romans.* Edinburgh: T & T Clark, 1911.

Sanders, E. P. "The Genre of Palestinian Jewish Apocalypses." Pages 447–459 in *Apocalypticism in the Mediterranean World and the Near East: Proceedings of the International Colloquium on Apocalypticism, Uppsala, August 12–17, 1979.* Edited by David Hellholm. Tübingen: Mohr Siebeck, 1983.

Sanders, E. P. *Jesus and Judaism.* Philadelphia: Fortress, 1985.

Sanders, E. P. *Paul, the Law, and the Jewish People.* Philadelphia: Fortress, 1983.

Sanders, James A. "Dissenting Deities and Philippians 2:1–11." *Journal of Biblical Literature* 88.3 (1969): 279–290.

Sanders, James A. "Text and Canon: Concepts and Method." *Journal of Biblical Literature* 98.1 (1979): 5–29.

Sarna, Nahum M. "Psalm 89: A Study in Inner-Biblical Exegesis." Pages 29–46 in *Biblical and Other Studies.* Edited by Alexander Altman. Cambridge, MA: Harvard University Press, 1963.

Sawyer, J. F. A. "Biblical Alternatives to Monotheism." *Theology* 87 (1984): 172–180.

Schäfer, Peter. *Rivalität zwischen Engeln und Menschen. Untersuchungen zur rabbinischen Engelvorstellung.* Studia Judaica 8. Berlin: de Gruyter, 1975.

Schenker, Adrian. "Le monothéisme israélite: un dieu qui transcende le monde et les dieux." *Biblica* 78 (1997): 436–448.

Schlier, H. *Principalities and Powers in the New Testament.* New York: Herder and Herder, 1961.

Schmithals, Walter. *The Apocalyptic Movement.* Nashville: Abingdon, 1975.

Schmitt, Rüdiger. *Der "Heilige Krieg" im Pentateuch und im deuteronomistischen Geschichtswerk: Studien zur Forschungs-, Rezeptions- und Religionsgeschichte von Krieg und Bann im Alten Testament.* Alter Orient und Altes Testament 381. Münster: Ugarit-Verlag, 2011.

Schnackenburg, Rudolf. *God's Rule and Kingdom.* Translated by John Murray. 2nd ed. New York: Herder and Herder, 1968.

Schoors, Antoon. "Isaiah, the Minister of Royal Anointment?" Pages 85–107 in *Instruction and Interpretation: Studies in Hebrew Language, Palestinian Archeology, and Biblical Exegesis.* Edited by H. A. Brongers. Oudtestamentische Studiën 20. Leiden: Brill, 1977.

Schultz, Brian. *Conquering the World: The War Scroll (1QM) Reconsidered.* Studies on the Texts of the Desert of Judah 76. Leiden: Brill, 2000.

Schweitzer, Albert. *The Mysticism of the Apostle Paul.* Translated by W. Montgomery. 2nd ed. Baltimore: Johns Hopkins University Press, 1998. German edition published in 1930.

Schweitzer, Albert. *The Quest for the Historical Jesus.* Translated by W. Montgomery. Mineola, NY: Dover, 2005. German edition published in 1906.

Schweizer, Eduard. "Slaves of the Elements and Worshippers of Angels: Gal 4:3, 9 and Col 2:8, 18, 20." *Journal of Biblical Literature* 107.3 (1988): 455–468

Scroggs, Robin. "Ernst Käsemann: The Divine Agent Provocateur." *Religious Studies Review* 11.3 (1985): 260–263.

Scurlock, JoAnn, and Richard Beal, eds. *Creation and Chaos: A Reconsideration of Hermann Gunkel's Chaoskampf Hypothesis.* Winona Lake, IN: Eisenbrauns, 2013.

Sedley, David. *Creationism and Its Critics in Antiquity.* Sather Classical Lectures 66. Berkeley: University of California Press, 2007.

Segal, Alan F. *Two Powers in Heaven: Early Rabbinic Reports About Christianity and Gnosticism.* Studies in Judaism in Late Antiquity 25. Leiden: Brill, 1977.

Seifrid, Mark A. "The Subject of Rom 7:14–25." *Novum Testamentum* 34.4 (1992): 313–333.

Seitz, Christopher R. "The Divine Council: Temporal Transition and New Prophecy in the Book of Isaiah." *Journal of Biblical Literature* 109.2 (1990): 229–247.

Sekki, Arthur Everett. *The Meaning of Ruaḥ at Qumran.* Society of Biblical Literature Dissertation Series 110. Atlanta: Scholars, 1989.

Seybold, Klaus. *Die Psalmen.* Handbuch zum alten Testament 15. Tübingen: Mohr Siebeck, 1996.

Shea, W. H. "Wrestling with the Prince of Persia: A Study on Daniel 10." *Andrews University Seminar Studies* 21.3 (1983): 225–250.

Skehan, Patrick K. *Studies in Israelite Poetry and Wisdom*. Catholic Biblical Quarterly Monograph Series 1. Washington, DC: Catholic Biblical Association of America, 1971.

Smend, Rudolf. *Yahweh War and Tribal Confederation: Reflections upon Israel's Earliest History*. Translated by M. G. Rogers. 2nd ed. New York: Abingdon, 1970.

Smit, Joop F. *About the Idol Offerings: Rhetoric, Social Context and Theology of Paul's Discourse in First Corinthians 8:1–11:1*. Contributions to Biblical Exegesis and Theology 27. Leuven: Peeters, 2000.

Smith, J. Z. "Differential Equations: On Constructing the Other." Pages 230–250 in *Relating Religion: Essays in the Study of Religion*. Chicago: University of Chicago Press, 2004.

Smith, J. Z. *Map Is Not Territory: Studies in the History of Religions*. Leiden: Brill, 1978. Reprint, Chicago: University of Chicago Press, 1993.

Smith, J. Z. "A Pearl of Great Price and a Cargo of Yams." Pages 90–101 in *Imagining Religion: From Babylon to Jonestown*. Chicago: University of Chicago Press, 1982.

Smith, J. Z. "Wisdom and Apocalypticism." Pages 101–120 in *Visionaries and Their Apocalypses*. Edited by Paul D. Hansen. Philadelphia: Fortress, 1983.

Smith, Mark S. *The Early History of God: Yahweh and Other Deities in Ancient Israel*. 2nd ed. Grand Rapids, MI: Eerdmans, 2002.

Smith, Mark S. "The Structure of Divinity at Ugarit and Israel." Pages 38–63 in *Text, Artifact, and Image: Revealing Ancient Israelite Religion*. Edited by Gary M. Beckman and Theodore J. Lewis. Brown Judaic Studies 346. Providence: Brown Judaic Studies, 2006.

Smith, Mark S. *The Origins of Biblical Monotheism: Israel's Polytheistic Background and the Ugaritic Texts*. Oxford: Oxford University Press, 2001.

Sommer, Benjamin D. "The Babylonian Akitu Festival: Rectifying the King or Renewing the Cosmos?" *Journal of the Ancient Near Eastern Society* 27 (2000): 81–95.

Sommerfeld, Walter. *Der Aufstieg Marduks: Die Stellung Marduks in der babylonischen Religion des zweiten Jahrtausends v. Chr.* Neukirchen-Vluyn: Neukirchener Verlag, 1982.

Sprague, R. K. "The Four Causes: Aristotle's Exposition and Ours." *Monist* 52.2 (1968): 298–300.

Staab, Karl. *Pauluskommentare aus der griechischen Kirche: aus Katenenhandschriften gasammelt und herausgeben*. Neutestamentliche Abhandlungen 15. Münster: Aschendorff, 1933.

Stambaugh, J. E. "The Functions of Roman Temples." Pages 554–608 in *Aufstieg und Niedergang der römischen Welt: Geschichte und Kultur Roms im Spiegel der neueren Forschung (ANRW)* 2.16.1. Edited by W. Haase. Berlin: de Gruyter, 1978.

Stanley, Christopher D., ed. *The Colonized Apostle: Paul Through Postcolonial Eyes*. Minneapolis: Fortress, 2011.

Stegemann, Hartmut. "Die Bedeutung der Qumranfunde für die Erforschung der Apokalyptik." Pages 495–530 in *Apocalypticism in the Mediterranean World and the*

Near East: Proceedings of the International Colloquium on Apocalypticism, Uppsala, August 12–17, 1979. Edited by David Hellholm. Tübingen: Mohr Siebeck, 1983.

Stegemann, Hartmut. "Zu Textbestand and Grundgedanken von 1QS III, 13–IV, 26." *Revue Qumran* 13 (1988): 95–130.

Sterling, Gregory E. "Prepositional Metaphysics in Jewish Wisdom Speculation and Early Christian Liturgical Texts." *Studia Philonica Annual* 19 (1997): 219–238.

Steudel, Annette. "The Eternal Reign of the People of God—Collective Expectations in Qumran Texts (4Q246 and 1QM)." *Revue de Qumran* 17 (1996): 507–525.

Stolz, Fritz. *Jahwes und Israels Kriege: Kriegstheorien und Kriegserfahrungen im Glauben des alten Israels.* Abhandlungen zur Theologie des Alten und Neuen Testaments 60. Zurich: Theologischer Verlag, 1972.

Stone, Michael E. "Lists of Revealed Things in the Apocalyptic Literature." Pages 414–452 in *Magnalia Dei: The Mighty Acts of God. Essays on the Bible and Archeology in Honor of G. Ernest Wright.* Edited by Frank Moore Cross, Werner E. Lemke, and Patrick D. Miller. Garden City, NY: Doubleday, 1976.

Stowers, Stanley. "Apostrophe, προσωποποιία, and Paul's Rhetorical Education." Pages 351–370 in *Early Christianity and Classical Culture: Comparative Studies in Honor of Abraham J. Malherbe.* Novum Testamentum Supplements 110. Edited by John T. Fitzgerald, Thomas H. Olbricht, and L. Michael White. Leiden: Brill, 2003.

Stowers, Stanley. "The Concept of 'Community' and the History of Early Christianity." *Method and Theory in the Study of Religion* 23 (2011): 238–256.

Stowers, Stanley. *The Diatribe and Paul's Letter to the Romans.* Society of Biblical Literature Dissertation Series 57. Chico, CA: Scholars Press, 1981.

Stowers, Stanley. "Does Pauline Christianity Resemble a Hellenistic Philosophy?" Pages 81–102 in *Paul Beyond the Hellenism-Judaism Divide.* Edited by Troels Engberg-Pedersen. Louisville, KY: Westminster John Knox, 2001.

Stowers, Stanley. "Paul and Self-Mastery." Pages 270–300 in vol. 2 of *Paul and the Greco-Roman World.* 2 vols. Edited by J. Paul Sampley. Harrisburg, PA: Trinity Press International, 2016.

Stowers, Stanley. "Paul's Four Discourses About Sin. " Pages 100–127 in *Celebrating Paul: Essays in Honor of Jerome Murphy O'Connor, O.P., and Joseph Fitzmyer, S. J.* Edited by Peter Spitaler. Catholic Biblical Quarterly Monograph Series 48. Washington, DC: Catholic Biblical Association of America, 2011.

Stowers, Stanley. *A Rereading of Romans: Justice, Jews, and Gentiles.* New Haven, CT: Yale University Press, 1994.

Stowers, Stanley. "Romans 7:7–25 as Speech-in-Character (προσωποποιία)." Pages 180–202 in *Paul in His Hellenistic Context.* Edited by Troels Engberg-Pedersen. Minneapolis: Fortress, 1995.

Stowers, Stanley. "What Is 'Pauline Participation in Christ'?" Pages 352–371 in *Redefining First-Century Jewish and Christian Identities: Essays in Honor of E. P. Sanders.* Edited by Fabien E. Udoh with Sussanah Heschel, Mark Chancey, and Gregory Tatum. Notre Dame, IN: Notre Dame University Press, 2008.

Stuckenbruck, Loren T. *Angel Veneration and Christology: A Study in Early Judaism and in the Christology of the Apocalypse of John.* Wissenschaftliche Untersuchungen zum Neuen Testament 2.70. Tübingen: J. C. B. Mohr (Paul Siebeck), 1995.

Stuckenbruck, Loren T. *1 Enoch 91–108.* Berlin: de Gruyter, 2007.

Stuckenbruck, Loren T. "The Interiorization of Dualism Within the Human Being in Second Temple Judaism: The Treatise on the Two Spirits (1QS III:13–IV: 26) in Its Tradition-Historical Context." Pages 145–168 in *Light Against Darkness: Dualism in Ancient Mediterranean Religion and the Contemporary World.* Edited by A. Lange, E. M. Meyers, B. H. Reynolds III, and R. Styers. Journal of Ancient Judaism Supplements 2. Göttingen: Vandenhoeck & Ruprecht.

Stuckenbruck, Loren T. "Overlapping Ages at Qumran and 'Apocalyptic' in Pauline Theology." Pages 309–326 in *The Dead Sea Scrolls and Pauline Literature.* Edited by Jean-Sébastien Rey. Leiden: Brill, 2014.

Stuhlmacher, Peter. *Paul's Letter to the Romans: A Commentary.* Translated by Scott J. Hafemann. Louisville, KY: Westminster/John Knox, 1994.

Sweeney, Marvin. "Habakkuk, Book of." Pages 2–5 in vol. 3 of *The Anchor Bible Dictionary.* Edited by David Noel Freedman. 6 vols. New York: Doubleday, 1992.

Tate, Marvin. *Psalms 51–100.* Word Biblical Commentary 20. Dallas: Word Books, 1990.

Tatum, W. Barnes. "The LXX Version of the Second Commandment (Exod 20, 3–6 = Deut 5, 7–10): A Polemic Against Idols, Not Images." *Journal for the Study of Judaism in the Persian, Hellenistic and Roman Period* 17.2 (1986): 177–195.

Testuz, Michel. *Les idées religieuses du Livre des Jubilés.* Geneva: Droz, 1960.

Theiler, W. *Die Vorbereitung des Neuplatonismus.* Berlin: Weidmann, 1964.

Thiessen, Matthew. *Paul and the Gentile Problem.* New York: Oxford University Press, 2016.

Thorsteinsson, Runar M. *Paul's Interlocutor in Romans 2: Function and Identity in the Context of Ancient Epistolography.* Coniectanea Biblica New Testament Series 40. Stockholm: Almqvist & Wiksell, 2003.

Thorsteinsson, Runar M. *Roman Christianity and Roman Stoicism: A Comparative Study of Ancient Morality.* New York: Oxford University Press, 2010.

Thorsteinsson, Runar M. "Stoicism as a Key to Pauline Ethics in Romans." Pages 15–38 in *Stoicism in Early Christianity.* Edited by Tuomas Rasimus, Troels Engberg-Pedersen, and Ismo Dunderberg. Grand Rapids, MI: Baker Academic 2010.

Tigchelaar, Eibert J. C. "The Evil Inclination in the Dead Sea Scrolls, with a Re-edition of 4Q468i (4QSectarian Text?)." Pages 347–357 in *Empsychoi Logoi: Religious Innovations in Antiquity: Studies in Honour of Pieter Willem van der Horst.* Edited by A. Houtman, A. de Jong, and M. Misset-van de Weg. Ancient Judaism and Christianity 73. Leiden: Brill, 2008.

Tigchelaar, Eibert J. C. "'These Are the Names of the Spirits of . . .': A Preliminary Edition of 4QCatalogue of Spirits (4Q230) and New Manuscript Evidence for the Two Spirits Treatise (4Q257 and 1Q29a)." *Revue Qumran* 21 (2004): 529–547.

Tigchelaar, Eibert J. C. *To Increase Learning for the Understanding Ones: Reading and Reconstructing the Fragmentary Early Jewish Sapiental Text 4QInstruction.* Studies on the Texts of the Desert of Judah 44. Leiden: Brill, 2001.

Tiller, Patrick A. *A Commentary on the Animal Apocalypse of 1 Enoch.* Early Judaism and Its Literature 4. Atlanta: Scholars, 1993.

Timmins, Will. "Romans 7 and Speech-in-Character: A Critical Evaluation of Stowers' Hypothesis." *Zeitschrift für die Neutestamentliche Wissenschaft und die Kunde der Alteren Kirche* 107.2 (2016): 94–115.

Tobin, Thomas H. "The Prologue of John and Hellenistic Jewish Speculation." *Catholic Biblical Quarterly* 52.2 (1990): 252–269.

Tobin, Thomas H. "The World of Thought in the Philippians Hymn (Philippians 2:6–11)." Pages 91–104 in *The New Testament and Early Christian Literature in Greco-Roman Context: Studies in Honor of David E. Aune.* Edited by John Fotopoulos. Supplements to Novum Testamentum 122. Leiden: Brill, 2006.

Toombs, L. E. "War, Ideas of." Pages 796–801 in *The Interpreter's Dictionary of the Bible.* Edited by G. A. Buttrick. New York: Abingdon, 1962.

Tov, Emanuel. *Textual Criticism of the Hebrew Bible.* Minneapolis: Fortress, 1992. Second rev. ed. 2001.

Trimm, Charles. "Recent Research on Warfare in the Old Testament." *Currents in Biblical Research* 10 (2012): 171–216.

Tsevat, Matitiahu. "Studies in the Book of Samuel IV: *YHWH Ṣeba'ot*." *Hebrew Union College Annual* 36 (1965): 49–58.

Tsumura, David T. *Creation and Destruction: A Reappraisal of the Chaoskampf Theory in the Old Testament.* Winona Lake, IN: Eisenbrauns, 2005.

Tucker, Paavo. "Reconsidering Βελιάρ: 2 Corinthians 6:15 in Its Anti-Imperial Jewish Apocalyptic Context." *Journal for the Study of Paul and His Letters* 4.2 (2014): 169–185.

Tugendhaft, Aaron. "Babel-Bible-Baal." Pages 190–198 in *Creation and Chaos: A Reconsideration of Hermann Gunkel's Chaoskampf Hypothesis.* Edited by JoAnn Scurlock and Richard Beal. Winona Lake, IN: Eisenbrauns, 2013.

Tugendhaft, Aaron. "Unsettling Sovereignty: Poetics and Politics in the Baal Cycle." *Journal of the American Oriental Society* 132.3 (2012): 367–384.

Urbach, E. E. "The Homiletical Interpretations of the Sages and the Expositions of Origen on Canticles, and Jewish-Christian Disputation." Pages 247–275 in *Studies in Aggadah and Folk-literature.* Edited by J. Heinemann and D. Noy. Scripta Hierosolymitana 22. Jerusalem: Magnes, 1971.

Urbach, E. E. *The Sages: Their Concepts and Beliefs.* Translated by I. Abrahams. 2 vols. Jerusalem: Magnes, 1975.

van der Deijl, Aarnoud. *Protest or Propaganda: War in the Old Testament Book of Kings and in Contemporaneous Ancient Near Eastern Texts.* Studia Semitica Neerlandica 51. Leiden: Brill, 2008.

Vanderhooft, David Stephen. *The Neo-Babylonian Empire and Babylon in the Latter Prophets.* Harvard Semitic Monographs 59. Atlanta: Scholars, 1999.

van der Horst, Pieter W. "'The Elements Will Be Dissolved with Fire': The Idea of Cosmic Conflagration in Hellenism, Ancient Judaism, and Early Christianity." Pages 271–292 in *Hellenism-Judaism-Christianity: Essays on Their Interaction*. 2nd ed. Contributions to Biblical Exegesis and Theology 8. Leuven: Peeters, 1998.

van der Horst, Pieter W. "'Thou Shalt Not Revile the Gods': The LXX Translation of Exod 22:28 (27), Its Background and Influence." *Studia Philonica Annual* 5 (1993): 1–8.

van der Horst, Pieter W. "Evil Inclination." Pages 317–319 in *The Dictionary of Deities and Demons in the Bible*. Edited by Karel van der Toorn, Bob Becking, and Pieter W. van der Horst. 2nd ed. Leiden: Brill, 1999.

VanderKam, James C. "The Angel Story in the Book of Jubilees." Pages 151–170 in *Pseudepigraphic Perspectives: The Apocrypha and Pseudepigrapha in Light of the Dead Sea Scrolls, Proceedings of the International Symposium of the Orion Center for the Study of the Dead Sea Scrolls and Associated Literature, 12–14 January, 1997*. Edited by E. Chazon and M. E. Stone. Studies on the Texts of the Desert of Judah 31. Leiden: Brill, 1999.

VanderKam, James C. "The *Aqedah, Jubilees*, and Pseudojubilees." Pages 241–261 in *The Quest for Context and Meaning: Studies in Biblical Intertextuality in Honor of James A. Sanders*. Edited by C. A. Evans and S. Talmon. Biblical Interpretation Series 28. Leiden: Brill, 1997.

VanderKam, James C. "The Demons in the Book of Jubilees." Pages 339–364 in *Die Dämonen: die Dämonologie der israelitisch-jüdischen und frühchristlichen Literatur im Kontext ihrer Umwelt* [Demons: The Demonology of Israelite-Jewish and Early Christian Literature in the Context of Their Environment]. Edited by Armin Lange, Hermann Lichtenberger, and K. F. Diethard Römheld. Tübingen: Mohr Siebeck, 2003.

VanderKam, James C. *Enoch: A Man for All Generations*. Studies on Personalities of the Old Testament. Columbia: University of South Carolina Press, 1995.

VanderKam, James C. *Enoch and the Growth of an Apocalyptic Tradition*. Catholic Biblical Quarterly Monograph Series 16. Washington, DC: Catholic Biblical Association, 1984.

VanderKam, James C. *Textual and Historical Studies in the Book of Jubilees*. Harvard Semitic Monographs 14. Missoula, MT: Scholars Press, 1977.

VanderKam, James C. "The Theophany of Enoch 1:3b–7, 9." *Vetus Testamentum* 23.2 (1973): 130–150.

VanderKam, James C. "Viewed from Another Angle: Purity and Impurity in the Book of Jubilees." *Journal for the Study of the Pseudepigrapha* 13.2 (2002): 209–215.

VanderKam, James C., and J. T. Milik. "4Qpseudo-Jubilees[a]." Pages 1–186 in *Qumran Cave 4. VIII: Parabiblical Texts, Part I*. Edited by Harold W. Attridge, Torleif Elgvin, Jozef Milik, Saul Olyan, John Strugnell, Emanuel Tov, James VanderKam, and Sidnie White. Discoveries in the Judaean Desert 13. Oxford: Clarendon, 1994.

van der Toorn, Karel. "The Babylonian New Year Festival: New Insights from the Cuneiform Texts and Their Bearing on Old Testament Study." Pages 331–344 in *International Organization for the Study of the Old Testament, Congress Volume, Leuven, 1989*. Edited by J. A. Emerton. Supplements to Vetus Testamentum 43. Leiden: Brill, 1991.

van der Toorn, Karel. *Family Religion in Babylonia, Syria, and Israel: Continuity and Change in the Forms of Religious Life*. Studies in the History and Culture of the Ancient Near East 7. Leiden: Brill, 1996.

van der Toorn, Karel. "The Theology of Demons in Mesopotamia and Israel: Popular Belief and Scholarly Speculation." Pages 61–83 in *Die Dämonen: die Dämonologie der israelitisch-jüdischen und frühchristlichen Literatur im Kontext ihrer Umwelt* [Demons: The Demonology of Israelite-Jewish and Early Christian Literature in the Context of Their Environment]. Edited by Armin Lange, Hermann Lichtenberger, and K. F. Diethard Römheld. Tübingen: Mohr Siebeck, 2003.

van der Toorn, Karel. "Yahweh." Pages 910–919 in *The Dictionary of Deities and Demons in the Bible*. Edited by Karel van der Toorn, Bob Becking, and Pieter W. van der Horst. 2nd ed. Leiden: Brill, 1999.

Vanstiphout, Herman L. J. "Enuma Elish as a Systematic Creed: An Essay." *Orientalia Lovaniensia Periodica* 23 (1992): 37–61.

Vielhauer, Philip, and Goerge Strecker. "Apocalyptic and Early Christianity." Pages 569–602 in vol. 2 of *New Testament Apocrypha*. 2 vols. Rev. ed. Edited by W. Schneemelcher, and English translation edited by R. McL. Wilson (1965, 1976 eds.). Louisville, KY: Westminster/John Knox, 1992.

Vollenweider, Samuel. "Der 'Raub' der Gottgleichheit: Ein religionsgeschichtlicher Vorschlag zu Phil 2.6(–11)." *New Testament Studies* 45.3 (1999): 413–433.

von der Osten-Sacken, Peter. *Gott und Belial: Traditionsgeschichtliche Untersuchungen zum Dualismus in den Texten aus Qumran*. Studien zur Umwelt des Neuen Testaments 6. Göttingen: Vandenhoeck & Ruprecht, 1969.

von Rad, Gerhard. *Holy War in Ancient Israel*. Translated and edited by Marva Dawn. Grand Rapids, MI: Eerdmans, 1991. Translation from the 3rd German edition published in 1958.

von Rad, Gerhard. *Old Testament Theology*. 2 vols. Translated by D. M. G. Stalker. New York: Harper and Row, 1965.

von Rad, Gerhard. "Origin of the Concept of the Day of Yahweh." *Journal of Semitic Studies* 4.2 (1959): 97–108.

von Rad, Gerhard. *Theologie des Alten Testaments*. 4th ed. Munich: Kaiser, 1965.

von Rad, Gerhard. *Wisdom in Israel*. Translated by James D. Martin. Nashville: Abingdon, 1972.

Walton, Francis. "The Messenger of God in Hecataeus of Abdera." *Harvard Theological Review* 48.4 (1955): 255–257.

Wambacq, B. N. *L'épithète divine Jahvé Ṣĕbaʾôt. Étude Philologique, historique, et éxegétique*. Bruges: Descleé, 1947.

Wasserman, "'An Idol Is Nothing in the World' (1 Cor 8:4): The Metaphysical Contradictions of 1 Corinthians 8:1–11:1 in the Context of Jewish Idolatry Polemics." Pages 201–227 in *Portraits of Jesus: Essays on Christology, Festschrift for Harold W. Attridge*. Edited by Susan Myers. Tübingen: Mohr Siebeck, 2012.

Wasserman, Emma. *The Death of the Soul in Romans 7: Sin, Death, and the Law in Light of Hellenistic Moral Psychology*. Wissenschaftliche Untersuchungen zum Neuen Testament 2.256. Tübigen: Mohr Siebeck, 2008.

Wasserman, Emma. "Paul Among the Philosophers: The Case of Sin in Romans 6–8." *Journal for the Study of the New Testament* 30.4 (2008): 387–415.

Wasserman, Emma. "Paul Beyond the Judaism/Hellenism Divide? The Case of Pauline Anthropology in Romans 7 and 2 Corinthians 4–5." Pages 259–279 in *Christian Origins and Hellenistic Judaism: Social and Literary Contexts for the New Testament*. Edited by Stanley E. Porter and Andrew W. Pitts. Leiden: Brill, 2012.

Wazana, Nili. "Anzu and Ziz: Great Mythical Birds in Ancient Near Eastern, Biblical, and Rabbinic Traditions." *Journal of the Ancient Near Eastern Society* 31 (2009): 111–135.

Weimar, Peter. "Die Jahwekriegserzählungen in Exodus 14, Joshua 10, Richter 4, und 1 Samuel 7." *Biblica* 57 (1976): 38–73.

Weinfeld, Moshe. "Divine Intervention in War in Ancient Israel and in the Ancient Near East." Pages 121–147 in *History, Historiography and Interpretation: Studies in Biblical and Cuneiform Literatures*. Edited by H. Tadmor and M. Weinfeld. Jerusalem: Magnes, 1983.

Weippert, Manfred. "Heiliger Krieg in Israel und Assyrien: Kritische Anmerkungen zu Gerhard von Rads Konzept des 'Heiligen Krieges im alten Israel.'" *Zeitschrift für die alttestamentliche Wissenschaft* 84 (1972): 460–493.

Weiss, Johannes. *Jesus' Proclamation of the Kingdom of God*. Translated and edited by Richard H. Hiers and David L. Holland. London: SCM, 1971. German edition published in 1892.

Weiss, K. "ἀρχή." Pages 161–163 in vol. 1 of *The Exegetical Dictionary of the New Testament*. 3 vols. Edited by Horst Balz and Gerhard Schneider. Grand Rapids, MI: Eerdmans, 1990.

Weiss, M. "The Origin of the 'Day of the Lord' Reconsidered." *Hebrew Union College Annual* 37 (1966): 29–72.

Weissert, Elnathan. "Creating a Political Climate: Literary Allusions to *Enūma eliš* in Sennacherib's Account of the Battle of Halule." Pages 191–202 in *Assyrien im Wandel der Zeiten: XXXIXe Rencontre Assyriologique Internationale, Heidelberg, 6–10 Juli, 1992*. Edited by Hartmut Waetzoldt and Harald Hauptmann. Heidelberger Studien zum Alten Orient 6. Heidelberg: Heidelberg Orientverlag, 1997.

Wellhausen, Julius. *Prolegomena to the History of Israel*. Gloucester, MA: Peter Smith, 1973. Reprint of *Prolegomena to the History of Israel*. Translated by J. Sutherland Black and Allan Menzies. Edinburgh: Adam and Charles Black, 1885. Translation of the 2nd German edition. Berlin: G. Reimar, 1883.

West, M. L. *The Orphic Poems.* Oxford: Clarendon, 1983.

Wildberger, Hans. *Isaiah 13–27: A Continental Commentary.* Translated by Thomas H. Trapp. Minneapolis: Fortress, 1997. From the 1978 German edition.

Willis, Wendell L. "1 Corinthians 8–10: A Retrospective After Twenty-Five Years." *Restoration Quarterly* 49.2 (2007): 103–112.

Wills, Lawrence M. "Ascetic Theology Before Asceticism? Jewish Narratives and the Decentering of the Self." *Journal of the American Academy of Religion* 74.4 (2006): 902–925.

Wilson, Robert R. "The Community of the Second Isaiah." Pages 53–70 in *Reading and Preaching the Book of Isaiah.* Edited by Christopher R. Seitz. Philadelphia: Fortress, 1988.

Wink, Walter. *Naming the Powers: The Language of Power in the New Testament.* Philadelphia: Fortress, 1984.

Winston, David. *The Wisdom of Solomon: A New Translation with Introduction and Commentary.* New York: Doubleday, 1979.

Wise, Michael O. "The Eschatological Vision of the Temple Scroll." *Journal of Near Eastern Studies* 49.2 (1990): 155–172.

Witherington, Ben, III. *Conflict and Community in Corinth: A Socio-Rhetorical Commentary on 1 and 2 Corinthians.* Grand Rapids, MI: Eerdmans, 1995.

Wolff, Hans Walter, Waldemar Janzen, and S. Dean McBride. *Joel and Amos: A Commentary on the Books of the Prophets Joel and Amos.* Philadelphia: Fortress, 1977.

Wright, Jacob L. "War, Ideas of." Pages 800–805 in vol. 5 of *The New Interpreter's Dictionary of the Bible.* 5 vols. Edited by Katharine Doob Sakenfeld. Nashville: Abingdon, 2009.

Wright, M. R. *Cosmology in Antiquity.* New York: Routledge, 1995.

Wright, N. T. *Jesus and the Victory of God.* London: SPCK, 1996.

Wyatt, N. "Arms and the King: The Earliest Allusions to the Chaoskampf Motif and Their Implications for the Interrelation of the Ugaritic and Biblical Traditions." Pages 833–882 in *"Und Mose schrieb diese Lied auf": Studien zum Alten Testament und zum alten Orient: Festschrift für Oswald Loretz zur Vollendung seines 70. Lebensjahres mit Beiträgen von Freunden, Schülern und Kollegen.* Edited by Manfried Dietrich und Ingo Kottsieper. Alter Orient und Altes Testament 250. Münster: Ugarit-Verlag, 1998.

Xeravits, Géza G., ed. *Dualism at Qumran.* Library of Second Temple Studies 76. New York: T & T Clark, 2010.

Yarbro Collins, Adela. "The Otherworld and the New Age in the Letters of Paul." Pages 189–207 in *Other Worlds and Their Relation to This World: Early Jewish and Ancient Christian Traditions.* Edited by Tobias Nicklas, Joseph Verheyden, Erik M. M. Eynikel, and Florentino García Martínez. Supplements to the Journal for the Study of Judaism 143. Leiden: Brill, 2010.

Yarbro Collins, Adela. "Psalms, Phil 2:6–11, and the Origins of Christology." *Biblical Interpretation* 11.3 (2003): 361–372.

Yarbro Collins, Adela. "The Worship of Jesus in the Imperial Cult." Pages 234–257 in *The Jewish Roots of Christological Monotheism: Papers from the St. Andrews Conference on the Historical Origins of the Worship of Jesus.* Edited by C. C. Newman, J. R. Davila, and G. S. Lewis. Supplements to the Journal for the Study of Judaism 63. Leiden: Brill, 1999.

Young, Norman H. "Paidagogos: The Social Setting of a Pauline Metaphor." *Novum Testamentum* 29.2 (1987): 150–176.

Younger, K. L. *Ancient Conquest Accounts: A Study in Ancient Near Eastern and Biblical History Writing.* Sheffield: Sheffield Academic, 1990.

Zeller, Dieter M. "The Life and Death of the Soul in Philo of Alexandria: The Use and Origin of a Metaphor." *Studia Philonica Annual* 7 (1995): 19–55.

General Index

Index of Ancient Sources